OXFORD STUDIES IN EUROPEAN LAW

The aim of this series is to publish important and original research on EU law. The focus is on scholarly monographs, with a particular emphasis on those which are interdisciplinary in nature. Edited collections of essays will also be included where they are appropriate. The series is wide in scope and aims to cover studies of particular areas of substantive and of institutional law, historical works, theoretical studies, and analyses of current debates, as well as questions of perennial interest such as the relationship between national and EU law and the novel forms of governance emerging in and beyond Europe. The fact that many of the works are interdisciplinary will make the series of interest to all those concerned with the governance and operation of the EU.

OTHER TITLES IN THIS SERIES

Fiscal State Aid Law and Harmful Tax Competition in the European Union
Dimitrios Kyriazis

The Abuse of Constitutional Identity in the European Union
Julian Scholtes

Judging European Democracy
The Role and Legitimacy of National Constitutional Courts in the EU
Nik de Boer

EU Values Before the Court of Justice
Foundations, Potential, Risks
Luke Dimitrios Spieker

Postnational Constitutionalism
Europe and the Time of Law
Paul Linden-Retek

The Legislative Priority Rule and the EU Internal Market for Goods
A Constitutional Approach
Eadaoin Ní Chaoimh

The Jurisprudence of Constitutional Conflict in the European Union
Ana Bobić

Reflexive Governance in EU Equality Law
Emma Lantschner

Enhanced Cooperation and European Tax Law
Caroline Heber

Legal Pluralism in European Contract Law
Vanessa Mak

Europe's Passive Virtues
Deference to National Authorities in EU Free Movement Law
Jan Zglinski

Accountability in EU Security and Defence
The Law and Practice of Peacebuilding
Carolyn Moser

Accountability in the Economic and Monetary Union
Foundations, Policy, and Governance
Menelaos Markakis

Official Secrets and Oversight in the EU
Law and Practices of Classified Information
Vigjilenca Abazi

Legislative Authority and Interpretation in the European Union

MARTIJN VAN DEN BRINK

OXFORD
UNIVERSITY PRESS

OXFORD
UNIVERSITY PRESS

Great Clarendon Street, Oxford, OX2 6DP,
United Kingdom

Oxford University Press is a department of the University of Oxford.
It furthers the University's objective of excellence in research, scholarship,
and education by publishing worldwide. Oxford is a registered trade mark of
Oxford University Press in the UK and in certain other countries

Published in the United States of America by Oxford University Press
198 Madison Avenue, New York, NY 10016, United States of America

British Library Cataloguing in Publication Data

Data available

Library of Congress Control Number: 2024932230

ISBN 9780198900085

DOI: 10.1093/9780198900115.001.0001

Printed and bound by
CPI Group (UK) Ltd, Croydon, CR0 4YY

FSC www.fsc.org MIX Paper | Supporting responsible forestry FSC® C013604

Preface

There is a very considerable literature on many central issues of EU law, and also on those of a more specialist nature. This is more especially so concerning the Court of Justice, where its reasoning has been analysed and dissected from multiple perspectives. Thus, there is a veritable library of literature concerning the way in which the CJEU interacts with national courts, the extent to which it does or does not accord them room for choice, and the extent to which it ought or ought not to do so.

It is then surprising that there is, by way of comparison, relatively little by way of in-depth study concerning the relationship between the CJEU and the EU legislature. The latter enacts a very considerable body of legislation, in the form of regulations and directives. It is commonplace for there to be legal contestation as to the interpretation of such measures, which result in cases being heard by the CJEU, either through preliminary rulings or by way of direct challenge. The CJEU decisions are then duly analysed by those interested in the relevant area. There is, nonetheless, little by way of more considered reflection as to the relationship between the CJEU and the EU legislature when it engages in such interpretive exercises.

The present book by Martijn van den Brink fills this important gap. It considers the horizontal relationship between the CJEU and the EU legislature. This is not only an issue of significance in its own right, it is, as the author rightly notes, central for evaluation of the proper vertical division of competence between the EU and the Member States in the many areas where there are not only primary Treaty provisions in play, but also EU legislation. In such situations, it is not possible to determine in isolation whether the CJEU should exercise its authority from a position of deference to national law, without taking some view, explicit or implicit, as to whether it must respect the EU legislation that covers the ground.

The author poses fundamental questions concerning the extent to which the CJEU accords deference to the EU legislature and the extent to which it ought to do so. The analysis considers when legislative decisions should be regarded as authoritative and how they should be interpreted if they are treated as authoritative. To this end, the first half of the book investigates the justifications for judicial deference to the choices of the EU legislature and the legitimacy of judicial review for violations of issues such as the division of competence and fundamental rights.

This is then complemented by the second half of the book, which examines how legislative intent can be ascertained in EU law. The book draws on literature from political science, and from constitutional, political, and legal theory.

The book addresses important issues concerning the nature of authority in the EU and will be of interest to all those studying EU law.

Paul Craig and Gráinne de Búrca

Acknowledgements

This book has been a long time in the making, and I have incurred many intellectual debts along the way. Its seeds were sown many years ago in the hills northeast of Florence, at the European University Institute in Fiesole, where I had the immense privilege of spending four years working on my doctoral dissertation. I arrived in 2013 with the plan to write a dissertation on the subject of European Union citizenship, but over the next few years, my interests moved on to the role of the legislature in European Union (EU) law, feeling that legal scholars had neglected the value and nature of the legislative process for too long. In the years since, I have thoroughly revised every aspect of my dissertation, and much has changed in my thinking about the EU legislature but not the feeling that its importance remains overlooked in legal scholarship still today. This book is an attempt to remedy that deficit.

I have many at the European University Institute to thank for their contributions to this book. First of all, Claire Kilpatrick, who was the best supervisor I could have wished for, always leaving me free to explore my own ideas, while providing the necessary guidance and pushback when these ideas were less well thought through than I imagined them to be. Thank you, also for your support in the following years. I am also very grateful to the members of my PhD committee, Richard Bellamy, Daniel Halberstam, and Niamh Nic Shuibhne, not only for their thorough engagement with my ideas at the time but also for their encouragement to develop them further. The chapter on legislative intent in EU law would not exist had I not been asked whether the legislature can form intentions during my defence. One of the many privileges of writing a doctoral dissertation at the European University Institute is that there is always someone to discuss one's ideas with and to rely on for support. My work benefited from feedback from many, but especially from Marcin Baranski, Filipe Brito Bastos, Leticia Diez Sanchez, Oliver Garner, Sophie Möller, and Bouke de Vries.

Two research stays enabled me to expand my knowledge and develop my ideas. Michigan Law School offered me a Grotius Fellowship and, more importantly, an intellectual home where I could explore and engage with debates in US constitutional law and work in all calm and quiet on my own research. The Department of European Public Law at the University of Zagreb proved to be the most critical, but also the most constructive, testing ground for my own ideas. I look back fondly on our discussions about the role of the EU legislature and the value of legislative rules and will never forget the warmth and hospitality I received during my first research stay and in later years. Thank you Nika Bačić Selanec, Tamara Ćapeta,

Melita Carević, Iris Goldner Lang, Antonija Ivanćan, Tamara Perišin, Davor Petric, Luka Petrović, and Snježana Vasiljević.

I am very grateful to Ayelet Shachar for taking me on as a member of the Department of Ethics, Law, and Politics at the Max Planck Institute for the Study of Religious and Ethnic Diversity in Göttingen immediately after completing my PhD. My two years in Göttingen gave me the time and freedom to develop and refine the arguments of my doctoral dissertation, which I was able to do as part of a highly interdisciplinary community, surrounded by many gifted and generous junior scholars. For our many discussions during colloquia, conferences, and lunches on the roof terrace, my warmest thanks go to Elisabeth Badenhoop, Benjamin Boudou, Derek Denman, Gün Gülay, Lisa Harms, Hans Leaman, Tania Pagotto, Stefan Salomon, Stefan Schlegel, Dana Schmalz, Samuel Schmid, Mia Seyfettinoglu, Barbara von Rütte, Bouke de Vries, Julius Yam, and Caleb Yong.

A sincere thank you also to the British Academy for generously supporting a two-year research stay at the University of Oxford, to the Department of Political and Social Sciences and Nuffield College for hosting and nurturing me during this period, and to Cécile Laborde for her generous mentorship at the time. While my British Academy Fellowship allowed me to pursue my interest in the regulation of religious discrimination within Europe, several of the ideas I developed in this period found their way into this book. My presence in Oxford was interrupted for over a year by the COVID-19 pandemic. I returned to Göttingen, where I was very fortunate to be 'adopted' by Ran Hirschl as a member of his research group. The overall framing of the book benefited greatly from discussions with him, Berihun Gebeye, Lisa Harms, Alex Hudson, and Mariana Velasco-Rivera.

The Jacques Delors Centre, Hertie School, in Berlin, has been my academic home for the past two years and the ideal environment to test some of the book's untested arguments and to cross all the t's and dot the many i's that come with finishing a book. Mark Dawson and Rónán Riordan were generous enough to comment on individual chapters more than once. Chapters II, III, and V have benefited from critical discussion by Romy Hansum, Markus Jachtenfuchs, Kinga Koranyi, Francesca Minetto, Christine Reh, Simona Stockreiter, Maria Uttenthal, and Antoine Vauchez.

I would finally like to express my gratitude to Dimitry Kochenov for introducing me to the academic discussion of EU law as a student in Groningen many years ago and for his continuous support ever since; Jan Zglinski for his generous comments on draft chapters in recent years; the University of Amsterdam, NOVA Law School, Pázmány University, and the University of Copenhagen for inviting me to present chapters of this book; Paul Craig and Gráinne de Búrca for accepting this book as part of the Oxford Studies in European Law series, the book manuscript reviewers and the Oxford University Press editorial team for their suggestions and their help, and Lisa and Frida for giving me the last push to bring this book across the finish line.

Contents

I. Introduction: Political Judgement 1
1. Introduction 1
2. European Courts in Context 7
3. The Methodology of Political Judgement 9
4. Structure of the Book 14

PART 1

II. The European Union's *Demoi*cratic Legislature: Legitimating Supranational Integration 21
1. Introduction 21
2. Conceptualising Political Legitimacy 23
3. The Limits of Output-Oriented Legitimacy 28
3.1 Legitimacy by effective governance 30
3.2 Legitimacy by containment 32
3.3 Legitimacy by just governance 35
4. The European Union's *Demoi*cratic Legislature 37
5. Legislating in the Judiciary's Shadow 45

III. Realising Legal and Social Change: A Theory of Judicial Deference 50
1. Introduction 50
2. Realising Legal Change 52
3. Realising Social Change 63
4. A Theory of Judicial Deference 68
4.1 Institutional legitimacy 72
4.2 Institutional capacity 72
4.3 Institutional collaboration 73
5. The Deferential Court 74
6. Adjudicating Minimum Harmonisation 81

IV. Legislated Treaty Rights and the Legitimacy of Judicial Review 86
1. Introduction 86
2. The Judicial Review of EU Legislation: Some Preliminaries 87
3. Legislative Process Review 90
4. *Ultra Vires* Review 93
5. Fundamental Rights Review 99
5.1 Legislated fundamental rights 101
5.2 The legitimacy of fundamental rights review 106
6. Appreciating Legislation 114

7. Primary Law in Legislative Interpretation 118
8. Legislated Treaty Rights 123
8.1 Mutual recognition 126
8.2 The *Laval* quartet 129
8.3 Out of the shadows 135

PART 2

V. Out of Many, One: Legislative Intent in European Union Law 141
1. Introduction 141
2. The Discursive Dilemma 144
3. Escaping the Discursive Dilemma 149
4. Rational Legislative Action 153
5. The Formation of EU Legislative Intent 156
6. The (Ir)Relevance of Individual Intentions for Legislative Intent 164

VI. Legislative Rules: The Means to an End 169
1. Introduction 169
2. EU Legislation as a System of Rules 170
3. The Value of Rules 172
4. Collaborating with the Legislative Plan 178
5. *Keck* and *Collins* 180
6. Rule Aversion in Legislative Interpretation 184

VII. Identifying Intent: A Theory of Legislative Interpretation 193
1. Introduction 193
2. Against Instrumentalist Interpretation 194
3. The Problem with Purposive Interpretation 199
4. Indeterminacy in EU Law 203
5. The Limits of Literal Interpretation 208
6. The Intended Meaning of EU Legislation 213

VIII. Conclusion: The Dignity of International Legislation? 224

Bibliography 231
Index 249

I
Introduction
Political Judgement

1. Introduction

In the past decades, the European Union (EU) has pursued an ambitious agenda of legislative harmonisation whereby it has penetrated deep into national legal orders and gradually regulated ever more sensitive terrain. Starting with free and fair competition and the mobility of goods, services, and persons, its regulations currently span areas as diverse as environmental and consumer protection, asylum and immigration law, and cooperation in criminal affairs. Estimates of the share of national law originating from 'Brussels' continue to vary, but it is safe to say that legislation has become the legal cornerstone of European integration.[1] Without the comprehensive legislative framework put in place, the Europeanisation of national law would not have gone as far, and without the legal precision this framework provides, the EU could not have guided the conduct of its Member States and their citizens so successfully. It is, indeed, political actors and their judgements that have grown dominant in shaping the course and content of EU law.

The decisive role of the legislature is not yet adequately reflected in the study of EU law and the story of its development as it is often told. It was, we often hear, the actions of courts, lawyers, and litigants that transformed Europe from a continent ruled by an ordinary international treaty to one with 'a basic constitutional charter',[2] and it is these actors that have been the object of much intellectual curiosity and scholarly attention ever since. International courts were not meant to rise above states and rein in their influence, but this is exactly what the Court of Justice of the European Union (CJEU) allegedly succeeded in doing. It is a fascinating story that has deservedly received much attention,[3] but this court, once 'tucked away in the fairyland Duchy of Luxembourg',[4] has so absorbed legal scholars that

[1] Anu Bradford, *The Brussels Effect: How the European Union Rules the World* (OUP 2020) ch 1.

[2] Case 294/83 *Les Verts* ECLI:EU:C:1986:166, para 23; Joseph HH Weiler, 'The Transformation of Europe' (1991) 100 Yale Law Journal 2403; G Federico Mancini, 'The Making of a Constitution for Europe' in Robert O Keohane and Stanley Hoffmann (eds), *The New European Community: Decisionmaking and Institutional Change* (Westview Press 1991).

[3] Weiler (n 2); Karen J Alter, *Establishing the Supremacy of European Law: The Making of an International Rule of Law in Europe* (OUP 2006); Alec Stone Sweet, *The Judicial Construction of Europe* (OUP 2004). For a very recent retelling of the story, Tommaso Pavone, *The Ghostwriters: Lawyers and the Politics behind the Judicial Construction of Europe* (CUP 2022).

[4] Eric Stein, 'Lawyers, Judges, and the Making of a Transnational Constitution' (1981) 75 American Journal of International Law 1, 1.

Legislative Authority and Interpretation in the European Union. Martijn van den Brink, Oxford University Press.
 DOI: 10.1093/9780198900115.003.0001

they have neglected the sweeping legal changes that were taking place in plain sight in the bustling metropolis of Brussels. The curious reality is that the EU legislature remains systematically marginalised in academic legal thought.

The issue is not, of course, that lawyers are unaware of the extensive legislative harmonisation that has taken place. Browsing through monographs or any of the specialist journals on the law of the European Union, one is likely to find detailed discussions of legislative provisions. The issue is, rather, that the legislature is rarely seen as an actor worthy of serious consideration in its own right. There has been very little concern for the legislature and its constitutional position in the EU legal order, and if we ask in what ways legal scholars have enriched our understanding of the legislative process or the nature of legislative acts, the answer is not much at all.[5] When we focus on the legislature, we are mostly interested in the shortcomings of the legislative process (that it is not democratic or effective enough or that it threatens to trample on the constitutional principles enshrined in EU primary law), and from there, our debates easily move on to a discussion of the proper limits on its authority. We rarely dwell, instead, on the virtues of the legislative process or the reasons why it might be better to regulate political issues through legislation than, say, case law.

This is, to be sure, not because all lawyers appreciate the value of EU legislation. Although the CJEU more or less recognises the legislature's legitimacy (it is generally reluctant to substitute its own views for those of the legislature and gives it wide discretionary powers when it is asked to make complex political, social, or economic choices[6]), its reasoning has been inconsistent and, at times, unintelligible: its case law is not, as we will see, informed by a complete and coherent moral justification of judicial deference. The academic debate hasn't fared any better. Recall the uproar when disputes over the right of EU citizens to claim social assistance in the host Member State began being resolved in accordance with the standards set by the legislature.[7] This represented 'a (dangerous) reversal of the institutional balance for rule-making in the European Union'.[8] The CJEU rescinded 'its duty of scrutiny over secondary law',[9] sacrificing 'EU citizenship in vain'.[10] One analysis was more condemning than the other, when all the CJEU had done was respect the choices of the legislature. These analyses may have been a product of their time (the Brexit referendum and its aftermath) and the inadequate

[5] See, however, Sacha Prechal, *Directives in EC Law* (2nd edn, OUP 2005).

[6] See Chapters III and IV.

[7] The social assistance case law from Case C-333/13 *Dano* ECLI:EU:C:2014:2358, which is discussed in more detail in Chapter III.

[8] Daniel Sarmiento and Eleanor Sharpston, 'European Citizenship and Its Union: Time to Move On?' in Dimitry Kochenov (ed), *EU Citizenship and Federalism: The Role of Rights* (CUP 2017) 237.

[9] Niamh Nic Shuibhne, 'Limits Rising, Duties Ascending: The Changing Legal Shape of Union Citizenship' (2015) 52 Common Market Law Review 889, 910.

[10] Charlotte O'Brien, 'The ECJ Sacrifices EU Citizenship in Vain: *Commission v. United Kingdom*' (2017) 54 Common Market Law Review 209, 209.

legal reasoning on display, but they show the controversies that can arise in the allocation of legislative and judicial authority. They also demonstrate the need for a principled approach to this relationship.

It is unsurprising that such an approach is lacking, as the nature of the legislative process and its place in the EU's institutional architecture has attracted little interest from EU lawyers. There are exceptions, such as conceptual work on the relationship between the legislature and the judiciary[11] or excellent studies on their collaboration in the regulation of the internal market and the governance of fundamental rights,[12] but these do not offer a systematic examination of the legislature's authority and its relationship to the judiciary either. There has, for instance, been a remarkable indifference to the justification of judicial deference to EU legislation, and even if we did know when legislation merits respect, we would not know what it means to respect it: while legislative interpretation is among the CJEU's core tasks, there has been virtually no discussion of how meaning must be ascribed to legislation.[13] The result is that EU lawyers have had curiously little to say about important issues that arise daily before the EU as well as national judiciaries. How wide should the legislature's discretionary powers be when it wants to draft new laws or amend existing ones? What is the relationship between legislation and the Treaties, as well as CJEU judgments ascribing meaning to Treaty law? How much weight must be assigned to the choices of the legislature when these are being reviewed or interpreted? And how must legislation be interpreted by those to whom its provisions are addressed? So far, these questions have been met with a deafening silence.

This silence speaks volumes, I think, about the state of the legal debate. It is hard to explain in full why the legislature has been sidelined to the extent it has, but several factors can be identified that offer a partial explanation. It is interesting to go by these briefly for what they tell us about the discipline of EU law. The first is obvious and hardly needs mentioning. When Jeremy Waldron admonished legal scholars that they were 'intoxicated by courts and blinded to almost everything

[11] Phil Syrpis, 'Theorising the Relationship between the Judiciary and the Legislature in the EU Internal Market' in Philip Syrpis (ed), *The Judiciary, the Legislature and the EU Internal Market* (CUP 2012); Phil Syrpis, 'The Relationship between Primary and Secondary Law in the EU' (2015) 52 Common Market Law Review 461; Gareth Davies, 'Legislative Control of the European Court of Justice' (2014) 51 Common Market Law Review 1579; Thomas Horsley, *The Court of Justice of the European Union as an Institutional Actor: Judicial Lawmaking and Its Limits* (CUP 2018).

[12] In respect of the internal market, Eadaoin Ní Chaoimh, *The Legislative Priority Rule and the EU Internal Market for Goods: A Constitutional Approach* (OUP 2022); Jan Zglinski, 'The Internal Market: From Judicial Politics to Ordinary Politics?' in Mark Dawson, Elise Muir, and Bruno De Witte (eds), *Revisiting Judicial Politics in the European Union* (Edward Elgar 2023). In respect of fundamental rights, Mark Dawson, *The Governance of EU Fundamental Rights* (CUP 2017); Elise Muir, *EU Equality Law: The First Fundamental Rights Policy of the EU* (OUP 2018); Elise Muir, 'The Fundamental Rights Implications of EU Legislation: Some Constitutional Challenges' (2014) 51 Common Market Law Review 219.

[13] For the same observation and a first effort to address this issue, Elke Cloots, *National Identity in EU Law* (OUP 2015) ch 10.

else by the delights of constitutional adjudication',[14] he might as well have been talking about EU lawyers. In fairness, their indifference to the legislative process is probably less the result of a deliberate choice than it is of internalised assumptions and orthodoxies that have shaped the field of EU law for decades.[15] In the same period that the CJEU promulgated the supremacy and direct effect of EU law, legal professionals wedded to this process of supranational integration began to promote the EU legal order as being a constitutional order—albeit a constitutional order of a different kind from that of Member States. Domestic constitutional doctrines such as legislative power, political accountability, and separation of powers were derided as 'outdated doctrines, incapable of reflecting the new forms of regional integration'.[16] Pierre Pescatore, the pre-eminent judge at the time, tried to convince interlocutors that the CJEU 'faced only its own legal conscience',[17] that is that it could develop EU law at its own motion without being subject to the same constraints as national courts. Few will hold such extreme views today, but the fact that the legislature is not taken more seriously would suggest that the influence of Pescatore and his contemporaries has been a lasting one.

Another likely explanation is that the EU is still implicitly treated as an ordinary international organisation, despite capacious attempts by EU lawyers to wrench their discipline from its international moorings. Viewed as an international organisation, the logical question to ask is how EU institutions influence and constrain national institutions or are, on the other hand, influenced and constrained by them; it is less interesting, in that case, to reflect on how EU institutions must be situated relative to one another. This vertical, top-down perspective used to put lawyers in the good company of political scientists: they too used to study the CJEU almost exclusively in relation to national actors.[18] But while political scientists have come to realise that their knowledge of the judicial process remains incomplete as long as they do not analyse its horizontal interaction with the legislative process,[19]

[14] Jeremy Waldron, *Law and Disagreement* (OUP 1999) 9.

[15] Pierre Bourdieu, 'The Force of Law: Toward a Sociology of the Juridical Field' (1987) 38 Hastings Law Journal 805. Applied to the EU, Antoine Vauchez, *Brokering Europe Euro-Lawyers and the Making of a Transnational Polity* (CUP 2018) 9–10.

[16] Vauchez, *Brokering Europe Euro-Lawyers* (n 15) 75.

[17] Antoine Vauchez, 'The Genie of Independence and the European Bottle. How Independence Became Europe's Most Contentious Political and Legal Category' (iCourts Working Paper No 2021/266, 2021) 15.

[18] Alter (n 3); Lisa J Conant, *Justice Contained: Law and Politics in the European Union* (CUP 2002); Rachel A Cichowski, *The European Court and Civil Society Litigation, Mobilization and Governance* (CUP 2007); Clifford J Carrubba and Matthew J Gabel, *International Courts and the Performance of International Agreements: A General Theory with Evidence from the European Union* (CUP 2015); Stone Sweet (n 3); R Daniel Kelemen, *Eurolegalism: The Transformation of Law and Regulation in the European Union* (Harvard UP 2011).

[19] Dorte Sindbjerg Martinsen, *An Ever More Powerful Court? The Political Constraints of Legal Integration in the European Union* (OUP 2015); Susanne K Schmidt, *The European Court of Justice and the Policy Process: The Shadow of Case Law* (OUP 2018); Olof Larsson and Daniel Naurin, 'Judicial Independence and Political Uncertainty: How the Risk of Override Affects the Court of Justice of the EU' (2016) 70 International Organization 377; Fabio Wasserfallen, 'The Judiciary as Legislator? How

lawyers have not yet sufficiently grasped this. To do so, however, they must reckon with two forces that still hold a powerful grip on their discipline.

The first is a bias in favour of substance over process. While I cannot speak about all areas of EU law, the main—and sometimes only—question asked in some areas is what the best substantive answer is to a given legal question. What gets overlooked or brushed aside is the question of *who decides*.[20] There is a logical explanation for this: the study of EU law is highly segmented along substantive lines, which means that legal questions tend to be analysed from within the prevailing frames of reference in specific substantive sub-disciplines. To give two examples, it is quite clear that labour lawyers approach EU law from a labour law paradigm and that EU citizenship lawyers do so from a citizenship paradigm. By this, I mean that the dominant standard for assessing the law is whether it protects labour relations or the interests of EU citizens. The result is that transversal institutional questions can get ignored or, alternatively, collapsed into considerations of a substantive nature. The debate on posted workers exemplifies what happens when they are ignored. Fixated on the substantive outcome of a handful of controversial judgments, the impression has been created that the standards governing the posting of workers were set by the CJEU, when in reality, the legislature's choices were respected in most of its judgments (section IV.8). The writings by EU citizenship lawyers show what happens when both considerations are collapsed. They are well aware of the institutional dynamics behind the law; they are just not too happy about it. They criticise judicial deference to legislative norms when these norms are unfavourable to EU citizens, while at the same time advocating deference when in the interest of those same citizens (section VII.2). The same outcome-oriented thinking is likely to be found in many other areas of EU law, but is no more satisfactory for that: the question is not only what is the best substantive answer to legal questions[21] but also who decides on that—the legislature, the judiciary, or some other authority?

The second force to be reckoned with is the historical lens through which EU lawyers view their discipline. EU law is hardly comparable in form and substance to that of a few decades ago, but narratives and assumptions of that era still shape its study today. One of them is the idea that EU law-making is subject to an imbalance between law and politics. This idea took root at a unique moment, namely the EU undergoing its process of constitutionalisation at a time of political stagnation.

the European Court of Justice Shapes Policy-Making in the European Union' (2010) 17 Journal of European Public Policy 1128.

[20] See also Ingo Venzke and Joana Mendes, 'The Idea of Relative Authority in European and International Law' (2018) 16 International Journal of Constitutional Law 75. The question of who decides has, in recent years, received more attention, as I show here: Martijn van den Brink, 'Institutional Choice in the Internal Market: A Review Essay' Modern Law Review (forthcoming).

[21] Chapter II refutes such outcome-oriented thinking.

Joseph Weiler warned even then that it would be deceptive to think 'that the cardinal material locus of change has been the realm of law and that the principal actor has been the European Court',[22] yet many scholars after him have assumed just that. It is a widely held belief that European integration is marked by an asymmetry between positive and negative integration,[23] and the concept of 'integration through law' has become quasi-synonymous with judge-made law.[24] Such ideas may still contain important truths today, but they no longer capture reality and can cloud our view of the EU legal order as it exists. Legislation is typically excluded from, or undervalued, by such studies, and our understanding of EU law—of how it is made, how it operates, and when it is complied with—is all the poorer for it.

This book intends to broaden the horizons of legal scholarship by bringing the EU legislature within its view. It seeks to deepen our appreciation for the nature of legislation and the qualities of the legislative process, and it asks how moving both of these from the sidelines to the centre of legal discourse should change our understanding of the judiciary's role in the EU's constitutional framework. What is the relative legitimacy and capacity of the legislature versus the judiciary and what should this entail for their law-making authority? How must judicial power be exerted in relation to legislative decisions? When and why should judges yield to the legislature's judgements and how should they discharge the task of legislative interpretation? This book answers these questions. Part I inquires into the allocation of authority between both branches, examining when judicial deference is due to legislation and when, conversely, its provisions should be subject to judicial review. Afterwards, we know when legislation deserves to be respected but not yet how to respect the choices of the legislature. Part II explores that question and provides an account of legislative interpretation that, by addressing several misunderstandings about the structure of the legislative process and the nature of legislative acts, identifies how legislative provisions can be interpreted in accordance with legislative intent.

[22] Weiler (n 2) 2417.

[23] Fritz Wilhelm Scharpf, *Governing in Europe: Effective and Democratic?* (OUP 1999); Fritz W Scharpf, 'The Asymmetry of European Integration, or Why the EU Cannot Be a "Social Market Economy"' (2010) 8 Socio-Economic Review 211. See, for an attempt to revisit the 'asymmetry thesis', Martijn van den Brink, Mark Dawson, and Jan Zglinski, 'Revisiting the Asymmetry Thesis: Negative and Positive Integration in the EU' (2023) Journal of European Public Policy 1.

[24] For the original idea, Mauro Cappelletti, Monica Seccombe, and Joseph H Weiler (eds), *Integration through Law: Methods, Tools and Institutions*, vol 1 (De Gruyter 1986). That it has come to be understood as quasi-synonymous with judge-made law is visible in recent criticism of the concept: Stefan Auer, Pepijn Bergsen, and Hans Kundnani, 'The Law as a Tool for Integration Could Be Ending' (2021) <www.chathamhouse.org/2021/10/law-tool-eu-integration-could-be-ending> accessed 3 July 2023; Nicole Scicluna and Stefan Auer, 'Europe's Constitutional Unsettlement: Testing the Political Limits of Legal Integration' (2023) 99 International Affairs 769.

2. European Courts in Context

Even those who find it self-evident that the legislature must be placed firmly at the centre of the study of EU law may not quite see why this is so important. It may be tempting to think of the legislature as just another actor vis-à-vis which the CJEU exercises its authority—alongside national governments, administrative actors, monetary institutions, and the like. But the legislative process is more important than that. In many situations, in fact, we cannot know how the CJEU must review the choices of EU executive actors or national governments unless we know whether it must assign weight to the choices of the legislature. Indeed, the appropriate allocation of EU legislative and judicial authority is a question that ultimately determines the proper relationship of the judiciary vis-à-vis executive institutions and national governments.

To illustrate why this is so, let us zoom in on a question that has attracted some attention in recent years: should national authorities be granted a margin of appreciation in the application of EU law?[25] Readers may be familiar with the margin of appreciation doctrine from the case law of the European Court of Human Rights (ECtHR), which it uses to adjust the intensity of judicial review of national measures. For instance, national authorities enjoy a margin of appreciation when they have greater democratic legitimation or are better placed to make certain decisions.[26] In setting the margin of appreciation that states enjoy, the ECtHR takes into account factors such as 'the nature of the Convention right in issue, its importance for the individual, the nature of the interference and the object pursued by the interference'.[27] Although the application of this doctrine has been criticised, many agree that it has a principled justification—that it provides a proper framework for dealing with disagreement over the rights protected by the Convention.[28]

For similar reasons, scholars have called for the application of a margin of appreciation doctrine in the adjudication of conflicts between EU and national law. For example, concerned that the CJEU currently has no adequate tools to accommodate pluralism among Member States, Janneke Gerards has argued that 'judicial review on the supranational level should start from a position of deference' to national actors.[29] She takes this view as national institutions may have greater democratic legitimacy or be in a better position to make certain decisions than the

[25] The book focuses not so much on the relationship between the EU legislative and executive branches. See, however, section IV.6.

[26] As is set out clearly in *SAS v France* App no 43835/11 (ECtHR, 1 July 2014) para 129.

[27] *S and Marper v UK*, App nos 30562/04 and 30566/04 (unreported) 4 December 2008, para 102.

[28] See, eg Bosko Tripkovic, 'A New Philosophy for the Margin of Appreciation and European Consensus' (2022) Oxford Journal of Legal Studies 207.

[29] Janneke Gerards, 'Pluralism, Deference and the Margin of Appreciation Doctrine' (2011) 17 European Law Journal 80, 115. See, similarly, Vilija Velyvyte, *Judicial Authority in EU Internal Market Law: Implications for the Balance of Competences and Powers* (Hart Publishing, an imprint of Bloomsbury Publishing 2022) 219.

EU judiciary. Likewise, in an excellent study of judicial deference in EU law, Jan Zglinski claims that because different institutions can determine what the Treaties mean, this task should be allocated to the institution with the greatest institutional capacity and legitimacy to regulate a specific matter. As he argues,

> The choice between centrally exercised substantive review, the margin of appreciation, and decentralized judicial review can therefore be translated into a choice between *the Court of Justice, national legislatures or executives, and national courts.* The lesson from plurality is that, at least in principle, each of these actors can decide what free movement law means, how it is to be reconciled with conflicting policy concerns, and which restrictions count as proportionate.[30]

In other words, on the basis of a comparative assessment of the qualities of the EU judiciary, on the one hand, and the qualities of the national branches of government—the legislature, the executive, or the judiciary—on the other, Zglinski seeks to determine whether deference is due to national interpretations of EU law.

However, while he rightly appeals to the importance of comparative institutional choice, his analysis is incomplete. It essentially evaluates the CJEU by the same metrics as the ECtHR, while these are, in fact, very different courts, embedded in a very different context. Two contextual factors are crucial here. First, the CJEU is embedded in a different and far more complex institutional structure: it exercises authority not only vertically, over national institutions, but also horizontally, relative to EU institutions—including, indeed, the EU legislature. Even more, the legislature is the most important of these institutions when it comes to determining when national institutions must be given a margin of appreciation. To see why, the second contextual factor matters. The good provided by the European Convention—safeguarding fundamental rights—can be realised by states on their own. In contrast, many of the goods the EU provides cannot be realised by states individually, not even in theory. Whether it is the creation of the internal market, the realisation of fair competition for firms operating in this market, environmental protection, or the mitigation of cross-border public health hazards, these goods can be attained only by the EU adopting a joint course of action that is binding on all national institutions. Thus, while each of the European Convention members could adopt a different standard for the protection of personal data, provided that their standard complies with the minimum protected by the Convention, the EU could not provide the goods it seeks to provide if it were to allow the same diversity. Tolerating such diversity would mean, as Anu Bradford argues, that 'the single market could not function effectively, as companies would face a different regulatory environment in each country'.[31]

[30] Jan Zglinski, *Europe's Passive Virtues: Deference to National Authorities in EU Free Movement Law* (OUP 2020) 159.

[31] Bradford (n 1) 9.

The conclusion is not that no national differentiation must be allowed. The analysis suggests that the CJEU should not, as a general rule, adjudicate disputes from a position of deference to national institutions. The EU needs a common course of action, which can, ostensibly, be most effectively realised through the legislative harmonisation of national standards, and so judicial review should instead start from a position of deference to EU legislation. Of course, it does not follow that the CJEU must always obey the legislature's choices; perhaps it should disregard these if it is better positioned to decide the EU's course of action.[32] But this shows that the question of how it should exert its authority vis-à-vis national institutions depends on a prior question, namely how it must exert its authority relative to the EU legislature. Indeed, the example makes clear that we cannot judge the CJEU adequately unless we place it in its proper institutional context. Whether it concerns its role in protecting the internal market, accommodating national constitutional identities, promoting fundamental rights, or determining the division of powers between the EU and the Member States, we cannot have such debates without an account of the appropriate allocation of legislative versus judicial authority. We cannot know, that is, what is proper judicial behaviour if we do not know what role the legislature should play, and we need to know both to be able to know how the EU should exert its authority over national governments.

3. The Methodology of Political Judgement

We now know why the legislature should become more central to our legal debates, but we do not yet know how to place it there, that is what methodological approach to take.[33] Legal training in Europe, and especially on the continent, is mostly about allowing lawyers to identify, understand, and systematise the positive legal material—its method is the doctrinal method according to which legal questions must be answered from within the legal system and the materials that constitute it.[34] This is not to belittle doctrinal legal analysis, which has immense practical value, but if the dominant way of thinking is that any legal dispute must, by virtue of the nature of law, be met with a legal judgement, then our ambitions to reflect on and settle the allocation of EU institutional authority in general, and of the EU legislature and judiciary in particular, will prove fruitless. What is required, instead, is to exercise political judgement.

[32] Which is what some EU lawyers believe, as we will see in Chapter II.

[33] This section draws on Martijn van den Brink, 'Political, Not (Just) Legal Judgment: Studying EU Institutional Balance' European Law Open (forthcoming).

[34] See, eg Armin von Bogdandy, 'The Past and Promise of Doctrinal Constructivism: A Strategy for Responding to the Challenges Facing Constitutional Scholarship in Europe' (2009) 7 International Journal of Constitutional Law 364; Armin Von Bogdandy, 'Founding Principles of EU Law: A Theoretical and Doctrinal Sketch' (2010) 16 European Law Journal 95.

The difficulties doctrinal reasoning faces in explaining and evaluating EU institutional practices were recently touched upon by Bruno de Witte. He argued that

> a positivist approach is appropriate for the study of EU law, provided that a sufficiently broad view is taken of what constitutes a legally relevant practice. . . . legal positivism and its corollary, the doctrinal legal method, should not be narrowly limited to the study and exposition of written legal norms, but should also include the study of institutional practices that are not, or only partially, based on legal norms. The reason for this is that positive EU law cannot properly be understood (and described) without knowledge of key institutional practices; the 'black letter' of EU law remains a dead letter without reflecting in its analysis the various practices which EU institutions develop in shaping and implementing the formal legal norms. These practices are not legal norms themselves, but are not unlawful either.[35]

This analysis is correct but only goes some way to appreciating the limits of the doctrinal method. A fuller appreciation would recognise that we not only need to understand key institutional practices to understand the positive law, or at least its application, but also that we cannot simply deduce from the positive law what is good institutional practice. This second conclusion will be harder to accept because it means accepting that the doctrinal method is insufficient for answering many legal questions.

The questions at the heart of this book show that we cannot escape this conclusion. Of course, the doctrinal method can shed some light on the EU legislature's constitutional position and its authority relative to the judiciary. An exploration of the provisions laid down in the Treaties allow us to identify the powers of EU institutions. We would learn that the European Parliament and Council can jointly exercise legislative functions (arts 14(1) and 16(1) of the Treaty on European Union, TEU), and as we leaf further through the Treaties, we will also learn about the procedures to be used for enacting legislation (eg art 294 of the Treaty on the Functioning of the European Union, TFEU). In this process, we will also discover the kind of powers the CJEU enjoys. It is entrusted with the task to 'ensure that in the interpretation and application of the Treaties the law is observed' (art 19(1) of the TEU), which can compel it to invalidate legislation for 'infringement of the Treaties or of any rule of law relating to their application' (art 263 of the TFEU). Moreover, as all institutions must 'practice mutual sincere cooperation' (art 13(2) of the TEU), we might develop a sense of how they must exercise their powers towards one another. Thomas Horsley has used the doctrinal method for such prescriptive and evaluative ends, invoking the Treaties 'as the principal touchstones

[35] Bruno De Witte, 'Legal Methods for the Study of EU Institutional Practice' (2022) 18 European Constitutional Law Review 637, 638.

for assessing the internal constitutionality, and hence legitimacy, of all Union institutional activity'.[36] His work nicely demonstrates how doctrinal reasoning can be applied to the relationship between the legislature and judiciary.

Yet, the doctrinal method will not allow us to identify what this relationship ought to be. By 'ought to be', I do not mean ought to be in the sense of abstract normative theory; I mean ought to be in the sense of the resolution of actual day-to-day legal disputes. Even if Horsley were right to suggest that internal constitutionality can be equated with legitimacy (Chapter II expresses some reservations), the Treaties underdetermine the allocation of legislative and judicial power. How much leeway must the legislature have in enacting provisions regulating (say) the internal market or fundamental rights? When must its decisions be struck down for violating the Treaties? By what standards and techniques should legislation be interpreted? What, in other words, is the proper balance of legislation versus case law? These are the sort of questions that underlie many of the disputes before the EU and national judiciary, and which the Treaties do not answer, no matter how often and closely we study them. Any EU lawyer who takes the doctrinal path to find answers to these questions will, sooner rather than later, get hopelessly lost. Indeed, legal judgement is not going to get us where we need to be.

Does it not? Some EU lawyers have devised a solution that, they believe, gets them out of this predicament—a rather formalistic but seemingly ingenious solution that invokes the hierarchy between EU primary law and secondary legislation. Observing a close connection between the interaction of legal norms and the allocation of authority, their solution is to prioritise the former and claim that the hierarchy of legal norms imposes a hierarchy of political authority. This solution rests on two premises: primary law (ie the Treaties) takes priority over secondary legislation, *and* the judiciary is the exclusive interpreter of primary law. It follows, they argue, that the CJEU stands on the highest rung of the law-making ladder: legislation must either be consistent with case law interpreting primary law or be annulled.[37] Not surprisingly, the CJEU likes this idea and has occasionally used it to circumvent the legislature's choices, which we see, for instance, in its response to the legislative distinction between flight delays and flight cancellations in terms of the kind of compensation to which passengers were entitled. While financial compensation was only due to passengers of cancelled flights,[38] the CJEU in *Sturgeon*

[36] Horsley (n 11). See also Velyvyte (n 29) 9 fn 30.

[37] The EU citizenship literature in nn 9 nd 10 rests on this view. For other examples, David Edward, 'Guest Editorial: Will There Be Honey Still for Tea?' (2006) 43 Common Market Law Review 623; Nicolas Rennuy, 'The Emergence of a Parallel System of Social Security Coordination' (2013) 50 Common Market Law Review 1221, 1243; Sacha Garben, 'Sky-High Controversy and High-Flying Claims? The Sturgeon Case Law in Light of Judicial Activism, Euroscepticism and Eurolegalism' (2013) 50 Common Market Law Review 15, 34; Ní Chaoimh (n 12).

[38] Articles 5 and 6 of Regulation (EC) No 261/2004 of the European Parliament and of the Council of 11 February 2004 establishing common rules on compensation and assistance to passengers in the event of denied boarding and of cancellation or long delay of flights (OJ L46/1).

erased the distinction ruling that it breached the principle of equality. It justified its decision by saying that legislative provisions must 'be interpreted in accordance with primary law as a whole'[39] or, at least, 'as far as possible, in such a way as not to affect its validity'.[40] Indeed, it suggested that since secondary legislation is subordinate to primary law, it had no choice but to disregard the choices made by the legislature.

Here lies the ingenuity of the solution: it almost entirely hides the political choices that go with it. One could almost hear the judges say in *Sturgeon*, 'Our hands are tied; we are merely ensuring that primary law is observed.'[41] It is 'constitutional law without politics',[42] or so the judges like us to believe. But, of course, they had a choice, they made a choice, and a political one at that. They could have easily maintained the distinction between flight delays and cancelations; it was not the least bit clear that the principle of equality was violated, as they found. This principle, like most provisions of primary law, is open-ended; that is, it is open to multiple plausible interpretations.[43] It follows that the interaction between the hierarchy of legal sources, on the one hand, and the allocation of political authority, on the other, is more complex than the formalistic solution assumes. Formally, the hierarchy of legal sources indeed places some organisation on the allocation of political authority: secondary legislation must be struck down when it conflicts with primary law. But primary law, at least those provisions whose meaning is typically in dispute, is open-ended, and so the all-important question is what discretionary powers the legislature ought to have within the scope of primary law.

This is not a legal question about the interaction of legal sources but a political one about the proper allocation of authority. Indeed, it is, for most purposes, not the interaction of legal sources that structures the allocation of political authority but the allocation of political authority that structures the interaction of legal sources. This has crucial implications for how lawyers should think about the relationship between the EU legislature and judiciary. Their formalistic solution isn't so ingenious after all. The allocation of EU authority cannot be settled by imposing a hierarchical legal framework on it, nor can it be resolved by legal judgement. Quite the contrary: as Martin Loughlin has made clear, many legal disputes 'invariably entail claims about the relative authority of case law versus legislation, of legislative will versus constitutional principles, of constitutional principles

[39] Joined cases C-402/07 and C-432/07 *Sturgeon* ECLI:EU:C:2009:716, para 48.

[40] ibid para 47.

[41] See, clearly, Koen Lenaerts, 'The Court's Outer and Inner Selves: Exploring the External and Internal Legitimacy of the European Court of Justice' in Maurice Adams and others (eds), *Judging Europe's Judges: The Legitimacy of the Case Law of the European Court of Justice* (Hart Publishing 2013). His work is exemplary of the inclination of judges to take refuge 'behind the appearance of a simple application of the law and who, when he or she does in fact perform work of judicial creation, tends to dissimulate this fact': Bourdieu (n 15) 823.

[42] Martin Shapiro, 'Comparative Law and Comparative Politics' (1980) 53 Southern California Law Review 537, 538.

[43] It is doubtful, moreover, whether the CJEU's interpretation was the most plausible (section III.3).

versus judicial precedents. These conflicts . . . cannot be resolved by legal method; they require the exercise of *political judgment*.'[44] It is not only the law that makes the political but also the political that makes the law, not just at the moment of its creation but also at the moment of its application.

It is important to spell out this claim clearly. It should not be confused with the legal realist claim that legal officials cannot keep their political beliefs at bay when applying the positive law. Rather, the point is that the relative authority of institutions and, relatedly, legal sources cannot be resolved without some form of political judgement. My claim should also not be interpreted as a repudiation of positivist legal thought.[45] We just saw that de Witte defends a positivist approach, along with its corollary, the doctrinal method, as appropriate for the study of EU law. However, without wishing to contribute to the debate on the nature of law, legal positivists are not committed to such 'positivistic adjudication'.[46] They are aware that judges have a responsibility to apply non-legal considerations when they cannot resolve disputes by the application of legal norms alone. They are aware, that is, of the limits of doctrinal reasoning. EU lawyers should be too. Doctrinal analysis cannot answer all questions of law; in which case, political judgement may be needed to render a legal judgment, including in cases involving disagreements about the correct allocation of political authority. Finally, my claim is not that the doctrinal method should be abolished or that legal reasoning can be reduced to political reasoning. Indeed, it is not that legal judgment is ultimately political judgement but that a significant number of legal judgments rest on, and cannot be made without, some kind of political judgement. The challenge, therefore, is to integrate the positivist with the political in a way to better understand, critique, and inform the political choices underlying EU constitutional principles and practices.[47]

It is now clear that the allocation of legislative and judicial authority is a matter of political judgement and not just legal judgement. This poses a further question: how to render the necessary political judgements to determine who decides what in EU law? This is the second methodological challenge that needs to be addressed. Roughly speaking, the challenge can be approached in two ways. The first possibility is to try to find ideal solutions to political questions unburdened by the context in which normative or political principles are invoked. This would amount to a form of ideal theorising that is unrestrained by existing social and political facts, such as, say, the existence of national communities with associated feelings of belonging and solidarity. The debate on the EU's democratic legitimacy often

[44] Martin Loughlin, *Political Jurisprudence* (OUP 2017) 6.

[45] I am agnostic on this issue, unlike Loughlin, who rejects legal positivism.

[46] John Gardner, 'Legal Positivism: 5½ Myths' (2001) 46 American Journal of Jurisprudence 199, 211–14.

[47] Michael Gordon, 'A Positivist and Political Approach to Public Law' in Dimitrios Kyritsis and Stuart Lakin (eds), *The Methodology of Constitutional Theory* (Hart Publishing 2022).

proceeds along such lines (Chapter II), with the result that it is affected by what Jo Shaw and Antje Wiener have called the 'touch of stateness'.[48] The normative baggage of domestic constitutional theory is carried into the EU debate without unpacking how the EU differs from national societies. This can produce valuable insights, but these are not always the most relevant for those interested in the here and now.

The second possibility would be to adopt a (more) realist approach that is attentive to the social and political context as it exists and the constraints it imposes on what is realistically feasible. The aim, then, is to identify what should be in light of what is or could be.[49] Much of the more interesting constitutional theory on the EU is realist in the proper sense of the term. It eschews moral idealism and takes seriously what Neil Walker called the difficulty of 'translating' normative concepts of constitutionalism from the state to the EU and other transnational settings more generally.[50] Motivated by similar concerns, Turkuler Isiksel has defended what she calls 'reflexive readjustment', which is a method that should allow constitutional concepts to be adapted to new contexts without losing the essential normative qualities that make constitutionalism valuable.[51] This book takes this approach: it identifies the appropriate allocation of EU legislative and judicial authority by examining if, and how, domestic constitutional concepts should be translated into the EU context.

4. Structure of the Book

Before I set out the structure of my argument, a remark about its scope is in order. Studying legislative decision-making in the EU is complicated by the fact that there is no single legislature or legislative process. Until the Lisbon Treaty, it was not even defined what institutions have legislative power and what acts are legislative acts. Despite the clarifications introduced, the problem has not disappeared. The standard procedure for passing legislation is the ordinary legislative procedure, which is initiated by the Commission when it submits a legislative proposal to the European Parliament and the Council of Ministers, who jointly exercise legislative power in this process. Some areas of EU law, however, are subject to special

[48] Jo Shaw and Antje Wiener, 'The Paradox of the "European Polity"' in Maria Green Cowles and Michael Smith (eds), *The State of the European Union: Risks, Reforms, Renewals, and Revival* (OUP 2000) 65.

[49] Robert Jubb, 'Realism' in Adrian Blau (ed), *Methods in Analytical Political Theory* (CUP 2017); David Schmidtz, 'Realistic Idealism' in Adrian Blau (ed), *Methods in Analytical Political Theory* (CUP 2017).

[50] Neil Walker, 'Postnational Constitutionalism and the Problem of Translation' in JHH Weiler and Marlene Wind (eds), *European Constitutionalism beyond the State* (CUP 2001).

[51] Turkuler Isiksel, *Europe's Functional Constitution: A Theory of Constitutionalism beyond the State* (OUP 2016) 24–25.

legislative procedures under which the Council and Parliament do not stand on equal footing. Usually, under these procedures, Parliament's powers vis-à-vis the Council are limited, and the passing of legislation requires unanimity (rather than qualified majority) in the Council. These procedures will not be discussed separately. Instead, when I zoom in on the legislative process, I focus on the ordinary legislative procedure. I believe that this book's argument is extendable to the other procedures (except perhaps the argument in Chapter II), but I will not explore this further.

The two parts of the book together offer a theory of legislative authority and interpretation in the EU. Chapters II–IV delineate the scope of the legislature's authority over EU law and the limits that primary law places on its authority. Chapters V–VII provide a theory of legislative interpretation that spells out how legal officials can ascertain the intentions in legislative acts.

Chapter II assesses the allocation of legislative and judicial authority against the value of political legitimacy. It gets to the root of so much scepticism about the value of the legislative process, namely that it lacks democratic legitimacy. Assuming that the EU suffers from a democratic deficit, EU lawyers have taken the view that the EU's political legitimacy must be output-oriented, a view that, implicitly or explicitly, detracts from the worth of the legislative process The chapter salvages legislative decision-making in two steps: first, by demonstrating that output-oriented standards are inadequate to legitimate the EU's authority; second, by making room for an input-oriented, *demoi*cratic conception of political legitimacy which shows that the value of political legitimacy weighs not against but in favour of bringing EU law within the province of legislation.

Chapter III builds on this argument by providing a theory of judicial deference to the choices of the legislature. It complements the account of institutional legitimacy in Chapter II with an account of institutional capacity. It is argued that the legislature has a greater capacity than the judiciary to initiate *legal change* and to realise *social change*. EU law can be trusted to be of higher quality and is more likely to generate its intended effects domestically when made by the legislature. These arguments are then integrated into a theory of judicial deference to legislation that rests on three principles: institutional legitimacy, institutional capacity, and institutional collaboration. More specifically, I defend a 'restrictive institutionalist' form of deference,[52] which favours deference to relatively precise legislative norms for reasons that we typically associate with the Rule of Law and democratic legitimacy. The final parts of the chapter clarify the implications of restrictive institutionalist adjudication and defend it against the criticism that is incompatible with primary law. It is not, and I will argue that it is the appropriate adjudicatory method in respect of both maximum and minimum harmonisation.

[52] Jeff King, *Judging Social Rights* (CUP 2012) 141–42.

Chapter IV discusses the limits that primary law places on the legislative process, focusing in particular on the question of the legitimacy of judicial review of legislation. To answer this question, I assess when judicial review can overcome the objections from institutional legitimacy and capacity set out in Chapters II and III, whereby a distinction is made between three grounds for review: legislative process review, *ultra vires* review, and fundamental rights review. First, legislative process review, which is exercised in disputes between the Parliament, the Council, and the Commission over the proper procedure for adopting legislation, is not vulnerable to these objections. No deference can be given to these actors in such disputes. In contrast, because *ultra vires* review and fundamental rights review are vulnerable to both objections, the legislature must enjoy a wide margin of discretion when it articulates the division of competences and individual fundamental rights. A discussion of the case law on the use of art 114 of the TFEU as the legal basis for internal market legislation shows that a correct standard of review is applied in *ultra vires* disputes. In contrast, a discussion of the case law in which fundamental rights review is exercised shows that the standard of review applied in these cases is too strict. Finally, to round off the discussion, I explain that primary law should not just be thought of as limiting the authority of the legislature. On the contrary, the rights enshrined in primary law are largely legislated rights. Not only does the CJEU not have exclusive interpretative authority over primary law, but also I will show, through a discussion of two unlikely cases (the principle of mutual recognition and the *Laval* quartet), that the legislature has exerted a much greater influence on the interpretation of primary law than is often recognised.

If legislation is to be treated as authoritative by other institutions, we need a theory that explains how it can be interpreted accordingly. This is the task of Chapters V–VII. Chapter V explains that it is plausible to think that legislative intent must be the object of legislative interpretation. It does so by showing that the intentions of individual legislators can be aggregated into joint legislative intentions. My theory challenges the notion that the legislative process is too complex and involves too many disjointed individual intentions for it to be able to form collective intentions. To demonstrate that legislative intent is an intelligible notion, the chapter draws on social choice theory and its application to legislative studies. A detailed study of the ordinary legislative procedure will show that the legislature is structured to facilitate joint action and generate coherent intentional attitudes. Of particular importance are the political parties and legislative committees in the Parliament and the hierarchical, consensus-based decision-making in the Council. Legislative intent is understood as the plan of action drawn up for the entire Union, which consists of both the ends the legislature wants to realise and the means to achieve these ends.

Chapter VI builds on this definition by exploring the nature and value of legislative rules. More specifically, singling out rules as the means by which the legislature intends to achieve its desired state of affairs, it explores the promises and pitfalls of rule-based decision-making. As exclusionary reasons for action, rules require their addressees to conform to these reasons and disregard factors not included in them. But because this can produce arbitrary results (ie results that are incompatible with the purpose behind the rule), there may be pressure to collapse rules into their background purpose. Since this would rob rules of their ability to guide and coordinate action, I defend compliance with legislative rules in legislative interpretation, even if the outcome is incompatible with their underlying purpose. Taking the judgments in the *Keck* and *Collins* cases as examples, I illustrate how the CJEU can succumb to pressure to collapse rules into the purpose behind them. Finally, using EU citizenship and consumer protection law, I show that concerns about arbitrariness can produce resistance to rule-based decision-making and, hence, judgments that violate legislative intent.

Chapter VII expands on Chapters V and VI by providing a theory of legislative interpretation. I reject instrumentalist interpretation (which wrongly assumes that interpretation is about achieving desirable outcomes) and purposive interpretation (which gives insufficient weight to the constraints of legislative rules and relies on too negative a view of legislative action). I then explain that while legislative interpretation involves considerable textualism, theories that advocate a literal reading of legislation underestimate the complexity of legislative language use. Legislation's intended meaning is not solely a function of linguistic conventions but is a pragmatically enriched version of the literal meaning of the words used. To identify legislative intent, the legislature must be treated as an ordinary language user, which requires that the literal meaning of legislation is read in its legislative context. Drawing on case law, I show that my theory is better than other theories at prescribing how meaning must be ascribed to EU law. Chapter VIII acts as a conclusion.

PART 1

II

The European Union's *Demoi*cratic Legislature

Legitimating Supranational Integration

1. Introduction

European Union (EU) institutions are engaged in a collaborative exercise: they work together in the development of EU law. But as with other collaborative relationships, questions can arise about which of the actors involved gets to take which decisions and how much respect and consideration each of them must have for decisions taken by the others. All EU institutions have an important role to play; so much is clear. But how authority should be allocated between them (and who gets to decide what political issues) are questions that easily spark a great deal of controversy. So too the question of which issues must fall within the purview of legislation and which should rather be left to adjudication and, relatedly, the question of whether the EU should ideally exercise its authority over national governments through the legislative or the judicial process. The relative authority of both branches is what will occupy us in Chapters II–IV. To decide when deference is due to legislation and when it can, instead, be struck down for violating the Treaties, the legislature's institutional legitimacy and capacity will be assessed against that of the judiciary.

The value of political legitimacy is the obvious place of departure for this inquiry. After all, in the areas in which it exerts its powers, the EU issues instructions that confer rights on national institutions and their citizens, as well as duties which, it claims, they are bound to obey. Where necessary, it will also seek to coerce those falling under its authority into obedience, either through its own modest means of enforcement or by calling on the law enforcement capacities of Member States. Hence, the question arises of the political legitimacy of its institutions and the authority they exert. When is the political authority the EU exercises justified?

This is a complex question with different dimensions, not all of which I will address in this chapter. For example, I will say almost nothing about legitimacy in relation to the EU's founding and will, instead, talk almost exclusively about legitimacy in relation to its ongoing governance and only to the extent necessary to identify the relative institutional legitimacy of the legislative versus the judicial process. I will do so without suggesting that the value of political legitimacy is the only yardstick for assessing the relationship between legislation and case law. On

Legislative Authority and Interpretation in the European Union. Martijn van den Brink, Oxford University Press.
 DOI: 10.1093/9780198900115.003.0002

the contrary, Chapter III assesses the relative institutional capacity of the legislature and judiciary (their capacity to initiate legal change and realise social change), which, together with the argument developed in this chapter, will provide a three-tiered account of judicial deference to the legislature's choices. It makes sense, however, for the value of political legitimacy to be the start of our inquiry, because it is not only normatively prior to institutional capacity but also allows us to better understand and address the still lingering scepticism among EU legal scholars regarding legislative decision-making.

A startling number of EU lawyers believe that the EU ideally exercises its authority through the judicial process.[1] Some have not given sufficient thought to the benefits of legislative decision-making; others have, yet still believe that it should ideally be for the Court of Justice of the European Union (CJEU) to decide on the content of EU law. This position is quite remarkable, not because it is obviously wrong—that case has yet to be made—but because it is clearly at odds with the widely held view that democratic legislatures, and not unelected judges, should hold the most comprehensive power to initiate legal change. For most political theorists, a plausible conception of legitimacy is a democratic one. In accordance, judicial constraints on democratic legislation, if legitimate at all, require weighty justification. As the leading democratic theorist, Robert Dahl, put it,

> There is necessarily an inverse ratio between the authority of quasi guardians and the authority of the demos and its representatives. . . . The broader the scope of rights and interests subject to final decision by the quasi guardians, the narrower must be the scope of the democratic process.[2]

The concern, in other words, is that the democratic process—and thus the legitimacy of state authority—is jeopardised when the authority of quasi guardians, such as courts, is too broad.

So why are many EU lawyers unperturbed by this concern? As we shall see, the reason for their divergent view is their undemocratic conceptions of legitimacy. They think that a democratic conception of legitimacy is so demanding that it can only be realised in societies that have a unified demos. And because there is no single European demos that is represented by the legislature, they believe that the CJEU's authority does not stand in inverse ratio to a democratic legislative process. Moreover, in their search for alternative sources of legitimation for EU law, they have started to embrace undemocratic conceptions of legitimacy: they either equate legitimacy with lawfulness or conflate it with output-oriented standards

[1] This chapter, except for section II.2, reuses material previously published in Martijn van den Brink, 'The European Union's Demoicratic Legislature' (2021) 19 International Journal of Constitutional Law 914.

[2] Robert A Dahl, *Democracy and Its Critics* (Yale UP 1991) 188.

like effectiveness or justice. Neither understanding favours legislative decision-making: the first holds that the CJEU acts legitimately as long as its rulings respect the limits of the powers conferred on it by the EU Treaties—no matter what the legislature has decided—and the second that its rulings are legitimate if they generate the right kind of political output so that overriding legislation is justified if this enhances the quality of the EU's political output.

My ambition is to make room for a *demoi*cratic conception of political legitimacy and to argue for its soundness. If this view is correct, the institutional implications will be considerable: the value of political legitimacy no longer furnishes reasons to curtail the legislature but rather provides a justification for assigning weight to its choices. To get to this point, much conceptual and normative work needs to be done. To start, section II.2 distinguishes three different usages of the concept of political legitimacy and explains why the justification of political authority is a normative and not a sociological or legal question. Next, I determine the proper content of this normative conception of political legitimacy. Although it is a widespread view that its content must be filled with output-oriented standards because of the EU's democratic deficit, I instead argue in section II.3 that the justification of EU political authority depends on input-oriented reasons. More specifically, a *demoi*cratic conception of political legitimacy will be defended and elaborated, according to which the national peoples must have shared and equal control over the EU to ensure that they are not dominated by its institutions. Finally, I will show that the conditions for *demoi*cratic legitimacy are met reasonably well by the legislature (and, in any case, better than by the judiciary), which gives us reason to favour legislative determinations of the content of EU law (within limits, defined in Chapter IV). It is also a reason to be concerned about evidence that the legislature at times operates in the judiciary's shadow (sections II.4 and II.5).

2. Conceptualising Political Legitimacy

Few concepts are as central to contemporary debate on the EU and its policies as the concept of political legitimacy. The 'quest for legitimacy in the European Union',[3] however, has been plagued by confusion about the path to take for the quest to succeed. Because there are 'many ways to cut the conceptual cake of legitimacy in the European Union',[4] our understanding of the concept has been muddled, leading to scepticism about its value in evaluating EU institutions. According to Michal Bobek, for example, disagreement on the CJEU's legitimacy is often

[3] Gráinne de Búrca, 'The Quest for Legitimacy in the European Union' (1996) 59 Modern Law Review 349.

[4] Neil Walker, 'The White Paper in Constitutional Context' (Jean Monnet Working Paper No 6/01, 2001).

reducible to 'personal, often culturally determined, convictions about what judges should and should not do'.[5] Along the same lines, Michael Dougan has asserted that 'any accusation of judicial activism against the Court ultimately rests upon certain unproven and ultimately unprovable assumptions about the proper nature of the Union's judicial function—and serves to underline the essentially selective and subjective nature of the judicial activism debate'.[6] If this were true, the quest might be better abandoned.

But that would be unattractive as well as unnecessary. Such pessimistic conclusions can, and should, be fought by more clearly marking the boundaries of the way forward in our quest. Christopher Thomas is right: 'if approached carefully... the concept of legitimacy can prove illuminating for international law scholarship and practice',[7] which it can be if we carefully dissect at least the following two questions: 'How should we conceptualise legitimacy?' and 'Under what conditions do political institutions exercise their authority legitimately?' This section discusses the first of both questions, while the argument that follows concerns the second. We will see that while the concept of legitimacy can be understood in multiple ways, these conceptions are not all equally valuable in terms of the evaluation of the allocation of EU authority.

Political legitimacy is the concept we use to define and describe when political authorities have the right to rule. Yet, different conceptions of legitimacy exist that can easily get mixed up if we proceed carelessly. Three such conceptions will be distinguished here: normative, sociological, and legal legitimacy.[8] Normative legitimacy is the conception used by those interested in the moral justification of political authority, that is the moral right of an institution to rule and create duties of obedience.[9] Legal legitimacy is a subcategory of normative legitimacy: it is used mainly by legal scholars to assess the 'internal qualities of the legal system'.[10] Sociological legitimacy stands apart from the other two conceptions: it is empirical and measurable rather than normative, held by political institutions whose subjects *believe* that they have the right to rule.[11] As I shall explain, legal and sociological conceptions cannot be used as yardsticks for determining the proper

[5] Michal Bobek, 'Of Feasibility and Silent Elephants: The Legitimacy of the Court of Justice through the Eyes of National Courts' in Maurice Adams and others (eds), *Judging Europe's Judges: The Legitimacy of the Case Law of the European Court of Justice* (Hart Publishing 2013) 200.

[6] Michael Dougan, 'The Bubble That Burst: Exploring the Legitimacy of the Case Law on the Free Movement of Union Citizens' in Adams and others (n 5) 131.

[7] Christopher A Thomas, 'The Uses and Abuses of Legitimacy in International Law' (2014) 34 Oxford Journal of Legal Studies 729, 732.

[8] ibid; Daniel Bodansky, 'Legitimacy in International Law and International Relations' in Jeffrey L Dunoff and Mark A Pollack (eds), *'Interdisciplinary Perspectives on International Law and International Relations': 'The State of the Art'* (CUP 2013).

[9] John Tasioulas, 'The Legitimacy of International Law' in Samantha Besson and John Tasioulas (eds), *The Philosophy of International Law* (OUP 2010); Allen Buchanan and Robert O Keohane, 'The Legitimacy of Global Governance Institutions' (2006) 20 Ethics & International Affairs 405.

[10] Bodansky (n 8) 323. See also Thomas (n 7) 735.

[11] Buchanan and Keohane (n 9); Bodansky (n 8) 327.

allocation and exercise of EU authority. Its justification depends not on whether its exercise is lawful (legal legitimacy) or believed to be legitimate (sociological legitimacy). Instead, it depends on there being a normative justification.

Sociological conceptions feature prominently in the academic debate on the legitimacy of EU institutions. This is partly due to widespread citizen dissatisfaction with the integration project, in relation to either specific areas of governance or the project as a whole. Its future clearly depends on citizens believing in its legitimacy, which is why Joseph Weiler has repeatedly stressed the need for a new 'political messianism'—a quintessentially sociological approach to legitimacy—that derives legitimacy 'not from process, as in classical democracy, or from result and success, but from the ideal pursued, the destiny to be achieved, the promised land waiting at the end of the road'.[12] Citizens must believe in the values the EU represents and share the ideals it promotes, and the EU must derive its legitimacy from such beliefs. In addition, academic interest in sociological legitimacy also stems from the responsibility that national institutions bear for the implementation and enforcement of EU law. Its effectiveness stands or falls on its social acceptance by national institutions. Although social acceptance of legal norms is, strictly speaking, separate from belief in their legitimacy, there may be significant overlap in practice: the EU has limited tools to enforce compliance so would not be able to govern effectively without a general belief among national institutions in the legitimacy of its political authority. This explains why EU law's social acceptance is often used as a benchmark for measuring EU institutions' legitimacy. For example, as Bobek noted, compliance by domestic courts is 'the perhaps most frequently invoked legitimising element for the Court's activity and its case law'.[13]

However, while the effectiveness of EU policy-making depends on subjective beliefs, its legitimacy does not. Historical examples abound of politically messianic regimes that were deeply illegitimate, because of their large-scale human rights violations, because of their undemocratic nature, or both.[14] Of course, subjective beliefs about the legitimacy of a regime may be influenced by the virtues of its institutions. It is very plausible, for instance, that popular dissatisfaction with the EU stems partly from the belief that its institutions suffer from a democratic deficit. However, citizens may hold such views towards the EU, when in reality its authority has sufficient democratic legitimacy (or vice versa). In other words, whether the EU has a right to rule does not depend on the subjective beliefs of the ruled but on the objective qualities of the ruler.[15] Indeed, the political legitimacy

[12] Joseph HH Weiler, 'The Political and Legal Culture of European Integration: An Exploratory Essay' (2011) 9 International Journal of Constitutional Law 678, 683.

[13] Bobek (n 5) 200.

[14] Of which Weiler is, of course, aware. See, for example, Joseph HH Weiler, 'Europe in Crisis—On "Political Messianism", "Legitimacy" and the "Rule of Law"' [2012] Singapore Journal of Legal Studies 248.

[15] Bodansky (n 8) 327.

of the EU is a normative question, not a sociological one that can be answered by gauging subjective beliefs.

Because legal legitimacy is a subset of normative legitimacy, EU lawyers may think that the EU's legitimacy depends on its authority being legally justified. Legal conceptions of legitimacy have been popular, especially in studies assessing judicial decision-making. The Court's legitimacy has been said to depend, for example, on case law providing 'clear, understandable, consistent and above all feasible guidance'.[16] That case law is judged according to such rule of law standards makes sense, especially given ongoing concerns about the style and quality of the Court's reasoning.[17] And yet the justification of its authority hardly depends on these values alone, especially since legal conceptions of legitimacy fall silent where an answer is most needed: How should judges exercise their authority relative to other EU institutions as well as domestic authorities? It simply makes no sense to try to answer this question in terms of rule of law values such as clarity and consistency.

For another legal conception, legitimacy means nothing else than lawfulness. It holds that EU institutions behave legitimately when their actions are lawful under the Treaty provisions that set out their powers. As an organisation subject to the principle of conferred powers, the scope of its authority is marked by the Treaties: EU institutions cannot act *ultra vires* (beyond the limits of their powers), in which case their actions are without legal authority.[18] Some have taken this to mean that EU institutions act legitimately insofar as they comply with the procedures laid down in the Treaties and observe the limits of the powers conferred on them. EU institutions would have legitimacy insofar as the Treaties grant them authority. It has been said, for example, that the CJEU can legitimately annul legislative acts because it has the power to review the validity of such acts.[19] But it is not as simple as that: such notions confuse legitimacy with legality. The point of political legitimacy is precisely to distinguish factual authority from moral justification. Establishing that an actor has the authority to do X is one thing; whether that actor is justified in doing X is quite another. These questions must be kept apart.

Those who believe that the moral justification of EU institutions can be derived from the Treaties may retort that the Treaties owe their legitimacy to the democratic consent of the Member States. They may argue that states are bound by international obligations they have consented to and that international institutions

[16] Bobek (n 5) 202.

[17] For an overview of complaints concerning the quality of legal reasoning, Mark A Pollack, 'The Legitimacy of the European Court of Justice' in Nienke Grossman and others (eds), *Legitimacy and International Courts* (CUP 2018) 156–58.

[18] Paul Craig, 'The ECJ and *Ultra Vires* Action: A Conceptual Analysis' (2011) 48 Common Market Law Review 395.

[19] Miguel Poiares Maduro, 'Interpreting European Law—On Why and How Law and Policy Meet at the European Court of Justice' in Henning Koch and others (eds), *Europe: The New Legal Realism: Essays in Honor of Hjalte Rasmussen* (Djøf Publishing 2010) fn 13.

cannot create morally binding obligations for states beyond their consent.[20] On that basis, they might want to claim that EU institutions can ground their legitimacy in Member State consent, provided they observe the limits of this consent. But again, things are not that simple. First, it is often not clear what was originally consented to: open-ended Treaty provisions, including the provisions that set out the authority of EU institutions, can be subject to reasonable interpretative disagreement. One can try using them 'as the principal statements on the internal constitutionality of all EU institutional activity',[21] but the Treaties do not specify how they should exercise their authority towards each other.[22] Second, as most EU law is made and approved not by national parliaments but by EU institutions, the democratic consent of national parliaments may be sufficient to legitimise the EU's founding—the Treaties—but not to justify its ongoing governance.[23]

What we need, in other words, is a normative conception of legitimacy that provides the circumstances that would legitimise the EU's ongoing governance and, hence, the proper allocation of authority between its institutions. Neither sociological nor legal conceptions of legitimacy allow a determination of how they should exercise their authority relative to one another and indirectly vis-à-vis national actors. Instead, as Paul Craig has said, institutional balance 'presumes by its very nature a normative and political judgment as to which institutions should be able to partake of . . . power, and it presumes also a view as to what constitutes the appropriate balance between them'.[24] Indeed, the proper exercise of EU authority can be settled neither by sociological fact nor by legal doctrine but only by normative argument.

The question that then naturally arises is by what standards the normative legitimacy of EU institutions must be assessed. I will address this question in what follows, but not before having clarified my understanding of the concept of legitimacy in two ways. First, the way we use it in our everyday language may suggest that it is a binary value that political institutions may or may not have. We tend to use it in an unyielding manner and say that something is legitimate or illegitimate. In my view, however, legitimacy is not an absolute value; it is a matter of degree. No political institution will be entirely legitimate; most are, to a greater or lesser degree. This brings me to my second point: institutional legitimacy—like institutional choice in general—is partly comparative.[25] The analysis in sections II.3 and

[20] On state consent, Andreas Follesdal, 'Survey Article: The Legitimacy of International Courts' (2020) 28 Journal of Political Philosophy 476, 482–83.

[21] Thomas Horsley, *The Court of Justice of the European Union as an Institutional Actor: Judicial Lawmaking and Its Limits* (CUP 2018) 9.

[22] See the introductory chapter of this volume for a more detailed argument in support of this view.

[23] See also, Allen Buchanan, 'The Legitimacy of International Law' in Besson and Tasioulas (n 9) 90–91.

[24] Paul Craig, 'Institutions, Power, and Institutional Balance' in Paul Craig and Gráinne de Búrca (eds), *The Evolution of EU Law* (2nd edn, OUP 2011) 42. See, in addition, my thoughts on the need for political judgement in the introductory chapter of this volume.

[25] Neil K Komesar, *Imperfect Alternatives: Choosing Institutions in Law, Economics and Public Policy* (University of Chicago Press 1997) 5.

II.4 will bear this out: no EU institution fully attains the value of legitimacy, but some do so more than others.

3. The Limits of Output-Oriented Legitimacy

If it has a choice, should the EU exercise its authority through the legislative or the judicial process? The answer to this question depends, to a considerable extent, on the conception of legitimacy that guides our answer. To demonstrate this, I will discuss various conceptions of normative legitimacy, following a distinction that most EU scholars will be familiar with: the distinction between input-oriented and output-oriented legitimacy.[26] Output-oriented conceptions care about the political performance of political institutions (the quality of their political output), whereas input-oriented conceptions cherish the fairness of the decision-making process, with fairness depending on the intrinsic qualities of the political process instead of the output it generates.[27]

Much academic writing on EU legitimacy implicitly assumes or explicitly argues that EU institutions cannot have input-oriented legitimacy; they can only aspire to enjoying output-oriented legitimacy. This assumption has led to extensive debate on the correct standards of output-oriented legitimacy. I will discuss three such standards with a twofold aim: to explain why many think that EU institutions can only have output-oriented legitimacy and to underline the inadequacy of this belief. However, I am not primarily interested in this debate for theoretical reasons. Instead, I want to question the institutional recommendations made by output-oriented conceptions of legitimacy, which typically strengthen the Court's authority at the expense of the legislature. In other words, my aim is to revisit these institutional claims by showing that their underlying moral assumptions prove inadequate.

The reason why many theories of EU legitimacy are output oriented is that the EU cannot, supposedly, be democratic. Input-oriented legitimacy is often equated with democratic legitimacy, so the belief that EU institutions cannot have democratic legitimacy has created the view that their authority can only be justified in output-oriented terms.[28] Now, it is also likely, given the persistent criticism of the EU's democratic deficit, that output-oriented theories have great appeal to the EU community for instrumental reasons. They allow the CJEU to respond to the critique that it has rendered undemocratic laws supreme over national

[26] I will not discuss 'throughput' legitimacy, which is sometimes added as a third value: Vivien A Schmidt, 'Democracy and Legitimacy in the European Union Revisited: Input, Output *and* "Throughput"' (2013) 61 Political Studies 2.

[27] On the distinction between input-oriented and output-oriented legitimacy, Fritz Wilhelm Scharpf, *Governing in Europe: Effective and Democratic?* (OUP 1999).

[28] For a clear statement to that effect, ibid 6–12.

democratic constitutions;[29] they allow the European Commission to pursue new forms of governance without concern for possible democratic costs;[30] and they provide scholars with the conceptual means to shield these institutions from criticism: their authority does not need to have democratic legitimacy but only needs to meet certain output-oriented standards to be justified. I do not mean this in a conspiratorial sense. It is undeniable, however, that output-oriented thinking has served the CJEU well.

This is very nicely illustrated by Floris de Witte's argument of how the EU must deal with the diversity of moral and ethical policies that exist in Europe. His argument is instructive because it both intelligently integrates multiple output-oriented standards into one theory and offers very clear institutional recommendations. He claims that the EU, in its choice of when to intervene with domestic policies, must mediate between two virtually incommensurate positions, which he calls 'the argument from self-determination' and 'the argument from containment'.[31] The first of these arguments cautions against intervention. It claims that '[t]he diversity in the moral and ethical policies that exist in Europe can both be explained and normatively defended with reference to the argument from (political) self-determination'.[32] The EU should respect national diversity since it lacks 'the basic institutional preconditions that would allow for self-determination at the transnational level',[33] that is the preconditions for democratic self-determination that could confer input legitimacy on the EU. In principle, he argues, 'a European public order, centred on majoritarian first principles, whether given shape through the EU's legislative process, through an overly strict application of the Charter of Fundamental Rights, or through the Court's case law, lacks legitimacy'.[34] In essence, the argument from self-determination is an argument for deference to national law.

The argument from containment diametrically opposes this conclusion. It rests on several output-oriented standards of legitimacy that supposedly justify EU intervention despite its input-oriented legitimacy deficit. According to the argument, the EU must seek 'to *constrain* national self-determination, so as to mitigate

[29] For such criticism, Weiler, 'The Political and Legal Culture of European Integration' (n 12) 690. For an attempt to legitimise the Court on output-oriented grounds, Koen Lenaerts, 'The Principle of Democracy in the Case Law of the European Court of Justice' (2013) 62 International and Comparative Law Quarterly 271.

[30] Commission of the European Communities, 'European Governance: A White Paper', Brussels 25 July 2001 (COM(2001) 428 final).

[31] Floris de Witte, 'Sex, Drugs & EU Law: The Recognition of Moral and Ethical Diversity in EU Law' (2013) 50 Common Market Law Review 1545, 1546.

[32] ibid.

[33] ibid 1551.

[34] ibid 1561. For similar views, Anthony Arnull, 'Judicial Review in the European Union' in Damian Chalmers and Anthony Arnull (eds), *The Oxford Handbook of European Union Law* (OUP 2015) 379; Jacob Öberg, 'The Rise of the Procedural Paradigm: Judicial Review of EU Legislation in Vertical Competence Disputes' (2017) 13 European Constitutional Law Review 248, 259.

what are regarded as its potential excesses: the exclusion of certain interests from the political process, and its capacity for sovereign violence in limiting permissible behaviour'.[35] So the EU may be able to derive legitimacy not from a democratic process but from its ability to curb the excesses of national democratic politics. Institutionally, it should do this by 'removing agency, or self-determination, from "the political" sphere, and re-allocating it to a different type of government, whether judicial . . . expert-based . . . administrative . . . or the individual'.[36] The EU legislative process is not fully discounted[37] but clearly sidelined. De Witte argues that the EU should attach 'legal significance to individual movement rather than collective policy decisions'.[38] His argument 'does not accept the national political process as the locus for the formation and re-negotiation of moral, ethical or cultural norms, but instead allocates this task to the transnational level, and *mainly its judiciary*'.[39] Indeed, his theory seeks to attain output-oriented legitimacy by transferring authority from EU and national legislative processes to various counter-majoritarian institutions, in particular the CJEU.

Interestingly, all output-oriented conceptions I am familiar with follow this logic or have this effect. The remainder of this section shows this by highlighting the defects of three different conceptions that have been defended over the past decades: *legitimacy by effective governance*, *legitimacy by containment*, and *legitimacy by just governance*. According to these standards, the EU acts legitimately when it, respectively, enhances policy effectiveness, contains unwanted domestic democratic policies, and promotes justice between citizens. All three standards prioritise the quality of political output over the fairness of political procedure on the assumption that the EU cannot attain input-oriented legitimacy. And all three have been used to defending the autonomy of the EU judiciary from the legislature. I do not contest that these are important standards for EU institutions to pursue—indeed, they should seek to promote social justice, curb the negative externalities caused by national institutions, and do so effectively—but they are not sufficient standards of legitimacy. As we shall see, these standards underestimate the degree of disagreement and contestation that exists over what constitutes desirable political output.

3.1 Legitimacy by effective governance

In the late 1990s, efficient and effective decision-making emerged as the dominant ideal for EU institutions to aspire to. The Commission earmarked 'governance' as

[35] De Witte, 'Sex, Drugs & EU Law' (n 31) 1551.
[36] ibid 1554.
[37] ibid 1556.
[38] ibid 1555.
[39] ibid 1555–56.

the EU's organising principle, reconceptualising most policy areas as involving fundamentally technical areas to be discussed by experts rather than the public.[40] Around the same time, Giandomenico Majone sought to recast the EU in similar terms, analysing it through the prism of the regulatory rather than the democratic state—a regime for which 'non-majoritarian sources of legitimacy—expertise, procedural rationality, transparency, and accountability by results—should be sufficient'.[41] He saw the EU as a functional regime with limited powers to which Member States delegate specific tasks in order to address collective problems more efficiently and credibly. They delegate tasks for 'efficiency-oriented' as opposed to 'redistributive' reasons, with the aim of increasing the aggregate welfare of society rather than the welfare of particular groups.[42] This is why, he argued, these tasks could be exercised without being democratically legitimated, provided that they are efficiency-oriented, are precisely and narrowly defined, and can be carried out 'more efficiently and/or credibly at the supranational level'.[43] As far as institutional balance is concerned, theories of legitimacy by effective governance justify 'the existence of the Court and the Commission as vigorous autonomous institutions',[44] in part because the Council was 'often swayed by short-term considerations' and the Parliament 'not yet institutionally suited to develop a coherent legislative strategy'.[45]

Effectiveness-based conceptions of legitimacy resurface occasionally,[46] but their popularity has waned significantly in recent decades, and they have been fully discredited since the outbreak of the economic and monetary crisis. The policies pursued in the aftermath of this crisis were strongly redistributive in character, so much so that even Majone has admitted that the EU can no longer be treated as a regulatory, efficiency-oriented regime.[47] But of course, his neat distinction between redistributive and efficiency-enhancing policy was always debatable.[48] His depiction of the EU as a regulatory regime may be valid in situations

[40] Commission of the European Communities (n 30). For a critical discussion, Cris Shore, '"European Governance" or Governmentality? The European Commission and the Future of Democratic Government' (2011) 17 European Law Journal 287.

[41] Giandomenico Majone, 'Europe's "Democratic Deficit": The Question of Standards' (1998) 4 European Law Journal 5, 28.

[42] ibid.

[43] ibid.

[44] Anand Menon and Stephen Weatherill, 'Democratic Politics in a Globalising World: Supranationalism and Legitimacy in the European Union' (LSE Law, Society and Economy Working Paper 2007/13, 2007) 3. In addition, Andrew Moravcsik, 'In Defence of the "Democratic Deficit": Reassessing Legitimacy in the European Union' (2002) 40 Journal of Common Market Studies 603.

[45] Majone, 'Europe's "Democratic Deficit"' (n 41) 23.

[46] For instance, Dominique Ritleng, 'The Independence and Legitimacy of the European Court of Justice' in Dominique Ritleng (ed), *Independence and Legitimacy in the Institutional System of the European Union* (OUP 2016) 108.

[47] Giandomenico Majone, 'From Regulatory State to a Democratic Default' (2014) 52 Journal of Common Market Studies 1216.

[48] Menon and Weatherill (n 44) 18.

when everyone benefits from cooperation or when the effective enforcement of the Treaties prevents freeriding by national governments. However, few EU policies are Pareto enhancing and without redistributive effects. EU policies mostly produce winners and losers, from the single market to agricultural subsidies and from competition law to cohesion policy.[49] It may be true that the legitimacy of political institutions depends on their ability to effectively promote the common interest, but there has always been much less agreement about what constitutes the EU common interest than efficiency-based accounts of legitimacy suggest.

3.2 Legitimacy by containment

When the limits of effectiveness-based accounts of legitimacy became apparent, those who were still unconvinced that input-oriented legitimacy could be claimed by the EU started developing more demanding output-oriented theories. Anand Menon and Stephen Weatherill, for example, accepted that effectiveness can 'run out of petrol as a legitimating factor',[50] yet remained 'sceptical of the existence at European level of essential pre-conditions for democratic governance' and thus '[t]he potential for strengthening mechanisms of input legitimacy'.[51] This is why they sought to justify the authority of the EU by reference to the value of containment. The theory of legitimacy by containment is a mixed conception of legitimacy that combines input-oriented with output-oriented features. It is, nonetheless, useful to illustrate its shortcomings here.

The theory of legitimacy by containment subscribes to the 'argument from transnational effects',[52] which presumes that the EU can justify its existence by properly guiding and taming the democratic state. It should especially seek to ensure that the interests of all people affected by domestic policies are represented in the domestic decision-making process.[53] Proponents of this theory argue that the domestic democratic process excludes two groups of people whose interests it affects: non-residents and residents without citizenship. They argue that the EU must, as far as possible, seek to mitigate these exclusionary effects by enhancing their representation in domestic politics.[54] It can do so by enforcing EU law, especially the right to free movement and the right to non-discrimination on grounds

[49] Andreas Follesdal and Simon Hix, 'Why There Is a Democratic Deficit in the EU: A Response to Majone and Moravcsik' (2006) 44 Journal of Common Market Studies 533, 542.

[50] Menon and Weatherill (n 44) 19.

[51] ibid 21.

[52] Alexander Somek, 'The Argument from Transnational Effects I: Representing Outsiders through Freedom of Movement' (2010) 16 European Law Journal 315; Alexander Somek, 'The Argument from Transnational Effects II: Establishing Transnational Democracy' (2010) 16 European Law Journal 375.

[53] On the all-affectedness principle, see, Robert E Goodin, 'Enfranchising All Affected Interests, and Its Alternatives' (2007) 35 Philosophy & Public Affairs 40.

[54] Miguel Maduro, *We the Court: The European Court of Justice and the European Economic Constitution* (Hart Publishing 1998) 169.

of nationality. In essence, the theory claims to kill two birds with one stone: it seeks to reaffirm the promises of output-oriented legitimacy and claims that allowing the EU to impose effective legal controls on the domestic democratic process would enhance the input-oriented legitimacy of Member States. In so doing, its proponents argue, the EU can play a 'potentially democracy-enhancing role',[55] by ensuring 'that there is no under-representation of the interests of nationals of other Member States in the national political process'.[56]

In unpacking these claims, it helps to distinguish between *internal* and *external* legitimacy. Political communities, such as states, have internal legitimacy when their domestic authority is justified, and they have external legitimacy when they observe their duty of non-interference with the legitimate authority of other political communities.[57] The aspects of the theory of legitimacy by containment that are worthwhile preserving relate to Member States' external legitimacy. As I show in section II.4, the EU can help strengthen their external legitimacy by preventing them from exerting undue foreign influence. However, the theory—and its institutional implications—are damaging to the internal legitimacy of both Member States and the EU. Let me explain.

As regards the internal legitimacy of Member States, the theory in the first place *overestimates the democratic gains* of restricting the authority of domestic institutions. Contrary to what it assumes, treating foreigners equally to nationals is not tantamount to representing their interests equally: the principle of non-discrimination on grounds of nationality may require domestic laws to be applied equally to foreigners, but that does not give them an equal voice in the democratic process.[58] So, whatever merits containment has, the boundaries of the demos are not, as a result, drawn more democratically, and the under-representation of foreign interests is not reduced. The theory also *underestimates the democratic costs* of containment. Even a straightforward application of the principle of non-discrimination can lead to significant social or political distortions, especially when used to open up access to scarce goods. *Commission v Austria* offers an illustrative example.[59] It gave non-Austrians equal access to medical training at Austrian universities, following which the percentage of German nationals studying medicine in Austria rose to around 25 per cent (and 50 per cent in psychology).[60] As many students returned to Germany following their studies, the case weakened the stability of Austria's public health care. As Martin Loughlin wryly observed, it is

[55] Menon and Weatherill (n 44) 20.

[56] Maduro, *We the Court* (n 54) 173.

[57] For this distinction, Bas van der Vossen, 'The Asymmetry of Legitimacy' (2012) 31 Law and Philosophy 565.

[58] Jan Zglinski, *Europe's Passive Virtues: Deference to National Authorities in EU Free Movement Law* (OUP 2020) 174.

[59] Case C-147/03 *Commission v Austria* ECLI:EU:C:2005:427.

[60] For criticism, Angelika Schenk and Susanne K Schmidt, 'Failing on the Social Dimension: Judicial Law-Making and Student Mobility in the EU' (2018) 25 Journal of European Public Policy 1522.

unclear 'whether the removal of nationality-based restrictions on access to medical schools in Austria—whatever other values it might serve—supports any version of democracy'.[61] Making matters worse, the principle of non-discrimination on grounds of nationality targets not only directly discriminatory but also indirectly discriminatory measures. As a result, Member States can be required to accept practices previously forbidden in their legal orders[62] so that the principle undermines rather than supports democratic decision-making at the national level: it 'maximizes negative integration at the expense of democratic self-determination in the national polity'.[63]

Another problem of the theory is that it fails to specify when foreign interests are wrongly excluded from national decision-making. Or rather, it seems to assume that the interests of foreign nationals must always count as equal to national citizens. As Jan Zglinski has observed,

> It may not be enough to ask whether non-national concerns are under-represented in domestic decisions. We have to address another question first: when should non-national concerns be represented at all? 'Always' is the answer advocates of European representation have given. In their view, every time non-nationals are put at a disadvantage, the Court of Justice should step in and double-check the substance of the Member State measure (even if it may eventually be justified). There is no scenario in which excluding the concerns of non-nationals from consideration, or lowering the weight which they are given in the decision-making process, would be desirable.[64]

However, one can easily imagine scenarios in which foreign citizens should not be treated as equals. It may be justified, for example, for Member States to grant nationals preferential access to their health-care or education systems, namely when such a discriminatory practice is needed to sustain the financial viability and accessibility of their domestic social provisions. For this reason, EU law applies a requirement of reciprocity as a condition of access to national social welfare, despite its discriminatory effects against foreigners without such reciprocal ties.[65] It does

[61] Martin Loughlin, 'Constitutional Pluralism: An Oxymoron?' (2014) 3 Global Constitutionalism 9, 27.

[62] Somek, 'The Argument from Transnational Effects I' (n 52) 329–30; Jukka Snell, 'The Internal Market and the Philosophies of Market Integration' in Catherine Barnard and Steve Peers (eds), *European Union Law* (OUP 2014) 302–303.

[63] Fritz W Scharpf, 'The Asymmetry of European Integration, or Why the EU Cannot Be a "Social Market Economy"' (2010) 8 Socio-Economic Review 211, 223.

[64] Zglinski (n 58) 178.

[65] Andrea Sangiovanni, 'Global Justice, Reciprocity, and the State' (2007) 35 Philosophy & Public Affairs 3; Andrea Sangiovanni, 'Justice and the Free Movement of Persons: Educational Mobility in the European Union and the United States' in Douglas A Hicks and Thad Williamson (eds), *Leadership and Global Justice* (Palgrave Macmillan 2012).

not seem credible, indeed, to think that the same weight must always be given to out-of-state as in-state interests.

The final problem with the theory is that it cares little for the institutional complexity of the EU. Its proponents just assume that the Court is best trusted to enforce free movement rights and therefore want its judges to decide how, and when, EU law contains national authorities.[66] Yet, because other EU institutions also decide on the containment of national actors, the question to be asked is which of these institutions should decide what standards of EU law bind national authorities. There is no escaping the question, especially not in the face of reasonable disagreement about how EU law must contain national actors, as well as uncertainty about the political and socio-economic consequences of doing so. For this reason, the question of which EU institution must decide the content of EU law is prior to the question of what this content should be.

3.3 Legitimacy by just governance

The third output-oriented conception conflates legitimacy with justice. This conflation also rests on the premise that the EU cannot be democratic and attain input-oriented legitimacy. According to Neyer, for example, '[a]pplying the democratic standard to the EU is nothing less than a categorical mistake'. Instead, we should 'substitute the discourse on the democratic deficit of the European Union with a discourse on its justice deficit'.[67]

Whereas theories of legitimacy by containment have mostly overlooked the legislative process, some of those who equate legitimacy with justice are downright sceptical of legislatures and have sought to diminish the EU legislature's authority. According to Charlotte O'Brien, 'judicial decisions and intellectual commentary, not legislation, have transformed conceptions of human rights and democracy'.[68] Not all proponents of justice-based conceptions of legitimacy may share this scepticism, yet it is almost inevitable that their theories will subvert the legislature's authority. This is not because legislation is, on average, less just than judicial choices—there is little empirical evidence that supports O'Brien's claims[69]—but

[66] See, eg Maduro, *We the Court* (n 54) 169–75; Menon and Weatherill (n 44) 8–9; de Witte, 'Sex, Drugs & EU Law' (n 31) 1552; Christian Joerges, 'European Law as Conflict of Laws' in Christian Joerges and Jürgen Neyer (eds), *'Deliberative Supranationalism' Revisited* (2006); Jürgen Neyer, *The Justification of Europe: A Political Theory of Supranational Integration* (OUP 2012).

[67] Neyer (n 66) 7. For a similar argument, Floris de Witte, *Justice in the EU: The Emergence of Transnational Solidarity* (OUP 2015) 52–69.

[68] Charlotte O'Brien, 'I Trade, Therefore I Am. Legal Personhood in the European Union' (2013) 50 Common Market Law Review 1643, 1680.

[69] See, eg Thomas Christiano, 'An Instrumental Argument for a Human Right to Democracy' (2011) 39 Philosophy & Public Affairs 142.

because justice-based conceptions of legitimacy will only treat legislative decisions as authoritative when just.

The response to recent case law on the right of EU citizens to claim social assistance in the host Member States shows that EU lawyers sometimes find that unjust legislative provisions do not bind the CJEU. Article 7(3)(c) of the Citizenship Directive (Directive 2004/38/EC) gives EU citizens who become involuntarily unemployed *during the first twelve months* the right to retain the status of worker for *no less than six months*. EU citizens with worker status are entitled to social assistance. Mrs Alimanovic and her daughter had worked in temporary jobs in Germany for eleven months and retained their status as worker for a period of six months after they became unemployed.[70] After that period, however, so decided the German authorities, they lost that status and, therefore, the right to social assistance. This decision was consistent with the Directive, as the CJEU rightly ruled in the *Alimanovic* case. But even though the judgment observed the conditions laid down in legislation, it was argued that it should have decided differently as a matter of social justice.[71] This implicitly suggests that it is legitimate for the CJEU to ignore legislative decisions that do not realise justice within the EU.

Like other output-oriented conceptions, justice-based conceptions also underestimate the disagreement that exists in our societies about what constitutes desirable output. Neither at the state nor at the EU level is there much agreement on the requirements of justice. To return to the example above, some will believe that the obligations of justice are so demanding that mobile EU citizens should have the right to immediate and full access to social assistance, while others will insist that EU citizens who have never exercised any economic activity can be refused social assistance without that injustice is done to them. Such disagreement happens in an environment where it seems practically impossible to identify correct principles of justice.[72] No one has an objective and complete view on such matters: our judgements about the nature and practical requirements of justice are shaped by our personal experiences as well as specific needs, talents, and desires.[73] Some people may be ignorant or driven by malicious intentions, but most disagreement is reasonable disagreement among reasonable people.

[70] Case C-67/14 *Alimanovic* ECLI:EU:C:2015:597.

[71] Päivi Johanna Neuvonen, *Equal Citizenship and Its Limits in EU Law: We the Burden* (Hart Publishing 2016); Charlotte O'Brien, *Unity in Adversity: EU Citizenship, Social Justice and the Cautionary Tale of the UK* (Hart Publishing 2017). To be sure, *Alimanovic* has been criticised on other grounds too, including, most importantly, for not clarifying how it is to be reconciled with precedent. See, eg Niamh Nic Shuibhne, 'Limits Rising, Duties Ascending: The Changing Legal Shape of Union Citizenship' (2015) 52 Common Market Law Review 889, 916.

[72] Jeremy Waldron, *Law and Disagreement* (OUP 1999) ch 8.

[73] Thomas Christiano, *The Constitution of Equality: Democratic Authority and Its Limits* (OUP 2008) 56–59; John Rawls, *Political Liberalism* (Columbia UP 1993) 54–58; Richard Bellamy, *Political Constitutionalism: A Republican Defence of the Constitutionality of Democracy* (CUP 2007).

Consequently, EU political decision-making is affected by what Jeremy Waldron famously called 'the circumstances of politics'.[74] Disagreement is an elemental condition under which politics takes place. It complicates political decision-making but also renders it necessary. On the one hand, disagreement will make it more difficult to agree on a joint course of action. On the other hand, it is crucial to settle on a shared framework of rules to guide citizens if their behaviour is not guided by a common understanding of justice. The EU is faced with a similar situation. A common vision of the wider ideals of European integration and how best to achieve them is lacking, so there is a clear need for an institution that sets the political course that must be followed by Member States and their citizens. In the face of disagreement, it will not do to say that this course should be laid out by the institution that can do so justly. The political choices made are supposed to settle our differences on these matters, which is why theories of legitimacy cannot be conflated with theories of justice. This is not to say that the substantive content of the EU's political decisions is irrelevant and not to be critically assessed, but only to say that our theories of legitimacy should complement our theories of justice.

4. The European Union's *Demoi*cratic Legislature

Since the EU cannot justify its authority merely by reference to the quality of its political output, the question is whether it can be legitimated by virtue of input-oriented reasons. Input-oriented legitimacy is usually equated with democratic legitimacy, the need for which is typically grounded in the circumstances in politics. As Thomas Christiano put it, the authority of democracy is justified by the fundamental interest of each citizen

> in being able to see that he is being treated as an equal in a society where there is significant diversity among persons in the conditions of well-being, and where there is disagreement about justice and wherein each citizen can acknowledge fallibility and cognitive bias in their capacities for thinking about their interests and about justice.[75]

Indeed, this assumes that the democratic process offers a legitimate framework for resolving deep-rooted differences between citizens by giving them an equal say in the decision-making process and by settling disagreements between them, or their representatives, using majority rule.[76]

[74] Waldron, *Law and Disagreement* (n 72) 101.
[75] Christiano, *The Constitution of Equality* (n 73) 56.
[76] Jeremy Waldron, 'The Core of the Case against Judicial Review' (2006) 115 Yale Law Journal 1246, 1387–88; Bellamy, *Political Constitutionalism* (n 73); Allen Buchanan, 'Political Legitimacy and Democracy' (2002) 112 Ethics 689; Albert Weale, *Democracy* (2nd edn, Palgrave Macmillan 2007) 62.

As we have seen, it is widely thought that the EU cannot walk this route. Because it would not have the capacity to be democratic, its authority cannot be legitimated by its input-oriented qualities; instead, it must be measured against output-oriented standards. And indeed, the EU's arrangements for collective decision-making seem to violate minimum conditions for democratic legitimacy: political equality and majority rule. The representation of EU citizens in the European Parliament is degressively proportionate, with a minimum of six and maximum of ninety-six seats per Member State (art 14(2) of the TEU).[77] Citizens of less populous Member States are overrepresented compared to citizens of any other Member State, negating the political equality of Union citizens. Qualified majority voting in the Council does so too (art 16(4) of the TEU).[78] The political inequality of EU citizens is one reason—along with pessimism about the existence of a collective European demos and a coherent European public sphere—that the democratic legitimacy of EU institutions has been rejected.[79] So, maybe, output-oriented legitimacy is as good as it gets. Maybe, as long as the preconditions for democratic decision-making are not in place, the justification of EU authority can only be assessed by reference to the output its institutions generate.

I shall offer an alternative vision which contends that the correct conception of legitimacy in the EU is input oriented. This alternative is not, however, grounded in the political equality of EU citizens. Indeed, as I will explain, EU decision-making is not designed to achieve political equality between its citizens, nor should it be.[80] As I will also explain, the fact that the EU deviates from the value of political equality does not mean that the preconditions for input-oriented legitimacy are not, or cannot be, met. This view rests on too narrow a conception of input-oriented legitimacy. I will explain all this using a *demoi*cratic conception of political legitimacy, which correctly values the constraints that weigh against instantiating political equality between EU citizens. *Demoi*cratic theory offers input-oriented requirements of legitimacy that, on the one hand, underline important features of the EU's political procedures and, on the other hand, enable us to assess whether the authority exercised thereby is justified.

The paramount *demoi*cratic value is the republican value of freedom as non-domination.[81] Notwithstanding what the term 'non-domination' may seem to

[77] European Council Decision of 28 June 2013 establishing the composition of the European Parliament 2013/312/EU.

[78] See Jürgen Habermas, 'Citizen and State Equality in a Supranational Political Community: Degressive Proportionality and the *Pouvoir Constituant Mixte*: Citizen and State Equality' (2017) 55 Journal of Common Market Studies 171; Jelena von Achenbach, 'The European Parliament as a Forum of National Interest? A Transnationalist Critique of Jürgen Habermas' Reconstruction of Degressive Proportionality' (2017) 55 Journal of Common Market Studies 193.

[79] BVerfGE 123, 267 *Lisbon Decision*, paras 273–95.

[80] For the opposite view, Dimitry Kochenov, 'Citizenship without Respect: The EU's Troubled Equality Ideal' (Jean Monet Working Paper No 08/10, 2011) fn 63.

[81] Miriam Ronzoni, 'The European Union as a Demoicracy: Really a Third Way?' (2017) 16 European Journal of Political Theory 210; Richard Bellamy, *A Republican Europe of States: Cosmopolitanism, Intergovernmentalism and Demoicracy in the EU* (CUP 2019).

imply, it does not object to political institutions interfering in citizens' lives. On the contrary, republican theory draws our attention to the fact that political institutions may need to exert their authority to prevent citizens from being dominated by each other or by private actors. Domination arises when individuals are subjected to arbitrary power or uncontrolled interference.[82] Thus, to avoid domination, political institutions must not interfere arbitrarily and uncontrollably in our lives, which can be avoided by 'binding power and making it controllable by those who are subject to it'.[83] At state level, the establishment of non-dominating relations between citizens requires that citizens be given democratic control over the political institutions to whose powers they are subject. They must have an equal say in the allocation of political authority and be in a position to participate effectively in the collective representative process.[84] At the transnational level, achieving non-dominating relations means that states cannot exercise arbitrary power over each other and that international organisations cannot interfere uncontrollably in the internal affairs of the state.[85] As the slogan of republican theory goes, citizens live freely within free states when their states are internally non-dominating and externally non-dominated.[86]

*Demoi*cratic theory provides a conceptual and a normative basis to study the EU, judging it by the value it seeks to provide—non-domination.[87] The theory escapes the narrow conception of input-oriented legitimacy that equates political legitimacy with nation-state democracy. Instead, it reveals that input-oriented legitimacy may be held not only by democratic regimes that function as 'government of the people' but also by *demoi*cratic regimes that function as 'government of the *peoples*'.[88] A *demoi*cratic polity consists of autonomous peoples that exercise joint political authority. They do so for two purposes: to counter the negative externalities that their individual decision-making processes can have on each other and to tackle problems that they cannot effectively address alone. The EU is one—and perhaps the main—example of a *demoi*cratic regime. By exercising joint authority through the EU institutions, the national peoples can seek to realise these purposes and reduce patterns of domination between and over them.[89] However, one form

[82] Philip Pettit, *On the People's Terms: A Republican Theory and Model of Democracy* (CUP 2012) 58; Cécile Laborde and Miriam Ronzoni, 'What Is a Free State? Republican Internationalism and Globalisation' (2016) 64 Political Studies 279, 279.

[83] Laborde and Ronzoni (n 82) 280.

[84] Pettit, *On the Peoples' Terms* (n 82); Cécile Laborde, 'Republicanism and Global Justice: A Sketch' (2010) 9 European Journal of Political Theory 48.

[85] Laborde and Ronzoni (n 82); Laborde (n 84); Philip Pettit, 'Legitimate International Institutions: A Neo-Republican Perspective' in Besson and Tasioulas (n 9).

[86] Quentin Skinner, 'On the Slogans of Republican Political Theory' (2010) 9 European Journal of Political Theory 95, 95–102.

[87] Ronzoni (n 81).

[88] Francis Cheneval, Sandra Lavenex, and Frank Schimmelfennig, '*Demoi-Cracy in the European Union*: Principles, Institutions, Policies' (2015) 22 Journal of European Public Policy 1, 2–3.

[89] ibid 4. It should be acknowledged, of course, that leaving is possible in a technical-legal sense for Eurozone Member States but close to impossible in a practical-material sense. See also Signe Rehling Larsen, *The Constitutional Theory of the Federation and the European Union* (OUP 2021) 168.

of domination should not be replaced by another: the alternative to unchecked interference between Member States should not be arbitrary power by the EU over them. To avoid this, the EU's authority should be made controllable to the national peoples, who should count as equal political subjects within the EU: they should have shared and equal control over the EU's political course of action.[90] Such control over EU institutions is a necessary condition for national citizens to be able live freely in free states.

This requires, first of all, that the national peoples can freely and democratically decide on EU membership and its corresponding obligations. This condition is met. National citizens can consent to the EU's terms of membership freely and democratically, influence these terms through the procedures for amending the Treaties, and revoke their membership through the withdrawal procedure.[91] However, as we saw in section II.2, the fact that the Treaties have been democratically agreed to is not enough to render the EU's ongoing governance legitimate. Indeed, for the EU not to exercise its powers arbitrarily, its ongoing governance must also be subject to the control of the national peoples. This means, as I illustrate next, that the EU should ideally exercise its authority through the legislative process.

The democratic equality of citizens is often considered a prerequisite for realising the ideal of non-domination.[92] It is only this, however, if citizens regard each other as equals and can influence the allocation of political authority in largely equal ways. Societies deeply segmented by religious or ethnic cleavages will not want to use decision-making procedures that ensure the formal political equality of all citizens, as this will enable the dominant group to promote its sectional interests at the expense of permanently insulated minority groups.[93] Thus, in some societies, giving citizens an equal political voice would carry the risk of domination. Moreover, even where sufficient cross-cutting cleavages exist to ensure that no majority can dominate insulated minorities, citizens must have a sufficient understanding of what is at stake in the political arena. If not, they will not be able to respond to and control decision-makers and therefore be able to exert equal power

[90] Kalypso Nicolaïdis, 'European Demoicracy and Its Crisis' (2013) 51 Journal of Common Market Studies 351, 359; Cheneval, Lavenex, and Schimmelfennig (n 88) 4.

[91] Francis Cheneval and Kalypso Nicolaidis, 'The Social Construction of Demoicracy in the European Union' (2017) 16 European Journal of Political Theory 235, 244; Nicolaïdis (n 90) 362–63; Antoinette Scherz, 'Representation in Multilateral Democracy: How to Represent Individuals in the EU While Guaranteeing the Mutual Recognition of Peoples' (2017) 23 European Law Journal 495, 495–508; Cheneval, Lavenex, and Schimmelfennig (n 88) 4.

[92] Bellamy, *Political Constitutionalism* (n 73) ch 4.

[93] Bellamy, *A Republican Europe of States* (n 81) 111–12; David Miller, 'Democracy's Domain' (2009) 37 Philosophy & Public Affairs 201, 212–13; Thomas Christiano, 'Democratic Legitimacy and International Institutions' in Besson and Tasioulas (n 9).

in the allocation of political power.[94] Hence, without a sufficiently strong collective demos and common public sphere, treating citizens as political equals may lead to domination instead of non-domination.

While some Member States have introduced measures to protect the autonomy of minority groups,[95] most of them meet the conditions under which majority rule among citizens is justified rather well. There is a relatively strong sense of community at the national level, and most Member States have a well-developed public sphere, consisting of national media, organised political parties, and a strong public discourse.[96] In contrast, feelings of identification and solidarity among Union citizens remain weak, and a European public sphere is still underdeveloped. European political parties may function in the same way as national political parties when it comes to internal legislative politics, but they play but a minimal role in the external electoral process, which includes providing voters with the necessary information to understand the views of political candidates.[97] Europe's linguistic diversity compounds these difficulties: it hinders the creation of a European mass media and public discourse.[98] Finally, the national *demoi* are constantly reinforced by national institutions and communication structures; there are no institutions at the EU level that can similarly mediate between citizens and the EU and contribute to the creation of a European *demos*.[99] It therefore seems almost inevitable that a European *demos* will remain 'secondary to the national *demoi*, and mediated by national identities, public spheres and political structures'.[100]

The Economic and Monetary Union (EMU) crisis has revealed the dangers of interfering with the equal political standing of the national peoples. The measures that were taken in the wake of the crisis mainly served the interests of financially stronger states at the expense of weaker ones. More powerful states succeeded in placing decision-making under their control by removing important political issues from the agendas of institutions under the shared and equal control of all Member States and by transferring such powers to unaccountable executives (the European Central Bank, European Commission, and International Monetary Fund) or to newly created institutions that gave Member States a degree

[94] Thomas Christiano, *The Rule of the Many: Fundamental Issues in Democratic Theory* (Westview Press 1996).

[95] Bellamy (n 81) 121.

[96] Admittedly, this glosses over a great deal of variation with respect to these prerequisites. See, on this point, Cormac Mac Amhlaigh, *New Constitutional Horizons: Towards a Pluralist Constitutional Theory* (OUP 2022) 170.

[97] Simon Hix, Abdul G Noury, and Gérard Roland, *Democratic Politics in the European Parliament* (CUP 2007).

[98] Will Kymlicka, *Politics in the Vernacular: Nationalism, Multiculturalism, and Citizenship* (OUP 2001).

[99] Francis Cheneval and Frank Schimmelfennig, 'The Case for Demoicracy in the European Union' (2013) 51 Journal of Common Market Studies 334, 338.

[100] ibid.

of influence commensurate with their financial position.[101] Financially weaker states were forced to implement sweeping economic and institutional reforms over which they had little control, with major consequences for their national welfare standards. The EMU crisis has thus accentuated the persistent dominance of the national cleavage and shown that, by removing the political course of action of the EU from shared and equal control of the national peoples, the EU risks producing 'consistent minorities and majorities split along national lines'.[102] Indeed, the EU should not treat its citizens as equal political subjects but the national peoples.[103]

Unlike post-crisis EMU governance, ordinary legislative decision-making meets the basic institutional conditions for *demoi*cratic representation reasonably well. Co-decision between the European Parliament and the Council helps the national peoples exercise shared and equal control over the EU's political direction.[104] The Council represents the positions of national governments, but the European Parliament is also structured in such a way as to promote the equality of national peoples instead of a European people.[105] The principle of degressive proportionality makes a twofold contribution to *demoi*cratic representation. First, it prevents larger Member States from jointly dominating smaller Member States. Second, it gives recognition to the diversity of views among national citizens. The national peoples are the fundamental political subjects of the EU, but they are not homogenous entities. The minimum threshold of six Members of the European Parliament per Member State ensures that even the electoral diversity of the least populous Member States can be represented in the European Parliament.[106] Finally, the Early Warning Mechanism (EWM), introduced by the Treaty of Lisbon, seeks to counter the erosion of parliamentary authority within the EU. National parliaments can now receive EU legislative proposals and review them for their compatibility with the principles of subsidiarity and proportionality.[107] This should enhance their ability to scrutinise national representatives sitting in the Council and thereby align European decision-making with the preferences of the national peoples.

EU institutions do not function perfectly, and much disagreement among *demoi*cratic theorists centres on questions of institutional design.[108] The importance attributed by *demoi*cratic theory to joint decision-making by the Council

[101] Mark Dawson and Floris de Witte, 'Constitutional Balance in the EU after the Euro-Crisis' (2013) 76 Modern Law Review 817; Kalypso Nicolaïdis and Max Watson, 'Sharing the Eurocrats' Dream: A Demoicratic Approach to EMU Governance in the Post-Crisis Era' in Damian Chalmers, Markus Jachtenfuchs, and Christian Joerges (eds), *The End of the Eurocrats' Dream: Adjusting to European Diversity* (CUP 2016).

[102] Bellamy (n 81) 121.

[103] Nicolaïdis (n 90) 356.

[104] Cheneval, Lavenex, and Schimmelfennig (n 88) 7. See also Cheneval and Nicolaidis (n 91) 244–45; Cheneval and Schimmelfennig (n 99) 342.

[105] Scherz (n 91); Nicolaïdis (n 90); Cheneval and Schimmelfennig (n 99).

[106] von Achenbach (n 78) 200. See also Scherz (n 91) 503–504.

[107] Article 12 of the TEU.

[108] Ronzoni (n 81).

and European Parliament can be disputed on two grounds, both of which question whether EU legislative institutions can function in such a way as to meet the *demoi*cratic value of non-domination between national peoples. One major concern will be that executive dominance in the Council poses an undue obstacle to public deliberation and democratic accountability.[109] Second, and more importantly, the EU has been said to function as a '*demoi*cracy without *demoi*crats',[110] as a community with functioning *demoi*cratic institutions but underdeveloped *demoi*cratic attitudes among its citizens. Because many citizens do not properly understand or identify with the EU's *demoi*cratic arrangement, it cannot adequately legitimate its decisions.[111]

One proposal has been to increase the influence of national parliaments on EU decision-making. Richard Bellamy, observing the *demoi*cratic disconnect between the Parliament and the European electorate and between the Council and the national peoples, has argued that giving national parliaments a greater say would both domesticate European politics and Europeanise domestic politics. The latter would happen as national parliaments can only exercise the powers conferred on them by the Treaty of Lisbon by cooperating with each other.[112] There are, indeed, indications that the EU has taken an important step in institutionalising *demoi*cracy by upgrading the position of national parliaments. The EWM allows them to exert greater influence on EU legislative proposals and can make the Council more responsive to public opinion and party politics at the national level.[113] At the same time, we must be careful not to overstate the capacity of national parliaments. The requirement for one-third of them to submit a reasoned opinion within eight weeks of the date of transmission of draft legislation remains a major obstacle to the EWM's effective use.[114] Second, national parliaments have full agendas, which means that their members lack the time to scrutinise the EU legislative process vigorously and not only the time but often also the resources or political incentives to do so.[115] Finally, democratic decline in some Member States may mean that not all parliaments can play their democratic role in a *demoi*cratic

[109] Deirdre Curtin, 'Challenging Executive Dominance in European Democracy' (2014) 77 Modern Law Review 1.

[110] Cheneval, Lavenex, and Schimmelfennig (n 88) 10. See, in addition, Achim Hurrelmann, '*Demoi*-Cratic Citizenship in Europe: An Impossible Ideal?' (2014) 22 Journal of European Public Policy 19, 29–31.

[111] Hurrelmann (n 110) 28.

[112] Bellamy, *A Republican Europe of States* (n 81) 123.

[113] Monika Mühlböck and Jale Tosun, 'Responsiveness to Different National Interests: Voting Behaviour on Genetically Modified Organisms in the Council of the European Union: Responsiveness to National Interests' (2018) 56 Journal of Common Market Studies 385.

[114] Tapio Raunio, 'Destined for Irrelevance? Subsidiarity Control by National Parliaments (WP)' (Real Institute Elcano Working Paper No 36/2010, 2010); Piotr Maciej Kaczyński, 'Paper Tigers or Sleeping Beauties? National Parliaments in the Post-Lisbon European Political System' (Centre for European Policy Studies Special Report, February 2011).

[115] Katrin Auel and Thomas Christiansen, 'After Lisbon: National Parliaments in the European Union' (2015) 38 West European Politics 261, 269.

Union.[116] The democratic decay is problematic from a *demoi*cratic point of view as the decisions of national governments have value only insofar as they reflect the preferences and interests of their citizens.[117]

However, while it seems unlikely that national parliaments alone can solve the *demoi*cratic deficit, it is not clear that they alone can make the EU more *demoi*cratically legitimate. Institutional shortcomings exist and have to be acknowledged, but the capacity of the Council and Parliament should not be underestimated either. Member States may sometimes be unwilling to recognise each other's legitimate interests, but major disagreements on salient issues aside, they are often willing to put aside their differences and avoid political stalemate by seeking compromise through policy linkage and exchange.[118] Moreover, the quality of European political representation is higher than is sometimes said. On important issues, political groups in the European Parliament adopt positions that reflect ideological differences between EU citizens.[119] Finally, a slow but certain Europeanisation of national public spheres is taking place that should increase citizens' interest in European politics and diminish the traditional second-order nature of European elections.[120]

Nevertheless, it is open to question whether the EU legislature adequately represents the interests and preferences of the national peoples and genuinely succeeds in placing the authority of the EU under their shared and equal control. But while the legislative process may not conform to idealised models of *demoi*cratic legitimacy, it contributes to realising non-dominating relations between the national peoples in two ways: it provides a process by which common European norms can be established that can reduce patterns of domination between them and that counts all Member States as roughly equal. Moreover, even if non-domination is only partially achieved, we should be able to agree on two things. First, it would be a mistake not to try to put in place institutional arrangements that can guarantee non-domination between EU citizens. Second, even if no institution fully meets the appropriate input-oriented standards of legitimacy, some will do better than others.

[116] R Daniel Kelemen, 'Europe's Other Democratic Deficit: National Authoritarianism in Europe's Democratic Union' (2017) 52 Government and Opposition 211.

[117] Ronzoni (n 81) 218.

[118] Adrienne Héritier, *Policy-Making and Diversity in Europe: Escape from Deadlock* (CUP 1999); Dorothee Heisenberg, 'The Institution of "Consensus" in the European Union: Formal versus Informal Decision-Making in the Council' (2005) 44 European Journal of Political Research 65.

[119] Zoe Lefkofridi and Alexia Katsanidou, 'Multilevel Representation in the European Parliament' (2014) 15 European Union Politics 108; Rory Costello, Jacques Thomassen, and Martin Rosema, 'European Parliament Elections and Political Representation: Policy Congruence between Voters and Parties' (2012) 35 West European Politics 1226.

[120] Thomas Risse-Kappen (ed), *European Public Spheres: Politics Is Back* (CUP 2015). On the second-order nature of European elections, Simon Hix and Michael Marsh, 'Second-Order Effects plus Pan-European Political Swings: An Analysis of European Parliament Elections across Time' (2011) 30 Electoral Studies 4.

5. Legislating in the Judiciary's Shadow

This brings us to the relationship between the EU legislature and judiciary. There have been two attempts to defend the legitimacy of the latter. First, as we saw in section II.3, legal scholars have tried to do this by invoking output-oriented standards of legitimacy, but these were not credible. Second, it has been argued that national governments' consent to the Treaties and appointment of judges is sufficient to legitimise the judicial development of EU law,[121] but this attempt is not convincing either. It ignores the fact that the Treaties are open-ended and therefore easily allow the CJEU to develop EU law outside the control of the national peoples. Rather, as I will show now, the value of political legitimacy requires that it is ideally the legislature that determines content of EU law.

Recall the theory of legitimacy by containment that was discussed in section II.3. It claims that the EU's legitimacy rests on its capacity to reduce patterns of domination between Member States, which it should do by containing their unchecked interference in each other's domestic affairs. However, while this theory has rightly emphasised that restraining national political actors can be a means of securing non-domination, it overlooks that the Court (for the theory's advocates the preferred institution to contain national actors) can be a source of domination itself. The theory therefore risks being self-defeating: if the EU wants to govern legitimately, it should not replace one form of domination—by Member States over one another—with its own. The Court can obstruct the EU's capacity to be *demoi*cratic in two ways: by undermining domestic democratic authority (and thus the capacity of Member States to be internally non-dominating) and by undermining the EU legislature's authority (and thus the capacity of the EU to be externally non-dominating).

Criticism of the CJEU often focuses on its impact on the domestic democratic process, on the fact that it has left 'deep marks on national law and politics'.[122] It is not clear, however, that this should be our primary concern. Reining in national political actors may be desirable, so the fact that its judgments have left their mark on domestic politics can hardly be a cause for concern in itself. The more important question is on what basis the CJEU interferes with national politics. As we see in Chapters III and IV, it often does so in line with prior legislative decisions, in which case there is, generally, no reason for criticism. Criticism is better directed at judgments that develop EU law against the legislature's will. Indeed, we should shift our attention from national to European politics to evaluate how the CJEU exerts its authority. The relevant question is not just how EU law should interfere with national law and politics but also, given reasonable disagreement on that issue, when and how it should do so. The relevant question is, therefore,

[121] This includes *demoi*cratic theorists: Cheneval and Schimmelfennig (n 99) 345.
[122] Dieter Grimm, *The Constitution of European Democracy* (OUP 2017) 96.

comparatively institutional: should EU legal rules binding national institutions be made by the legislature or judiciary?

The CJEU operates—and is supposed to operate—outside the control of those affected by its decisions: its decisions must not be subject to political influence. Consequently, the EU is much more likely to exercise arbitrary power over Member States when it exerts power through the judicial rather than legislative process. The latter renders EU decision-making accountable to the national peoples, while the former is shielded from such political control mechanisms. This is why the judicial process is inferior to the legislative process in terms of *demoi*cratic legitimacy. It is as simple as that, and it cannot be countered that the Treaties, as interpreted by the CJEU, have been approved by the national peoples. Most of their provisions are open-ended and do not meaningfully constrain judicial behaviour. Moreover, as their amendment process is notoriously cumbersome, the CJEU has ample opportunity to develop the Treaties outside of the provisions required for their amendment and to remove political power from the shared and equal control of the national peoples.

From this perspective, it would be concerning if the ability of the national peoples to act jointly via the legislative process were limited by the judicial process. In recent years, there have been indications that the Court has, at times, restricted the influence the legislature could exercise over the content of EU law. The scope of application of the Treaties is very wide. Not only do they regulate what national constitutions regulate, namely the fundamental rights that public institutions must observe and the division of powers between the branches of government, but they also include provisions to facilitate the creation of a common market, such as economic freedoms and competition law.[123] The result is a highly constitutionalised legal order, which some say is 'over-constitutionalised'.[124] This concept gives expression to the concern that the Court, by interpreting the Treaties, could place these areas outside the purview of legislative politics. The legislature is expected to act in accordance with the Treaties (including, this concern assumes, their judicial interpretation), so it would have little choice but to codify case law in the legislative acts it adopts.[125]

123 Fritz W Scharpf, 'Legitimacy in the Multi-Level European Polity' in Petra Dobner and Martin Loughlin (eds), *The Twilight of Constitutionalism?* (OUP 2010) 104; Grimm (n 122) 10; Stefano Bartolini, *Restructuring Europe: Centre Formation, System Building and Political Structuring between the Nation-State and the European Union* (OUP 2005) 164–65.

124 Grimm (n 122) 97–101; Martin Höpner and Susanne K Schmidt, 'Can We Make the European Fundamental Freedoms Less Constraining? A Literature Review' (2020) 22 Cambridge Yearbook of European Legal Studies 182, 184–93.

125 Grimm (n 122) 100; Scharpf, 'The Asymmetry of European Integration' (n 63); Sacha Garben, 'The Constitutional (Im)Balance between "the Market" and "the Social" in the European Union' (2017) 13 European Constitutional Law Review 23, 37–38; Jacquelyn Veraldi and Matthew Hassall, 'Corporate Power and the Constitutionalisation of the EU Internal Market Project' in Mark V Tushnet and Dimitry Kochenov (eds), *Research Handbook on the Politics of Constitutional Law* (Edward Elgar 2023).

Chapter IV considerably nuances this argument, showing that the legislature has retained a great deal more autonomy than this narrative suggests. Yet, it cannot be denied that case law has, at times, exerted such an impact on the content of legislative provisions that the legislature indeed appears as an 'agent' of the CJEU.[126] The influence of judicial decisions is visible in areas as diverse as internal market law, competition law, public procurement law, EU citizenship law, and non-discrimination law—all areas where the legislature has, at times, been involved in 'the art of codifying complex case law'.[127] The preambles to certain legislative acts illustrate this clearly. The Merger Regulation was drafted 'without prejudice to the case law of the Court of Justice,[128] and the Patients' Rights Directive sought to effect 'a more general, and also effective, application of principles developed by the Court of Justice on a case-by-case basis'.[129] As a result, legislative provisions are, at times, strikingly similar 'to the language of the Court in key judgments'.[130] For instance, art 14(3) of the Citizenship Directive corresponds almost fully to the verdict in the *Grzelczyk* case that expulsion measures shall not 'become the automatic consequence of [EU citizens] having recourse to the host Member State's social assistance system'.[131] It is but one example, though one that illustrates well that the legislature may be deprived of many policy choices if it must stay within the judiciary's shadow.

Moreover, when manoeuvring between its own preferences and those possibilities already closed off by case law, the legislature could not always avoid legal contradictions. The Citizenship Directive once again serves as a case in point. While art 14(3) of the Directive provides that expulsion cannot be an 'automatic consequence of . . . having recourse to the host Member State's social assistance system', art 14(1) of the Directive determines that the right of residence is subject to not becoming 'an unreasonable burden on the social assistance system of the host Member State'.[132] Both provisions are difficult to square. In addition, the Directive

[126] Gareth Davies, 'The European Union Legislature as an Agent of the European Court of Justice: EU Legislature as an Agent of the ECJ' (2016) 54 Journal of Common Market Studies 846.

[127] Stephane de la Rosa, 'The Directive on Cross-Border Healthcare or the Art of Codifying Complex Case Law' (2012) 49 Common Market Law Review 15.

[128] Recital 40 of Council Regulation (EC) No 139/2004 of 20 January 2004 on the control of concentrations between undertakings (OJ L24/1). See, additionally, Recital 27 of Council Regulation (EC) No 1/2003 of 16 December 2002 on the implementation of the rules on competition laid down in Articles 81 and 82 of the Treaty (OJ L1/1).

[129] Recital 8 of Directive 2011/24/EU of the European Parliament and of the Council of 9 March 2011 on the application of patients' rights in cross-border healthcare (OJ L88/45).

[130] Davies (n 126) 854–55.

[131] Case C-184/99 *Grzelczyk* ECLI:EU:C:2001:458, para 43. In justifying the amendment, the legislature said it wanted to integrate 'in the text the case-law of the Court of Justice in case C-184/99, Grzelczyk'. See Common Position (EC) No 6/2004 of 5 December 2003 adopted by the Council, acting in accordance with the procedure referred to in Article 251 of the Treaty establishing the European Community, with a view to adopting a directive of the European Parliament and of the Council on the right of citizens of the Union and their family members to move and reside freely within the territory of the Member States amending Regulation (OJ C54/12).

[132] Alexander Somek, 'Solidarity Decomposed: Being and Time in European Citizenship' (2007) 32 European Law Review 787.

paradoxically allows Member States to deny social assistance to EU citizens who have resided on their territory for more than three months to find work but not citizens that are unemployed and not seeking employment.[133] This paradox arose after the proposed Directive was amended in response to expansive judicial interpretations of the EU citizenship provisions in the Treaties.[134] Finally, nothing may better indicate the extent to which the legislature at times feels bound by case law interpreting the Treaties than the Parliament trying to amend the Directive in a way that was inconsistent with other elements of the proposal, solely to comply with and implement the case law.[135]

As EU patient mobility law shows, the codification of case law can create inconsistencies not just within but also between legislative acts.[136] EU citizens had been given a conditional right to receive health care abroad under the Social Security Coordination Regulation.[137] The CJEU then created a second avenue for patients to do so through its interpretation of the freedom to provide services.[138] The legislature subsequently tried to reassert control over patient mobility by codifying the case law in the Patients' Rights Directive.[139] However, as the relationship between the Directive and Regulation was not clarified, two parallel and partially inconsistent legislative regimes are still in force.[140] So, like the Citizenship Directive, EU patient mobility suggests that a requirement that legislation must comply with case law will have the effect of not only depriving the legislature of control over important policy domains but possibly also adopting irrational and incoherent legislation.

[133] Case C-133/13 *Dano* ECLI:EU:C:2014:341, Opinion of AG Wathelet, para 116.

[134] For a more detailed analysis of how case law shaped the Directive, Martijn van den Brink, 'Justice, Legitimacy and the Authority of Legislation within the European Union' (2019) 82 Modern Law Review 293; Fabio Wasserfallen, 'The Judiciary as Legislator? How the European Court of Justice Shapes Policy-Making in the European Union' (2010) 17 Journal of European Public Policy 1128.

[135] Amendment 38 of the European Parliament Report of 23 January 2003 on the proposal for European Parliament and Council Directive on the right of citizens of the Union and their family members to move and reside freely within the territory of the Member States—Committee on Citizens' Freedoms and Rights, Justice and Home Affairs (2001/0111(COD)). Responding to Amendment 38, the Council decided not to include it 'in the common position, because the Council considers it contradictory to Article 10': Common Position (EC) No 6/2004 (n 131).

[136] Susanne K Schmidt, 'Governing by Judicial Fiat? Over-Constitutionalisation and Its Constraints on EU Legislation' (European Union Studies Association International Biennial Conference, Denver, 9–11 May 2019).

[137] Regulation (EC) No 883/2004 of the European Parliament and of the Council of 29 April 2004 on the coordination of social security systems (OJ L166/1).

[138] Starting in Case C-120/95 *Kohll* ECLI:EU:C:1998:167 and Case C-158/96 *Decker* ECLI:EU:C:1998:171.

[139] Directive 2011/24/EU (n 129).

[140] Grega Strban and others, 'FreSsco Analytical Report 2016: Access to Healthcare in Cross-Border Situations' (European Commission 2017); Frans Pennings, 'The Draft Patient Mobility Directive and the Coordination Regulations of Social Security' in Johan W van de Gronden, Erika Szyszczak, and Ulla Neergaard (eds), *Health Care and EU Law* (TMC Asser Press 2011).

The shadow of case law that hovers over legislation should trouble us for another reason. It not only puts into jeopardy the quality of EU law but also endangers its legitimacy. The legislature might fall short of meeting standards of *demoi*cratic legitimacy in full, but it meets these to a greater extent than the judiciary. As such, the value of political legitimacy dictates that it must ideally be the legislature that defines the EU's political course of action: it should not be required to legislate in the shadow of the judiciary. In this light, the empirical evidence discussed just now is disconcerting: it paints a picture of a legislature subservient to the judiciary, contrary to what we should want the allocation of legislative versus judicial authority to be. But let's not judge too soon, not before a more complete view has been obtained of how the legislature and judiciary exercise authority relative to each other. In Chapters III and IV, I will improve and, in part, correct the picture just drawn, which is more complex and less one-dimensional than the examples just discussed may suggest. We will see that EU Treaty rights are, in large part, legislated rights.

Studying the relative authority of the legislature versus the judiciary against the value of political legitimacy, this chapter has shown that the determination of the content of EU law should ideally lie within the domain of legislation. It refuted three output-oriented conceptions of legitimacy, which have been used to support judicial supremacy, and argued instead that the EU can lay claim to input-oriented legitimacy. On this *demoi*cratic conception of legitimacy, in the exercise of its authority, the EU should not dominate over the national peoples, which is why the legislature must be the main source of EU law-making. Conversely, as Chapter III affirms, the value of political legitimacy militates in favour of the CJEU exercising its power in deference to the choices of the legislature.

III

Realising Legal and Social Change

A Theory of Judicial Deference

1. Introduction

Chapter II taught us that the comparative advantage of the legislature over the judiciary lies in its political legitimacy—in its ability to establish non-dominating relations between national citizens by placing European Union (EU) decision-making under their shared and equal control. In showing this, I focused on the quality of these institutions' decision-making procedures rather than the political output they generate. A concern with such a procedural conception of political legitimacy may be that it is too fragile to support the legislature's authority, first because there may be a gap between the stated ideal and actual legislative practice, and second because political institutions serve values other than procedural ones. Performance matters: claims of procedural fairness will ring hollow if political institutions fail to achieve what they exist for. The same goes for EU institutions: we want them to perform well and reach good political decisions, whatever that means. The legislature may offer the fairest process for settling the content of EU law, but we also expect it to formulate good laws and policies.

Concern about the fragility of procedural conceptions of legitimacy can be cashed out in different ways. Some would say that the legitimacy of our political arrangements depends on not only their intrinsic but also their instrumental value: on their ability to perform well, or at least better than alternative arrangements.[1] Others have argued that political institutions should be evaluated having regard to not only their *institutional legitimacy* but also their *institutional capacity*.[2] Taking the second route, this chapter complements the account of institutional legitimacy set out in Chapter II with an account of institutional capacity.[3] Together, these arguments provide a theory of judicial deference to the choices of the legislature.

[1] David M Estlund, *Democratic Authority: A Philosophical Framework* (Princeton UP 2009); Hélène Landemore, *Democratic Reason: Politics, Collective Intelligence, and the Rule of the Many* (Princeton UP 2017).

[2] See Jeff King, *Judging Social Rights* (CUP 2012) 130, including the literature to which he refers.

[3] I do so not because I disagree that an institution's ability to make good decisions is unrelated to its legitimacy but because my assessment will include measures of capacity that should probably be kept separate from normative evaluations of legitimacy (such as the capacity of EU institutions to get Member States to comply with EU law).

Legislative Authority and Interpretation in the European Union. Martijn van den Brink, Oxford University Press.
 DOI: 10.1093/9780198900115.003.0003

The capacity to make good decisions is not the same as the capacity to make just or correct decisions. Chapter II has addressed the moral and practical difficulties of justice-based conceptions of legitimacy. Our societal debates are characterised by serious disagreement about justice, much of which seems reasonable. It has, moreover, been impossible to identify objectively correct standards of justice, which is why it cannot be thought that EU institutions act legitimately provided they observe accepted principles of justice. There is also a more practical problem of thinking that political authority is legitimate only when it is exercised justly. If that were true, the legitimacy of political institutions would be fragmented and depend on whether the decisions reached are just, which is something about which people subject to their authority will disagree. Using justice as the measure of legitimacy will thus have problematic implications for the stability of our political arrangements.

However, we can be concerned with the outcomes of political institutions without having to invoke contentious standards of justice. Certain institutions may be expected to perform better in specific respects because of how their decision-making procedures are structured, because of the kind or number of people involved, because of the information they have access to, or for other reasons. We can evaluate and compare the instrumental value of political institutions looking at such institutional qualities. The question, then, is not whether the decisions they take are correct but whether they can reliably be trusted to take better decisions than other institutions, given their capacities. This chapter follows this approach with a view to evaluating and comparing the relative institutional capacity of the EU legislature and judiciary. It focuses on two types of institutional capacity and explains that the legislature is better equipped to initiate *legal change* and to realise *social change*. The first means that it is a better lawmaker than the Court of Justice of the European Union (CJEU) so that EU law can be trusted to be of higher quality when made by legislation than case law (section III.2). The second means that legislation is more likely to generate its intended social effects domestically: legal addressees of EU law are more likely to adjust their laws and practices in response to legislation than case law (section III.3).

These conclusions lend further support to the position defended in Chapter II: the EU must be able to decide its course of action through the legislative process. Indeed, the arguments of both chapters combined provide a robust basis for the application of a principle of judicial deference to the legislature. In section III.4, I develop a theory of judicial deference that rests on three principles: institutional legitimacy, institutional capacity, and institutional collaboration. More specifically, I defend a form of judicial deference that is in line with so-called restrictive institutionalism,[4] which favours the imposition of, and adherence to, relatively

[4] King (n 2) 141–42.

precise legislative rules for reasons typically associated with the Rule of Law and democratic legitimacy. After it has been argued that restrictive institutionalism is most appropriate in the EU, I show, in sections III.5 and III.6 that this approach is compatible with EU primary law—the Treaties and the Charter of Fundamental Rights—and appropriate not just where the legislature has fully harmonised an area of law but also in the adjudication of minimum harmonisation.

2. Realising Legal Change

The Court has left a clear mark on the content as well as the study of EU law. As Daniel Augenstein and Mark Dawson observe, its judgments have strongly influenced the 'Integration through Law' school, whose core assumptions have, in turn, 'shaped the contours of EU law as an academic discipline'.[5] It should not surprise, therefore, that many legal scholars find integration through case law desirable: they assume that the CJEU is an institution well placed to decide on the development of EU law.[6] This section paints a more realistic picture by showing that the EU judiciary misses the capacities competent lawmakers such as the legislature have. As I will explain, the legislature is better equipped to initiate legal change by reference to the *epistemic qualities* of the legislative process and the *rule of law qualities* of legislative acts.

First, however, let me be clear about what my argument is not. My argument is not that the content of EU law should never be made by judges. Not only should it be uncontroversial that they may not be able to avoid creating law in the process of legal interpretation, but also federal-type systems may not be able to function properly without a judiciary that arbitrates conflicts between the centre and the states.[7] The EU has, at times, needed its judiciary to promote and protect the foundations of its multi-level legal order.[8] Furthermore, it is inevitable that the CJEU will be asked to settle complex questions of politics, just as it is unavoidable that the legislature will have to deal with intricate questions of law. It is sometimes said, by contrast, that courts should not adjudicate complex disputes whose consequences

[5] Daniel Augenstein and Mark Dawson, 'Introduction: What Law for What Polity? "Integration through Law" in the European Union Revisited' in Daniel Augenstein (ed), *'Integration through Law' Revisited: The Making of the European Polity* (Routledge 2016) 1.

[6] Recall the arguments in favour of judicial decision-making discussed in Chapter II.

[7] See also Cécile Fabre, 'The Dignity of Rights' (2000) 20 Oxford Journal of Legal Studies 271, 273. Moreover, as I explain in Chapter IV, the CJEU is indispensable as arbiter in conflicts between legislative institutions.

[8] Think, for example, of the legal principles governing the application of EU law in the Member States, such as supremacy and direct effect, but also of more recent case law establishing principles for the protection of the rule of law in the Member States. For an overview of these judgments, Dimitry Kochenov and Laurent Pech, 'Respect for the Rule of Law in the Case Law of the European Court of Justice: A Casebook Overview of Key Judgments since the Portuguese Judges Case' (Swedish Institute for European Policy Studies Report, 2021).

are unpredictable yet significant for people not represented in the judicial process (so-called polycentric disputes). But as Jeff King has shown, such disputes are common as well as inevitable. EU law 'provides a wealth of examples of the adjudication of polycentric problems of mind-boggling proportions'.[9] Think of legal disputes on the division of competences between the EU and the Member States, on the authority of the European Central in monetary and economic issues, or on the proper balance between national labour law and cross-border movement in an integrated internal market—all polycentric disputes of the highest order.

This is not to say that the CJEU should bear such responsibilities or discharges them properly; one may, indeed, question how desirable it is for courts to decide such issues. However, the point is that the CJEU cannot 'decline to adjudicate a dispute on grounds of polycentricity if it is centrally within the class of disputes its mandate requires it to address'.[10] It is neither conceptually compelling nor practically possible to determine in advance which issues are justiciable and which are not, for example by demarcating domains that are exclusively for courts (law or principle) or exclusively for legislatures (politics or policy).[11] The dividing line between law and politics can be unclear, and courts have a clear mandate to deal with complex political issues: they cannot decline jurisdiction on the ground that their rulings would involve complex moral or empirical judgements. The relevant question, therefore, is not whether but how the CJEU should deal such disputes.

One way of dealing with the uncertainty that comes with such cases is to develop the law incrementally. Incrementalism has enormous appeal for judges who need to adjudicate complex cases under conditions of bounded rationality. It allows them to adjust their decisions in response to criticism or to new information about the consequences of earlier judgments, and it leaves room for other institutions to intervene and draw up different or more detailed legal norms.[12] Naturally, the CJEU has been attracted to incrementalism as a method of adjudication too. As any observer of EU law knows, it often answers the preliminary questions it receives using vague legal principles without spelling out clearly what legal changes are needed in observation of these principles: the more general implications of its judgments often remain unclear until future decisions.[13] Especially when the rules under consideration are imprecise and their interpretation requires controversial moral or empirical judgement, incrementalism may be an appropriate judicial response. However, while there are good reasons to think that incrementalism is a method judges can use to develop the law, it is not the case that judges are best

[9] King (n 2) 199.
[10] ibid 200.
[11] Ronald Dworkin, *Taking Rights Seriously* (Bloomsbury 2013) 90.
[12] King (n 2) ch 10.
[13] Susanne K Schmidt, *The European Court of Justice and the Policy Process: The Shadow of Case Law* (OUP 2018) 197. See also Loïc Azoulai, 'The European Court of Justice and the Duty to Respect Sensitive National Interests' in Mark Dawson, Bruno de Witte, and Elise Muir (eds), *Judicial Activism at the European Court of Justice* (Edward Elgar 2013) 1339–40.

placed to develop the law or that incrementalism is the best method for doing so. If other decision-makers have already expressed their view on a matter and adopted legal rules to that effect, another way for the CJEU to resolve a dispute is to assign weight to these views and yield to these rules.[14] Judicial deference to legislative choices can be justified on different grounds (section III.4), one of which is the legislature's superior law-making capacities.

Establishing the framework of rules that applies across all Member States is a difficult task. To be carried out successfully, the responsible actors must have the capacity to process complex and highly technical information on a wide range of subjects, the capacity to identify and respond to societal problems requiring legal change, the capacity to deliberate openly and on the basis of all relevant information on the state of affairs to be achieved, and the capacity to put in place the legal norms required to realise the desired state of affairs.[15] The legislature has these capacities both in absolute terms and relative to the CJEU. This is not because of some institutional defect but because realising legal change is, in the first place, a legislative task for which courts are not as well equipped. The primary purpose of courts, instead, is to settle legal disputes; the legal change they generate is incidental to the process of adjudication.[16]

One reason why the legislature is a better lawmaker is that its decision-making process is epistemically more secure. It has access to a wide range of information on a broad variety of issues, including the social and political conditions in the Member States, the scientific and technological matters relating to the issues to be resolved, and possible trade-offs between alternative courses of action. It can rely on the vast expertise available to EU officials, including specialised agencies and research departments that can be asked to provide independent advice. Their knowledge facilitates the impact assessments carried out by the Commission before it submits a legislative proposal, in which it assesses the necessity and desirability of legal change and which enable the legislature institutions to have an informed debate on the economic, social, and environmental consequences of alternative policies.[17] Besides in-house expertise, the legislature can also call on external experts, domestic civil servants, and those most directly affected by the proposals under discussion for information and advice.[18]

[14] Aileen Kavanagh, 'Deference or Defiance?: The Limits of the Judicial Role in Constitutional Adjudication' in Grant Huscroft (ed), *Expounding the Constitution: Essays in Constitutional Theory* (CUP 2008) 186.

[15] For similar accounts, Richard Ekins, *The Nature of Legislative Intent* (OUP 2012) ch 5; Paul Yowell, *Constitutional Rights and Constitutional Design: Moral and Empirical Reasoning in Judicial Review* (Hart Publishing 2018) ch 5.

[16] See also Ekins (n 15) 121–22.

[17] Commission of the European Communities, 'European Governance: A White Paper', Brussels 25 July 2001 (COM(2001)) 428. See further Anne CM Meuwese, *Impact Assessment in EU Lawmaking* (Wolters Kluwer Law 2008).

[18] Åse Gornitzka and Ulf Sverdrup, 'Access of Experts: Information and EU Decision-Making' (2011) 34 West European Politics 48.

By comparison, the judicial process tends to exhibit greater epistemic uncertainty. Judges cannot, as Krajewski notes, rely on 'experts, recognised methods, advisory committees, delegated national experts, and the like. Constrained by the adversarial procedure, they usually examine the claims and evidence adduced by the parties, relinquishing their own investigatory powers.'[19] First, the judicial process is subject to significant constraints of information and expertise. The expertise of judges is in questions of law and rarely adequate for taking the complex political, economic, and social choices that our political institutions are called upon to take. Judicial officials can, of course, rely on the expertise of the research services at their disposal or the arguments submitted by the parties to a dispute, but such information is normally geared towards the resolution of disputes and may not provide enough insights into related societal questions and the most appropriate response thereto. Moreover, they cannot choose which cases to hear and must dispose of a relatively large number of cases.[20] This means they work under considerable constraints of time and are compelled to decide cases in a reasonable manner, within the shortest possible time.[21] It is unlikely, therefore, that they can adequately consider the wider social and political implications of their decisions.

Moreover, research in psychology suggests that large and diverse groups are, all things being equal, better at processing complex information than small and homogeneous groups. As Landemore says, 'deliberation among more-inclusive groups is likely to produce better results than deliberation among less-inclusive groups, even if those less-inclusive groups include smarter people.'[22] The two relevant variables are deliberation and inclusiveness. Deliberation enables group members to learn from each other's experience and expertise, broadening the knowledge and information they can draw from. Inclusiveness increases the cognitive diversity of groups and thereby the perspectives on the issues to be discussed and decided. If it is true that deliberation by cognitively diverse groups increases the probability of good decision-making, then we have an additional reason to think that the EU must ideally exercise its authority through the legislative process. It provides a relatively inclusive process for debating political issues, in which people from different walks of life and with different kinds of experience and expertise make political decisions together. Internal legislative structures may limit the capacity for

[19] Michal Krajewski, 'Judicial and Extra-Judicial Review: The Quest for Epistemic Certainty' in Merijn Chamon and others (eds), *The Boards of Appeal of EU Agencies: Towards Judicialization of Administrative Review?* (OUP 2022). See also Hanns Peter Nehl, 'Judicial Review of Complex Socio-Economic, Technical, and Scientific Assessments' in Joana Mendes (ed), *EU Executive Discretion and the Limits of Law* (OUP 2019); Vilija Velyvyte, *Judicial Authority in EU Internal Market Law: Implications for the Balance of Competences and Powers* (Hart Publishing 2022).

[20] Though see Arthur Dyevre, Monika Glavina, and Michal Ovadek, 'Raising the Bar: The Development of Docket Control on the Court of Justice' (2021) Zeitschrift für öffentliches Recht 523.

[21] See also Adrian Vermeule, *Judging under Uncertainty: An Institutional Theory of Legal Interpretation* (Harvard UP 2006); Yowell (n 15) ch 5.

[22] Landemore (n 1) 90. See also Estlund (n 1) 181.

deliberation,[23] but members involved in the deliberations on a legislative proposal must hear and respond to alternative views, whether from members of the same institution or committee or from other institutions. If all is well, the legislation that gets passed has been deliberated on by a sizeable number of people, which, if the findings of psychological research hold true for decision-making by EU institutions, should increase the likelihood of good law-making.

The CJEU is made up of more like-minded individuals who do not have the same capacity as the legislature to deliberate on the content of EU law. As Paul Yowell reminds us, constitutional adjudication is subject to an important paradox: it requires relatively unconstrained reasoning about the moral and empirical justifications of the law, however, by judges who want to uphold their reputation for impartiality by defending their judgments as properly guided and constrained by legal rules.[24] The CJEU is subject to this paradox too. We can see this in, for example, the extrajudicial writings of Koen Lenaerts, its current President. Aware of the far-reaching influence 'his' court has exerted on the development of EU law, he is, on the one hand, inclined to defend judge-made law, asserting that judicial incrementalism is 'the right way of building a solid edifice to the rights' of EU citizens.[25] On the other hand, to deflect accusations of improper judicial behaviour, he tries to downplay its influence by denying that judges ever 'go beyond their duty of saying "what the law is"'. This would rob their verdicts of 'legitimacy as they intrude into the political process'.[26] He obviously cannot have it both ways,[27] but his comments are interesting for a different reason: they point to a tension in the judicial process. Lenaerts obviously understands that the choices of him and his colleagues cannot all be objectively deduced from the law, yet he tries to give the impression that their decisions do not turn on extrajudicial moral and factual concerns. Although he may have good reasons for this, the deliberative capacity of judges is limited by the expectations they face. They may feel compelled to reason as if controversial rulings rest on the only possible interpretation of EU law, but that does not make for good law-making.

The second reason why the legislature must have authority over EU law is that legislation is more conducive to the rule of law. Conversely, essential rule of law values—such as that the law must be stable, clear, coherent, and workable in practice—risk being compromised when judges take on too much responsibility

[23] See Chapter IV.

[24] See also Yowell (n 15) 113. For similar arguments, Jeremy Waldron, 'Judges as Moral Reasoners' (2008) 7 International Journal of Constitutional Law 2; Wojciech Sadurski, 'Judicial Review and the Protection of Constitutional Rights' (2002) 22 Oxford Journal of Legal Studies 275.

[25] Koen Lenaerts, 'The Court's Outer and Inner Selves: Exploring the External and Internal Legitimacy of the European Court of Justice' in Maurice Adams and others (eds), *Judging Europe's Judges: The Legitimacy of the Case Law of the European Court of Justice* (Hart Publishing 2013) 59.

[26] ibid 13.

[27] JHH Weiler, 'Epilogue: Judging the Judges—Apology and Critique' in Adams and others (n 25).

for the development of EU law.[28] This is, in large part, due to the incremental style of decision-making of the Court and its frequent use of vague legal norms, both of which create uncertainty for those to whom the law is addressed. This problem is exacerbated by the Court's erratic use of precedent. Previous decisions are rarely overturned;[29] instead, they are, as Anthony Arnull observed,

> normally only cited by the Court in support of its argument: authorities which point the other way are rarely mentioned. Indeed, they are sometimes presented by the Court as if they support the line it has chosen to take. This practice is liable to cause serious confusion among those who have the task of giving effect to the Court's judgments and may as a result jeopardize the proper application of Community law.[30]

Indeed, it is a practice that is likely to jeopardise EU law's capacity to guide the conduct of citizens and, as we see in section III.3, partly explains why Court-initiated legal change is less likely to lead to social change.

The legislature's capacity to change EU law does not depend on the disputes that arise and the legal questions they raise. It can remedy the shortcomings it identifies in EU law by means of comprehensive reform, that is by amending any legal norm that stands in the way of its intended state of affairs. Moreover, it can focus on the general state of EU law, rather than the more specific circumstances of particular disputes, and thereby determine the content of EU law at the level of generality needed for its proper application to millions of EU citizens. It can also change the law in a way that appropriately guides the behaviour of those whom it addresses. Particularly important in this respect is the fact that legislation is 'replete with detailed, highly constraining, judicially enforceable provisions'.[31] This is the case not only for Regulations but also for Directives, even though they are officially binding only 'as to the result to be achieved'.[32] Still, they are typically 'so detailed that . . . the Member States are left with very little latitude'.[33] Daniel Kelemen has offered a simple explanation for this:

[28] More generally, Maris Köpcke Tinturé, *Legal Validity: The Fabric of Justice* (Hart Publishing 2018) 110–14 and 129.

[29] The exceptions are Case C-10/89 *HAG II* ECLI:EU:C:1990:359, para 10; Case C-127/08 *Metock* ECLI:EU:C:2008:449; Case C-209/03 *Bidar* ECLI:EU:C:2005:169, paras 28–32, and some say, Joined cases C-267/91 and C-268/91 *Keck and Mithoard* ECLI:EU:C:1993:905. See further, Marc A Jacob, *Precedents and Case-Based Reasoning in the European Court of Justice: Unfinished Business* (CUP 2014) ch 6.

[30] Anthony Arnull, 'Owning Up to Fallibility: Precedent and the Court of Justice' (1993) 247 Common Market Law Review 247, 253. See also Margaret McCown, 'The European Parliament before the Bench: ECJ Precedent and EP Litigation Strategies' (2003) 10 Journal of European Public Policy 974, 979.

[31] R Daniel Kelemen, *Eurolegalism: The Transformation of Law and Regulation in the European Union* (Harvard UP 2011) 41.

[32] Article 288 of the Treaty on the Functioning of the European Union (TFEU).

[33] Sacha Prechal, *Directives in EC Law* (2nd edn, OUP 2005) 14.

> The EU has limited administrative capacity but strong courts. EU lawmakers (the principals) rely primarily on national administrations (their agents) to implement EU policy, but lawmakers realise that these agents often will have incentives to shirk. Therefore, EU lawmakers seek to craft detailed, judicially enforceable laws that will limit discretion in implementation.[34]

The European Parliament, in particular, has actively sought to introduce amendments that increase the detail and precision of legislation, all in order to reduce 'the discretion of the national agents in charge of policy execution'.[35] It explains why legislation can reliably be trusted to offer better protection of essential rule of law values.

A sceptical reader might want to interject at this point and pose the obvious question: where is the evidence to back up the claim that the legislature is better positioned to realise legal change? Let's face the facts, she could go on, without the CJEU neither the content of EU law nor its binding force in the Member States would be remotely what it is today. Am I really denying that the CJEU has been instrumental in the development of EU law? I am not, of course, and do not wish to downplay its influence. However, the fact that the CJEU has been an influential lawmaker does not prove that it is a good lawmaker. In fact, our understanding of successful law-making would be impoverished if success is measured by influence alone.

So let's face the facts and examine the above arguments. This is best done by comparing legislative and judicial law-making in the same area of EU law. To allow for a proper comparison, the selected area must be one in which both institutions have tried exerting significant influence, which excludes many areas of EU law. The CJEU typically affords considerable deference in areas regulated by legislation, while areas where case law has left its imprint are not always characterised by much legislative activity. An important exception is the legal regulation of EU citizenship, which therefore provides a suitable case study. There always have been detailed legislative provisions that set out the rights of EU citizens who move to a country other than that of their nationality. For a considerable period of time, however, the CJEU refused to respect these provisions, particularly those setting out the conditions under which citizens can claim social assistance in the host state. Instead, it sidestepped the provisions and replaced them with alternative norms of its own, making this area an ideal testing ground for a comparison between legislation and case law.[36]

[34] Kelemen (n 31) 43.

[35] Fabio Franchino, *The Powers of the Union: Delegation in the EU* (CUP 2007) 256.

[36] For a more extensive discussion of the legal development of the right of EU citizens to claim social assistance, Martijn van den Brink, 'Off Track, Again? EU Citizenship and the Right to Social Assistance' (2023) 11 Hungarian Yearbook of International and European Law 18.

This area of law also provides a good case study because the case law supposedly discredits my arguments. As we saw earlier, Koen Lenaerts believes that case law can offer a good foundation to build a solid edifice of rights, which is a claim he supported with reference to the EU citizenship case law. He is certainly not the only one who thinks this way. In fact, many others agree that the Court's activities in this area are an example of sound law-making attesting to its capacity to realise legal change and have defended its interventionist approach in this area.[37] I will explain that they are mistaken: the case law has all the shortcomings we should expect from judge-made law.

In the early 1990s, a few years before EU citizenship's introduction, legislation was adopted, granting the right to move and reside freely throughout the EU to economically inactive persons such as students and pensioners.[38] However, this right came without the right to claim social assistance in the host state: it was made conditional on citizens having sufficient resources not to become a burden on the social assistance system. Although there were no indications that these legislative acts became obsolete with the introduction of EU citizenship in 1993, the CJEU began to use this concept in the late 1990s to rewrite the regulation of the right to free movement of persons, granting EU citizens *without* sufficient resources the right to social assistance. It did not do this, however, based on a coherent political vision and in response to identified shortcomings in the law. It did so, instead, on an ad hoc basis and in response to singular disputes, whereby sympathy for litigants has often seemed to be the main determinant for how disputes were settled.[39]

This process started with the judgment in *Martínez Sala*. Mrs Martínez Sala had been legally resident in Germany for approximately twenty-five years and employed on several occasions. Still, her application for a child-raising allowance was rejected because she lacked a residence permit at the time.[40] The CJEU helped her out, ruling that the Treaties attach to the status of EU citizenship the right not to suffer discrimination on grounds of nationality.[41] Next came *Grzelczyk*, which

[37] For example, Dora Kostakopoulou, 'European Union Citizenship: Writing the Future' (2007) 13 European Law Journal 623; Dimitry Kochenov and Sir Richard Plender, 'EU Citizenship: From an Incipient Form to an Incipient Substance? The Discovery of the Treaty Text' (2012) 37 European Law Review 369; Ferdinand Wollenschläger, 'A New Fundamental Freedom beyond Market Integration: Union Citizenship and Its Dynamics for Shifting the Economic Paradigm of European Integration' (2011) 17 European Law Journal 1; Síofra O'Leary, 'Putting Flesh on the Bones of European Union Citizenship' (1999) 24 European Law Review 68; Michael Dougan, 'The Constitutional Dimension to the Case Law on Union Citizenship' (2006) 31 European Law Review 613.

[38] Council Directive 93/96/EEC of the Council of 29 October 1993 on the right of residence for students (OJ L317/59); Council Directive 90/365/EEC of 28 June 1990 on the right of residence for employees and self-employed persons who have ceased their occupational activity (OJ L180/28). See also Council Directive 90/364/EEC of 28 June 1990 on the right of residence (OJ L180/26).

[39] Gareth Davies, 'Has the Court Changed, or Have the Cases? The Deservingness of Litigants as an Element in Court of Justice Citizenship Adjudication' (2018) 25 Journal of European Public Policy 1442, 1445; Niamh Nic Shuibhne, '(Some of) The Kids Are All Right: Comment on McCarthy and Dereci' (2012) 39 Common Market Law Review 349.

[40] Case C-85/96 *Martínez Sala* ECLI:EU:C:1998:217, paras 13–16.

[41] ibid para 63.

extended the scope of *Martínez Sala*. At the time, Member States could, in accordance with EU legislation, deny students the right to reside in their country if they risked becoming a burden on their social assistance system because of insufficient financial resources.[42] However, by ruling that any situation involving the exercise of the right to free movement fell within the material scope of EU law,[43] the CJEU allowed mobile citizens lawfully resident in another state to invoke the principle of non-discrimination on grounds of nationality. In addition, it limited the right of Member States to revoke the right of lawful residence, saying that it could not be an 'automatic consequence of a national of another Member State having recourse to the host Member State's social assistance system'.[44] The full potential of these judgments became visible in *Trojani*. Once again, the CJEU circumvented the applicable legislation,[45] this time by allowing a French national without adequate financial means to benefit from the principle of equal treatment during his lawful residence in Belgium.[46] Since the possibility of revoking the right to reside from persons claiming social assistance was restricted,[47] the early social assistance case law came close to establishing a right of equal treatment for all citizens with a right of residence in the host country.

Regardless of our view of what social rights mobile citizens should have, we should be able to see that this is not an ideal way to bring about legal change: the CJEU seemingly had little regard for the more general financial and economic implications of its decisions. That the expansion of the right to free movement has not, on a large scale, eroded collective social welfare does not alter this conclusion.[48] Not only have some EU citizenship rulings adversely affected the provision of certain social benefits (namely, those whose enjoyment was not subject to any conditions),[49] but also such rulings may well significantly affect the national allocation of resources without bringing welfare states to the brink of collapse.[50] Introducing such major legal changes without a proper assessment of the likely consequences is far from desirable.

[42] Council Directive 93/96/EEC (n 38).
[43] Case C-184/99 *Grzelczyk* ECLI:EU:C:2001:458, para 33.
[44] ibid para 43.
[45] Council Directive 90/364/EEC (n 38).
[46] Case C-456/02 *Trojani* ECLI:EU:C:2004:488, para 40
[47] ibid para 45.
[48] Dorte Sindbjerg Martinsen and Gabriel Pons Rotger, 'The Fiscal Impact of EU Immigration on the Tax-Financed Welfare State: Testing the "Welfare Burden" Thesis' (2017) 18 European Union Politics 620; Dorte Sindbjerg Martinsen and Benjamin Werner, 'No Welfare Magnets—Free Movement and Cross-Border Welfare in Germany and Denmark Compared' (2019) 26 Journal of European Public Policy 637.
[49] Angelika Schenk and Susanne K Schmidt, 'Failing on the Social Dimension: Judicial Law-Making and Student Mobility in the EU' (2018) 25 Journal of European Public Policy 1522.
[50] Christopher Newdick, 'Citizenship, Free Movement and Health Care: Cementing Individual Rights by Corroding Social Solidarity' (2006) 43 Common Market Law Review 1645; Maurizio Ferrera, *The Boundaries of Welfare: European Integration and the New Spatial Politics of Social Protection* (OUP 2005).

Moreover, one reason why the three judgments did not affect collective welfare rights more substantially is that they were subsequently construed more narrowly. Shortly after *Trojani*, the CJEU began to introduce tests that integrated the extent of social integration in the host state into the examination of whether EU citizens should be granted social assistance.[51] Perhaps aware of the possible far-reaching implications of earlier judgments, it allowed Member States to condition their treatment of non-national EU citizens as equal to their nationals on 'a real link [with] the geographic employment market'[52] or on 'a certain degree of integration into the society of the host State'.[53] Since then, applications for social assistance by citizens who did not meet these conditions could be refused.

The granted discretion may have been desirable from the point of view of the sustainability of social welfare, but these criteria generated new problems. They show how much judges can be fixated on the individual cases before them in developing the law at the expense of the overall state of the law. And they show how little they may be aware of the challenges involved in the law's administration and implementation. Deciding very few cases, judges have the capacity to carry out a separate examination for each individual applicant. Yet, the requirement to carry out such individualised assessments may place unacceptable burdens on national authorities dealing with larger number of cases. This is certainly so if, as was once required, Member States must take into consideration all sorts of 'representative elements'[54]—including 'family,[55] employment, language skills or the existence of other social and economic factors';[56] the place where citizens went to school;[57] and any chances of a future link with society.[58] As Floris de Witte rightly remarked, we have reason to be concerned about such requirements 'for reasons of legal certainty, the risk of endless litigation, administrative burdens, and added legislative complexity'.[59]

Now compare these criteria with the legislative rules conditioning access to social assistance. According to the Citizenship Directive, citizens are not entitled to

[51] Floris de Witte, *Justice in the EU: The Emergence of Transnational Solidarity* (OUP 2015) 131; Charlotte O'Brien, 'Real Links, Abstract Rights and False Alarms: The Relationship between the ECJ's "Real Link" Case Law and National Solidarity' (2008) 33 European Law Review 125; Michael Dougan, 'The Court Helps Those Who Help Themselves . . . The Legal Status of Migrant Work-Seekers under Community Law in the Light of the Collins Judgment' (2005) 7 European Journal of Social Security 7.

[52] Case C-224/98 *D'Hoop* ECLI:EU:C:2002:432, para 38; Case C-258/04 *Ioannidis* ECLI:EU:C:2005:559, para 30; Case C-367/11 *Prete* ECLI:EU:C:2012:668, para 33.

[53] *Bidar* (n 29) para 57; Case C-158/07 *Förster* ECLI:EU:C:2008:630, para 49.

[54] Case C-75/11 *Commission v Austria* ECLI:EU:C:2012:605, para 62; Case C-503/09 *Stewart* ECLI:EU:C:2011:500, para 95.

[55] *Prete* (n 52) para 48; *Stewart* (n 54) para 100.

[56] Case C-523/11 *Prinz and Seeberger* ECLI:EU:C:2013:524, para 38.

[57] Joined cases C-11/06 and C-12/06 *Morgan and Bucher* ECLI:EU:C:2007:626, para 45.

[58] Case C-20/12 *Giersch* ECLI:EU:C:2013:411, para 67; Case C-542/09 *Commission v The Netherlands* ECLI:EU:C:2012:346, para 77.

[59] de Witte (n 51) 137–38. See also Michael Blauberger and Susanne K Schmidt, 'Welfare Migration? Free Movement of EU Citizens and Access to Social Benefits' (2014) 1 Research & Politics 1.

social assistance during their first three months of residence, while they can claim social assistance for a period of no less than six months when they are in duly recorded involuntary unemployment after a period of employment of less than a year and indefinitely when they have been employed for more than a year.[60] In terms of clarity and applicability, these conditions are manifestly superior to those laid down in the case law (and the Citizenship Directive is not even considered a well-drafted legislative act).[61] They clearly provide under what circumstances it is possible to claim social assistance and enable national authorities, as well as citizens, to determine with relative ease and certainty whether the relevant conditions have been met.

In recent years, the CJEU has become more deferential to the provisions of the Citizenship Directive.[62] It has dropped the requirement to examine applicants' genuine links with the labour market and their degree of integration in their society.[63] It has also adopted a definition of social assistance more in line with the Directive.[64] However, it has changed course exactly as described by Arnull earlier. Instead of making the break with previous case law explicit, it left the impression that it followed precedent.[65] As Niamh Nic Shuibhne commented, 'The Court neither reconciled rooted case law on conditions and limits with its revised logic, nor openly reversed it. The result is a distorted and unconvincing jurisprudence.'[66] The result is confusion about the rights of Union citizens, among national administrations, judicial officials, and citizens themselves. This could have been avoided if the CJEU had consistently respected the legislature's choices.

Thus, contrary to Lenaerts' belief, the incremental construction of EU citizenship has not resulted in 'a solid edifice of rights'. Quite the opposite: the case law is difficult to understand or explain. Moreover, what is troubling is that this conclusion applies not only to the jurisprudence on social assistance but also to case law on the right of citizens to family reunification and the right of states to expel citizens—two more domains in which the CJEU ruled contrary to the legislature's

[60] These rules are found in arts 24(2), 7(3)(b), and 7(3)(c) of Directive 2004/38 of the European Parliament and of the Council of 29 April 2004 on the right of citizens of the Union and their family members to move and reside freely within the territory of the Member States (OJ L158/77).

[61] For a critical discussion, Alexander Somek, 'Solidarity Decomposed: Being and Time in European Citizenship' (2007) 32 European Law Review 787.

[62] Case C-333/13 *Dano* ECLI:EU:C:2014:2358; Case C-67/14 *Alimanovic* ECLI:EU:C:2015:597; Case C-411/20 *S v Bundesagentur für Arbeit* ECLI:EU:C:2022:602; Case C-709/20 *CG* ECLI:EU:C:2021:602.

[63] For lengthier discussion, Niamh Nic Shuibhne, 'Limits Rising, Duties Ascending: The Changing Legal Shape of Union Citizenship' (2015) 52 Common Market Law Review 889; Daniel Thym, 'The Elusive Limits of Solidarity: Residence Rights of and Social Benefits for Economically Inactive Union Citizens' (2015) 52 Common Market Law Review 17; Herwig Verschueren, 'Preventing "Benefit Tourism" in the EU: A Narrow or Broad Interpretation of the Possibilities Offered by the ECJ in Dano?' (2015) 52 Common Market Law Review 363; Charlotte O'Brien, 'Civis Capitalist Sum: Class as the New Guiding Principle of EU Free Movement Rights' (2016) 53 Common Market Law Review 937.

[64] For an overview, van den Brink (n 36).

[65] See eg *Alimanovic* (n 62) para 46.

[66] Nic Shuibhne, 'Limits Rising, Duties Ascending' (n 63) 916.

intentions.[67] Given the constraints on the judicial process, it should not be a surprise that things turned out this way, but they did not have to end up this way. The CJEU may not be able to avoid making complex moral or empirical judgements where there is no legislation governing a particular matter, but it could have yielded to the legislature's judgements in the cases just discussed. Instead, it decided to assume enormous responsibility for the development of the law, causing the expected shortcomings.

3. Realising Social Change

This is particularly problematic for EU law's addressees. This section examines how differences between legislation and case law affect the EU's capacity to realise social change. By this, I mean their capacity to induce compliance with EU law, by Member States and other persons to whom its provisions are addressed. Compliance means addressees adapting their legal provisions, their behaviour, or both in response to changes in EU law, in line with the expectation that they comply with, and adjust their conduct, in response to such changes. We know that compliance with EU law is influenced by various factors that interact in complex ways, including the compatibility of EU law with pre-existing national laws, the political preferences of national governments, the cost of non-compliance, and the administrative capacity of Member States.[68] As I will explain, however, another factor influencing compliance is the EU institution issuing legal instructions. All things being equal, the legislature is better than the judiciary at realising social change, which is a third ground upon which to advocate judicial deference to the choices of the legislature, assuming, of course, that compliance with EU law is an important good.

The CJEU was once regarded as a powerful and potent driver of social change.[69] However, scepticism about its capacity to effect change has grown, especially since Lisa Conant's pioneering study on the domestic effects of case law.[70] She found that national courts referring preliminary questions usually comply with CJEU

[67] Martijn van den Brink, 'Is It Time to Abolish the Substance of EU Citizenship Rights Test?' (2021) 23 European Journal of Migration and Law 13; Nic Shuibhne, '(Some of) The Kids Are All Right' (n 39) 379.

[68] Oliver Treib, 'Implementing and Complying with EU Governance Outputs' (2014) 9 Living Reviews in European Governance; Mariyana Angelova, Tanja Dannwolf, and Thomas König, 'How Robust Are Compliance Findings? A Research Sythesis' (2012) 19 Journal of European Public Policy 1269.

[69] Satisfying Rosenberg's description of a 'dynamic court': Gerald N Rosenberg, *The Hollow Hope: Can Courts Bring about Social Change?* (University of Chicago Press 2008) ch 1.

[70] Lisa J Conant, *Justice Contained: Law and Politics in the European Union* (CUP 2002); Lisa Conant, 'Compliance and What EU Member States Make of It' in Marise Cremona (ed), *Compliance and the Enforcement of EU Law* (OUP 2012).

rulings[71] but that these rulings rarely act as a catalyst for social change. This is because Member States tend towards 'contained compliance', especially when civil society groups are unable to put pressure on national authorities to transpose case law into national legislation or to amend their administrative practices.[72] It has since been shown that the contained compliance thesis is incomplete (ie judgments requiring major and costly changes cannot always be contained)[73] but also that it is not incorrect. Domestic strategies of contained compliance can inhibit the effectiveness of EU law; the important question is when they do. As we will see, there is evidence to suggest that this depends, in part, on the institution issuing EU law: such strategies are more likely to succeed in respect of case law that is unsupported by legislation. Let me illustrate this with some examples.

The case law on adequate remedies for breach of EU law has highlighted the shortcomings of purely judicial solutions to political problems.[74] As early as the 1990s, scholars observed that the lack of legislative harmonisation in this area undermined the effectiveness of EU legal remedies.[75] The guidelines developed by the CJEU proved difficult to realise, especially in legal systems where courts considered it beyond their authority to offer remedies not provided for in national law.[76] The *Köbler* principle of state liability for judicial infringements of EU law perhaps provides the best example. It has been so widely disregarded that Michael Bobek called it a 'virtual' principle, existing only 'in a few pronouncements of the CJEU and in EU law textbooks recounting the Luxembourg orthodoxy'.[77] One would think that this problem could be remedied, at least in part, by legislation establishing clear and uniform procedural rules. These would make it harder for national authorities to contain remedies for breach of EU law.

Non-compliance can also be a problem that arises when EU law is not interpreted the way the legislature intended. In the period of one year, from June 2013 to

[71] As they usually do: Stacy A Nyikos, 'The Preliminary Reference Process: National Court Implementation, Changing Opportunity Structures and Litigant Desistment' (2003) 4 European Union Politics 397.

[72] Conant, 'Compliance and What EU Member States Make of It' (n 70) 26; Rachel A Cichowski, *The European Court and Civil Society Litigation, Mobilization and Governance* (CUP 2007); Michael Blauberger, 'National Responses to European Court Jurisprudence' (2014) 37 West European Politics 457.

[73] See the examples given by Schmidt, *The European Court of Justice and the Policy Process* (n 13) 203–206. See also, Michael Blauberger and Susanne K Schmidt, 'The European Court of Justice and Its Political Impact' (2017) 40 West European Politics 907, 913; Michael Blauberger, 'With Luxembourg in Mind . . . the Remaking of National Policies in the Face of ECJ Jurisprudence' (2012) 19 Journal of European Public Policy 109.

[74] This paragraph draws on, Conant, *Justice Contained* (n 70) 62.

[75] Christopher MG Himsworth, 'Things Fall Apart: The Harmonisation of Community Judicial Procedural Protection Revisited' (1997) 22 European Law Review 292.

[76] Gráinne de Búrca, 'Giving Effect to European Community Directives' (1992) 55 Modern Law Review 215, 239.

[77] Case C-224/01 *Köbler* ECLI:EU:C:2003:513. Michal Bobek, 'EU Law in National Courts: *Viking*, *Laval* and Beyond' in MR Freedland and Jeremias Prassl (eds), *Viking, Laval and beyond* (Hart Publishing 2016) 334. See also Zsófia Varga, *The Effectiveness of the Köbler Liability in National Courts* (Hart Publishing 2020).

June 2014, three German courts asked preliminary questions with a view to clarifying when mobile citizens can claim social assistance in the host state.[78] Their decision to stay proceedings and ask questions was not evident: the German authorities that rejected the requests for social assistance had acted in accordance with the conditions laid down in the Citizenship Directive. The applicants in *García-Nieto* had applied for assistance during the first three months of their stay which, under art 24(2) of the Directive, need not be granted during that period. The applicants in *Alimanovic* had worked for eleven months, one month less than the one-year period that entitles an involuntarily unemployed person to retain their status as a worker and be eligible for the receipt of social assistance under art 7(3)(b) of the Directive. The applicant in *Dano* had never been employed or tried to find work in Germany. However, while the German authorities complied with the applicable legislative provisions, their decisions seemed contrary to settled case law at the time. As we saw in section III.2, it used to be the rule that benefits could be claimed by jobseekers with 'real links to the labour market'.[79] To my knowledge, it had not been examined whether the applicants met this condition, even though some of them had established links with the labour market.[80] It appears, therefore, that the German authorities continued to deal with social assistance claims as required by the Citizenship Directive. For almost a decade, conflicting case law was interpreted narrowly or simply ignored.[81]

A third example that illustrates the uncertainty and backlash that can be caused by case law that goes against express legislative rules is the *Sturgeon* case. The Air Passenger Rights Regulation sets out when air carriers must offer assistance and when they must offer financial compensation to passengers who are delayed or stranded. Financial compensation is due only in the event of flight cancellations, while assistance—but no financial compensation—can be claimed in the event of long delays.[82] In *Sturgeon*, this distinction was erased: financial compensation was to be awarded also in the event of long delays. The CJEU found the differential treatment between cancellations and delays to be incompatible with the general principle of equality, since 'the damage sustained by air passengers in cases of cancellation or long delay is comparable'.[83] This finding met with vehement criticism by courts in Germany, the United Kingdom, and the Netherlands. Some of them even refused to comply with *Sturgeon*, taking the view that the CJEU had not acted

[78] *Dano* (n 62); *Alimanovic* (n 62); Case C-299/14 *García-Nieto* ECLI:EU:C:2016:144).

[79] Joined cases C-22/08 and C-23/08 *Vatsouras and Koupatantze* ECLI:EU:C:2009:344, para 40.

[80] Especially, the applicants in *Alimanovic* (n 62) had established such links.

[81] See also Schmidt, *The European Court of Justice and the Policy Process* (n 13) 223; Dion Kramer, 'EU-Studenten en de Nederlandse Studiefinanciering: Assertiviteit in de Schaduw van Het Europees Hof van Justitie' [2020] Nederlands Tijdschrift voor Onderwijsrecht en Onderwijsbeleid 29.

[82] Articles 5 and 6 of Regulation (EC) No 261/2004 of the European Parliament and of the Council of 11 February 2004 establishing common rules on compensation and assistance to passengers in the event of denied boarding and of cancellation or long delay of flights (OJ L46/1).

[83] Case C-432/07 *Sturgeon* ECLI:EU:C:2009:716, para 60.

as a legitimate court should.[84] Other lower courts continued to apply the legislative provisions, not out of protest but due to a lack of familiarity with the judgment.[85]

These examples buoy the contained compliance thesis. Yet, more importantly, I think, they support Susanne Schmidt's thesis that the 'implications of European integration differ depending on whether they are caused by the impact of secondary law or by court rulings'.[86] She believes, correctly it seems, that case law generates 'weaker adjustment pressures for member states than positively prescribed EU policies'.[87] Of course, national authorities will not always manage to evade unwelcome judgments; they sometimes engage in 'anticipatory obedience' to shield their policies from further legal incursions.[88] On balance, however, the compliance pull of EU law seems to be stronger when it is laid down in legislation than in case law, and it pulls more strongly on not only public but also private actors. As Stacy Nyikos has shown, the voluntary compliance of private actors with preliminary rulings increases 'as the amount of EU legislation that characterises a particular legal area increases'.[89] This is so, she assumes, because of the precision of legislative rules.[90] Since litigants can be fairly certain that national courts will follow case law interpreting such rules, they are more likely to comply voluntarily so as not to waste unnecessary time and resources.

How can we explain why legislation is better than case law in bringing about social change? One of the reasons is most likely a traditional view of the separation of powers and the associated legitimacy beliefs of national actors. The reception of the *Sturgeon* case in national courts shows that some find it inappropriate for the EU judiciary to arrogate legislative power to itself.[91] The *Landgericht Köln* asked, in no uncertain terms, whether it violated the separation of powers by erasing the distinction between flight delays and flight cancellations.[92] The *Rechtbank 's-Hertogenbosch* simply refused to implement *Sturgeon*. It said that 'the CJEU does not constitute the European legislature and is therefore not competent to legislate by means of its case law'.[93] However, there are other explanations for why

[84] Sacha Garben, 'The Turbulent Life of Regulation 261: Continuing Controversies Surrounding EU Air Passenger Rights' in Michal Bobek and Jeremias Prassl (eds), *Air Passenger Rights: Ten Years On* (Hart Publishing 2016) 268–70.

[85] A problem that has been observed within France and the United Kingdom: Fabien Le Bot, 'France: Air Passengers Facing Long-Haul Judicial Journeys' in Bobek and Prassl (n 84); Benjamin Jones, 'United Kingdom and Ireland: Passenger Protection Turns a Corner' in Bobek and Prassl (n 84).

[86] Susanne K Schmidt, 'Beyond Compliance: The Europeanization of Member States through Negative Integration and Legal Uncertainty' (2008) 10 Journal of Comparative Policy Analysis: Research and Practice 299, 304.

[87] Blauberger and Schmidt, 'The European Court of Justice' (n 73) 913. See also Diana Panke, 'The European Court of Justice as an Agent of Europeanization? Restoring Compliance with EU Law' (2007) 14 Journal of European Public Policy 847, 854–56.

[88] Blauberger, 'National Responses to European Court Jurisprudence' (n 72).

[89] Nyikos (n 71) 411.

[90] ibid 404.

[91] Garben, 'The Turbulent Life of Regulation 261' (n 84).

[92] Case C-413/11 *Germanwings* ECLI:EU:C:2013:246.

[93] Rechtbank 's-Hertogenbosch, *X v Ryanair Limited*, 774709, LJN BV1931 (19 January 2012). The translation is by Garben, 'The Turbulent Life of Regulation 261' (n 84) 270.

legislation is more likely to generate social change that are unrelated to the legitimacy beliefs of national actors. In particular, the reasons that explain why the legislature is better at initiating legal change (section II.2) also explain why it is more likely to realise social change.

First, legislative acts are more likely to be complied with because they establish relatively certain codes of conduct that limit the interpretative freedom of legal addressees, thereby facilitating the correct enforcement of EU law.[94] Legislation is typically more comprehensive, detailed, and precise than case law—all factors that strengthen the authority of EU law.[95] To give an example, the vague judicial standards that conditioned access to social assistance—'a certain degree of integration' or 'effective and genuine economic activities'—were fairly easy to contain for national authorities.[96] Precise norms not only discourage such behaviour but also make it easier to restore compliance with EU law. For example, it has been easier to end non-compliance with EU social policy than with environmental law, as Diane Panke has shown, because '[t]he social policy directive is more precise and less complex regarding its aims and applicatory scope than the environmental directive'.[97] Finally, legal precision allows national courts to enforce EU law without submitting a request for a preliminary reference,[98] which matters especially in countries where judges are less inclined to initiate the preliminary reference procedure.[99]

Second, legislation is more likely to induce compliance as it is more accessible than case law. The correct implementation of EU law depends, for the most part, on national institutions, so their knowledge of the law is essential for its proper application. A Commission study on the implementation of the Unfair Terms in Consumer Contracts (UTCC) Directive (93/13/EEC) once showed that many legal disputes were settled under national law without reference to the Directive. The conclusion Conant drew from this study is that litigants were 'utterly dependent on the correct and timely transposition of this directive into national law, because only a precious few national courts were applying the directive directly,

[94] See further Rachel A Cichowski, 'Introduction: Courts, Democracy, and Governance' (2006) 39 Comparative Political Studies 3, 9; Kelemen (n 31) 43; Kenneth W Abbott and others, 'The Concept of Legalization' (2000) 54 International Organization 401, 413; Wayne Sandholtz and Alec Stone Sweet, 'Integration, Supranational Governance, and the Institutionalization of the European Polity' in Wayne Sandholtz and Alec Stone Sweet (eds), *European Integration and Supranational Governance* (OUP 1998) 10.

[95] See also Schmidt, *The European Court of Justice and the Policy Process* (n 13) 201; Fabio Wasserfallen, 'The Judiciary as Legislator? How the European Court of Justice Shapes Policy-Making in the European Union' (2010) 17 Journal of European Public Policy 1128, 1133.

[96] Kramer (n 81).

[97] Panke (n 87) 854.

[98] Jesse Claassen, 'Attitude or Aptitude? Explaining the Lack of Preliminary References in Dutch Competition Law Cases' in Clara Rauchegger and Anna Wallerman (eds), *The Eurosceptic Challenge: National Implementation and Interpretation of EU Law* (Hart Publishing 2019).

[99] Marlene Wind, 'The Nordics, the EU and the Reluctance towards Supranational Judicial Review' (2010) 48 Journal of Common Market Studies 1039.

indirectly, vertically, or horizontally'.[100] She also suggested that 'judges who do invoke European provisions in their decisions are likely to interpret the treaties, regulations, and directives without any explicit reliance on ECJ case law'.[101] The problem, as interviews with national judges have made clear, is that they often lack the training and the time to familiarise themselves with EU law,[102] which is a problem that increases as the rules they need to interpret become more complex and less accessible. This chimes with earlier findings that national courts did not always apply the legislative provisions regulating the rights of EU citizens and air passengers in light of the relevant case law. Of course, neither Regulations nor Directives guarantee that EU law is applied uniformly in all Member States.[103] It seems, however, that these are sources of law that can be easier applied, on the whole, than case law. Due to the constraints under which domestic courts operate, they will try not to invest more time and effort in settling legal disputes than strictly necessary.[104] This will require them to stay close to legal sources they are most familiar with—first and foremost, national law and then EU legislation.

4. A Theory of Judicial Deference

Let's take stock of the argument so far. I have identified three reasons why the content of EU law should ideally be determined by the legislature. Chapter II established that the legislature is more politically legitimate than the judiciary, and this chapter has shown that it has a greater capacity to initiate legal change and realise social change. The question is what these findings should entail for the allocation of authority between both actors. In this section, I provide an important part of the answer. Assuming that political institutions must recognise the constraints they operate under in their behaviour towards one another, I argue that the findings so far militate for judicial modesty in areas of EU law governed by legislation. Indeed, where the legislature has expressed its view, it is normally appropriate for the judiciary to respect this view. To support this point, I will defend a theory of judicial deference to legislation that rests on three principles: institutional legitimacy, institutional capacity, and institutional collaboration.

My analysis builds on excellent scholarship on judicial deference by Aileen Kavanaugh and Jeff King. According to Kavanaugh, deference is 'a matter of assigning weight to the judgment of another, either where it as at variance with one's own assessment, or where one is uncertain of what the correct assessment should

[100] Conant, *Justice Contained* (n 70) 82.

[101] ibid.

[102] Tommaso Pavone, *The Ghostwriters: Lawyers and the Politics behind the Judicial Construction of Europe* (CUP 2022) 56–78.

[103] Michal Bobek, 'Uniform Rights? The Nature of Regulations Revisited' in Bobek and Prassl (n 84).

[104] For similar remarks, Bobek, 'EU Law in National Courts' (n 77) 331–32.

be'.[105] Weight can be assigned to the judgements of others, she argues, for one of two reasons. The main reason is epistemic: I have good reason to respect the judgements of another person when that person 'has some skill, expertise, or knowledge that [I do] not possess, or at least not to the same degree'.[106] Second, one can have non-epistemic reasons to assign weight to the views of another person, namely as 'a way of showing respect to [someone] whose relationship one values'.[107] Applied to the separation between the branches of government, these reasons entail a requirement of 'interinstitutional comity—the requirement of mutual respect between the branches of government'.[108]

King has elaborated on this theory by supplementing the requirement of 'interinstitutional comity' with the requirement of 'institutional collaboration'. By this, he means that judicial deference to legislation is appropriate not just when the legislature has some skill or expertise that courts do not have or when the relationship with the legislature is one that courts should value. A third ground for courts to assign weight to the choices of the legislature is that the

> primary branches of government essentially collaborate in the general promotion of commonly accepted public values such as fairness, autonomy, welfare, transparency, efficiency, and so on. Parliament, the executive, and courts are on this vision part of a joint enterprise for the betterment of society. Conflicts between them are subsumed within one vision of governance.[109]

These three grounds—the two that establish the requirement of institutional comity and the requirement of institutional collaboration—are separate yet interrelated. Together, as I will explain, they call for extensive judicial deference to the choices of the EU legislature.

The three grounds for deference identified by Kavanaugh and King overlap quite neatly with the reasons I have identified; just the terminology is different. First, in line with what they argue, weight should be assigned to the choices of the legislature because it has certain skills and expertise that the judiciary does not possess, or at least not to the same degree. As I explained in section III.2, the legislature is owed a degree of deference for reasons of *institutional capacity*. Second, also when the CJEU doubts the skills and expertise of the legislature, it has reason to show respect to its choices as they are inherently valuable. This is so, we saw in Chapter II, because the legislative process offers a fairer process for setting the EU's political course of action. The second reason for applying a principle of deference, then, is that of *institutional legitimacy*. Third, the EU is made up of distinct

[105] Kavanagh (n 14) 185.
[106] ibid 187.
[107] ibid 188.
[108] ibid.
[109] King (n 2) 139.

institutions that should collaborate with one another to promote a shared vision of EU governance. The effectiveness of EU law depends on such collaboration, if only, as we saw in section III.3, since discrepancies between legislation and case law affect the domestic implementation of EU law.[110] The third reason for granting judicial deference to legislation is thus that of *institutional collaboration*. Finally, while collaborative relationships can be non-hierarchical, the three reasons together provide strong reasons to think that the judiciary should, in principle, follow the course set out by the legislature.

People may agree that deference is a virtue that courts must aspire to but disagree about the weight that should be given to legislation in specific cases. King distinguishes two competing views of the role of courts in public law adjudication among scholars who take seriously the relative institutional facilities of the branches of government: contextualist institutionalism and restrictive institutionalism. Contextualist institutionalists believe that in determining how much weight to assign to the choices of other institutions, courts must consider and contextualise all institutional factors that may be relevant to the resolution of a dispute. Restrictive institutionalists, on the other hand, fear that such unfettered public law adjudication is inappropriate and ill advised in light of the shortcomings in the democratic legitimacy and institutional capacity of courts. They, therefore, prefer retaining 'bright-line rules that lessen the use of judicial discretion, either in pre-designated areas ... or simply as a more general posture of judicial discretion'.[111]

These are not distinct models but opposite ends of a spectrum.[112] For example, a contextualist institutionalist may believe that upholding constitutional norms is, in the first place, a judicial task while advocating deference to legislative decisions as a general rule. In relation to EU law, such a position has been defended by Paul Craig. He argues that the CJEU should, in principle, yield to legislation but also ensure that legislation respects the limits of primary law. Legislation that cannot be reconciled with primary law should be set aside.[113] Restrictive institutionalists may oppose granting such powers to the Court but still believe that the legislature is subject to some judicial constraints. Phil Syrpis has taken this view regarding EU law:

> The Court should only exercise its power to review the acts of the Union institutions in extreme circumstances, where for example, the legislature has 'manifestly', or 'manifestly and gravely', exceeded the limits of its powers. It should, as far as possible, try to read secondary legislation literally. It should also be

[110] Similarly, though with respect to the US government, Alexander M Bickel, *The Least Dangerous Branch: The Supreme Court at the Bar of Politics* (2nd edn, Yale UP 1986) 261.
[111] King (n 2) 141.
[112] ibid 142.
[113] Paul Craig, *The Lisbon Treaty: Law, Politics, and Treaty Reform* (OUP 2013) 228–29.

> prepared to adjust its own interpretation of Treaty texts in the light of the stance adopted by the legislature.[114]

This shows, indeed, that the views of contextualist institutionalists and restrictive institutionalists need not be miles apart. At the same time, their disagreements are more than just theoretical: it matters whether the CJEU takes one position or the other. To see this, let us re-examine some of the judgments discussed earlier.

Consider again *Sturgeon*. The CJEU ruled, contrary to the Air Passenger Rights Regulation, that compensation must be awarded to passengers not just in the event of flight cancellations but also in the event of long delays. Until then, nothing suggested that the distinction between flight delays and flight cancellations was incompatible with the Treaties. Nor was there reason to think that the legislature had acted unreasonably in drawing this distinction—that it had manifestly exceeded the limits of its powers. Restrictive institutionalists like Syrpis will therefore most likely take the view that this choice should have been within the margin of discretion normally available to the legislature in deciding such complex questions. The CJEU, however, found the Regulation to violate the principle of equal treatment after it interpreted the provisions 'in accordance with primary law as a whole'.[115] It ruled that passengers should receive financial compensation in the event of long delays as well because 'the damage sustained by air passengers in cases of cancellation or long delay is comparable'.[116] A contextualist institutionalist like Craig is more likely to defend such a ruling as a legitimate exercise of judicial discretion, meant to ensure the compatibility of legislation with primary law.

Contextualist institutionalists and restrictive institutionalists might also disagree about the merits of the social assistance case law discussed in section III.2. As we saw, the legislative conditions for access to social assistance were revised through their interpretation in accordance with primary law, in particular the right of non-discrimination on grounds of nationality and the right to freedom of movement for workers.[117] Contextualist institutionalists are more likely to support such verdicts than restrictive institutionalists due to their belief that it is legitimate for the judiciary to impose its vision of primary law on the legislature.

Yet, knowing the shortcomings of the social assistance case law, we can begin to understand the defects of contextualist institutionalism. As these judgments show, the consequences of giving legislation a Treaty-conform interpretation can be far-reaching: the result was not at all what the legislature intended. They also show that it is not at all respectful of the legislature to say that its decisions are due

[114] Phil Syrpis, 'The Relationship between Primary and Secondary Law in the EU' (2015) 52 Common Market Law Review 461, 484.
[115] *Sturgeon* (n 81) para 48.
[116] ibid para 60.
[117] See, eg Case C-138/02 *Collins* ECLI:EU:C:2004:172; *Vatsouras and Koupatantze* (n 79).

deference unless they violate primary law. The scope of primary law is so wide and its content so vague that the CJEU will always be able to find a provision of primary law to amend legislation if it wishes. The problem of contextualist institutionalism, then, is that it leaves the judiciary too much discretion. It rests on the premise that deference should not be presumed but earned anew in every case; that the CJEU may use its discretion on a case-by-case basis to adjust the applicable legislation or otherwise leave it to national actors to decide whether to enforce the rules or not. Instead, as I explain now, the three grounds for judicial deference support a more restrictive adjudicative approach that assigns more weight to the choices of the legislature.

4.1 Institutional legitimacy

As we just observed, courts authorised to read legislation in the light of higher constitutional norms can potentially approach any legal dispute as a legislative task that may require a revision of the legislature's choices.[118] Since it would permit the revision of any legislative provision in accordance with some norm of primary law, a contextualist institutionalist approach to adjudication can seriously undermine the EU legislature's authority and, with that, the legitimacy of EU law. The CJEU has the power to interpret legislation in the light of primary law, but the relevant question is whether it should make use of this power. As we have seen in Chapter II, the value of political legitimacy dictates that it should ideally exercise restraint in order not to prejudice legislation.[119] EU law's legitimacy is more secure, in other words, under a restrictive institutionalist approach to adjudication that attributes significant weight to legislative provisions.

4.2 Institutional capacity

Restrictive institutionalism values the superior epistemic qualities of the legislature; it recognises that EU law is more likely to be based on an incomplete understanding of the relevant empirical and moral considerations when developed through the judicial process. One example that shows that the CJEU may not see the full range of empirical and moral considerations relevant to the legislative task was discussed in section III.2—EU citizenship law. Another example is the *Sturgeon* judgment. The CJEU justified its decision that passengers are entitled to financial compensation in the event of both cancellations and long delays on

[118] See also Tom Campbell, *The Legal Theory of Ethical Positivism* (Dartmouth 1996) 116.

[119] In section III.2, I explain that it is fine to rely on primary law in legislative interpretation where this does not adversely affect the choices of the legislature.

the ground that 'the damage sustained by air passengers in cases of cancellation or long delay is comparable'.[120] This conclusion seems correct but cannot be the sole consideration in deciding which passengers should have this right. Equally relevant are questions such as are delays and cancellations caused by the same degree of negligence on the part of air carriers and would the equal treatment of flight cancellations and delays impose excessive costs on air carriers?[121] The CJEU paid no attention to these considerations. The negotiation of the new Air Passengers Rights Regulation shows, on the other hand, that the legislature is able to gain a fuller view of the relevant moral and empirical issues before taking such decisions.[122] It shows, in other words, that a more deferential attitude can reduce the chances of ill-informed judicial decisions.

4.3 Institutional collaboration

The effective application of EU law is facilitated by collaboration between EU institutions. Restrictive institutionalism promotes institutional collaboration while contextualist institutionalism reinforces the uncertainty that characterises case law. As Bobek has rightly remarked, only judgments 'which can be applied by normal, mortal judges, and do not require judicial Euro-Hercules in terms of zeal, capacity and resources, tend to be accepted and followed'.[123] In support of this claim, he cites case law on state liability for breach of EU law and on the horizontal direct effect of Directives, which set standards that are impracticable and difficult to enforce. He could just as well have cited some of the judgments discussed earlier in this chapter, especially those that ask national courts to interpret legislation in accordance with primary law. Determining whether national law is compatible with EU legislation is often hard enough for national judges. Asking them to also interpret legislation in the light of primary law betrays a clear lack of awareness of what can reasonably be expected of them and of how best to ensure the effective application of EU law in the national legal orders.[124] EU law will not be able to provide the necessary certainty if its application too often depends on unpredictable legal principles such as those laid down in primary law. A restrictive institutionalist method of adjudication facilitates collaboration between EU institutions and thereby also the uniform and effective functioning of EU law.

120 *Sturgeon* (n 83) para 60.
121 Weiler (n 27) 245.
122 See Commission Proposal for a Regulation of the European Parliament and of the Council amending Regulation (EC) No 261/2004 (COM(2013) 130 final). For an excellent discussion of some of the challenges ahead, Jeremias Prassl, 'Tackling Diversity through Uniformity? Revisiting the Reform of Regulation 261/2004' in Bobek and Prassl (n 84).
123 Bobek, 'EU Law in National Courts' (n 77) 331.
124 For similar criticism, Ulf Bernitz, 'Epilogue' in Freedland and Prassl (n 77) 341.

5. The Deferential Court

Sceptics of judicial deference may argue that restrictive institutionalist adjudication is inconsistent with the Treaties. The idea flies in the face of the traditional view of the relationship between the legislature and judiciary, according to which the latter stands on a higher rung of the law-making ladder. According to its proponents, legislation must be consistent with the Court's interpretation of primary law or else be struck down.[125] The traditional view is so pervasive that even those who worry that the Court interferes too extensively with national politics rarely question it. They, too, believe that the legislature must abide by the judicial articulation of the Treaties so that only a de-constitutionalisation of EU law can allow for its de-judicialisation.[126]

It is time to dispel the traditional view. As we saw in the introductory chapter, this view correctly emphasises that a close connection exists between the interaction of legal norms and the allocation of authority. But then it wrongly assumes that the hierarchy between primary law and secondary legislation translates into a hierarchy between judicial and legislative authority. Although I argued in Chapter I that this view is wrong, I have not yet properly explained where it goes wrong. It rests on two premises, namely that primary law enjoys priority over secondary legislation and that the judiciary is the exclusive interpreter of primary law. The first seems correct, but the second is patently not. Constitutionalisation does not equal judicialisation: it leaves open the question of who decides on the meaning of the constitution, in our case primary law. The mere fact that the judiciary is authorised to interpret primary law does not entail that it is the exclusive interpreter.[127] On the contrary, it co-interprets primary law together with the legislature. This is also the view we (increasingly) find in case law, which suggests that the traditional view draws the wrong conclusions from the Treaties—conclusions not even the judges share.

Repudiating the traditional view is important not just in its own right. It also creates the legal space to accommodate a restrictive institutionalist form of

[125] *Sturgeon* (n 83) para 47; Joined cases C-391/16, C-77/17, and C-78/17, *M* ECLI:EU:C:2019:403, para 77; Case C-601/15 PPU *JN* ECLI:EU:C:2016:84, para 48; Case C-12/11 *McDonagh* ECLI:EU:C:2013:43, para 44. See also David Edward, 'Guest Editorial: Will There Be Honey Still for Tea?' (2006) 43 Common Market Law Review 623; Nicolas Rennuy, 'The Emergence of a Parallel System of Social Security Coordination' (2013) 50 Common Market Law Review 1221, 1243.

[126] Dieter Grimm, *The Constitution of European Democracy* (OUP 2017) 100; Fritz W Scharpf, 'The Asymmetry of European Integration, or Why the EU Cannot Be a "Social Market Economy"' (2010) 8 Socio-Economic Review 211; Sacha Garben, 'The Constitutional (Im)Balance between "the Market" and "the Social" in the European Union' (2017) 13 European Constitutional Law Review 23, 37–38; Jacquelyn Veraldi and Matthew Hassall, 'Corporate Power and the Constitutionalisation of the EU Internal Market Project' in Mark V Tushnet and Dimitry Kochenov (eds), *Research Handbook on the Politics of Constitutional Law* (Edward Elgar 2023).

[127] This point is made extensively in Chapter IV. See also Gareth Davies, 'Legislative Control of the European Court of Justice' (2014) 51 Common Market Law Review 1579, 1584.

adjudication, which is compatible with the Treaties and realisable without their amendment. The Court observes its duty to uphold primary law when it yields to the legislature's choices and, in fact, adheres to this approach most of the time: it is a highly deferential court. To show this, I first discuss three areas of EU law where it has started to assign greater weight to the choices of the legislature in recent years before showing that the relevant judgments, while sometimes controversial, are consistent with its overall adjudicative approach.

One area of law where judicial deference is increasingly being practiced is the area of EU citizenship. We saw in section III.2 that legislative provisions denying economically inactive citizens the right to claim social assistance were, for some time, ignored by the CJEU. The legislature at the time made a distinction between workers and jobseekers: workers enjoyed the same social and tax advantages as nationals of the host state,[128] while jobseekers were only entitled to the assistance provided by employment offices.[129] The introduction of EU citizenship into the Treaties led to a belief among the members of the CJEU that legislative acts regulating the mobility of persons could be legitimately reconsidered.[130] The *Collins* case illustrates this clearly. It ruled that the distinction between workers and jobseekers could no longer be maintained: jobseekers could suddenly also claim certain social assistance benefits on the condition that they had established a genuine link with the labour market of the state where they claimed benefits.[131] It declined to yield to the legislature and continued doing so for quite some years. Shortly after *Collins*, the legislature passed the Citizenship Directive, which again allowed Member States to deny social assistance to jobseekers, seemingly overruling the judgment.[132] The CJEU was unruffled, however, by this legislative amendment: it upheld its own case law and thereby the right of jobseekers to claim assistance in *Vatsouras and Koupatantze*, defying the legislature for a second time.[133]

Times have changed and so has the case law, quite dramatically in fact. In *Dano*, *Alimanovic*, and *García-Nieto*, the CJEU showed a clear appreciation for the virtues of judicial deference.[134] The applicant in *Dano* had never had or looked for work in the host state; the applicants in *Alimanovic* had been employed for eleven months, one month less than required for involuntary unemployed persons to qualify for social assistance under art 7(3)(b) of the Citizenship Directive; and the applicant in *García-Nieto* had applied for assistance during the first three months

[128] Article 7(2) of Regulation No 1612/68.

[129] Compare art 7(2) with art 5 of Regulation No 1612/68.

[130] Until then, the case law had followed the distinction: those moving in search of employment 'qualify for equal treatment only as regards access to employment': Case C-316/85 *Lebon* ECLI.EU.C.1987:302, para 26; Case C-278/94 *Commission v Belgium* [1997] ECR I-1035, para 17.

[131] *Collins* (n 117) paras 69–70.

[132] Article 24(2), in conjunction with art 14(4)(b), of Directive 2004/38/EC.

[133] *Vatsouras and Koupatantze* (n 79).

[134] *Dano* (n 62); *Alimanovic* (n 62); *García-Nieto* (n 78).

of her stay, which need not be awarded during that period according to art 24(2) of the Directive. The decision of the German authorities to reject their applications for social assistance was consistent with the Directive but not with the verdicts in *Collins* and *Vatsouras and Koupatantze*. Nevertheless, yielding to the conditions set out in the Directive, the CJEU ruled in favour of the German authorities in all three cases. The crucial difference with earlier judgments is that legislative provisions are no longer interpreted in the light of primary law. Instead, since *Dano*, the legislature is treated as a co-interpreter of primary law. The CJEU justified its deference to the legislative provisions as follows:

> the principle of non-discrimination, laid down generally in Article 18 TFEU, is *given more specific expression* in Article 24 of Directive 2004/38 in relation to Union citizens who, like the applicants in the main proceedings, exercise their right to move and reside within the territory of the Member States. That principle is also given more specific expression in Article 4 of Regulation (EC) No 883/2004 in relation to Union citizens, such as the applicants in the main proceedings, who invoke in the host Member State the benefits referred to in Article 70(2) of the regulation.[135]

Indeed, accepting that the Citizenship Directive gives more specific expression to the Treaties, it yielded to the conditions laid down therein.

We can observe similar dynamics in the regulation of social security coordination between Member States. Regulation No 1408/71 laid down the rules determining which state's social security schemes apply to mobile workers. It set out, inter alia, which benefits could be exported to another state and which could be claimed by workers only in the territory of the state in which they reside. The benefits listed in Annex IIa could only be claimed by persons residing in the territory of the conferring state, while unemployment benefits could be exported by those who moved elsewhere 'to seek employment' (art 69) and those who 'during his last employment, was residing in the territory of a Member State other than the competent State' (art 71). However, by applying the Treaties in parallel with the Regulation, the CJEU also allowed the export of social security benefits in other circumstances. It did so in three judgments. The *Hendrix* case concerned benefits listed in Annex IIa, while the *De Cuyper* and *Petersen* cases concerned benefits that fell outside the scope of arts 69 and 71. Had the CJEU applied the Regulation on its face, it should have ruled that there was no obligation to allow the export of the benefits. Instead, it applied the Regulation in the light of art 45 of the TFEU on the free movement of workers (*Hendrix* and *Petersen*) and art 21 of the TFEU on the free movement of EU citizens (*De Cuyper*).[136] On this basis, national rules that were compatible with

[135] *Dano* (n 62) para 61 (italics mine). See also *CG* (n 62) para 66.

[136] Case C-287/05 *Hendrix* ECLI:EU:C:2007:494, para 52; Case C-406/04 *De Cuyper* ECLI:EU:C:2006:491, para 39; Case C-228/07 *Petersen* ECLI:EU:C:2008:494, para 52.

the Regulation would be prohibited if they restricted free movement in a way that was not 'objectively justified and proportionate to the aim pursued'.[137]

In more recent decisions, the CJEU distanced itself from the idea that secondary legislation coordinating the application of social security schemes must be interpreted in the light of primary law. In *von Chamier-Glisczinski*, the legislature was given a wide margin of discretion in choosing the measures most suitable for protecting the freedom of movement of workers. It had made use of its discretion appropriately by 'setting up a system allowing workers to overcome any obstacles which may arise for them from national rules in the field of social security, that is by adopting Regulation 1408/71.[138] In *Commission v Spain*, the CJEU ruled that no obligations other than the ones laid down in secondary legislation should be applied, since that 'would ultimately undermine the very fabric of the system which Regulation 1408/71 sought to establish'.[139] Finally, in *van Delft*, it declined to interpret the Regulation in the light of art 21 of the TFEU.[140] As Herwig Verschueren observed, these judgments 'suggest that the Court is indeed, and perhaps more so than in the past, deferential to the specific provisions in Regulation 1408/71'.[141]

A similar change of attitude is noticeable, thirdly, in case law concerning claims affecting the national constitutional identities of the Member States, which the EU shall respect according to art 4(2) of the Treaty on European Union (TEU). Until recently, the CJEU was inclined to uphold such claims against legislation restricting national conceptions of constitutional identity. In *Groener* and *Michaniki*, for example, it allowed Member States to invoke their national identity to justify derogations from the applicable legislative provisions, provided that national law respected the principle of proportionality.[142] By contrast, in *Melloni* and *Taricco II*, it seemed to have ruled that the decision of whether or not to accommodate national constitutional law will depend on whether the contested norm of EU law is one that was adopted by the legislature.[143] In *Melloni*, the CJEU refused to accommodate Spanish constitutional law as the contested decision 'effects a harmonisation of the conditions of execution of a European arrest warrant in the event of a conviction rendered *in absentia*, which reflects the consensus reached by all the Member States'.[144] In contrast, in *Taricco II*, it allowed Italy 'to apply national

[137] *Hendrix* (n 136) para 54; *Petersen* (n 136) para 54. See also *De Cuyper* (n 136) para 40. For excellent analysis, Herwig Verschueren, 'The EU Social Security Co-ordination System: A Close Interplay between the EU Legislature and Judiciary' in Philip Syrpis (ed), *The Judiciary, the Legislature and the EU Internal Market* (CUP 2012). See, in addition, Rennuy (n 125).

[138] Case C-208/07 *von Chamier-Glisczinski* ECLI:EU:C:2009:455, paras 64–65.

[139] Case C-211/08 *Commission v Spain* ECLI:EU:C:2010:340, para 79.

[140] Case C-345/09 *van Delft* ECLI:EU:C:2010:610.

[141] Verschueren, 'The EU Social Security Co-ordination System' (n 137) 201.

[142] Case C-379/87 *Groener* ECLI:EU:C:1989:599; Case C-213/07 *Michaniki* ECLI:EU:C:2008:731. For further discussion, Elke Cloots, *National Identity in EU Law* (OUP 2015) 340–43.

[143] For more detailed analysis, Clara Rauchegger, 'National Constitutional Rights and the Primacy of EU Law: M.A.S.' (2018) 55 Common Market Law Review 1521, 1532–34.

[144] Case C-399/11 *Melloni* ECLI:EU:C:2013:107, para 62.

standards of protection of fundamental rights' because 'the limitation rules applicable to criminal proceedings relating to VAT *had not been harmonised by the EU legislature*'.[145]

Some of these judgments have proven highly controversial. An oft-heard criticism is that the CJEU failed to observe primary law by giving in so unconditionally to secondary legislation. It is a criticism that has been directed, most notably, at the social assistance case law from *Dano* onwards.[146] Yet, this criticism is misguided. First, it wrongly suggests that affording deference to legislation risks withering primary law of its content, when, in reality, it is merely given a different content—one that is consistent with the wishes of the legislature. Second, it is misleading because it suggests that it is a constitutional anomaly to allow the legislature to decide on the content and contours of primary law, while, in fact, this has always been an important legislative prerogative. Indeed, the decision to apply deference in the three areas just discussed was not the exception but the rule; that is, it was an established principle of adjudication.

What illustrates this well is the interplay between the legislature and judiciary in the regulation of free movement law. Especially in free movement of goods case law, there is a long history of treating the legislature as the co-interpreter of primary law. As regards the existence of legislation, the CJEU said the following as early as 1974 in *Dassonville*:

> *In the absence of a Community system guaranteeing for consumers the authenticity of a product's designation of origin*, if a Member State takes measures to prevent unfair practices in this connexion, it is however subject to the condition that these measures should be reasonable and that the means of proof required should not act as a hindrance to trade between Member States and should, in consequence, be accessible to all Community nationals.[147]

As Laurence Gormley observes, the phrase 'in the absence of a Community system' indicates that reasonable national measures will be allowed until the legislature 'takes steps to offer protection at the European level, which will replace the need and justification for national measures in the fields concerned'.[148] It has, indeed, been the norm that EU legislation pre-empts not just the application of national legislation but also the need to review national measures under EU primary law. As Eadaoin Ní Chaoimh has shown, since the *Bauhaus* and *Tedeschi* verdicts, harmonising legislation has steadily become the standard of reference

[145] Case C-42/17, *MAS and MB* ECLI:EU:C:2017:936, para 44.

[146] Such criticism we find in O'Brien, 'Civis Capitalist Sum' (n 63); Nic Shuibhne, 'Limits Rising, Duties Ascending' (n 63).

[147] Case C-8/74 *Dassonville* ECLI:EU:C:1974:82, para 6 (italics added).

[148] Laurence W Gormley, 'Free Movement of Goods and EU Legislation in the Court of Justice' in Syrpis, *The Judiciary, the Legislature and the Internal Market* (n 137) 51.

for the resolution of disputes between EU and national law.[149] In *Bauhaus*, legislation was regarded as an appropriate instrument for reconciling market integration with public interests,[150] while *Tedeschi* established that national measures no longer need to be reviewed under art 34 of the TFEU when the case is governed by secondary legislation. In that case, instead, they should be reviewed solely by reference to the enacted legislative provisions.[151] As a result of harmonisation, we read in *Bennekom*, 'recourse to Article [34 TFEU] must gradually become unnecessary',[152] which is, indeed, what has happened.[153] Since 'secondary legislation enjoys a general presumption of constitutionality',[154] it is, in large part, legislation and not case law that has guided the development of the free movement of goods. It is settled case law, for instance, that 'where a matter is regulated in a harmonised manner at EU level, any national measure relating thereto must be assessed in the light of the provisions of that harmonising measure and not of those of the [EU] Treaty'.[155] In these circumstances, national authorities may not cite the grounds of public morality, public policy, or public security, set out in art 36 of the TFEU, to deviate from legislation that fully harmonises an area of law.[156] The fact that this approach has been extended beyond the internal market of goods to the other economic freedoms shows that it is secondary legislation that, in principle, provides the standard against which the legality of national measures is assessed.[157] Seen in this light, the most recent case law on the right to claim social assistance, the coordination of social security, and the accommodation of national constitutional law is nothing exceptional. Deference has always been the default rule.

Supporters of the traditional view may want to criticise this default rule in a last attempt to save their position. Yet, no one genuinely believes that all these cases were wrongly decided—and indeed, there is no reason to think they were. Contrary to what the traditional views assumes, therefore, the Treaties are generally co-interpreted and co-owned by the legislature and judiciary, alongside several other institutions. The legislature has, for a long time, been allowed to give

[149] Eadaoin Ní Chaoimh, *The Legislative Priority Rule and the EU Internal Market for Goods: A Constitutional Approach* (OUP 2022) 12–13.

[150] Case 46/76 *Bauhaus* ECLI:EU:C:1977:6.

[151] Case 5/77 *Tedeschi* ECLI:EU:C:1977:144, para 35.

[152] Case 227/82 *Bennekom* ECLI:EU:C:1983:354, para 14.

[153] Jan Zglinski, 'The End of Negative Market Integration: 60 Years of Free Movement of Goods Litigation in the EU (1961–2020)' [2023] Journal of European Public Policy 1.

[154] Ní Chaoimh (n 149) 71.

[155] Case C-257/06 *Roby Profumi* EU:C:2008:35, para 14; Case C-324/99 *DaimlerChrysler* EU:C:2001:682, para 32; Case C-309/02 *Radlberger Getränkegesellschaft and S Spitz*, 2004 I-11763, para 53; Case C-91/18 *Commission v Greece* ECLI:EU:C:2019:600, para 44.

[156] *DaimlerChrysler* (n 155) para 32; Case C-132/08 *Lidl Magyarország Kereskedelmi bt* ECLI:EU:C:2009:281, para 42; C-37/92 *Vanacker and Lesage* ECLI:EU:C:1993:836, para 9; Case C-322/01 *Deutscher Apothekerverband* ECLI:EU:C:2003:664, para 64.

[157] See, eg Case C-569/07 *HSBC Holdings* EU:C:2009:594, para 26; Case C-265/16 *VCAST Limited* ECLI:EU:C:2017:913, para 26; Case C-573/16 *Air Berlin* ECLI:EU:C:2017:772, para 28.

'more specific expression'[158] and 'concrete form'[159] to its provisions. This is not to say that legislation should always be respected. Perhaps some of the disputes discussed here were wrongly decided, but this is not a conclusion one can reach by pointing out that primary law ranks above secondary legislation. This is a trivial observation with little practical relevance for the relationship between the legislature and judiciary.

The question, instead, is who is entitled to decide on the meaning of primary law. It cannot be derived from the fact that primary law ranks above secondary legislation that the Court alone can do so. In fact, this question cannot be answered by reference to the Treaties alone. It is true that art 19 of the TFEU places the Court under an obligation to ensure that 'the law is observed' in the application of the Treaties, and that art 267 of the TFEU grants it the power to review the legality of legislative acts, but the relevant question is when it may use such powers. Recall from Chapter II that legality does not equal legitimacy: it may be lawful to exercise the power of judicial review, but that does not make it legitimate. Moreover, being under an obligation to ensure that the law is observed does not make it unlawful to interpret Treaty provisions in accordance with the wishes of the legislature. The most frequently litigated provisions are among the most indeterminate, about which there can be reasonable disagreement as to their proper meaning. Thus, in most legal disputes, it is not clear what it means for primary law to be observed: different interpretations are plausible. One may thus think that the legislature should have interpreted primary law differently, but this does not mean that it has done so unreasonably.

For all we know, the default rule in the adjudication of EU legal disputes is one of judicial deference to legislation. Contrary to the traditional view on the relationship between the judiciary and legislature, the former is not, and does not think of itself as, the exclusive interpreter of primary law. The Court is prepared to share interpretative responsibility with the legislature and, in most cases, accepts the latter's preferred understanding of primary law. This picture is considerably more complex than the one painted by the traditional view, but it corresponds far better to reality and is normatively more compelling.[160] The traditional view must be refuted as a matter of legal and normative principle, which means that restrictive institutionalist adjudication is entirely consistent with the Treaties.

[158] *Dano* (n 62) para 61; *CG* (n 62) para 66; Case C-507/18 *NH* ECLI:EU:C:2020:289, para 38; Case C-414/16 *Egenberger* ECLI:EU:C:2018:257, para 47.

[159] Joined cases C-704/20 and C-39/21 *Staatssecretaris van Justitie en Veiligheid v C and B* ECLI:EU:C:2022:858, para 83; Joined cases C-924/19 PPU and C-925/19 PPU *FMS* ECLI:EU:C:2020:367, paras 192 and 289.

[160] See also Thomas Horsley, *The Court of Justice of the European Union as an Institutional Actor: Judicial Lawmaking and Its Limits* (CUP 2018).

6. Adjudicating Minimum Harmonisation

The CJEU must, in principle, defer to the choices of the legislature in disputes that are governed by legislation. Where no harmonisation has taken place, it may have to apply EU law in the way it deems most appropriate: it cannot yield to any legislative provisions in such disputes, but it cannot decline to adjudicate such disputes either. But what about minimum harmonisation? What if the legislature only partially harmonises an area of law—when it enacts minimum standards below which national law may not fall but which allow Member States to adopt more stringent national norms?[161] Minimum harmonisation is, one could say, a halfway house between no and full harmonisation—a difficult case which my argument has not yet fully addressed. The choice for minimum harmonisation may stem from the inability to agree on more extensive harmonisation, from a principled commitment to respect social and moral diversity between Member States, or simply from the limitations the Treaties place on the EU's capacity to harmonise national law.[162] In any case, the question is how stricter national norms that go beyond the legislative minimum must be assessed: only in the light of the legislative minimum or also in the light of relevant norms of primary law?

Most of the time, the CJEU will respect the choice to only harmonise an area in part, but its response has partially depended on the type of minimum harmonisation in question: on whether it adjudicates *legislative minimum harmonisation* or *constitutional minimum harmonisation*.[163] We speak of constitutional minimum harmonisation when the Treaties protect the right of Member States to adopt more stringent standards, that is where they expressly prohibit maximum harmonisation. According to arts 169(4) and 193 of the TFEU, for example, legislative measures that are adopted to protect consumer interests or the environment 'shall not prevent Member States from maintaining or introducing more stringent protective measures'. Recognising that maximum harmonisation is constitutionally prohibited in these areas, the CJEU has tolerated more stringent national norms: it assesses their validity only in the light of the legislative minimum. In the *Deponiezweckverband* case, for example, it would not subject the stricter national measure to a proportionality assessment. It ruled that 'the wording and broad logic of [the legislative] provisions make it clearly apparent that they set a minimum reduction to be achieved by the Member States and they do not preclude the adopting by the latter of more stringent measures'.[164] In the *TSN* case,

[161] Stephen Weatherill, 'The Fundamental Question of Minimum or Maximum Harmonisation' in Sacha Garben and Inge Govaere (eds), *The Internal Market 2.0* (Hart Publishing, an imprint of Bloomsbury Publishing 2020).

[162] Nina Boeger, 'Minimum Harmonisation, Free Movement and Proportionality' in Syrpis, *The Judiciary, the Legislature and the Internal Market* (n 137) 66–68.

[163] Marcus Klamert, 'What We Talk about When We Talk about Harmonisation' (2015) 17 Cambridge Yearbook of European Legal Studies 360, 362.

[164] Case C-6/03 *Deponiezweckverband* ECLI:EU:C:2005:222, para 31.

similarly, it declined to apply the Charter of Fundamental Rights to stricter national social policy standards—an area in which Member States may not be prevented, according to art 153(4) of the TFEU, 'from maintaining or introducing more stringent protective measures compatible with the Treaties'.[165] National rules that exceed the legislative minimum are not governed by EU law and therefore fall 'outside the scope of the Charter'.[166] Here, too, deference to legislation is the judicial default rule.

The CJEU sometimes follows a different approach in cases involving legislative minimum harmonisation. We speak of legislative minimum harmonisation when the legislature is left free by the Treaties to choose between minimum and maximum harmonisation and where it has made the choice to harmonise an area only partially. It has this choice, for example, under art 114 of the TFEU, the legal basis that provides the power to adopt legislative measures 'which have as their object the establishment and functioning of the internal market'. In this area, the CJEU has not always yielded to the minimum legislative standards in force. It permits stricter national measures provided 'they respect the fundamental freedoms guaranteed by the Treaty'.[167] To assess this, legislative measures have, at times, been subjected to an incisive proportionality test[168] whereby the minimum legislative standards have sometimes been turned from a floor below which national measures may not fall into a ceiling above which they may not go. A perfect illustration is the *Alemo Herron* judgment,[169] where the CJEU invoked the Charter of Fundamental Rights to turn legislative minimum harmonisation into maximum harmonisation (in contrast to its decision in *TSN* to place national measures that exceed constitutional minimum harmonisation outside the scope of the Charter). Article 8 of Directive 2001/23 provides that the Directive does not affect the right to 'apply or introduce laws . . . which are more favourable to employees'.[170] Nevertheless, the more favourable national rules were found to be incompatible with the right to freedom to conduct a business laid down in art 16 of the Charter of Fundamental Rights.[171] The minimum rule was thereby rendered 'redundant by a judicial fiat'.[172]

[165] Joined cases C-609/17 and C-610/17 *TSN* ECLI:EU:C:2019:981, para 48.

[166] ibid para 53. See also Case C-198/13, *Julián Hernández* EU:C:2014:2055, para 35. For analysis, Maxime Tecqmenne, 'Minimum Harmonisation and Fundamental Rights: A Test-Case for the Identification of the Scope of EU Law in Situations Involving National Discretion?' [2020] European Constitutional Law Review 20.

[167] Case C-222/07 *UTECA* ECLI:EU:C:2009:124, para 18; Case C-500/06 *Dermoestética* ECLI:EU:C:2008:421, para 31; Case C-6/98 *ARD* ECLI:EU:C:1999:532, para 49.

[168] Boeger (n 162) 77–78.

[169] Case C-341/05 *Laval un Partneri* ECLI:EU:C:2007:809 is often cited as the paramount example. As we will see in section IV.8, however, the provision in question in the *Laval* judgment did not entail minimum harmonisation.

[170] Council Directive 2001/23/EC of 12 March 2001 on the approximation of the laws of the Member States relating to the safeguarding of employees' rights in the event of transfers of undertakings, businesses or parts of undertakings or businesses (OJ L82/16).

[171] Case C-426/11 *Alemo Herron* ECLI:EU:C:2013:521, para 31.

[172] Klamert (n 163) 370. See also Boeger (n 162) 72.

Is the distinction that is, at times, drawn between legislative and constitutional minimum harmonisation justified? Exceptionally, one reads that national measures exceeding the legislative minimum are not yet scrutinised strictly enough. Jan Jans asks,

> if the standards of the directive provide an adequate level of protection, how can stricter national measures be necessary? Surely it must be assumed that a Member State infringes the principle of proportionality when in fact there is nothing to protect.[173]

Surely, however, this is the wrong approach. As Nina Boeger explains, Jans 'applies a debatable assumption that by setting an EU minimum standard the EU legislature determines what would, and should, be considered a proportionate regulatory standard across the EU'.[174] Indeed, he blurs the distinction between minimum and maximum harmonisation for no apparent reason. Minimum harmonisation allows Member States to raise their regulatory standards above the EU minimum, even if their more stringent standards are not strictly necessary. It does so on the view that national governments may legitimately hold different views on such issues as labour law or environmental protection and that maintaining these standards is justified even if they run counter to certain objectives pursued by the EU.

In fact, the assessment of national measures exceeding minimum harmonisation is too strict rather than too lenient. At times, Boerger argues, 'the EU minimum standard carries . . . little independent normative weight'.[175] Instead, deference must become the default rule, also in respect of legislative minimum harmonisation. The Court must respect and give effect to legislative efforts to accommodate socio-economic and moral diversity among Member States. There is no apparent justification for decisions like *Alemo Herron*. The CJEU interpreted the more favourable national rule in the light of the right to freedom to conduct a business in art 16 of the Charter, as the rule was 'liable to undermine the fair balance between the interests of the . . . employer, on the one hand, and those of the employees, on the other'.[176] But what constitutes a fair balance in this context is clearly something on which national governments might reasonably disagree, which is why the legislature thought it proper to leave them some discretion in this matter. The judges may have different ideas on legitimate national diversity, but disagreement with the legislature is hardly a sufficient reason to discard its choices. It would therefore

173 Jan Jans, 'Minimum Harmonisation and the Role of the Principle of Proportionality' in Martin Führ and Eckard Rehbinder (eds), *Umweltrecht und Umweltwissenschaft: Festschrift für Eckard Rehbinder* (Schmidt 2007).
174 Boeger (n 162) 76.
175 ibid 77–78.
176 *Alemo Herron* (n 171) para 29.

have been more convincing if, as in the *TSN* case, national measures going beyond the legislative minimum had been regarded as falling outside the Charter's scope.[177] At the very least, the legislature must be given wide discretionary powers to determine what restrictions on Charter rights are permissible.[178]

Someone might argue, instead, that national measures exceeding the EU minimum must be subject to judicial scrutiny if they threaten to undermine central EU interests such as the internal market and its fundamental freedoms. The imposition of more favourable national rules may make it less attractive for undertakings to engage in cross-border economic activities. But again, the question arises: why not yield to minimum harmonisation and allow national authorities to exceed the norms laid down therein, even if this means less economic freedom? Surely, the internal market is not so sacrosanct that national diversity is something to be frowned upon. And surely, it is not so fragile that national restrictions—not least those permitted by the legislature—must be subject to incisive scrutiny. The proper balance between the internal market and national regulatory freedom is an open question, about which there is empirical uncertainty and reasonable disagreement. It would therefore be better to leave the determination of this balance to legislation. Rather than subjecting more favourable national measures to a strict proportionality test, the Court should permit such measures whenever legislation does.

So, even if minimum harmonisation is, in some sense, halfway between no and maximum harmonisation, the CJEU must treat minimum legislative norms as it treats full harmonisation. National measures that relate to minimum harmonisation must be assessed in the light of the harmonising measure and not primary law. In this respect, it should not matter whether legislative provisions constitute legislative or constitutional minimum harmonisation. Both seek to establish Europe-wide regulatory minimum norms that leave national authorities free to adopt more stringent measures. The CJEU must accept the legislative intention in such acts and defer to the minimum standard rather than treating these measures as a ceiling beyond which Member States may not regulate. Also here, it must adhere to the restrictive institutionalist adjudicative method.

Building on Chapter II's assessment of the political legitimacy of the EU legislature and judiciary, this chapter discussed which of these actors should bear the primary responsibility to make and amend EU law by studying their relative capacity to initiate legal change and realise social change. My findings supported the conclusion

[177] For further discussion, Tecqmenne (n 166).

[178] The reason for this is given in section IV.5. The CJEU offered the legislature such a wide discretion with respect to the right to freedom to conduct a business in Case C-544/10 *Deutsches Weintor* ECLI:EU:C:2012:526 and Case C-283/11 *Sky Österreich* ECLI:EU:C:2013:28. For further analysis, Eduardo Gill-Pedro, 'Freedom to Conduct Business in EU Law: Freedom from Interference or Freedom from Domination?' (2017) 9 European Journal of Legal Studies; Stephen Weatherill, 'Use and Abuse of the EU's Charter of Fundamental Rights: On the Improper Veneration of "Freedom of Contract"' (2014) 10 European Review of Contract Law 167.

of Chapter II that the determination of EU law is better left to the legislature. This provides a tripartite account of judicial deference to legislation, supporting a restrictive institutionalist form of adjudication, for reasons of institutional legitimacy, institutional capacity, and institutional collaboration. This approach is consistent with primary law and is to be adhered to in all public law adjudication, with respect to provisions of both maximum and minimum harmonisation.

IV

Legislated Treaty Rights and the Legitimacy of Judicial Review

1. Introduction

We can conceive of the Treaties of the European Union (EU) both in negative and in positive terms. Many of our debates focus on the negative legal constraints that the Treaties impose on the EU and its institutions, as well as their enforcement by judicial institutions—on how the Treaties should be applied to safeguard national governments from the EU encroaching on their competences and individual citizens from undue interference with their rights and freedoms. Just as important, however, is the Treaties' positive function: they constitute EU authority by enumerating its competences and empowering its institutions.[1] They therefore limit the exercise of transnational authority but also enable it, and they do so precisely to allow the EU to act when certain objectives cannot be adequately achieved by Member States alone.[2] This shift in our attention to EU constitutionalism's positive dimension broadens our institutional horizon. It reminds us that the realisation and preservation of the rights, principles, and objectives set out in the Treaties require a set of institutions that can prevent the EU from taking certain decisions but also facilitate the successful exercise of its powers.

The Treaties cannot be reduced to their negative dimension either in discussions about the role of the legislative process. The Treaties limit the exercise of legislative power but also facilitate it, precisely to allow the EU to protect and advance the rights and objectives set out in the Treaties. This chapter is interested in EU constitutionalism's negative and positive dimensions as applied to the relationship between the legislature and the judiciary. On the one hand, it is interested in the justification of judicial review. The Court of Justice of the European Union (CJEU) has, in accordance with art 263 of the Treaty on the Functioning of the European Union (TFEU), the power to 'review the legality of legislative acts'. My aim is to establish when it can legitimately exercise this power and when legislation should be struck down for violating the Treaties. On the other hand, the

[1] On the negative and positive dimension of constitutionalism, NW Barber, *The Principles of Constitutionalism* (OUP 2018).

[2] Indeed, the principle of subsidiarity also has both a negative and a positive dimension. For discussion, Paul Craig, 'Subsidiarity: A Political and Legal Analysis' (2012) 2012 Journal of Common Market Studies 72; Thomas Horsley, 'Subsidiarity and the European Court of Justice: Missing Pieces in the Subsidiarity Jigsaw?' (2012) 50 Journal of Common Market Studies 267.

Legislative Authority and Interpretation in the European Union. Martijn van den Brink, Oxford University Press.
 DOI: 10.1093/9780198900115.003.0004

legislature is presented as an actor that actively shapes the content and contours of the Treaties. Building on Chapters II and III, I will stress that interpretative authority over the Treaties is shared between institutions, as a result of which the legislature can more autonomously steer the course of the Treaties than is often thought. Treaty rights can be, and often are, legislated rights.

The first part of this chapter discusses the question of how the EU judiciary should exercise its power of judicial review in relation to legislation. Section IV.2 addresses some preliminaries, after which the three sections that follow zoom in on three specific grounds of judicial review: legislative process review, *ultra vires* review, and fundamental rights review. The exercise of legislative process review is shown to be unproblematic. *Ultra vires* review and fundamental rights review, by contrast, are vulnerable to objections from institutional legitimacy and capacity. Analysing the relevant case law, I demonstrate that judicial review for fundamental rights violations is currently too strict, while *ultra vires* review is conducted using appropriately deferential standards. Following this discussion, section IV.6 pinpoints the legislature's unique position in the EU institutional framework. Comparing the position of the legislature with that of national institutions and the EU executive, I explain that the legislature must be given wider discretionary powers than other actors whose choices may be subject to review by the CJEU. This argument brings to the fore the contentious role of primary law in legislative interpretation, which is addressed in section IV.7. I argue that primary law may be invoked when this amounts to a reasonable reading of legislative intent but not to compromise the intentions of a legislative act. The legislature must be able to legislate Treaty rights. Section IV.8 reinforces this conclusion by showing that legislation has more extensively steered the course of EU Treaty law than many believe. By analysing two unlikely cases, the principle of mutual recognition and the '*Laval* quartet', I show that the legislature has been able to negotiate or push back against unwanted judicial interpretations of Treaty rights, including crucial internal market doctrines. Once we understand how much influence the legislature can exercise over the content of EU law, we can see that any remaining imbalances between the EU legislature and judiciary can be addressed without radical institutional reform.

2. The Judicial Review of EU Legislation: Some Preliminaries

That the EU judiciary has compelling reasons to abide by the choices of the legislature does not entail, evidently, that yielding to these choices is always right. In Chapter III, I argued that the legislature must be allowed to give more specific expression to primary law by means of the provisions it enacts. Nevertheless, the question remains what limits, if any, the Treaties place on its authority—a question that concerns not the existence but the legitimate exercise of judicial power.

Article 263 of the TFEU empowers the CJEU to review legislative provisions 'on grounds of lack of competence, infringement of an essential procedural requirement, infringement of the Treaties or of any rule of law relating to their application, or misuse of powers'. Yet, this provision addresses only the 'if', not the 'when and how', of judicial review; nor are these covered by any other Treaty provisions.

The limits of legislative authority should be set having regard to something else, namely the institutional legitimacy and capacity of the legislature versus the judiciary. This suggests, given the legislature's institutional advantages in EU law-making, that these limits should be so broad that they do not unjustifiably encroach on the legislature's authority. However, we do not yet know how broad, whether they should be broad in every situation, and what those situations are. Sections IV.3, IV.4, and IV.5 discuss the 'when and how' of judicial review, that is in what situations, and using what standards, the CJEU should exercise its power to review the legality of legislative acts and invalidate legislative provisions. This section offers some preliminary thoughts and clarifications.

A good starting point for this inquiry into the legitimacy of judicial review of EU legislation was recently set by Ní Chaoimh. After cautioning against judicial supremacy, she argued that

> legislative supremacy also poses risks, this time by placing too much control in the hands of political institutions, which would undermine the judicial role of ensuring *lawfulness, fairness, and justifiability*, and thus the rights of constitutional subjects... If the Court cannot review resulting decisions, or if its review is too light, *individual rights could be severely curtailed* with limited redress, while Member States might rely on secondary legislation to undermine Treaty provisions. Limiting judicial review could also *threaten the delicate federal balance between Member States and the EU*, and *between the EU institutions themselves*.[3]

This statement provides a good starting point for our discussion because it shows at once how we should and how we should not assess the justification of judicial review. It will not do to discuss this question in terms of lawfulness, fairness, and justifiability. In the first place, it is not clear how these values make a positive case for judicial review. As Chapters II and III told us, the legislative process contributes to fairness in EU decision-making and helps the EU assess the lawfulness and justifiability of national practices and thus safeguard the rights of its citizens. Moreover, the validity of EU legislation is rarely contested on the basis of abstract values like fairness and justifiability but rather on any of the more specific grounds Ní Chaoimh mentions, namely that they unduly curtail individual rights, threaten the federal balance between the EU and Member States, or violate the EU institutional

[3] Eadaoin Ní Chaoimh, *The Legislative Priority Rule and the EU Internal Market for Goods: A Constitutional Approach* (OUP 2022) 60.

balance. If legislative measures are (deemed) unlawful, unfair, or unjustified, it is generally on these grounds. Therefore, the following sections discuss the justification of judicial review with reference to three grounds for review—*legislative process review*, ultra vires *review*, and *fundamental rights review*.[4]

The relevant question, then, is what standard of review should be applied in reviewing the legality of legislation, that is how strict the applicable standard of review should be. Determining this requires that we first know what speaks against the exercise of judicial review. Judicial review of legislation is potentially vulnerable to two important objections. The first, and most common, objection is that of democratic legitimacy: laws must have a democratic basis, that is be made by institutions that are accountable to a democratic process. Since judicial review does not meet that standard, it is democratically illegitimate.[5] The second objection involves concerns of institutional capacity: the judicial process is burdened by constraints of time, knowledge, and resources, which act as a limitation on judges' capacity to review the complex political and socio-economic assessments underlying many legislative choices. This is why such decisions are best left to the legislative process.[6] Both objections are consistent with the argument in Chapters II and III that judicial encroachment on the legislative process is objectionable for reasons of institutional legitimacy and institutional capacity.[7] Therefore, the appropriate standard of judicial review of EU legislation depends on when judicial review is vulnerable to these objections in practice.

This requires us to understand both objections in more detail. The objection from institutional legitimacy rests on *three propositions*.[8] The first is that rights are moral concepts that are subject to pervasive disagreement. Such disagreement is inevitable, especially when it comes to their more precise articulation and application, and—most of the time—reasonable.[9] Second, the very fact that rights are contested concepts means that our constitutions express them in vague and abstract terms. As a consequence, the actors responsible for their interpretation and application enjoy extensive moral and political discretion. Third, the most pivotal

[4] There might be other grounds that I will not consider here, such as, perhaps, constitutional identity review.

[5] Two influential proponents of this view are Jeremy Waldron, 'The Core of the Case against Judicial Review' (2006) 115 Yale Law Journal 1246 and Richard Bellamy, *Political Constitutionalism: A Republican Defence of the Constitutionality of Democracy* (CUP 2007).

[6] Two protagonists of this institutional view are Adrian Vermeule, *Judging under Uncertainty: An Institutional Theory of Legal Interpretation* (Harvard UP 2006) and Paul Yowell, *Constitutional Rights and Constitutional Design: Moral and Empirical Reasoning in Judicial Review* (Hart Publishing 2018).

[7] Note that the reasons against judicial review are narrower than the reasons for judicial deference. The justification for judicial deference was threefold: institutional legitimacy, the capacity to realise legal change, and the capacity to realise social change. The third plays no role in assessing the justification of judicial review. For if judicial review of legislation is justified, it should not be complied with—that is, it should not generate social change.

[8] Summarised clearly by Adrienne Stone, 'Judicial Review without Rights: Some Problems for the Democratic Legitimacy of Structural Judicial Review' (2008) 28 Oxford Journal of Legal Studies 1, 7.

[9] Jeremy Waldron, *Law and Disagreement* (OUP 1999) 176–86; Bellamy (n 5) 20–26.

proposition is that judges have no superior skills or knowledge that would make them better than legislatures at the kind of moral reasoning involved in articulating constitutional rights.[10] Therefore, the value of democratic legitimacy militates in favour of leaving this task to legislatures. The objection from institutional capacity reinforces this third proposition by emphasising that courts, for various reasons, lack the capacity to undertake the complex policy assessments needed in the articulation of constitutional rights. Hence, courts should either not be empowered to exercise judicial review or be reluctant in exercising this power.

The crucial question on which the legitimacy of judicial review of EU legislation depends is to what extent these arguments against judicial review hold in the EU setting. As is well known, some of the most astute voices in constitutional theory have argued that these objections constitute knockout arguments against judicial review. They claim that the exercise of judicial review is, per se, objectionable regardless of the circumstances.[11] My argument follows a different trajectory. I argue that the objections from institutional legitimacy and institutional capacity are not the death knell to the justification of judicial review, at least not within the EU.[12] Instead, its justification is partly context-dependent, which is to say, dependent on the specific ground for review. As I will argue, legislative process review is not vulnerable to the objections of institutional legitimacy and institutional capacity, whereas *ultra vires* review and fundamental rights review are. This calls for extensive judicial deference to legislation that gives expression to the EU's division of competences or fundamental rights.

3. Legislative Process Review

The European Commission initiates the legislative process by submitting a legislative proposal to the Parliament and the Council, which jointly exercise legislative functions.[13] However, their ability to influence legislation, and hence the balance of power between them, depends on the procedure used for the enactment of legislation. Most proposals are dealt with under the ordinary legislative procedure that treats Parliament and Council as co-legislatures, but some proposals are subject to different legislative procedures that change the institutional balance of power. Which procedure applies depends on the choice of legal basis, which, in turn, depends on the aim and content of the legislative proposal in question. While it is

[10] Jeremy Waldron, 'Judges as Moral Reasoners' (2008) 7 International Journal of Constitutional Law 2.

[11] See the literature cited in nn 5 and 6.

[12] I will not speculate about the legitimacy of judicial review in other settings because the legitimacy of judicial review seems to me to be partly context-dependent, meaning that it cannot be determined in the abstract without considering the specific features of the legal system and societal environment in which it takes place.

[13] Articles 14(1), 16(1), and 17(2) of the TFEU.

usually clear what is the correct legal basis and legislative procedure, the legislative institutions sometimes disagree on these issues. This has led to protracted legal battles over the appropriate legal basis and the correct legislative procedure, and it has led to the invalidation of legislation for being adopted under the wrong legal basis and wrong legislative procedure. This section examines the legitimacy of legislative process review.

Intra-legislative disputes first peaked after the entry into force of the Single European Act (SEA).[14] The SEA introduced a specific legal basis for environmental legislation, which co-existed with a legal basis for internal market legislation. This became a source of institutional conflict, as the legislative procedures used for the adoption of internal market and environmental legislation differed. Internal market legislation could be adopted by the Council acting by qualified majority on a proposal from the Commission and after obtaining the Parliament's opinion, which could approve, amend, or reject the Council's position. Introduced amendments could then be approved or rejected by the Commission, after which the re-examined proposal returned to the Council, which could adopt it by qualified majority or amend it unanimously.[15] By contrast, the procedure used for adopting environmental legislation required unanimity in the Council, after consulting the Parliament.[16] As a result, the choice of whether a legislative proposal intended to regulate the internal market or the environment mattered to the respective powers of the legislative institutions. When a legislative measure concerned both the functioning of the internal market and the protection of the environment, Parliament, and sometimes the Commission, had an interest in using the internal market as the legal basis for its enactment, while the Council could protect its influence on the legislative process by using the legal basis for environmental protection. This led to extensive litigation in the years following the adoption of the SEA, through which Parliament and the Commission sought to protect their legislative prerogatives.[17]

This process has repeated itself with subsequent amendments of the legislative procedures or their applicability within specific areas of law, culminating in the years following the entry into force of the Treaty of Lisbon.[18] Despite the

[14] For a lengthier discussion, Kieran St Clair Bradley, 'Powers and Procedures in the EU Constitution: Legal Bases and the Court' in Paul Craig and Gráinne de Búrca (eds), *The Evolution of EU Law* (2nd edn, OUP 2011).

[15] This was the so-called cooperation procedure, laid down in art 252 of the Treaty on European Community.

[16] Article 130s of the SEA.

[17] Case C-300/89 *Commission v Council* ECLI:EU:C:1991:244; Case C-187/93 *Parliament v Council* ECLI:EU:C:1994:265; Case C-155/91 *Commission v Council* ECLI:EU:C:1993:98.

[18] For an excellent overview, Miriam Hartlapp, 'Power Shifts via the Judicial Arena: How Annulments Cases between EU Institutions Shape Competence Allocation: Power Shifts via the Judicial Arena' (2018) 56 Journal of Common Market Studies 1429, 1434. See also María-Luisa Sánchez Barrueco, 'Litigation as a Means to Solve Conflicts between the European Parliament and the Council: One Size Does Not Fit All' in Paul James Cardwell and Marie-Pierre Granger (eds), *Research Handbook on the Politics of EU Law* (Edward Elgar 2020).

simplifications the Treaty introduced, subjecting most legislative proposals to joint decision-making between the Council and Parliament,[19] the number of intra-institutional legislative disputes increased steeply in the following years, largely due to conflicts between both actors over influence in EU external affairs.[20] EU external affairs includes both the Common Foreign and Security Policy (CFSP), where Parliament's influence is limited,[21] and the Area of Freedom, Security, and Justice (AFSJ), where co-decision between Parliament and the Council is the norm.[22] Parliament filed cases against the Council, arguing that the CFSP cannot be the exclusive legal basis for adopting international agreements with ramifications for AFSJ.[23] The Commission, at times, joined the battle by lodging complaints against the Council for violating the balance of power between the legislative institutions in the field of external affairs.[24]

As it is the appropriateness of legislative process review that concerns us here, this is not the place to examine these disputes and the respective judgments in detail. Intra-legislative disputes usually arise from a decision of the Council to legislate using a procedure that limits Parliament's influence. The latter then resorts to litigation to preserve or expand its powers. The Commission may join Parliament or bring its own case for incorrect use of legal basis. It is then for the CJEU to review whether the legal basis chosen is appropriate considering the objectives and content of the contested legislative act and to annul the act if it finds that its enactment was supported by an incorrect legal basis.

The demand for legislative process review shows why it is crucial that the CJEU has been given the power of judicial review. Unlike *ultra vires* and fundamental rights review (see sections IV.4 and IV.5), legislative process review is not vulnerable to the standard objections to judicial review. After all, it would beg the question at the heart of such disputes to argue that deference should be afforded to the legislature in such cases, namely who is the legitimate legislature? Whose views on what is the correct legal basis should prevail: those of Parliament, those of the

[19] For a detailed analysis, Michael Dougan, 'The Treaty of Lisbon 2007: Winning Minds, Not Hearts' (2008) 45 Common Market Law Review 617.

[20] There were other disputes as well at the time, such as Case C-48/14 *Parliament v Council* ECLI:EU:C:2015:91, concerning the complaints lodged by Parliament against the Council for basing measures on the Euratom Treaty rather than environmental policy.

[21] Article 218(6) of the TFEU.

[22] Title V of the TFEU.

[23] See, eg Case C-263/14 *Parliament v Council* EU:C:2016:435; Case C-658/11 *Parliament v Council* (Mauritius) EU:C:2014:2025; Case C-130/10 *Parliament v Council* EU:C:2012:472; Joined cases C-103/12 and C-125/13 *Parliament and Commission v Council* EU:C:2014:2400. For a detailed analysis, Soledad R Sánchez-Tabernero, 'The Choice of Legal Basis and the Principle of Consistency in the Procedure for Conclusion of International Agreements in CFSP Contexts: *Parliament v. Council* (Pirate-Transfer Agreement with Tanzania)' (2017) 54 Common Market Law Review 899; Ramses Wessel, 'Legality in EU Common Foreign and Security Policy: The Choice of the Appropriate Legal Basis' in Claire Kilpatrick and Joanne Scott (eds), *Contemporary Challenges to EU Legality* (OUP 2021).

[24] Case C-377/12 *Commission v Council* EU:C:2014:1903; *Parliament and Commission v Council* (n 23); Case C-244/17 *Commission v Council* ECLI:EU:C:2018:662.

Council, or, possibly, those of the Commission? Since the legislative institutions could not agree on the adjudicated questions, it makes no sense to try to settle such disputes through the operation of a principle of deference.

Of course, such disputes could be resolved by systematically placing one of the institutions above the others. The Council has argued in the past that it should be competent to determine the correct legal basis, and the Commission once took the view that it should be allowed to select the legislative procedure to be followed by the other two institutions.[25] Yet, these positions were hardly conceivable then, when Parliament's legislative prerogatives were not equal to those of the Council, let alone now. Parliament's position would be seriously undermined if it could not challenge the legal basis chosen by the Council; it would no longer be an equal partner in the legislative process. For similar reasons, it should not be for the Commission to determine the legal basis, which would make an independent assessment of the Council's and Parliament's positions impossible. The only option, therefore, is to let such disputes be settled by a third party, for which the CJEU is the most obvious candidate. Precisely to protect the integrity of the legislative process, the EU judiciary must be able to intervene in, and settle, such intra-legislative disputes, which is why its decision that 'the choice of the legal basis of a European Union act must rest on objective factors amenable to judicial review' has been the right one.[26]

This is not to say that the CJEU has always correctly assessed the choices of the legislative institutions and determined the correct legal basis. It seems incontestable, however, that judicial review of legislation is desirable when the legislative institutions cannot agree among themselves on the correct course of action. The alternative, applying a principle of deference to the choices made by the legislative institutions, would jeopardise the institutional balance between them and between the Council and Parliament in particular. The only way to guarantee their status as co-legislatures is to subject the choice of legal basis to judicial review and to annul legislation that has not been enacted following the correct procedural requirements.

4. *Ultra Vires* Review

Legislative process review is an easy case. Things become more complex when the legislative institutions agree on the choice of legal basis and legislative procedure, as well as the enactment of legislative provisions. Then the question of whether legislation must be respected, or its validity challenged, gets more acute. This section

[25] St Clair Bradley (n 14) 91.

[26] Case C-263/14 *Parliament v Council* (n 23) para 43; Case C-300/89 *Commission v Council* (n 17) para 10; Case C-130/10 *Parliament v Council* (n 23) para 42.

considers this question in relation to *ultra vires* review, that is the review of legislative acts for violation of the limits of EU competence. My analysis focuses specifically on the review of internal market legislation.

Three principles govern the limits and use of EU competence: the principles of conferral, subsidiarity, and proportionality.[27] In accordance with the principle of conferral, the EU may not act outside the limits of competences conferred on it by the Treaties. The principle of subsidiarity requires that the EU acts only if and insofar as the objectives pursued cannot be properly achieved by the Member States. Under the principle of proportionality, the EU shall ensure that the content and form of its actions shall not exceed what is necessary to achieve these objectives. The EU acts *ultra vires* when it acts in an area where it has no competence or when its actions violate the principles of subsidiarity and proportionality.[28] All EU institutions can act *ultra vires*, but this section focuses only on the *ultra vires* review of legislative measures.

To understand what limits the Treaties impose on legislative competence, one must first know whether the EU has exclusive or shared competence over the subject matter the legislature wishes to regulate. When the Treaties confer exclusive competence in a specific area, only the EU may legislate and take legally binding decisions. When competence is shared in a specific area, both the EU and the Member States may act, but the latter only insofar as the EU has not exercised its shared competence.[29] The principle of subsidiarity does not apply to areas of exclusive competence.[30] Second, one must know the limits on the exercise of legislative authority in different areas of law according to the legal bases scattered across the Treaties. These limits are relatively clear when it comes to sector-specific competences, such as public health and the environment, which 'confer a relatively clear-cut and tightly-defined competence to legislate on the EU',[31] and therefore rarely spark litigation. Less clear-cut are the limits of functionally driven competences. The most notable example of a functional competence is art 352 of the TFEU, which can be used to pass legislation if 'necessary, within the framework of the policies defined in the Treaties, to attain one of the objectives set out in the Treaties, and the Treaties have not provided the necessary powers'. However, since this provision requires the Council to act unanimously, it rarely triggers litigation either. The functional competence that has caused more controversy is the legislative competence in art 114 of the TFEU to adopt measures for the approximation of

[27] Article 5 of the Treaty on European Union (TEU).

[28] Paul Craig, 'The ECJ and *Ultra Vires* Action: A Conceptual Analysis' (2011) 48 Common Market Law Review 395, 425–26.

[29] Article 2(1) and (2) of the TFEU.

[30] Article 5(3) of the TEU.

[31] Stephen Weatherill, 'The Limits of Legislative Harmonization Ten Years after *Tobacco Advertising*: How the Court's Case Law Has Become a "Drafting Guide"' (2011) 12 German Law Journal 827, 831. See also Gareth Davies, 'Democracy and Legitimacy in the Shadow of Purposive Competence' (2015) 22 European Law Journal 2.

national standards 'which have as their object the establishment and functioning of the internal market'. One reason why this provision has proven controversial is that it provides that '*any* national measure may be harmonized provided that leads to an improvement in the functioning of the internal market'.[32] In addition, such measures may be adopted by the Council acting by a qualified majority, which means that this competence can be exercised contrary to the wishes of a small minority of Member States. For these reasons, and for the fact that the use of art 114 of the TFEU has caused extensive litigation, this provision will be the focus of my analysis.

There is general agreement that the legislature has acted at the outer limits of art 114 of the TFEU and that the CJEU has policed the limits of this legislative competence very loosely. It is settled case law that under art 114 of the TFEU,

> the legislature must be allowed *a broad discretion* in an area such as that involved in the present case, which entails political, economic and social choices on its part, and in which it is called upon to undertake complex assessments. The legality of a measure adopted in that sphere can be affected only if the measure is *manifestly inappropriate* having regard to the objective which the competent institutions are seeking to pursue.[33]

Only once, in the first *Tobacco Advertising* judgment, was a legislative decision struck down because it did not 'genuinely have as its object the improvement of the conditions for the establishment and functioning of the internal market'.[34] This judgment is the exception to the rule that the CJEU is 'extraordinarily permissive of legislative discretion'.[35] It is by now settled, for example, that

> While a mere finding of disparities between national rules and the abstract risk of infringements of fundamental freedoms or distortion of competition is not sufficient to justify the choice of Article [114 of the TFEU] as a legal basis, the [EU] legislature may have recourse to it in particular where there are differences between national rules which are such as to obstruct the fundamental freedoms and thus

[32] Weatherill, 'The Limits of Legislative Harmonization' (n 31) 831.

[33] Case C-58/08 *Vodafone v Secretary of State* ECLI:EU:C:2010:321, para 52; Case C-380/03 *Germany v Parliament and Council* ECLI:EU:C:2006:772, para 145; C-491/01 *British American Tobacco* ECLI:EU:C:2002:741, para 123; Joined cases C-154/04 and C-155/04 *Alliance for Natural Health* ECLI:EU:C:2005:449, para 52 (italics mine).

[34] Case C-376/98 *Germany v Parliament and Council* ECLI:EU:C:2000:544, para 84.

[35] For this statement and an excellent analysis of the case law, Weatherill, 'The Limits of Legislative Harmonization' (n 31) 837. For further analysis, Robert Schütze, 'Limits to the Union's "Internal Market" Competence(s)' in Loïc Azoulai (ed), *The Question of \Competence in the European Union* (1st edn, OUP 2014).

> have a direct effect on the functioning of the internal market or to cause significant distortions of competition.[36]

Provided that these criteria are fulfilled, there is nothing that prevents the legislature from relying on art 114 of the TFEU, even if it acts to ban a specific product from the market[37] or if another consideration such as 'public health protection is a decisive factor in the choices to be made'.[38]

Because of the permissive nature of these criteria, it may seem as if the CJEU is unprepared to adequately police the limits of EU competence. Jacob Öberg, for instance, argues that the choice to grant the legislature such broad discretion has 'resulted in poor enforcement' of arts 5 of the TEU and 114 of the TFEU.[39] Such criticism does not convince, however, because it assumes what it is trying to establish: that broad legislative discretion compromises the proper enforcement of the limits of EU competence; that is, to prove that the exercise of EU competence must be subject to more exacting scrutiny, it is insufficient to show that the legislature has wide discretionary powers. It must instead be shown that it has been given *too* wide a margin of discretion. Critics assume but rarely try to establish this, and on closer examination, their assumption seems dubious. As I will argue, the wide legislative discretion in the governance of the internal market is justified.

First, *ultra vires* review is vulnerable to the objection from institutional capacity. As Paul Craig noted, the CJEU, in reviewing whether legislation complies with the principle of subsidiarity, must assess the evidence on which the legislature acted and thus 'adjudicate on what may be a complex socio-economic calculus'.[40] Critics of light-touch *ultra vires* review might want to argue that no such complex assessments are needed to establish whether the principle of conferral has been breached, since 'the identification of a competence to legislate in the first place is *not* in the gift of the legislature'.[41] But while it is, indeed, not a legislative prerogative to amend the limits of EU competence, the contours of art 114 of the TFEU, and thus the limits of EU competence, are vague and do not neatly delimit

[36] *Vodafone v Secretary of State* (n 33) para 32; Case C-380/03 *Germany v Parliament and Council* (n 33) para 37.

[37] Case C-151/17 *Swedish Match* ECLI:EU:C:2018:938.

[38] *Alliance for Natural Health* (n 33) para 30; *British American Tobacco* (n 33) para 62.

[39] Jacob Öberg, 'The Rise of the Procedural Paradigm: Judicial Review of EU Legislation in Vertical Competence Disputes' (2017) 13 European Constitutional Law Review 248, 254. For further criticism, Alexander Somek, *Individualism: An Essay on the Authority of the European Union* (OUP 2008) ch 7; Weatherill, 'The Limits of Legislative Harmonization' (n 31); Derrick Wyatt, 'Could a "Yellow Card" for National Parliaments Strengthen Judicial as Well as Political Policing of Subsidiarity?' (2006) 2 Croatian Yearbook of European Law and Policy 1; Christoph Ritzer, Marc Ruttloff, and Karin Linhart, 'How to Sharpen a Dull Sword—The Principle of Subsidiarity and Its Control' (2006) 7 German Law Journal 734.

[40] Craig, 'The ECJ and *Ultra Vires* Action' (n 28) 427. Some critics of the standard of review applied by the CJEU have recgnised as much: Öberg (n 39) 254; Weatherill, 'The Limits of Legislative Harmonization' (n 31) 843–46.

[41] Weatherill, 'The Limits of Legislative Harmonization' (n 31) 847.

the legislature's authority.[42] The question that arises, therefore, is how much discretion the legislature must be given in determining the contours of this provision.

A more detailed examination of the objection from institutional legitimacy answers this question: it shows that the legislature has rightly been given extraordinary discretion in its choice to use art 114 of the TFEU. Because this objection is usually levelled against rights-based review, it must first be established that it can also be invoked against *ultra vires* review. The question, in other words, is whether the three propositions underlying the case against rights-based review (outlined in section IV.2) are equally applicable to disputes over the constitutional division of powers. Adrienne Stone has compellingly argued that they are.[43] First, constitutional provisions regulating the division of powers between the different levels of government are often just as imprecise as constitutional rights provisions. As a result, the institutions responsible for their application enjoy considerable latitude in determining how to set and enforce the division of powers. The same is true for the constitutional division of powers within the EU: the limits of art 114 of the TFEU and those of similar provisions, such as the flexibility clause in art 352 of the TFEU, are difficult to establish. Second, the interpretation of such provisions requires moral judgement. As Wojciech Sadurski has argued, 'it is not the case that reasoning oriented toward rights articulation is any *more* moral than many non-rights-oriented authoritative public decisions'.[44] The determination of the division of competences between the EU and the Member States proves that non-rights-oriented decisions can be fraught with moral controversy—think of questions such as when the EU should accommodate national diversity and when it must subject retained national competences to EU law.[45] Third, the CJEU is not better placed than the legislature to make such moral judgements, so it is justified to afford a great margin of deference to legislation in *ultra vires* disputes.

The third point needs further elaboration. According to the democratic critique of judicial review, most of our moral disagreements about the correct interpretation

[42] ibid 847–48. See also Craig, 'The ECJ and *Ultra Vires* Action' (n 28) 406–407.

[43] Stone, 'Judicial Review without Rights' (n 8); Adrienne Stone, 'Democratic Objections to Structural Judicial Review and the Judicial Role in Constitutional Law' (2010) 60 University of Toronto Law Journal 109. Stone draws a distinction between rights-based and structural review. In my view, the concept of structural review is too broad and includes different types of disputes that may be incomparable. For example, legislative process review and *ultra vires* review would both be encompassed by it, even though they pose distinct normative questions. However, this does not detract from Stone's argument that division of powers review (one component of structural review) is vulnerable to the argument from democracy. For a useful differentiation between different types of structural review, Jeffrey Goldsworthy, 'Structural Judicial Review and the Objection from Democracy' (2010) 60 University of Toronto Law Journal 137.

[44] Wojciech Sadurski, 'Rights and Moral Reasoning: An Unstated Assumption' (2008) 7 International Journal of Constitutional Law 25, 44. See also Stone, 'Judicial Review without Rights' (n 8) 11–17.

[45] Loïc Azoulai, 'The European Court of Justice and the Duty to Respect Sensitive National Interests' in Mark Dawson, Bruno de Witte, and Elise Muir (eds), *Judicial Activism at the European Court of Justice* (Edward Elgar 2013); Bruno de Witte, 'Exclusive Member State Competences—Is There Such a Thing?' in Sacha Garben and Inge Govaere (eds), *The Division of Competences between the EU and the Member States: Reflections on the Past, the Present and the Future* (Hart Publishing 2017).

of abstract constitutional rights are reasonable. Coupled with the fact that courts are not better at getting to the truth of these concepts, such disagreements must, for reasons of democratic fairness, be settled using the legislative process.[46] But what fairness requires may, of course, vary across contexts, and I have not yet shown that it is fair to leave the demarcation of EU competences to the legislature. So, is this fair? It is, provided that the legislative process offers sufficient safeguards for these limits, which it does if the exercise of EU competence is controlled not only by the centre (ie the EU) but also by the national peoples or their representatives.[47] The EU legislative process meets this condition: it provides 'a system of political safeguards of federalism'[48] that attaches much weight to national interests in determining the federal balance of powers between the EU and the Member States. It therefore offers a fair process for demarcating the boundaries of EU competence, which means that the legislature is rightly given a wide margin of discretion in relation to the political and socio-economic choices to be made in using the competence under art 114 of the TFEU to regulate the internal market.

But are these safeguards adequate when legislation is adopted against the wishes of one or more Member States? The exercise of competence under art 114 of the TFEU is subject to qualified majority rule, so there is always a possibility that Member States find themself on the losing side. However, as Stone has emphasised, we must 'distinguish between those who simply lose in the resolution of political disputes and those who lose unjustly because of their effective exclusion from politics'.[49] A Member State that is defeated in a vote on the demarcation of EU competence exceptionally belongs to the losing minority; it is not thereby unjustly excluded from the political process. It could protect its interests and express its objections; it just so happens that these were not shared by a qualified majority of other Member States. This does not amount to unjust political exclusion, nor is it a reason to plead for a more stringent *ultra vires* review.

What, then, about the first *Tobacco Advertising* judgment, in which the regulation of tobacco advertising and sponsorship was annulled for being wrongly based on art 114 of the TFEU? In my view, this decision unduly curtailed the legislature's discretion in using this provision. The CJEU held that a reading of art 114 of the TFEU that would vest 'in the Community legislature a general power to regulate the internal market would ... be contrary to the *express wording* of the provision'.[50] It suggested that the provision could be used to liberalise the market but not for other forms of market regulation. The problem with this reading is that it finds no support in art 114 of the TFEU's 'express wording', which licenses legislative

[46] Famously: Waldron, 'The Core of the Case against Judicial Review' (n 5).
[47] Goldsworthy (n 43) 139–40; Stone, 'Democratic Objections to Structural Judicial Review' (n 43) 115.
[48] St Clair Bradley (n 14) 109.
[49] Stone, 'Democratic Objections to Structural Judicial Review' (n 43) 129.
[50] Case C-376/98 *Germany v Parliament and Council* (n 34).

provisions that have 'as their object the improvement of the conditions for the establishment and functioning of the internal market'. This clearly does not rule out that it can serve as the legal basis for market regulation,[51] so the CJEU construed this provision too narrowly in *Tobacco Advertising* and corrected its mistake in subsequent judgments by allowing art 114 of the TFEU to form the basis for market regulation, including legislative provisions regulating the authorisation of products or banning their marketing altogether.[52] Had it interpreted this provision equally plausibly in *Tobacco Advertising*, the legislative measures in question would most likely have survived review.

But let's not get too hung up on a single judgment. My ambition was to show that it is appropriate to apply a lenient standard of review in *ultra vires* disputes such as those involving the use of art 114 of the TFEU. The legality of legislative acts that have this provision as their legal basis should, indeed, be affected only if they are 'manifestly inappropriate having regard to the objective which the competent institution is seeking to pursue'.[53] Their legality may be sooner compromised if the limits of EU competence are demarcated more precisely than in (say) art 114 of the TFEU.[54] Apart from that, there are no reasons to revisit the legislature's extensive discretion and exercise a more exacting *ultra vires* review of legislation. The legislative process offers a fair process for settling the EU division of powers.

5. Fundamental Rights Review

Academic debate on the legitimacy of judicial review has centred mainly on the protection of fundamental rights. Volumes have been written about whether courts should have the power to invalidate legislation for violating individual rights and the appropriate exercise of that power. Proponents of judicial review usually defend it as an essential part of constitutional government, as a way to protect minority groups from domination by the political majority, and therefore as a vital tool to ensure the political equality of citizens and therewith the democratic legitimacy of government as such.[55] Critics, in contrast, may be quick to point out that constitutional courts have failed to live up to the lofty expectations of the advocates of judicial review. Moreover, and more fundamentally, doubts remain about the

[51] ibid para 45, for Parliament, the Council, and the Commission making the same point.

[52] *Swedish Match* (n 37) para 34. See also Case C-547/14 *Philip Morris Brands* EU:C:2016:325, para 14; *Swedish Match* (n 37) para 72. For discussion, Weatherill, 'The Limits of Legislative Harmonization' (n 31).

[53] *Vodafone v Secretary of State* (n 33) para 52; *Alliance for Natural Health* (n 33) para 52; *British American Tobacco* (n 33) para 123.

[54] Although this will depend on deeper questions of constitutional interpretation, such as whether precise provisions should be interpreted in accordance with the general scheme of the Treaties. This is not the place to go into such questions, but see Craig, 'The ECJ and *Ultra Vires* Action' (n 28) 399. More generally, Stone, 'Judicial Review without Rights' (n 8) 9–10.

[55] See, famously, John Hart Ely, *Democracy and Distrust* (Harvard UP 1981).

compatibility of the practice of judicial review with the principle of democratic legitimacy.[56]

Interestingly, the legitimacy of fundamental rights review has not been much discussed by EU lawyers. Perhaps this is because, throughout most of its history, the CJEU has been timid—critics might say 'pusillanimous'[57]—in the exercise of fundamental rights review of legislation. In the past decade, however, it has become more assertive, annulling legislative provisions on four occasions.[58] In *Digital Rights Ireland*, it ruled that the legislature exceeded the limits of its authority under the EU Charter of Fundamental Rights, specifically the right to respect for private life in art 7 and the right to the protection of personal data in art 8, by adopting the Data Retention Directive.[59] In the three other cases, the CJEU struck down individual legislative provisions. In *Volker und Markus*, it found a provision mandating the disclosure of information about the beneficiaries of agricultural funds to violate the right to respect for private life and the right to the protection of personal data.[60] In *WM and Sovim*, it reached the same verdict in respect of a provision requiring the disclosure of information on the beneficial ownership of companies to members of the general public.[61] Finally, in *Test-Achats*, a provision that allowed sex to be a factor in the calculation of insurance premiums was struck down for violating the principle of non-discrimination between men and women.[62]

The most striking part of these judgments is the apparent enthusiasm with which the CJEU is now exerting fundamental rights review. Earlier, we saw that the legislature has an extraordinary discretion in its choice of how to regulate the internal market. Because this is an area that 'entails political, economic and social choices on its part, and in which it is called upon to undertake complex assessments',[63] its decisions survive review unless they are manifestly inappropriate. The legislature does not enjoy nearly the same discretion when it interferes with

[56] Waldron, 'The Core of the Case against Judicial Review' (n 5); Bellamy (n 5).

[57] Damian Chalmers, Gareth Davies, and Giorgio Monti, *European Union Law: Cases and Materials* (2nd edn, CUP 2010) 251. For similar views, Benedikt Pirker, *Proportionality Analysis and Models of Judicial Review: A Theoretical and Comparative Study* (Europa Law Publishing 2013) 251–54; Albertina Albors-Llorens, 'Edging towards Closer Scrutiny? The Court of Justice and Its Review of the Compatibility of General Measures with the Protection of Economic Rights and Freedoms' in Anthony Arnull and others (eds), *A Constitutional Order of States? Essays in EU Law in Honour of Alan Dashwood* (Hart Publishing 2011). Examples of this timid approach include Case 44/79 *Hauer* ECLI:EU:C:1979:290; Case C-540/03 *Parliament v Council* ECLI:EU:C:2006:429; Case C-303/05 *Advocaten voor de Wereld* ECLI:EU:C:2007:261. The CJEU has also exercised restraint in some recent judgments: Case C-291/12 *Michael Schwarz* ECLI:EU:C:2013:670; Case C-401/19 *Poland v Parliament and Council* ECLI:EU:C:2022:297.

[58] In the same period, however, it has also upheld the validity of legislative provisions on several occasions: Case C-18/16 *K v Staatssecretaris van Veiligheid en Justitie* ECLI:EU:C:2017:680.

[59] Joined Cases C-293/12 and C-594/12 *Digital Rights Ireland* EU:C:2014:238. There have been similar verdicts in challenges against Commission decisions: Case C-362/14 *Schrems I* EU:C:2015:650; Case C-311/18 *Schrems II* ECLI:EU:C:2020:559.

[60] Joined cases C-92/09 and C-93/09 *Volker und Markus* ECLI:EU:C:2010:353.

[61] Case C-37/20 *WM and Sovim* ECLI:EU:C:2022:912.

[62] Case C-236/09 *Test-Achats* ECLI:EU:C:2011:100.

[63] See n 33.

fundamental rights. It seems settled case law by now that derogations from fundamental rights are lawful only insofar as they are 'strictly necessary'.[64] In *Digital Rights Ireland*, for instance, it was held that the 'legislature's discretion is reduced, with the result that review of that discretion should be strict'.[65] In this respect, there is a curious discrepancy in the applicable standards of review: broad discretion to legislate the internal market translates into lenient *ultra vires* review, while limited discretion to legislate fundamental rights translates into strict fundamental rights review. This discrepancy is all the more remarkable since decisions to restrict fundamental rights do not necessarily involve less complex choices than decisions regulating the internal market. Far from it: deciding on how to balance the right to data protection with the objective of crime prevention is a hugely complex matter, both in terms of the value trade-offs it entails and the technical considerations it requires. And yet, at no point did the CJEU recognise the complexity of such choices in *Digital Rights Ireland*, nor did it in other judgments involving fundamental rights review.

This does not show that the standard by which the CJEU assesses the legality of legislative provisions restricting fundamental rights is too strict, but the discrepancy between *ultra vires* review and right-based review poses several important questions. Is fundamental rights review vulnerable to the objections from institutional legitimacy and institutional capacity? How wide a discretionary power must the legislature have in balancing and restricting fundamental rights? And how strictly must the CJEU review such legislative provisions? The remainder of this section determines how fundamental rights review should be exercised. To anticipate the argument that follows, the legislative process functions in such a way that scepticism about its capacity to take fundamental rights seriously can be put to rest. It offers a fair basis for settling disagreements about fundamental rights (section IV.5.1). But this does not exclude the possibility that the CJEU may be in a better position to decide such issues. On my account, the justification for fundamental rights review is not predicated on distrust of the legislature but on it not being infallible and omniscient. It follows, however, that this type of review must be exercised by way of exception and under more deferential standards of review than those currently in place (section IV.5.2).

5.1 Legislated fundamental rights

The objection from institutional legitimacy to judicial review provides a systematic starting point for answering these questions. As we know from sections IV.3 and IV.4, this objection rests on three propositions, namely that rights are moral

[64] ibid para 52; *Volker und Markus* (n 60) para 77; *Poland v Parliament and Council* (n 57) para 67.
[65] *Digital Rights Ireland* (n 59) para 48.

concepts about which there is pervasive but reasonable disagreement; that rights are therefore formulated in abstract terms, giving those responsible for their articulation substantial political discretion; and that legislatures are at least as good as judges at the kind of moral reasoning required for exercising such discretion responsibly. The first two of these propositions strike me as uncontroversial. First, the rights laid down in EU primary law are formulated in abstract language, which means that they leave substantial political discretion to the institution interpreting them. Second, moral disagreement about the value of fundamental rights and their proper balancing against each other and against various public policy interests, can create serious disagreements about their interpretation. For the most part, such disagreement amounts to disagreement between reasonable people, who may be well meaning and well informed and yet differ on the proper application of fundamental rights in concrete situations. Therefore, the answer to the questions raised in the above paragraph depends largely on the truth of the third proposition, that is on the relative institutional capacity and legitimacy of the institutions that bear responsibility for the articulation and application of fundamental rights.

Sympathy for judicial review often rests on the view that democratically elected majorities cannot be trusted to take seriously the fundamental rights of those affected by their decisions. This view has been articulated in the famous slogan that unchecked legislative authority would lead to a 'tyranny of the majority' in government, that is to political majorities exercising their powers unfazed by the interests and rights of (mostly vulnerable) societal minorities. In this view, courts must have the power to overrule the decisions of political majorities to protect marginalised groups from tyranny and domination. EU lawyers have argued the same. According to Anthony Arnull, for example, the CJEU should have the power of judicial review since 'there is a danger that the voices of minorities (even substantial ones) may be drowned out by the very size of the Union'.[66] This, however, does not provide a sound justification for fundamental rights review within the EU for the simple reason that the articulation of fundamental rights through the EU legislative process will not create majoritarian tyranny. Let me explain why.

For a start, fundamental rights often cannot be considered 'minority rights'.[67] Many of the rights laid down in the EU Charter benefit the entire class of citizens, and some, such as the freedom to conduct a business under art 16 and the right to private property under art 17, are more likely to benefit powerful economic interests. The right to respect for private life and the right to the protection of personal data—the two rights that have been central to the CJEU's exercise of fundamental rights review—do not necessarily protect minority groups either. The ruling in

[66] Anthony Arnull, 'Judicial Review in the European Union' in Damian Chalmers and Anthony Arnull (eds), *The Oxford Handbook of European Union Law* (OUP 2015) 400. See also Elise Muir, *EU Equality Law: The First Fundamental Rights Policy of the EU* (OUP 2018) 32.

[67] Wojciech Sadurski, 'Judicial Review and the Protection of Constitutional Rights' (2002) 22 Oxford Journal of Legal Studies 275, 293.

Digital Rights Ireland, for example, protected not a specific group but, as the CJEU said itself, 'practically the entire European population'.[68] And the judgment in *Volker und Markus* protected recipients of EU agricultural subsidies, while it was entrepreneurs that benefited most from the *WM and Sovim* verdict—not exactly vulnerable minorities either. And because the beneficiaries of these judgments did not coincide with a vulnerable minority group, the judicial review carried out in these cases cannot be justified by the need to protect vulnerable minorities from domination by the political majority.

More importantly, it is an unavoidable fact of political decision-making that it produces winners and losers; nothing tyrannical happens to anyone merely because their will is not followed by the winning majority.[69] Indeed, political losers are not, by virtue of that fact alone, victims of majoritarian tyranny that must be repairable by judicial review. And if they were, that would hardly make the case for judicial review, which creates losers just the same; often enough, losers that are among the more vulnerable and marginalised in our society. This is no argument against judicial review, but it shows that any plausible argument for it must 'distinguish between *mere* losers and minorities that lose because they cannot protect themselves in politics'.[70] So let us make this distinction and ask ourselves the following question: what is the risk of minorities being unable to protect themselves in EU politics because their interests are drowned out in the legislative process?

There is little evidence pointing to the existence of such a risk. This is partly because the legislative process is not a strictly majoritarian one. It is an inclusive process that represents a wide variety of actors with different attitudes and interests, who cannot enact legislation until they have reached a high degree of consensus. It is designed precisely to allow a wide array of preferences to be voiced and to protect more vulnerable groups from domination.[71] Moreover, legislative alliances vary, so EU legislation is 'not the product of a homogeneous majority imposing its will upon a consistent minority, but of a series of compromises brokered by winning coalitions of different minorities'.[72] In addition, fundamental rights carry considerable weight in the legislative process. The impact assessments that are conducted before legislative proposals are tabled identify the fundamental rights impact of the proposed legislation,[73] and the Fundamental Rights Agency may offer advice on the constitutional implications of legislative decisions.[74] Such advice helps the

[68] *Digital Rights Ireland* (n 59) para 56.

[69] Waldron, 'The Core of the Case against Judicial Review' (n 5) 1398.

[70] Mark V Tushnet, *Taking the Constitution Away from the Courts* (Princeton UP 1999) 159.

[71] See Chapter I.

[72] Bellamy (n 5) 241. He reached this conclusion in respect of domestic legislation; it certainly holds in respect of EU legislation.

[73] Communication from the Commission, 'Strategy for the Effective Implementation of the Charter of Fundamental Rights by the European Union' (COM(2010) 673 final). For more discussion, Mark Dawson, *The Governance of EU Fundamental Rights* (CUP 2017) 89–94.

[74] Article 4(2) of Council Regulation (EC) No 168/2007 establishing a European Union agency for Fundamental Rights (OJ L53/1).

legislative institutions fulfil their commitment to observe the fundamental rights enshrined in the Charter.[75] They tend to take the advice they receive seriously and correct each other when the rights implications of their decisions risk being neglected.[76] For these reasons, as Mark Dawson has argued, 'the very diversity of the EU's institutional system—and the need for a high level of consensus between actors—makes efforts to erode [fundamental rights] protection via EU legislation difficult'.[77]

It is also worth recalling the major contribution EU legislation makes to the promotion and protection of fundamental rights in Europe, including the rights of vulnerable minorities. The extensive anti-discrimination framework established over the past three decades provides the best illustration of the central role the legislature has played in this process.[78] In addition to setting Europe-wide anti-discrimination standards, it facilitates their application within the national legal orders by setting up public institutions at the national level that help tackle discrimination and by instituting procedures that allow victims to challenge unlawful practices.[79] Similar developments have occurred in the field of data protection law, where the legislature has assumed a central role in the development of substantive fundamental rights and the creation of a domestic infrastructure that supports their enforcement.[80] No EU institution other than the legislature can make such a contribution to the domestic enforcement of fundamental rights.

One may, of course, disagree with the choices made and chide the enacted provisions. The legislative articulation of fundamental rights may be inconsistent with our own conception of morality, and the legislature will, from time to time, disregard the concerns expressed in the impact assessments of the Commission or the recommendations it receives from the Fundamental Rights Agency.[81] It does not follow, however, that it then acts unreasonably or unjustly. Fundamental rights are not absolute and must be weighed against public interests, such as public security and public health, as well as against each other. This requires complex political choices to which there are no easy and uniquely correct answers. The legislature may then also come to a different view than other EU institutions or legal experts on what the right balance is without this being an improper or illegitimate view.

The following example clarifies this point. The right to equality is guaranteed by all national constitutions but is interpreted differently everywhere. Member States

[75] See, eg Communication from the Commission (n 74). For discussion of the European Parliament's efforts to promote fundamental rights, read Federico Camporesi, 'The European Parliament and the EU Charter of Fundamental Rights' in Giacomo Di Federico (ed), *The EU Charter of Fundamental Rights: From Declaration to Binding Instrument* (Springer 2011). More generally, Dawson, *The Governance of EU Fundamental Rights* (n 73) 87–114.

[76] Dawson, *The Governance of EU Fundamental Rights* (n 73) ch 3.

[77] ibid 87.

[78] Muir (n 66).

[79] ibid ch 5. See also Dawson, *The Governance of EU Fundamental Rights* (n 73) 121–26.

[80] For a discussion of these parallels, Muir (n 66) 136–40.

[81] For more detail, Dawson, *The Governance of EU Fundamental Rights* (n 73) 91–94 and 135–41.

have different views, for example, on the correct interaction of the right to equality and the right to religious freedom.[82] Under German and Austrian constitutional law, religious employers—be they churches, hospitals, or kindergartens—enjoy sweeping exemptions from the prohibition of discrimination,[83] offering them considerable freedom to discriminate against non-believers in employment matters. This is unthinkable in Sweden and the Netherlands, where the exemption from the prohibition of discrimination for religious employers is more narrowly drawn.[84] Such constitutional divergences can pose thorny problems for the EU. Indeed, the legislature faced the impossible task of forging a compromise out of these disparate understandings of the right to equality when it tried to enact anti-discrimination legislation.[85] The CJEU faced a similar problem when it was asked to interpret the relevant provisions.[86] Those on the losing side of these decisions may feel that they have been wronged, but that does not mean that the decisions were unreasonable—let alone tyrannical—or that the EU institutions lack the moral facilities to give concrete expression to fundamental rights.

Instead, the example shows what we already know: the articulation of fundamental rights is subject to serious yet reasonable disagreement. There is no single understanding of fundamental rights across the national legal orders, nor a single method for the resolution of the moral questions that their articulation entails. The definition of fundamental rights will then also differ across the national legal orders. These differences, as Joseph Weiler observed, 'reflect fundamental societal choices and form an important part in the different identities of polities and societies'.[87] And yet, the EU often has no choice but to form its own views on such moral questions in order to exercise its regulatory mandate. In so doing, it may try finding a middle ground between the divergent fundamental right conceptions of the Member States, but its choices will inevitably differ to a greater or lesser extent

[82] The tension that exists between these rights is discussed in Martijn van den Brink, 'When Can Religious Employers Discriminate? The Scope of the Religious Ethos Exemption in EU Law' (2022) 1 European Law Open 89.

[83] For a good overview of the state of the law in these countries, European Equality Law Network, 'Germany—Country Report on Non-Discrimination 2020' (2020) 56–62 <www.equalitylaw.eu/downloads/5226-germany-country-report-non-discrimination-2020-1-96-mb> accessed 1 March 2024 and European Equality Law Network, 'Austria—Country Report on Non-Discrimination 2020' (2020) 43–44 <www.equalitylaw.eu/downloads/5264-austria-country-report-non-discrimination-2020-1-37-mb> accessed 1 March 2024.

[84] European Equality Law Network, 'Sweden—Country Report on Non-Discrimination 2019' (2019) 51 <www.equalitylaw.eu/downloads/4973-sweden-country-report-non-discrimination-2019-pdf-1-44-mb> accessed 1 March 2024.

[85] The compromise we find in art 4(2) of Council Directive 2000/78/EC of 27 November 2000 establishing a general framework for equal treatment in employment and occupation (OJ L303/16). As a result of this compromise, this provision is 'possibly one of the most opaque to be found on any statute book': Evelyn Ellis and Philippa Watson, *EU Anti-Discrimination Law* (2nd edn, OUP 2012) 394.

[86] Case C-414/16 *Egenberger* ECLI:EU:C:2018:257; Case C-68/17 *IR v JQ* ECLI:EU:C:2018:696. For discussion, van den Brink, 'When Can Religious Employers Discriminate?' (n 82) 101.

[87] Joseph HH Weiler, 'Fundamental Rights and Fundamental Boundaries: On Standards and Values in the Protection of Human Rights' in Nanette A Neuwahl and Alan Rosas (eds), *The European Union and Human Rights* (Martinus Nijhoff 1995) 51.

from those made at the national level. This alone gives the EU good reason to settle disagreements pertaining to fundamental rights through the legislative process, namely because it involves the Member States and gives them the opportunity to express their view on how best to decide these questions. This specific reason ties in with the more general reason for doing so. The legislature provides a legitimate basis for settling moral disagreements on fundamental rights, not only because of the diversity of views it represents but also because of its proven ability to exercise moral judgment on fundamental rights.

5.2 The legitimacy of fundamental rights review

That the legislative process establishes a legitimate framework for the articulation of fundamental rights does not mean that judicial review is never justified; that is, it does not mean the CJEU is never in a better position to decide the content of fundamental rights. It is entirely consistent to think that the legislature can be trusted in the articulation of fundamental rights and can occasionally err in the decisions it takes. Both can be true: trust need not be blind. A lack of foresight, an act of omission, or an unexpected combination of circumstances—legislative choices may exceptionally violate fundamental rights despite the guardrails the legislative process provides. As I will explain, however, legislative fundamental rights articulations should be assessed with more respect than the case law currently allows.

Due to the diversity of the legislative process and the value that is attached to fundamental rights by the institutions involved, it is unlikely that the fundamental rights impact of the decisions taken is overlooked. However, if the fundamental rights implications of legislative decisions are not properly considered, the legislature is not exercising its capacity for good moral judgement on fundamental rights questions competently, in which case judicial intervention is justified. Such omissions will be rare and occur more out of negligence than malice, yet two examples show that they do happen.

The first is the *Saint Prix* judgment,[88] which concerned the status of pregnant women under art 7(3) of the Citizenship Directive. This provision provides that citizens who are no longer employed in the host state can retain the status of worker and claim social assistance in specific situations, such as when they are temporarily unable to work due to illness or when they are involuntarily unemployed after a period of prior employment.[89] The problem that arose was that the legislature had not made any provision for people who are temporarily out of work due to

[88] Case C-507/12 *Saint Prix* ECLI:EU:C:2014:2007.

[89] Article 7(3) of Directive 2004/38 of the European Parliament and of the Council of 29 April 2004 on the right of citizens of the Union and their family members to move and reside freely within the territory of the Member States (OJ L158/77).

their pregnancy, whereby it put them at risk of being without social protection at a moment of great vulnerability. That such situations were left out of the scope of art 7(3) is most likely solely because it had been overlooked that pregnant women may need to cease work due to the physical constraints of their pregnancy. Still, the omission left pregnant women in a vulnerable position, potentially breaching the principle of non-discrimination on grounds of sex as laid down in art 23 of the Charter of Fundamental Rights.[90] It did not say so in so many words,[91] but the CJEU ruled that women who must give up work 'because of the physical constraints of the late stages of pregnancy and the aftermath of childbirth retain the status of "worker"',[92] and therefore also the right to claim social protection.

The second example is the *CG* judgment.[93] The applicant arrived in Northern Ireland with her partner in 2018. She separated from him on account of domestic violence, after which she moved to a women's shelter with her two children. She never worked in the United Kingdom and had no means to support herself and her children. Her application for social assistance was refused by the local authorities because she did not meet the requirements that would make her eligible. In line with the Citizenship Directive, the CJEU ruled that economically inactive citizens cannot claim equal access to social assistance.[94] But in this case, this would have meant depriving an already isolated and impoverished parent of the means to ensure the well-being of her children,[95] thus violating her right to family life and the children's right to the necessary care for their well-being under arts 7 and 24 of the Charter of Fundamental Rights. To avoid this, the CJEU held that, for the duration of their right of residence in the territory of the host state, they must be able to live in dignified conditions that respect their family life and are in the best interests of the child.[96]

No legislative provision was declared invalid, but both judgments were contrary to what could be reasonably inferred from the legislative provisions. The fundamental rights of the citizens concerned were upheld, albeit through legislation's supplementation rather than its invalidation. To understand why this was justified, the two main objections to judicial review must be re-examined: the objections from institutional capacity and institutional legitimacy. Both normally militate for judicial deference, but of course, on the condition that the legislature acted competently and exercised good moral judgement. If fundamental rights violations result from oversight, as in *Saint Prix*, the legislature failed to act competently. If they

[90] Case C-507/12 *Saint Prix*, ECLI:EU:C:2013:841, Opinion of AG Wahl, para 35.

[91] For criticism, Samantha Currie, 'Pregnancy-Related Employment Breaks, the Gender Dynamics of Free Movement Law and Curtailed Citizenship: *Jessy Saint Prix*' (2016) 53 Common Market Law Review 543, 553–57.

[92] *Saint Prix* (n 88) para 47.

[93] Case C-209/20 *CG* ECLI:EU:C:2021:602.

[94] ibid paras 65–83.

[95] Case C-209/20 *CG*, ECLI:EU:C:2021:515, Opinion of AG Richard De La Tour, para 109.

[96] *CG* (n 93) paras 88–90.

result from rare circumstances that were almost unforeseeable when legislation was passed, as in *CN*, the legislature was in no better position to take such decisions. Reactive institutions such as courts are then at an advantage. The objection from institutional capacity is no longer valid in such situations, nor is the objection from institutional legitimacy. In the first chapter, we saw that the legitimacy of legislative decision-making is grounded in the value of non-domination. But to be non-dominating, political institutions must respect the most basic rights and liberties of their citizens.[97] If their decisions restrict fundamental rights severely to the point of domination, they are void of legitimacy. Had the CJEU not supplemented the provisions of the Citizenship Directive to ensure the fundamental rights of vulnerable mobile citizens, this might well have happened.

While the legislature violated fundamental rights seemingly inadvertently in the two cases just discussed, it restricted the right to respect for private life and the right to protection of personal data deliberately and after careful consideration when it passed the provisions that were later struck down in *Digital Rights Ireland*, *Volker und Markus*, and *WM and Sovim*, namely with a view to ensure public security, promote transparency in the use of public money, and combat money laundering and terrorist financing, respectively. Likewise, it knowingly infringed on the right to equality when it allowed insurers to take sex into account in the calculation of insurance premiums in a provision invalidated in *Test Achats*. The question is by what standards such fundamental rights restrictions must be reviewed—restrictions that are not the result of oversight or exceptional circumstances but that are intentional and motivated by a desire to protect a legitimate public interest. It cannot be readily concluded that the legislature acted incompetently: the balance that was found between the affected fundamental rights and the competing public policy goals was arrived at after careful legislative deliberation. The question, therefore, is how and when fundamental rights review should be exercised in such cases.

The clearest and most comprehensive elaboration on that question by the CJEU we find in *Digital Rights Ireland*. That the Data Retention Directive was annulled was no surprise. A revolt had arisen in domestic courts against the Directive, so the CJEU was caught between the rock of 'the primacy of EU law' and the hard place of 'mutual institutional respect'. Predictably, it chose the former.[98] But the way it reached that conclusion was unfortunate. It held that

> in view of the important role played by the protection of personal data in the light of the fundamental right to respect for private life and the extent and seriousness

[97] Philip Pettit, *Republicanism: A Theory of Freedom and Government* (OUP 1999) 180–82.

[98] Orla Lynskey, 'The Data Retention Directive Is Incompatible with the Rights to Privacy and Data Protection and Is Invalid in Its Entirety: *Digital Rights Ireland*' (2014) 51 Common Market Law Review 1789, 1799.

> of the interference with that right , , „ the EU legislature's discretion is reduced, with the result that review of that discretion should be strict.[99]

Here, we see what happens to the standard of review when the legislature's discretionary powers are reduced: fundamental rights derogations are lawful only if they are 'strictly necessary'.[100] It has since been clarified in *WM and Sovim* that this requires that 'where there is a choice between several measures appropriate to meeting the legitimate objectives pursued, recourse must be had to the least onerous'.[101]

This is the wrong standard, based on a wrong appraisal by the CJEU of its own limitations vis-à-vis those of the legislature. The complexity of the questions at issue in such cases requires a more prudent approach than it was willing to take. The issue is not simply whether lawmakers should have recourse to policies that are the least restrictive of fundamental rights. The greater problem is that it may not be clear what solution is least onerous to fundamental rights. It may not be possible to determine this in the abstract without practical knowledge of the problems a specific provision was meant to address and without a careful assessment of how a policy works in practice. This, in turn, may require an assessment of complex scientific and technical evidence and a thorough appreciation of the broader political and societal context in which a policy operates. Seeing its rulings in *Digital Rights Ireland* and *WM and Sovim*, it is very much the question of whether the CJEU has the capacity to undertake such complex assessments.

The second of these decisions proved the most controversial. *WM and Sovim* struck down the requirement in art 1(15)(c) of the Fifth Anti-Money Laundering Directive that information on the beneficial ownership of companies must be made accessible to any member of the general public.[102] This led to the closure of beneficial ownership registers across the EU, which made transparent who owned and benefited from a company and thereby aided the fight against corruption and money laundering. The requirement of full transparency was introduced precisely because the requirement in the Fourth Anti-Money Laundering Directive that such information be accessible only to those 'that can demonstrate a legitimate interest' proved ineffective.[103] Indeed, it was introduced because it was considered

[99] *Digital Rights Ireland* (n 59) para 47.

[100] ibid para 52. See, similarly, *Volker und Markus* (n 60) para 77; Case C-601/15 PPU *JN* ECLI:EU:C:2016:84, para 56; Joined cases C-511/18, C-512/18 and C-520/18, *La Quadrature du Net* ECLI:EU:C:2020:791, para 113.

[101] *WM and Sovim* (n 61) para 65. See also Case C-401/19 *Commission v Poland* ECLI:EU:C:2022:297, para 65.

[102] Directive (EU) 2018/843 of the European Parliament and of the Council of 30 May 2018 amending Directive (EU) 2015/849 on the prevention of the use of the financial system for the purposes of money laundering or terrorist financing, and amending Directives 2009/138/EC and 2013/36/EU (OJ L156/43).

[103] Directive (EU) 2018/843 of the European Parliament and of the Council 0f 20 May 2015 on the prevention of the use of the financial system for the purposes of money laundering or terrorist financing, amending Regulation (EU) No 648/2012 of the European Parliament and of the Council,

strictly necessary to prevent money laundering and corruption. The CJEU was aware of this justification but failed to thoroughly engage with it.[104] Instead, it argued that 'the fact that it may be difficult to provide a detailed definition of the circumstances and conditions under which the public may access information on beneficial ownership is no reason for the EU legislature to provide for the general public to access that information'.[105] The appreciation shown here for the reasons for allowing the public to access such information is woefully inadequate. First, the legislature may have drafted the provision in indeterminate language knowing that it could not determine *ex ante* when beneficial ownership information is needed. It thereby allowed national authorities, which may be in a better position to do so, to determine when access to beneficial ownership information must be granted. Second, it may have replaced the words 'any person or organisation that can demonstrate a legitimate public interest' with 'any member of the public' because the former created unwanted barriers to access to the information in the registers. Failing to reflect on the underlying practical challenges, the CJEU dealt a serious blow to the fight against cross-border corruption.

The difficulty of the questions at issue in *Digital Rights Ireland* was of an even greater order: how to balance the rights to privacy and data protection with the general interest of maintaining public security and preventing crime? And how to do so in an era of increasing technological progress. While the complexity of the factual assessments and value judgements needed to make these choices would normally translate into a wide legislative discretion, the discretion granted in *Digital Rights Ireland* was, as we have seen, strictly reduced; unsurprisingly, since the complexity of the issues at stake went mostly unacknowledged. The CJEU listed the manifold ways in which the Data Retention Directive restricted the rights laid down in arts 7 and 8 of the Charter and presumed this was sufficient to prove its unlawfulness.[106] The judgment reads as if the judges made an instinctive decision and then constructed a chain of reasoning to justify it, and their assessment was not combined with a sound appreciation of the aims such restrictions may serve. They were not wrong to claim that the Directive affects 'in a comprehensive manner, all persons using electronic communications services, but without the persons whose data are retained being, even indirectly, in a situation which is liable to give rise to criminal prosecutions'.[107] Nor were they mistaken in saying

and repealing Directive 2005/60/EC of the European Parliament and of the Council and Commission Directive 2006/70/EC (OJ L141/73). For analysis, Maxime Lassalle, 'Op-Ed: "Who Cares about Financial Privacy?: The Court of Justice in *WM, Sovim SA v Luxembourg Business Registers* (C-37/20 and C-601/20)"' [2022] European Law Live 3.

[104] *WM and Sovim* (n 61) paras 68–72. Contrary to Joined cases C-37/20 and C-601/20 *WM and Sovim* ECLI:EU:C:2022:43, Opinion of AG Pitruzzella, paras 172–77.

[105] *WM and Sovim* (n 61) para 72.

[106] *Digital Rights Ireland* (n 59) paras 58–65.

[107] ibid para 58.

that it applies 'to persons for whom there is no evidence capable of suggesting that their conduct might have a link, even an indirect or remote one, with serious crime'.[108] Yet, this alone is not a conclusive argument. The question is also whether such a generalised form of data retention was necessary for the fight against crime. Perhaps the information collected allows law enforcement officials to act before a criminal offence is committed or to gather the necessary evidence after its commission.[109] If that is the case, it may be necessary to cover 'in a generalised manner, all persons and all means of electronic communication'.[110] Moreover, finding the proper balance between privacy and security is not simply a matter of objective fact. It requires intractable value trade-offs that are hard to make or evaluate under a proportionality assessment. Thus, the issues at stake called for a very different assessment from that in *Digital Rights Ireland*. Rather than painting an ominous picture of the legislation under review, the CJEU should have tried to appreciate the political choices, practical challenges, and technical issues involved in combating serious crime. It is doubtful, however, how well suited it is to undertake such tasks.

By what standards must the compatibility of legislative provisions with fundamental rights then be reviewed? First, as may be uncontroversial, the European Convention on Human Rights establishes the floor of protection that all EU action must comply with. The restrictions that may be imposed on the fundamental rights recognised under EU law should not exceed those tolerated by the European Court of Human Rights (ECtHR).[111] The advantage of using the Convention as the floor of protection is threefold. The first is legal: it is consistent with the requirement under art 52(3) of the Charter that 'in so far as this Charter contains rights which correspond to rights guaranteed by the Convention for the Protection of Human Rights and Fundamental Freedoms, the meaning and scope of those rights shall be the same as those laid down by the said Convention'. Second, it adheres to the moral view defended so far that the legitimacy of political authority is conditional on respect for the most basic rights and liberties of citizens. Third, the EU would be sending the wrong message if it refused to adhere to the rights enshrined in the Convention, especially in the face of the growing backlash against the Convention.

Legislation that is consistent with this minimum level of protection should benefit from a larger margin of discretion than it does now. The strict standard that currently guides fundamental rights review is, as we have seen, inappropriate. Here too, the CJEU should take inspiration from the ECtHR, whose margin of appreciation doctrine is predicated on the belief that certain decisions are better left to

[108] ibid.
[109] Richard A Epstein, 'The ECJ's Fatal Imbalance: Its Cavalier Treatment of National Security Issues Poses Serious Risk to Public Safety and Sound Commercial Practices' (2016) 12 European Constitutional Law Review 330, 337.
[110] *Digital Rights Ireland* (n 59) para 57.
[111] See, to this effect, *Volker und Markus* (n 60) para 52.

other authorities for *democratic* and *epistemic* reasons; that is, the ECtHR usually affords a wide margin of appreciation to authorities that enjoy direct democratic legitimation and that are better placed than an international judiciary to undertake certain assessments.[112] While the CJEU is embedded in a different institutional context,[113] it has, as we saw in Chapter III, the same democratic and epistemic reasons to afford the legislature extensive discretionary powers. This conclusion also applies to legislative choices derogating from fundamental rights, especially where the underlying factual assessments were complex. When reviewing such choices, the CJEU should be mindful of the fact that the legislature has greater democratic legitimacy to articulate fundamental rights and was most likely in a better position to evaluate the complexity of the issues at stake and determine the extent to which an infringement of certain rights is necessary to realise the aims of its policies. Broad discretion thus seems more appropriate than strict scrutiny.

This does not yet settle the question of whether the annulled legislative provisions should have been struck down. Judicial review is equifinal: different standards of review can produce the same result—the intensity of judicial review should dictate the discretion afforded in a particular case, not necessarily its outcome.[114] It is safe to say, however, that the CJEU exceeded the limits of judicial power in its *WM and Sovim* ruling. The annulled provision had been carefully considered and drafted. Moreover, while the requirement of transparency of beneficial ownership information constituted a restriction on the right to privacy, the magnitude of that restriction was limited and incomparable to, for example, the restriction on that right by the Data Retention Directive struck in *Digital Rights Ireland*. Given that this provision served an eminently sensible public policy goal, it probably should have passed even strict scrutiny, let alone a more deferential standard of review.

A definite assessment of *Digital Rights Ireland* is harder to give. While the CJEU overstepped the limits of its competence there too by failing to recognise the complexity of the issues involved, it is another question whether it reached the wrong conclusion. In comparison with the provision reviewed in *WM and Sovim*, the Data Retention Directive interfered with fundamental rights more severely, while being less well drafted. Moreover, while the CJEU may not be in the best position to examine the complex and controversial decisions involved in settling the balance between the interest of public security and the right to privacy, it was clear that the Directive provided few safeguards for the proper usage of data. The Directive sought to harmonise national laws on the obligations of data providers to retain data generated or processed by them but left the procedures and conditions for

[112] See, eg Application No 43835/11, *SAS v France* 1 July 2014, para 102.

[113] As I explain in Chapter I of this book.

[114] Joined cases C-293/12 and C-594/12 *Digital Rights Ireland* ECLI:EU:C:2013:845, Opinion of AG Cruz Villalón, para 96. See also Paul Craig, 'Judicial Review and Judicial Deference' in Miroslava Scholten and AFM Brenninkmeijer (eds), *Controlling EU Agencies: The Rule of Law in a Multi-Jurisdictional Legal Order* (Edward Elgar 2020) 100.

access to that data almost entirely up to the Member States.[115] That the CJEU found that the legislature exceeded the limits of its authority by establishing common requirements for data retention without also providing common standards for access to, and use of, the retained data can arguably be justified. The CJEU went further, of course, in condemning the legislative framework, but had it limited its review to the mismatch between the extensive requirements on data retention and the minimal safeguards on data usage, the annulment of the Directive would not have impaired the legislature's prerogative to strike a balance between public security and the right to privacy. The legislature would then have been free to elaborate a similar regime on the condition that it also laid down conditions for data usage.

The CJEU acted more appropriately in *Volker und Markus* when it ruled the publication of information on the beneficiaries of agricultural funds to be unlawful. Publishing such information was not impermissible per se. Instead, the provision requiring publication was invalidated for lack of a substantial connection between the end of guaranteeing transparency in the use of EU funding and the kind of information published on its beneficiaries.[116] Thus, the legislature was left free to introduce another provision requiring the publication of information on the beneficiaries of EU funds, but on the condition that this provision establishes a rational connection between the ends pursued and the means employed.[117] When it took this liberty, the legislature said the same:

> The Court did not contest the legitimacy of the objective of reinforcing public control of the use of the money from the Funds. However, the Court did emphasise the need to consider methods of publishing information relating to the beneficiaries concerned which are consistent with the objective of such publication.[118]

This is more appropriate judicial behaviour than that seen in the *Digital Rights Ireland* and *WM and Sovim* verdicts. It accepted that the legislature is the proper institution to make public policy choices that involve fundamental rights, provided that the imposed restrictions on such rights are properly related to the objectives that are pursued. Of course, this assessment was facilitated by the fact that *Volker und Markus* was an easy case compared to *WM and Sovim* and *Digital Rights Ireland*, which made assessing whether a rational connection exists between

[115] As was set out clearly in *Digital Rights Ireland* (n 59) paras 58–65.

[116] *Volker und Markus* (n 60) paras 81–83. The CJEU seemingly followed AG Sharpston in her conclusion that there was no rational connection between the objectives pursued and the way information was published: Joined cases C-92/09 and C-93/09 *Volker und Markus* ECLI:EU:C:2010:353, Opinion of AG Sharpston, paras 114–17.

[117] Michal Bobek, 'Joined cases C-92 & 93/09, *Volker und Markus Schecke GbR and Hartmut Eifert*, Judgment of the Court of Justice (Grand Chamber) of 9 November 2010' (2011) 48 Common Market Law Review 2005.

[118] Recital 73 of Regulation (EU) No 1306/2013 of the European Parliament and of the Council of 17 December 2013 on the financing, management and monitoring of the common agricultural (OJ L347/549).

the means chosen for the objectives pursued easier. Where the underlying empirical and factual assessments are more difficult to undertake, the legislature must enjoy wider discretionary powers as regards the means it chooses for the objectives it pursues. Strict review is, in any case, the wrong standard to apply in fundamental rights review of legislation.

6. Appreciating Legislation

The aim of my entire argument so far has been to determine how much appreciation there should be for the legislature, both in general and in specific areas of EU law. Another way to clarify this is through comparative institutional analysis. By comparing the position of the EU judiciary vis-à-vis the EU legislature with the position it holds versus national legislatures or EU executive actors, we can better understand the unique position the EU legislature occupies in the EU's institutional landscape. The CJEU has been vested with the power to review the decisions of all these actors, but it does not necessarily subject them to the same intensity of scrutiny. It is well known that EU legislation is subject to less rigorous review than national legislation. Most commentators accept this discrepancy, and I concur with their assessment. I will also argue, however, that the standards of review applicable to different EU institutions may have to vary depending on the institution in question. The EU legislature should enjoy wider discretionary powers than the EU executive, just as it enjoys a larger discretion than national legislatures.

Formally, the structure of the review of EU and national measures is very similar. As far as their proportionality goes, it is examined whether they serve a *legitimate interest* and whether the adopted rules are *suitable* and *necessary* to secure that interest. Yet, the review of national legislation is generally more intrusive in practice. The assessment of EU legislation is often preceded by the observation that the legislature must be given broad discretionary powers, especially because its choices rest on complex political, economic, or technical calculations. While the choices underlying national legislation can be equally complex, national legislatures are given a considerably narrower discretion.[119] Some have taken issue with this discrepancy. Norbert Reich, for instance, has queried why 'broad discretion'

[119] Although there are areas where the CJEU has left them a considerable discretion. One such areas is the regulation of games of chance. See, eg Case C-156/13 *Digibet* ECLI:EU:C:2014:1756, para 24; Case C-42/07 *Liga Portuguesa de Futebol Profissional* ECLI:EU:C:2009:519, para 57; Joined cases C-186/11 and C-209/11 *Stanleybet International* ECLI:EU:C:2013:33, para 24. See, for discussion, Daniel Thym, 'The Constitutional Dimension of Public Policy Justifications' in Panos Koutrakos, Niamh Nic Shuibhne, and Phil Syrpis (eds), *Exceptions from EU Free Movement Law: Derogation, Justification and Proportionality* (Hart Publishing 2016). More generally, Jan Zglinski, *Europe's Passive Virtues: Deference to National Authorities in EU Free Movement Law* (OUP 2020).

isn't 'also applied to Member state legislation in areas where it involves complex (and controversial!) choices'.[120]

However, there is a straightforward justification for affording the EU legislature a wider discretion than national actors. As Ní Chaoimh explains, the justification 'lies in the substantive differences between EU and national legislators, in terms of the interests they represent and their position in the Treaty'.[121] National authorities are likely to pursue narrow national interests and aspirations and as such may 'exert a protectionist effect between Member States'.[122] In contrast, EU legislation reflects the interests of all Member States and can therefore substitute motivations of political and economic nationalism for substantive European policies. How broad the discretion of national legislatures should be might depend on a variety of factors, but all things being equal, their discretion must be more narrowly drawn than that of the EU legislature. It should be especially narrowly construed in areas that are subject to harmonising legislation.[123] The national legislature simply occupies a different political position from the EU legislature and it would therefore be inappropriate to apply the same standards to them.[124]

By comparison, the EU legislature and executive actors occupy a more similar, namely European, political context. It could be inferred that EU institutions should be reviewed according to similar standards. This might be the CJEU's thinking. Its case law may not espouse a coherent vision of judicial review,[125] but it eschews an explicit distinction between different EU institutions in the applicable standards of review.[126] Instead, it has transposed these standards directly between institutional contexts, which is to say that the choice of standards in one context is often justified

[120] Norbert Reich, 'How Proportionate Is the Proportionality Principle? Some Critical Remarks on the Use and Methodology of the Proportionality Principle in the Internal Market Case Law of the ECJ' in Hans-W Micklitz and Bruno de Witte (eds), *The European Court of Justice and the Autonomy of the Member States* (Intersentia 2012).

[121] Ní Chaoimh (n 3) 92.

[122] Stephen Weatherill, 'Justification, Proportionality and Consumer Protection' in Koutrakos, Nic Shuibhne, and Syrpis (n 118) 258.

[123] Or, vice versa, leave Member States a margin of discretion in the absence of harmonisation. See, eg Case C-446/08 *Solgar Vitamin's France* ECLI:EU:C:2010:233, para 35; Case C-333/08 *Commission v France* ECLI:EU:C:2010:44, para 85; Case C-496/01 *Commission v France* ECLI:EU:C:2004:137, para 55; Case C-345/09 *van Delft* ECLI:EU:C:2010:610, para 84; Case C-922/19 *Stichting Waternet* ECLI:EU:C:2021:91, para 45.

[124] Jukka Snell, 'Economic Justifications and the Role of the State' in Koutrakos, Nic Shuibhne, and Syrpis (n 118) 25–26.

[125] The inconsistencies observed in sections 4 and 5 exist just as much in regard to the judicial review of executive measures: Marta Morvillo and Maria Weimer, 'Who Shapes the CJEU Regulatory Jurisprudence? On the Epistemic Power of Economic Actors and Ways to Counter It' (2022) 1 European Law Open 510, 537.

[126] See, eg Case C-425/08 *Enviro Tech (Europe)* ECLI:EU:C:2009:635, para 47; Case T-70/99 *Alpharma Inc* ECLI:EU:T:2002:210, paras 177–80. For more general discussion, Jürgen Bast, 'Is There a Hierarchy of Legislative, Delegated, and Implementing Acts?' in Carl Fredrik Bergström and Dominique Ritleng (eds), *Rulemaking by the European Commission: The New System for Delegation of Powers* (OUP 2016).

by reference to another context.[127] The apparent result is that the executive seemingly enjoys a similar discretion to the legislature. A good example of this institutional crossover of standards can be found in the review of the European Central Bank's (ECB) monetary decisions. In *Gauweiler* and *Weiss*, the CJEU ruled that 'since the ESCB [European System of Central Banks] is required . . . to make choices of a technical nature and to undertake forecasts and complex assessments, it must be allowed, in that context, a broad discretion'.[128] Therefore, the standard of review was whether the ESCB had made 'a manifest error of assessment'.[129] This was a literal transplant from the legislative to the executive domain, justified by reference to the standards of review of legislative measures.[130] Similarly, the requirement that fundamental rights derogations are permissible only when strictly necessary was transferred directly from the executive to the legislative context.[131] Indeed, EU institutions are often reviewed indiscriminately, without regard to their different political functions.

This makes sense to the extent that the legislature is not the only institution that must make difficult choices in the political decisions it takes. As the monetary measures reviewed in *Gauweiler* and *Weiss* illustrate, the executive is often also required to do so. The CJEU understandably regards these as lying outside the scope of its expertise, knowing that it lacks the capacity to second-guess executive decisions that require considerable scientific and technical know-how.[132] Its practice of giving EU institutions a wide margin of discretion in such situations and limiting its review to 'the manifest error of assessment test' shows its recognition of the fact that other institutions may be better placed to make such choices.[133] Therefore, to the extent that the complexity of the subject matter is the only factor determining the margin of discretion, the CJEU may occupy the same position towards the executive as it does towards the legislature and be justified in applying the same standard of review to both.

However, the position of the executive and legislature is incomparable in another respect. The executive may be able to justify the authority it exercises on account of its expertise, but its decisions lack democratic legitimation (unless derived from the legislative process). The legislature has the resources to make complex

[127] Stefania Baroncelli and Annelieke AM Mooij, 'What Kind of Judicial Review for the European Central Bank?: All Institutions Are Equal But Some Are More Technical Than Others' (2022) 29 Maastricht Journal of European and Comparative Law 413, 415.

[128] Case C-62/14 *Gauweiler* ECLI:EU:C:2015:400, para 68; Case C-493/17 *Weiss* ECLI:EU:C:2018:1000, para 73.

[129] *Gauweiler* (n 127) para 74; *Weiss* (n 127) para 78.

[130] Such as the reference in *Gauweiler* (n 127) para 68 to Case C-343/09 *Afton Chemical Limited* ECLI:EU:C:2010:419, para 28 and Case C-203/12 *Billerud Karlsborg* ECLI:EU:C:2013:664, para 35.

[131] *Volker und Markus* (n 60) para 77.

[132] Mark Dawson, Adina Maricut-Akbik, and Ana Bobić, 'Reconciling Independence and Accountability at the European Central Bank: The False Promise of Proceduralism' (2017) 23 European Law Journal 118.

[133] For a detailed analysis, Morvillo and Weimer (n 124) 521–25.

decisions but, in addition, derives democratic legitimacy directly from the legislative process. Without this notion, the value of legislative decision-making, both in absolute terms and relative to other EU institutions, cannot be adequately appreciated. It provides an additional, democratic justification for legislative discretion in matters of EU law.[134] That this notion is absent from the case law is surprising and suggests that the CJEU's appreciation for the legislature is incomplete.[135]

How should this translate in practice? A first implication is that the intensity of the review of executive measures may legitimately vary depending on whether the legislature has delegated discretion to the executive in the application of EU law. The CJEU should not substitute its own assessment of the desired discretion of the executive for that of the legislature.[136] This entails a positive and a negative obligation. On the positive side, the CJEU must strike down executive decisions that violate the limits delegated to the executive by the legislature, such as the limits of the powers delegated to the Commission under art 290(1) of the TFEU. According to this provision, 'a legislative act may delegate to the Commission the power to adopt non-legislative acts of general application to supplement or amend certain non-essential elements of the legislative act'. Thus, when reviewing the exercise of delegated powers, it must be ascertained

> whether the EU authorities have exceeded the powers conferred on them by the enabling act, bearing in mind in particular that such a delegated power must in any event comply with the essential elements of the enabling act and come within the regulatory framework as defined by the basic legislative act.[137]

The negative obligation is that the CJEU must not, in principle, limit the Commission's discretion below what the delegating act stipulates. This does not mean that scrutiny of the exercise of its discretion is impermissible. It may be checked that discretionary powers are not exercised arbitrarily or in a way incompatible with accepted principles of EU law.[138] In principle, however, the Commission must retain the freedom delegated to it by the legislature. This means that the review of such delegated powers should not be too incisive. In this spirit, the CJEU set aside the *Alrosa* verdict of the Court of First Instance (CFI) on the

[134] Chapters II and III discuss this justification extensively.

[135] A distinction is sometimes made between 'political' and 'technical' discretion, but this distinction is unrelated to that between executive and legislative power. For critical discussion, Joana Mendes, 'Bounded Discretion in EU Law: A Limited Judicial Paradigm in a Changing EU: Bounded Discretion in EU Law' (2017) 80 Modern Law Review 443.

[136] For a more extensive discussion of this issue, Miro Prek and Silvère Lefèvre, 'Administrative Discretion, Power of Appraisal and Margin of Appraisal in Judicial Review Proceedings before the General Court' (2019) 56 Common Market Law Review 339, 366–68.

[137] Case C-44/16 P *Dyson* ECLI:EU:C:2017:357, para 53. See also Case C-427/12 *Commission v Parliament and Council* EU:C:2014:170, para 38; Case C-286/14 *Parliament v Commission* EU:C:2016:183, para 30.

[138] Prek and Lefèvre (n 135) 365–66.

ground that it construed the powers delegated to the Commission for the implementation of competition rules more narrowly than the delegating act provided.[139] It ruled that the CFI had wrongly 'substituted its own assessment for that of the Commission, thereby encroaching on the discretion enjoyed by the Commission instead of reviewing the lawfulness of its assessment'.[140]

Another more important implication is that the CJEU should not necessarily subject all EU institutions to the same level of scrutiny. According to Advocate General Emiliou, an implicit distinction is already made between legislative and executive institutions in terms of the standards of review applied to them.[141] The standards can be phrased in very similar terms ('manifestly inappropriate' for legislative review versus 'manifest error' for executive review), but the first test sets the bar higher for applicants than the second.[142] His claim may find support in the fact that a review of executive measures is usually accompanied by 'a more searching review of both the scientific evidence and the administrative reasoning'.[143] When reviewing legislation, on the other hand, the CJEU is known to draw on 'the evidence of those directly and partially implicated in the adoption of the measure in the first place—the Commission, the Council and States who had voted in favour of the measure in Council'.[144] The fact that applicants might face a more uphill battle to challenge legislative than executive measures is justified by the fact that different courses of action are usually open to the legislature, with the choice for one over the other alternative depending not only on an assessment of scientific evidence but also on a range of more fundamental political and moral choices. In contrast, the exercise of delegated powers often relies more on technical assessments. These may be complex, but it can at least be expected that the Commission's assessments have a solid scientific basis.[145] In any case, if legislation is implicitly already subject to lower scrutiny than executive power, this is justified by the democratic legitimacy of legislation.

7. Primary Law in Legislative Interpretation

Several aspects of the argument developed so far have implications for the role primary law should play in legislative interpretation. In Chapter III, I argued that the EU judiciary should, in all but exceptional situations, yield to the choices of the legislature even if these differ from its own. In these situations, it should not invoke

[139] Case T-170/06 *Alrosa* ECLI:EU:T:2007:220.
[140] Case C-441/07 P *Alrosa* ECLI:EU:C:2010:377, para 67. See further, Prek and Lefèvre (n 135) 368.
[141] Case C-389/21 P *European Central Bank v Crédit Lyonnais* ECLI:EU:C:2022:844, Opinion of AG Emiliou, para 64 and references.
[142] ibid fn 56.
[143] Morvillo and Weimer (n 124) 523.
[144] Weatherill, 'The Limits of Legislative Harmonization' (n 31) 840.
[145] Opinion of AG Emiliou (n 140) para 66.

primary law to contradict legislative intent. I explained that this view is consistent with the hierarchy of norms between EU primary and secondary law. It is consistent with this hierarchy, that is to allow the legislature to legislate Treaty rights. But what about the role of primary law in legislative interpretation more generally? It is settled case law that EU measures 'must be interpreted, as far as possible, in such a way as not to affect its validity and in conformity with primary law as a whole'.[146] Do I call into question this principle? Not in essence, as I shall explain, but it depends on how it is understood and applied.

One might intuitively think that the most intellectually coherent approach on this issue is an all-or-nothing approach, that is that either primary law must not be relied on at all in legislative interpretation or that all principles of primary law relevant to a dispute must be applied. In this view, the CJEU would be acting selectively, and perhaps even disingenuously, if it relied on some, but not all, principles of primary law. However, taking the example of the 'headscarf judgments',[147] I will explain why this view is both incorrect and impractical. The application of primary law in legislative interpretation is not always problematic, and the challenge is to distinguish problematic from unproblematic forms of this interpretative practice.

The headscarf judgments narrowly construed the prohibition of religious discrimination in relation to headscarf bans at work.[148] In *Achbita*, the most controversial of these rulings, the CJEU held that a company policy banning the manifestation of religious, philosophical, or political beliefs at work was compatible with the Equal Treatment Framework Directive (Framework Directive).[149] Such policies, while worded in neutral terms, are particularly detrimental to women wearing the Islamic headscarf; they may even be adopted with a view to accommodating the Islamophobic prejudices of customers.[150] And yet, while tolerating such policies would 'defeat the very purpose of discrimination law',[151]

[146] Joined cases C-391/16, C-77/17 and C-78/17 *M* ECLI:EU:C:2019:403, para 77; Case C-601/15 PPU *JN* ECLI:EU:C:2016:84, para 48; Case C-12/11 *McDonagh* ECLI:EU:C:2013:43, para 44.

[147] Case C-157/15 *Achbita* ECLI:EU:C:2017:203; Case C-188/15 *Bougnaoui* ECLI:EU:C:2017:204; Joined cases C-804/18 and Case C-341/19 *IX v Wabe and MH Müller Handels* ECLI:EU:C:2021:594; Case C-344/20 *LF v SCRL* ECLI:EU:C:2022:774. For analysis of these judgments, Martijn van den Brink, 'The Protected Grounds of Religion and Belief: Lessons for EU Non-Discrimination Law' (2023) 24 German Law Journal 855.

[148] For criticism, JHH Weiler, 'Je Suis Achbita!' (2017) 15 International Journal of Constitutional Law 879; Stéphanie Hennette-Vauchez, 'Equality and the Market: The Unhappy Fate of Religious Discrimination in Europe' (2017) 13 European Constitutional Law Review 744; Erica Howard, 'Islamic Headscarves and the CJEU: *Achbita* and *Bougnaoui*' (2017) 24 Maastricht Journal of European and Comparative Law 348; Aqilah Sandhu, 'Das EU-Antidiskriminierungsrecht zwischen ökonomischer und sozialer Integration: Zu den Grenzen unternehmerischer Freiheit—Anmerkung zu EuGH, Rs. C-188/15 (Bougnaoui) und C-157/15 (Achbita)' (2017) 50 Kritische Justiz 517.

[149] Directive 2000/78/EC (n 85).

[150] Case C-188/15 *Bougnaoui* ECLI:EU:C:2016:553, Opinion of AG Sharpston, para 133. See also Lucy Vickers, '*Achbita* and *Bougnaoui*: One Step Forward and Two Steps Back for Religious Diversity in the Workplace' (2017) 8 European Labour Law Journal 232, 251; Sandhu (n 148) 527.

[151] Elke Cloots, 'Safe Harbour or Open Sea for Corporate Headscarf Bans? *Achbita* and *Bougnaoui*' (2018) 55 Common Market Law Review 589, 613–14.

the CJEU held that they could be justified under the freedom to conduct a business employers enjoy in accordance with art 16 of the Charter of Fundamental Rights.[152] By interpreting the provisions of the Framework Directive in the light of primary law, specifically the freedom to conduct a business, it prejudiced the protection the Directive seeks to provide to vulnerable religious groups.[153]

In an apparent attempt to rectify this wrong, the Commission argued, in its submissions in the follow-up *IX v Wabe* case, for a more selective application of primary law: that the Framework Directive should be interpreted in light of the prohibition on discrimination laid down in art 21 of the Charter but not in accordance with the freedom to conduct a business in art 16 or any other Charter provision.[154] This argument was dismissed by Advocate General Sharpston, who regarded it as 'misconceived and intellectually flawed'.[155] She countered that the full scope of the prohibition of religious discrimination cannot be determined by looking at art 21 of the Charter alone. To 'define what "religion or belief" means',[156] account must also be taken of art 10 of the Charter on the right to religious freedom and of the interpretation of this right by the European Court of Human Rights.[157] More generally, she opined that the CJEU should take 'all relevant rights under the Charter into account'.[158]

While her criticism of the Commission's approach is compelling, her own approach is not. A first problem is that disagreement can arise about what principles of primary law must be taken into consideration in the resolution of a particular dispute. The headscarf cases attest to this. Advocate General Sharpston limited her analysis to the right to non-discrimination (art 21), the right to religious freedom (art 10), and the freedom to conduct a business (art 16), which she believed had to be subject to a careful balancing exercise.[159] Others, however, will add that the right to education in art 14 of the Charter should also be taken into account, as the case concerned the principle of religious neutrality at school.[160] And perhaps there is also a relation to the freedom of expression or the right to engage in work in arts 11 and 15 of the Charter. So there is an uncertain number of relevant Charter rights, all of which must be weighed in a structured but ultimately open-ended

[152] *Achbita* (n 147) para 38. The CJEU's review became stricter in subsequent cases, probably in response to the criticism it received: *IX v Wabe* and *MH Müller Handels* (n 147) para 83; *LF v SCRL* (n 147) para 51.

[153] *Achbita* (n 147) para 38.

[154] *IX v Wabe* and *MH Müller Handels* (n 147).

[155] Joined cases C-804/18 and Case C-341/19 *IX v Wabe and MH Müller Handels* ECLI:EU:C:2021:594, Shadow Opinion of former AG Sharpston: headscarves at work, para 63 <http://eulawanalysis.blogspot.com/2021/03/shadow-opinion-of-former-advocate.html> accessed 1 March 2024.

[156] ibid para 65.

[157] ibid para 73.

[158] ibid para 76.

[159] ibid.

[160] *IX v Wabe* and *MH Müller Handels* (n 147) para 65.

balancing exercise that can go both ways: the side of the employer who seeks to protect its business interest or the side of the employees who were discriminated against.

Therefore, another more serious problem with weighing all relevant provisions of primary law in the interpretation of legislation is that it would create significant uncertainty for the parties involved. One could argue that the CJEU is, like other supranational courts, well equipped to carry out such a balancing exercise, but this ignores that the legislature already struck a balance between competing rights and interests when it enacted the Framework Directive and that it is the CJEU's task to interpret the legislature's choices in cases such as the headscarf judgments.[161] It would, for the reasons given in Chapter III, be improper for the CJEU to revisit this task and strike a different balance from the one the legislature intended. Of course, discrimination disputes may call on it to balance competing rights and interests within the confines of the Framework Directive, especially under the open-ended justification for indirect discrimination,[162] but the Directive constrains the CJEU more than the approach advocated by Advocate General Sharpston. The Directive gives 'specific expression' to the general prohibition of discrimination,[163] not to employers' freedom to conduct a business.[164] Thus, the main problem with weighing all relevant principles of primary law is that it may allow the CJEU to revisit the legislature's choices, which it apparently did in the headscarf judgments by giving so much weight to the freedom to conduct a business.

However, while her own preferred approach is flawed, Advocate General Sharpston rightly rejected the Commission's position that only the prohibition of discrimination in art 21 of the Charter was to be applied. It would, indeed, be odd to ignore the right to religious freedom and the relevant case law interpreting concepts such as religion and belief in religious discrimination disputes;[165] that is, it would be strange not to consider, and possibly apply, art 10 of the Charter. But if this is so, we seemingly face a dilemma. It might be sensible to take some Charter rights into account but improper to apply all fundamental rights pertaining to a dispute. Is this inconsistent? If not, how do we solve this conundrum?

[161] Council Directive 2000/78/EC of 27 November 2000 establishing a general framework for equal treatment in employment and occupation (OJ L303/16).

[162] There is no indirect discrimination when a provision or practice is 'objectively justified by a legitimate aim and the means of achieving that aim are appropriate and necessary': art 2(2)(b)(i) of the Framework Directive.

[163] Case C-507/18 *NH* ECLI:EU:C:2020:289, para 38; *Egenberger* (n 86) para 47.

[164] Shadow Opinion of former AG Sharpston (n 155) para 76. Sharpston was evidently aware of this and highly critical of the CJEU's use of the freedom to conduct a business. It is not the case, indeed, that her approach necessarily leads to the outcome the CJEU reached in the headscarf cases, but it does not protect against it either.

[165] Even though the meaning of 'religion or belief' may be different under the right to religious freedom than under the right to be free from religious discrimination, as both rights pursue different objectives: Tarunabh Khaitan and Jane Calderwood Norton, 'The Right to Freedom of Religion and the Right against Religious Discrimination: Theoretical Distinctions' (2019) 17 International Journal of Constitutional Law 1125.

The solution is to recognise that provisions of primary law may stand in different relations to different legislative acts, some in a more harmonious relation and others in a more antagonistic one. If the proper judicial task is to ascertain and act upon the intention in a legislative act, as my argument for judicial deference suggests, it would be improper for the CJEU to subject all relevant Charter rights to a balancing exercise—a task already performed by the legislature, after all. As a matter of principle, the judiciary should thus exercise restraint in applying primary law in legislative interpretation. But this is not to say that primary law should not be invoked at all. Advocate General Sharpston was right that the Equal Treatment Framework Directive does not define how 'religion' and 'belief' must be understood, that is which personal beliefs are covered by the prohibition of discrimination on grounds of religion and belief. To clarify this, it may, indeed, be appropriate to consider how these concepts have been understood in, for example, ECtHR religious freedom cases. This would be a reasonable way of settling this question *because it is consistent with legislative intent.* Having regard to other fundamental rights—such as the freedom to conduct a business—may not be. In other words, the fact that it may sometimes be appropriate to have regard to principles of primary law does not mean that all such principles must always be considered in legislative interpretation. The assumption that if one fundamental right is considered, other relevant fundamental rights must be as well is the crucial fallacy on which Sharpston's argument is built.

This point is true in general and relevant beyond the headscarf cases. It is settled case law that legislative interpretation 'must be undertaken in the light of the fundamental rights guaranteed by the Charter'.[166] Similarly, it is well established that 'if the wording of secondary ... law is open to more than one interpretation, preference should be given to the interpretation which renders the provision consistent with the ... Treaty rather than to the interpretation which leads it to being incompatible with the Treaty'.[167] These principles are not inherently inconsistent with the respect that is due to legislative acts. For example, when legislation lends itself to two or more different interpretations, the most reasonable interpretation may be that which is compatible with prevailing interpretations of primary law. However, there is a crucial difference between invoking principles of primary law to justify a result that is a reasonable inference of legislative intent and invoking such principles when they compromise the intended effects of legislation. The former is justified since it treats legislation as worthy of respect, while the latter does not. In other words, it is not necessarily objectionable to rely on primary law in legislative interpretation; it is problematic only when it prejudices legislative intent.

[166] Case C-311/18 *Data Protection Commissioner* ECLI:EU:C:2020:559, para 99.

[167] Case C-305/05 *Ordre des barreaux francophones et germanophone* ECLI:EU:C:2007:383, para 28; Case C-135/93 *Spain v Commission* ECLI:EU:C:1995:201, para 37; Case C-90/92 *Dr Tretter GmbH ECLI:EU:C:1993:264*, para 11.

8. Legislated Treaty Rights

The picture I have painted of the legislature is quite different from the one that has emerged in the course of the past decades. We have become accustomed to claims that the legislature would act 'in the shadows' or be an 'agent' of the judiciary.[168] Judicial constraints on the legislative process would be so tight 'that the legislature is more akin to a subordinate implementing regulator than to an autonomous political policy-maker'.[169] In contrast, my analysis reveals that these constraints are often incredibly loose. The CJEU is a very deferential court that normally refuses to substitute the legislature's choices for its own. Instead, it permits the legislature to 'bring about'[170] or give 'specific expression'[171] and 'concrete form'[172] to the Treaties, and it usually adjudicates disputes solely in the light of provisions of legislation where the issue before it is 'regulated in a harmonised manner at EU level'.[173] The picture that has emerged, therefore, is one of Treaty rights as partially being legislated rights.

The obvious response from those who remain unconvinced by this conclusion would be to reply that the passing of legislation often involves little more than the codification of case law.[174] If this were true, the exercise of judicial deference would only mean that the CJEU defers to its own principles as consolidated by legislation. We saw in section II.5 that this argument is supported by empirical evidence and that sound theoretical reasons exist to believe that it is plausible. First, the Treaties effectively operate as the EU's constitution, which is why the CJEU is deemed to hold 'an effective monopoly . . . in the substantive interpretation of European law'.[175] It would follow that judicial rulings just as much bind the EU legislature as they do national governments so that the only way to revoke case law would be to amend the Treaties. Second, case law could change 'the bargaining constellation' between legislative actors,[176] who need to legislate on a

[168] Susanne K Schmidt, *The European Court of Justice and the Policy Process: The Shadow of Case Law* (OUP 2018); Gareth Davies, 'The European Union Legislature as an Agent of the European Court of Justice: EU Legislature as an Agent of the ECJ' (2016) 54 Journal of Common Market Studies 846.

[169] Davies, 'The European Union Legislature as an Agent of the European Court of Justice' (n 166) abstract.

[170] Case C-346/06 *Rüffert* ECLI:EU:C:2008:189, para 36.

[171] Case C-333/13 *Dano* ECLI:EU:C:2014:2358; para 61; *CG* (n 93) para 66; *NH* (n 163) para 38; *Egenberger* (n 86) para 47.

[172] Joined cases C-704/20 and C-39/21 *Staatssecretaris van Justitie en Veiligheid v C and B* ECLI:EU:C:2022:858, para 83; Joined cases C-924/19 PPU and C-925/19 PPU *FMS* ECLI:EU:C:2020:367, paras 192 and 289.

[173] Case C-257/06 *Roby Profumi* EU:C:2008:35, para 14; Case C-324/99 *DaimlerChrysler* EU:C:2001:682, para 32, Case C-309/02 *Radlberger Getränkegesellschaft and S Spitz* 2004 I-11763, para 53; Case C-91/18 *Commission v Greece* ECLI:EU:C:2019:600, para 44.

[174] See section II.5.

[175] Fritz Wilhelm Scharpf, *Governing in Europe: Effective and Democratic?* (OUP 1999) 55. Similarly, Dieter Grimm, *The Constitution of European Democracy* (OUP 2017) 31–32.

[176] Fritz W Scharpf, 'The Asymmetry of European Integration, or Why the EU Cannot Be a "Social Market Economy"' (2010) 8 Socio-Economic Review 211, 224. See also Sacha Garben, 'The

canvas partly filled with judicial precedent. So even if case law can be overridden by legislation, those with a different view from the CJEU must fight an uphill battle to enshrine their preferences in EU law: national governments must find a qualified majority to pass their preferences, while those with preferences aligning with CJEU jurisprudence only need to find a blocking minority to prevent case law from being overruled. This, it is believed, degenerates the legislature into an impotent appendage of the judiciary.

This view has been voiced by leading scholars of EU law and governance. For example, assuming that interpretations of primary law can only be corrected by means of Treaty revision and that overruling interpretations of secondary law is hindered by the veto points in the legislative process, Fritz Scharpf reached the following conclusion:

> Given the ever-increasing diversity of national interests and preferences, such corrections were and are in theory improbable and in practice nearly impossible. In other words, ECJ interpretations of European law are much more immune to attempts at political correction than is true of judicial legislation at the national level.[177]

In the same vein, Gareth Davies, expressing even greater pessimism about the legislature's ability to shape the trajectory of EU law, argued that

> There has been little attempt to autonomously steer the course of integration, at least of economic integration. Market-building legislation from the EU is overwhelmingly an implementation of an agenda which is little more than the extrapolation of a few key judgments. Serious thought about what a market should be, and indeed what a union of peoples should be, beyond the banalities of ever more, ever closer, ever freer, has not emerged from the EU legislative institutions.[178]

They are but two voices in what has become a large chorus lamenting that political override of judicial decisions is near impossible.[179]

Constitutional (Im)Balance between "the Market" and "the Social" in the European Union' (2017) 13 European Constitutional Law Review 23, 42.

[177] Scharpf, 'The Asymmetry of European Integration' (n 174) 217.

[178] Gareth Davies, 'Legislative Control of the European Court of Justice' (2014) 51 Common Market Law Review 1579, 1606–607.

[179] See, eg Schmidt, *The European Court of Justice and the Policy Process* (n 166); Garben (n 174); Grimm (n 173).

And yet, while there is some evidence that supports these arguments, their empirical and conceptual foundations are shakier than is often believed. For a start, we can dispel the notion that the EU judiciary has a monopoly over the interpretation of EU law. Far from it: as we have seen, the legislature has wide discretionary powers to articulate the meaning of primary law. In addition, there is not nearly enough case law to support the full range of legislation that has emerged in the past decades. If we shift our focus beyond the internal market to other areas of EU law, case law and legislation most likely interact according to dynamics that are favourable to the legislature.[180] But even within the internal market, the area on which most observations concerning a law–politics imbalance in EU law are based, there has always been ample room for autonomous legislative intervention.[181] In the past decades, the legislative acquis governing the internal market has steadily increased; it has quadrupled in the period from the Treaty of Maastricht until now.[182] This is not because the legislature has wished to systematise existing case law. Many of these acts cover policy areas in relation to which there was little case law, which made it possible to legislate on a mostly empty canvas.

Finally, as I explain now in more detail, even when regulating areas that are saturated with case law, the legislature often has the means to successfully navigate and negotiate judicial interpretations of EU law. I will illustrate this by reference to two unlikely cases: the principle of mutual recognition (section IV.8.1) and the '*Laval* quartet' (section IV.8.2). This discussion reinforces my argument that Treaty rights are, in large part, legislated rights. The CJEU enjoys no monopoly over the interpretation of EU law, and the legislature has been able to push back against and override case law, including some of the main doctrines and judgments shaping the internal market. These lessons will be used to assess the desirability of two sets of proposals that have been put forward to strengthen the authority of the legislature (or, conversely, weaken that of the CJEU) over EU law. Once we understand how much influence the legislature can exercise over the course and content of EU law, we can see that there is no need for radical legal or institutional reform. It is time to abandon this (German)[183] notion that EU law needs to be deconstitutionalised. Simpler institutional reforms will do to address any remaining imbalances between the legislature and judiciary (section IV.8.3).

[180] Martijn van den Brink, Mark Dawson, and Jan Zglinski, 'Revisiting the Asymmetry Thesis: Negative and Positive Integration in the EU' (2023) Journal of European Public Policy 1.

[181] Mark Dawson, 'Re-Visiting Europe's "Law–Politics Imbalance"' in Mark Dawson, Elise Muir, and Bruno de Witte (eds), *Revisiting Judicial Politics in the European Union* (Edward Elgar 2023).

[182] Jan Zglinski, 'The End of Negative Market Integration: 60 Years of Free Movement of Goods Litigation in the EU (1961–2020)' [2023] Journal of European Public Policy 1.

[183] For the claim that this has been a very German debate, Martin Höpner and Susanne K Schmidt, 'Can We Make the European Fundamental Freedoms Less Constraining? A Literature Review' (2020) 22 Cambridge Yearbook of European Legal Studies 182, 196.

8.1 Mutual recognition

To see that the constitutionalisation of EU law does not necessarily remove important legal and political issues from the reach of the legislative process, let us examine an unlikely case: the *Cassis de Dijon* verdict and the evolution of the principle of mutual recognition. Although not the first case to broadly interpret the Treaty provisions on the free movement of goods,[184] *Cassis de Dijon* is forever linked to the introduction of the principle of mutual recognition in EU internal market law. It was held that Member States have no valid reasons to prohibit the sale of products 'lawfully produced and marketed' in another Member State.[185] The importance of this judgment and, more generally, the principle of mutual recognition of national regulations is clear. Not only was the duty of mutual recognition transposed from the free movement of goods to the other economic freedoms in the decades that followed, creating considerable convergence between these areas,[186] but also, in the 1980s, the Commission seized upon the judgment to promote 'a new approach to harmonisation'.[187] It favoured the mutual recognition of national rules over the harmonisation of laws where possible; where not, it required mutual recognition of national rules, while European Standards were being developed, in its efforts to remove barriers to trade and 'complete the internal market'.[188]

The importance of the judgment is clear but also easy to overstate. The development of internal market law has naturally been a path-dependent process,[189] but the implementation of mutual recognition in different areas of free movement law is subject to significant variation.[190] Some of this variance is court-made,[191] but it is also due to legislative negotiation and resistance against the principle's application. A great example is Regulation No 1576/89, which was adopted many years

[184] See, especially, Case 8-74 *Dassonville* ECLI:EU:C:1974:82.

[185] Case C-120/78 *Rewe (Cassis de Dijon)* ECLI:EU:C:1979:42, para 14.

[186] Famously, Case C-76/09 *Säger* ECLI:EU:C:1991:331 and Case C-55/94 *Gebhard* ECLI:EU:C:1995:411. See, for discussion, Christine Janssens, *The Principle of Mutual Recognition in EU Law* (OUP 2013).

[187] For a discussion of the Commission's strategy, Sophie Meunier and Karen J Alter, 'Judicial Politics in the European Community: European Integration and the Pathbreaking Cassis de Dijon Decision' (1994) 26 Comparative Political Studies 535.

[188] Commission of the European Communities, 'Completing the Internal Market: A White Paper', from the Commission to the European Council, Milan, 28–29 June 1985 (COM/85/0210 final). For a detailed discussion, Josef Falke and Christian Joerges, 'The New Approach to Technical Harmonization and Standards, Its Preparation through ECJ Case Law on Articles 30, 36 EEC and the Low-Voltage Directive, and the Clarification of Its Operating Environment by the Single European Act' (2010) 6 Hanse Law Review 289.

[189] Susanne K Schmidt, 'Who Cares about Nationality? The Path-Dependent Case Law of the ECJ from Goods to Citizens' (2012) 19 Journal of European Public Policy 8.

[190] Contrary to expectations, such variation seems hard to explain based on the presence/absence of a clear CJEU ruling in favour of mutual recognition and is also evident in the area of the free movement of goods: Adrienne Héritier, 'Mutual Recognition: Comparing Policy Areas' (2007) 14 Journal of European Public Policy 800.

[191] Janssens (n 186) 23–24.

after the *Cassis de Dijon* ruling, and several after the Commission had outlined its new approach to harmonisation, but which regulated the same matter as that before the CJEU in *Cassis de Dijon*—the minimum alcoholic strength of beverages. The CJEU had ruled against the fixing of alcohol contents, but the Regulation harmonised European alcohol standards by prescribing in detail the (alcoholic) content spirit drinks should have.[192] By passing this act, 'the CJEU's most famous free movement ruling was simply "legislated away"'.[193]

This act has since been revised, but EU law still broadly follows the same regulatory approach. Regulation (EC) No 110/2008 on the definition, description, presentation, labelling and the protection of geographical indications of spirit drinks still contains detailed prescriptions on the content of alcoholic beverages.[194] And art 5(1)(a) of Directive 2000/13/EC on the labelling, presentation, and advertising of foodstuffs provides for host country control over the name under which a product is sold in the absence of EU legislation regulating the matter.[195] In other words, even if the CJEU occasionally ignored these provisions by imposing a duty of mutual recognition on national governments,[196] the EU legal regime on foodstuffs and alcoholic drinks is quite different from what *Cassis de Dijon* once suggested it would be. This is not to say that the legislature necessarily ignored this ruling; it may also have heeded the invitation it had previously received in *Dassonville*, that the CJEU will not independently assess whether national rules are a hindrance to trade if these are compatible with legislative harmonisation.[197] In any case, these examples support Ní Chaoimh's conclusion that 'the EU legislature can genuinely influence the contours of the internal market's various regulatory regimes . . . thus impacting the scope of and limitations to free movement of goods'.[198]

A similar story emerges when we look at other areas of free movement law. Legislative harmonisation has often honoured the central role of mutual recognition in the internal market[199] but, at times, also thwarted attempts to implement

[192] In more detail, Stephen Weatherill, 'Did *Cassis de Dijon* Make a Difference?' in Albertina Albors-Llorens, Catherine Barnard, and Brigitte Leucht (eds), *Cassis de Dijon: 40 Years On* (Hart Publishing, an imprint of Bloomsbury Publishing 2021).

[193] Jan Zglinski, 'The Internal Market: From Judicial Politics to Ordinary Politics?' in Dawson, Muir, and de Witte, *Revisiting Judicial Politics* (n 181).

[194] Regulation (EC) No 110/2008 on the definition, description, presentation, labelling and the protection of geographical indications of spirit drinks and repealing Council Regulation (EEC) No 1576/89 (OJ L39/16).

[195] Directive 2000/13/EC of the European Parliament and of the Council of 20 March 2000 on the approximation of the laws of the Member States relating to the labelling, presentation and advertising of foodstuffs (OJ L109/29).

[196] For a discussion, Ní Chaoimh (n 3) 83.

[197] *Dassonville* (n 184) para 6.

[198] Ní Chaoimh (n 3) 73. See also Zglinski, *Europe's Passive Virtues* (n 118) 58: the legislature 'takes the driver's seat when it comes to internal market governance'. Additionally, Zglinski, 'The Internal Market' (n 193). For a detailed discussion of this literature, Martijn van den Brink, 'Institutional Choice in the Internal Market: A Review Essay' Modern Law Review (forthcoming).

[199] See, eg the discussion in Janssens (n 186) 77–81.

(an overbroad understanding of) the principle. For example, the Commission was committed to making mutual recognition a reality in the freedom of services when it presented its 2002 proposal for a Services Directive. Member States would be allowed to subject services providers 'only to the national provisions of their Member State of origin'.[200] This caused such an outcry that the proposal was watered down to the point that 'the letter, if not unambiguously the spirit, of mutual recognition [was] sacrificed'.[201] All references to the country-of-origin principle had been removed by the time a compromise was reached and replaced by the narrower 'principle of freedom to provide services'.[202] Likewise, the country-of-origin principle has been rejected as the guiding principle in the area of consumer law. Whereas the proposal for the Unfair Commercial Practices Directive provided that 'traders shall only comply with the national provisions . . . of the Member State in which they are established',[203] the enacted legislative act does not mention the principle and, instead, limits itself to a more generic requirement that Member States shall 'neither restrict the freedom to provide services nor restrict the free movement of goods for reasons falling within the field approximated by this Directive'.[204] Finally, where legislation does endorse the country-of-origin principle, it usually supplements this principle with provisions that leave certain safeguard mechanisms to the host state.[205] To be sure, these provisions do not usually conflict with case law, which only ever applied 'a principle of conditional or non-absolute mutual recognition'.[206] However, the examples do illustrate, as Dorte Martinsen noted, that 'EU politics, despite its multitude of actors and their diverse perceptions, interests and interpretations, is not too fragmented to respond'.[207] The legislature has a lot of leeway in developing EU law, even in an area as replete with case law as the internal market.

[200] Article 16(1) of the Proposal for a Directive of the European Parliament and of the Council on services in the internal market (COM/2004/0002 final).

[201] Kalypso Nicolaïdis and Susanne K Schmidt, 'Mutual Recognition "on Trial": The Long Road to Services Liberalization' (2007) 14 Journal of European Public Policy 717, 728.

[202] Article 16 of Directive 2006/123/EC of the European Parliament and of the Council of 12 December 2006 on services in the internal market (OJ L376/36). For lengthier discussion, Janssens (n 186) 75–76.

[203] Article 4(1) of the Proposal for a Directive of the European Parliament and of the Council concerning unfair business-to-consumer commercial practices in the Internal Market (COM/2003/0356 final).

[204] Article 4 of Directive 2005/29/EC of the European Parliament and of the Council of 11 May 2005 concerning unfair business-to-consumer commercial practices in the internal market (OJ L 149/22).

[205] Janssens (n 186) 91–94.

[206] Stephen Weatherill, 'The Principle of Mutual Recognition: It Doesn't Work Because It Doesn't Exist' (2018) 43 European Law Review 224. Similarly, in relation to the Services Directive, Bruno de Witte, 'Setting the Scene: How Did Services Get to Bolkestein and Why?' (European Union Institute Working Paper Law 2007/20 8, 2007).

[207] Dorte Sindbjerg Martinsen, *An Ever More Powerful Court? The Political Constraints of Legal Integration in the European Union* (OUP 2015) 229.

8.2 The *Laval* quartet

These findings are confirmed by another unlikely example: the *Laval* quartet.[208] The decisions in *Viking* and *Laval*,[209] and their successors *Commission v Luxembourg* and *Rüffert*,[210] sent shockwaves through the EU legal community nearly two decades ago. Due to their alleged attack on domestic labour relations, *Viking* and *Laval* were immediately dubbed Europe's '*Lochner* moment'.[211] They are still seen as the epitome, the absolute high—or rather low—point, of the constitutionalisation of EU law and of the deregulatory, neoliberal drift that supposedly accompanies this process.[212] However, no matter how compelling this narrative has been, it could hardly be more misleading. Not only does it essentialise EU law on the basis of a handful of judgments,[213] but it also ignores the institutional dynamics behind EU law[214] and therefore the avenues available for the re-interpretation and reorientation of EU law outside the judicial process.

The whole saga confirms what we saw earlier, namely that the content of internal market law is largely a product of legislation. The central act in this saga is the Posted Workers Directive (PWD), which, in all its versions, has sought to strike a balance between two potentially competing aims: facilitating the cross-border provision of services, on the one hand, and protecting employees, on the

[208] A Koukiadaki, 'The Far-Reaching Implications of the Laval Quartet: The Case of the UK Living Wage' (2014) 43 Industrial Law Journal 91. It is doubtful that this is really a quartet, especially given the variance in the institutional dynamics underlying the cases. Most of all, Case C-438/05 *Viking* ECLI:EU:C:2007:772 has little in common with Case C-319/06 *Commission v Luxembourg* ECLI:EU:C:2008:350 and *Rüffert* (n 170)

[209] Case C-341/05 *Laval un Partneri* ECLI:EU:C:2007:809; *Viking* (n 208).

[210] *Commission v Luxembourg* (n 208); *Rüffert* (n 170).

[211] Danny Nicol, 'Europe's Lochner Moment' (2011) Public Law 308.

[212] See, eg Michael A Wilkinson, *Authoritarian Liberalism and the Transformation of Modern Europe* (1st edn, OUP 2021) 191; Cormac Mac Amhlaigh, *New Constitutional Horizons: Towards a Pluralist Constitutional Theory* (OUP 2022) 153; Turkuler Isiksel, *Europe's Functional Constitution: A Theory of Constitutionalism beyond the State* (OUP 2016) 143–45; Wolfgang Streeck, 'Progressive Regression' (2019) 118 New Left Review 117, 134; Hauke Brunkhorst, 'A Curtain of Gloom Is Descending on the Continent: Capitalism, Democracy and Europe' (2017) 23 European Law Journal 335, 343; Joe Guinan and Thomas M Hanna, 'Forbidden Fruit: The Neglected Political Economy of Lexit' (2017) 24 Institute for Public Policy Research Progressive Review 14, 18.

[213] *Viking*, which is not discussed, should, indeed, be regarded 'as a corruption of the Court's orthodox approach to free movement law, not as typical of it': Stephen Weatherill, 'The Beauty and the Beast: Is EU Internal Market Law Over-Constitutionalised?' in Tamara Ćapeta, Iris Goldner Lang, and Tamara Perišin (eds), *The Changing European Union: A Critical View on the Role of Law and the Courts* (Hart Publishing 2022).

[214] As, for that matter, have more nuanced views. See, in this respect, the summary of the main criticisms of *Viking* and *Laval* by Catherine Barnard, 'The Calm after the Storm: Time to Reflect on EU (Labour) Law Scholarship following the Decisions in *Viking* and *Laval*' in Alan Bogg, Cathryn Costello, and ACL Davies (eds), *Research Handbook on EU Labour Law* (Edward Elgar 2016). The interplay between the legislature and judiciary, as well as other national and EU actors, is not among this criticism. For an important exception, however, Claire Kilpatrick, 'Internal Market Architecture and the Accommodation of Labour Rights: As Good as It Gets?' (European Union Institute Working Paper Law 2011/04, 2011).

other.[215] What has changed over the years is how this balance was struck. The legislative proposal for the original PWD leaned most towards the aim of promoting the provision of cross-border services. It stipulated that foreign undertakings 'observe a minimum "hard core" of protective working conditions in force in the host country' while being subject 'to the bulk of the labour law in force in the country of origin'.[216] During its negotiations, however, the application of the home state principle was watered down, most notably by the decision to remove the provision that the host state's minimum rate of pay and paid holidays do not apply during the first three months of posting.[217] The result of the negotiations was, as one commentator said at the time, 'a Directive which was highly protective of domestic labour regulation'.[218]

The academic response to the *Laval* quartet has been such that it is now accepted that it was the CJEU who jeopardised these protective provisions, when, in fact, the legislative standards agreed upon were mostly upheld. This we can see by examining the *Laval* judgment from up close. A key question was when Member States could impose on undertakings posting workers on their territory an obligation to pay minimum wages. Article 3 of the PWD requires that posted workers, in accordance with the law or collective agreement in the Member State where the work is carried out, be guaranteed minimum terms and conditions of employment in relation to the matters listed in art 3(1), including maximum work periods and minimum rates of pay, rest periods, and holidays. However, as Sweden had not laid down minimum rates of pay by law or collective agreement, it was clear that it could not invoke this provision to oblige undertakings posting workers to pay minimum wages.[219] More controversial was the interpretation of art 3(7) of the PWD, according to which art 3 'shall not prevent application of terms and conditions of employment which are more favourable to workers'. This provision has been read as a minimum harmonisation clause allowing the *host* state to apply more favourable employment standards to posted workers than the minimum standards set out in art 3(1).[220] Yet, this is not the case. The intention of this provision was 'to guarantee the application of the more favourable working conditions provided

[215] Paul Davies, 'Posted Workers: Single Market or Protection of National Labour Law Systems?' (1997) 34 Common Market Law Review 571.

[216] Proposal for a council directive concerning the posting of workers in the framework of the provision of services (COM/91/230FINAL) para 19.

[217] Article 3(2) of Directive 96/71/EC of the European Parliament and of the Council of 16 December 1996 concerning the posting of workers in the framework of the provision of services (OJ L18/1).

[218] Davies, 'Posted Workers' (n 215) 591.

[219] *Laval un Partneri* (n 207) paras 62–72. This is true even if 'the consensual and negotiation-based Swedish labour system did not fit the directive': Gareth Davies and Dion Kramer, 'The Posting of Workers' in Robert Schutze and Takis Tridimas (eds), *Oxford Principles of European Union Law Vol 2: The Internal Market* (OUP forthcoming).

[220] Nina Boeger, 'Minimum Harmonisation, Free Movement and Proportionality' in Philip Syrpis (ed), *The Judiciary, the Legislature and the EU Internal Market* (CUP 2012) 72; Kilpatrick (n 214) 5.

for by the law applicable, usually the law of the *home* country'.[221] In this respect, the CJEU rightly ruled that art 3(7) could not 'be interpreted as allowing the host Member State to make the provision of services in its territory conditional on the observance of terms and conditions of employment which go beyond the mandatory rules for minimum protection'.[222] As Stein Evju explains, the CJEU's 'stance could hardly come as a surprise. Quite apart from the drafting history, from a free movement of services perspective, host State freedom on this point could easily undermine the effective exercise of the freedom.'[223] The judgment was perfectly in line with the legislative intention in these provisions.

Of the judgments that are part of the *Laval* quartet, *Commission v Luxembourg* might be the only ruling that was inconsistent with the enacted legislative standards. The Commission alleged that Luxembourg had violated the PWD by requiring undertakings posting workers to its territory to adjust wages to the cost of living and to comply with domestic rules on part-time and fixed-term work. As these requirements were more favourable than the terms and conditions of employment set out in art 3(1), they could not be justified by reference to this provision. This is why Luxembourg invoked the public policy exception in art 3(10). Subject to the requirement of equal treatment between undertakings posting workers and domestic undertakings, this provision licences the application of 'terms and conditions of employment on matters other than those referred to in [art 3(1)] in the case of public policy provisions'. In some Member States, the concept of public policy plays but a minor role in the regulation of industrial relations, but others consider almost all their labour law to be a matter of public policy.[224] Article 3(10) was introduced to meet the concerns of Member States who feared that the PWD would lead to social regression if the list of minimum terms and conditions in art 3(1) were exhaustive. At the time, the view was that art 3(10) made the list in art 3(1) non-exhaustive, allowing Member States to extend the concept of public policy quite liberally to undertakings posting workers.[225] The CJEU ruled differently, however: it said that, as a derogation from the freedom to provide services, the public policy exception had to 'be interpreted strictly'.[226] The derogation could 'be relied on only if there is a genuine and sufficiently serious threat to a fundamental interest of society'.[227] This definition, drawn from case law that

[221] Amended proposal for a Council Directive concerning the posting of workers in the framework of the provision of services (OJ C187/5), explanatory memorandum on Article 3 (italics are mine). I thank Rónán Riordan for bringing this to my attention. See further, Stein Evju, 'Revisiting the Posted Workers Directive: Conflict of Laws and Laws in Contrast' (2010) 12 Cambridge Yearbook of European Legal Studies 151, 158–59.

[222] *Laval un Partneri* (n 209) para 80.

[223] Evju (n 221) 174.

[224] ibid 155.

[225] Marco Biagi, 'Guest Editorial—Fortune Smiles on the Italian EU Presidency: Talking Half-Seriously about the Posted Workers and Parental Leave Directives' (1996) 12 International Journal of Comparative Labour Law and Industrial Relations 97, 104.

[226] *Commission v Luxembourg* (n 208) para 30.

[227] ibid para 50.

essentially equates public policy with public security,[228] is so strict that, as Claire Kilpatrick pithily observed, 'it is difficult to imagine the host-state labour law rules typically at stake in posted workers' cases falling under such a definition'.[229] This was not the intention at the time that art 3(10) was adopted.

The *Rüffert* ruling was, just as the *Laval* verdict, consistent with the PWD's provisions. At issue was the compatibility of the public procurement law of one of the German *Länder* with EU law. The public contract awarded to the company in question contained a declaration of compliance with collective agreements, including the agreed-upon minimum wage. The contract was terminated when it was found that workers had been employed at a lower wage. Asked whether this was compatible with art 56 of the TFEU on the freedom to provide services, the CJEU recognised that art 3(1) of the PWD, read in conjunction with art 3(8) of the PWD, acts as a limitation on that freedom. These provisions essentially require undertakings posting workers to guarantee rights such as minimum rates of pay, either when these rates are laid down by law or administrative provision or when they are laid down in collective agreements that have been 'declared universally applicable'.[230] However, since the minimum wage was laid down neither in law nor in a collective agreement declared universally applicable, the CJEU found that the German *Land* could not rely on these provisions.[231] It also ruled that the minimum rate of pay 'cannot be considered to be a term and condition of employment which is more favourable to workers within the meaning of Article 3(7)' of the PWD.[232] Repeating what it had decided earlier in *Laval*, it held that this provision 'cannot be interpreted as allowing the host Member State to make the provision of services in its territory conditional on the observance of terms and conditions of employment which go beyond the mandatory rules for minimum protection'.[233] None of this was surprising considering the text and objectives of the PWD. The German authorities had not used the opportunities offered by the PWD to protect workers and so could not take advantage of them without first amending their domestic legislation.[234] There was nothing more to it than that.

The *Laval* quartet was not the culmination of a ceaseless process of constitutionalisation. On the contrary, the saga belies the belief that CJEU case law

[228] Case C-54/99 *Église de scientologie* ECLI:EU:C:2000:124, para 17; Case 30/77 *Bouchereau* ECLI:EU:C:1977:172, paras 31–35.

[229] Kilpatrick (n 214) 12. See also C Barnard, 'The UK and Posted Workers: The Effect of Commission v Luxembourg on the Territorial Application of British Labour Law: Case C-319/06 Commission v Luxembourg, Judgment 19 June 2008' (2009) 38 Industrial Law Journal 122, 129.

[230] That is, where there is a 'system for declaring collective agreements . . . to be of universal application'.

[231] Similarly, *Rüffert* (n 170) paras 24–31.

[232] ibid para 32.

[233] Ibid para 33.

[234] It was only after *Rüffert* that German *Länder* introduced minimum wage legislation: Dorte Sindbjerg Martinsen and Michael Blauberger, 'The Court of Justice of the European Union and the Mega-Politics of Posted Workers' (2021) 84 Law and Contemporary Problems 29, 54.

constitutes a 'perpetual momentum . . . that is consistently extending the domain of constitutionally protected individual rights'.[235] The verdicts mostly rested on a reasonable legislative interpretation: except for, arguably, the interpretation of the concept of public policy in *Commission v Luxembourg*, the CJEU upheld the balance struck by the PWD between the aim of facilitating the cross-border provision of services, on the one hand, and the aim of protecting posted workers, on the other—a balance that, incidentally, was criticised when the law was passed for not sufficiently promoting the free movement of services.[236]

Not only that, but also the rulings marked not the end of a process of *judicial* constitution-making but the beginning of an ongoing *political* conversation on the interpretation of the EU Treaties, specifically about what is the proper balance between the social rights of workers and EU market freedoms. The judgments immediately attracted fierce backlash. National authorities took steps to contain their effects,[237] and a host of actors (including trade unions, the European Parliament, and national governments) called for political action to overturn problematic aspects of the law.[238] Of these steps, the most important ones have come from the legislature. The first attempt at legislative change failed: the *Monti II* Regulation sought to reconcile the right to take collective action with the freedom of establishment and the freedom to provide services[239] but was withdrawn after over one-third of national parliaments triggered the 'yellow card' procedure against the proposal for violating the principle of subsidiarity.[240] The second attempt, however, proved more successful.

In 2018, the legislature was able to agree on revisions to the PWD,[241] partially overruling *Commission v Luxembourg* and *Rüffert* through two legislative amendments. First, the words 'minimum rates of pay' in art 3(1)(c) were replaced by 'remuneration'. As a result, undertakings posting workers can now be required to respect all rates of remuneration, including rates higher than the minimum rates of pay set by domestic legislation or collective agreements. Second, the revised Directive expands the kind of collective agreements that can be applied to undertakings posting workers. Under the old art 1(8) of the PWD, if there was

[235] Fritz W Scharpf, 'Perpetual Momentum: Directed and Unconstrained?' (2012) 19 Journal of European Public Policy 127, 134.

[236] Biagi (n 225) 103.

[237] Martinsen and Blauberger (n 234) 54; Andreas Hofmann, 'Resistance against the Court of Justice of the European Union' (2018) 14 International Journal of Law in Context 258, 267–89.

[238] For a longer discussion, Dorte Sindbjerg Martinsen, 'The European Union and EU Legislative Politics' in Frank Vandenbroucke, Catherine Barnard, and Geert de Baere (eds), *A European Social Union after the Crisis* (CUP 2017).

[239] Proposal for a Council Regulation on the exercise of the right to take collective action within the context of the freedom of establishment and the freedom to provide services (COM/2012/0130 final).

[240] Ian Cooper, 'A Yellow Card for the Striker: National Parliaments and the Defeat of EU Legislation on the Right to Strike' (2015) 22 Journal of European Public Policy 1406.

[241] Directive (EU) 2018/957 of the European Parliament and of the Council of 28 June 2018 amending Directive 96/71/EC concerning the posting of workers in the framework of the provision of services (OJ L173/16).

a system for declaring collective agreements to be of universal application, national authorities could not enforce terms and conditions of employment under collective agreements that had not been declared universally applicable on such undertakings—which was confirmed in *Rüffert*. The amended art 1(8) of the PWD gives national authorities that failed to declare a collective agreement to be universally applicable an escape route. It says that national authorities may enforce collective agreements that have not been declared to be of universal application 'in the absence of, *or in addition to*, a system for declaring collective agreements . . . to be of universal application'.[242] Consequently, the terms and conditions of employment set forth in collective agreements can be imposed on undertakings posting workers even if these agreements have not been declared to be of universal application. By thus amending the law, the legislature has remedied some of the perceived shortcomings of the CJEU's interpretations of the first PWD.

Since *Rüffert*, the CJEU has kept its course of deference to legislation. In *ESA*, it adopted a broad conception of minimum rates of pay,[243] yet one that is consistent with art 3 of the PWD. In *Regiopost*, national authorities were allowed to enforce such rates provided they are laid down in legislation.[244] This followed directly from the wording of art 3 of the PWD, as did the *Rüffert* decision at the time. In other words, the reason that case law has become more favourable to posted workers is not that the CJEU's attitude towards the political balance struck by the PWD has changed but because the legislative provisions were more favourable this time. This matters not only for our assessment of the judgments but also for future cases. If the CJEU maintains its deferential stance, *Commission v Luxembourg* and *Rüffert* will have been effectively reversed, and the balance struck by the PWD will be more favourable to posted workers than it was initially.

To the extent that the *Laval* quartet rulings harmed domestic labour relations, the blame can hardly be placed on the CJEU alone, which acted in accordance with the legislative provisions in most of its rulings. This also means that the cause of any harm that was done hardly lies in the (over-)constitutionalisation or juridification of EU law. Not at all: these cases demonstrate the control the legislature could exercise over the content of EU internal market law and how it has used its power to defend domestic social provisions against encroachments by the freedom to provide services. The original PWD rested on a compromise that rejected the application of a broad home state principle, by which the legislature already protected domestic labour law to a high degree. The amended PWD has only increased this protection, remedying shortcomings in the original PWD as laid bare by the CJEU. In other words, and contrary to what one often reads, the area of posted workers was shaped mostly by the legislature. The CJEU largely took a back seat and, except

[242] Italics mine.
[243] Case C-396/13 *Elektrobudowa Spolka Akcyjna* ECLI:EU:C:2015:86.
[244] Case C-114/14 *Regiopost* ECLI:EU:C:2015:760.

for *Commission v Luxembourg*, ruled in accordance with the legislature's political choices in the area.

8.3 Out of the shadows

All in all, there is plenty of evidence to suggest that case law casts a much weaker shadow over the legislative process than one might think when reading the academic literature on the over-constitutionalisation of EU law. As we just saw, the legislature retains ample room to define the reach and scope of the economic freedoms underpinning the internal market. This includes the power to bring EU law out of the judiciary's shadow by revising settled case law. Not even a ruling as famous and important as *Cassis de Dijon* was immune to legislative override. This section reinforces this point by providing additional examples before discussing how findings discussed in earlier sections and chapters should inform the ongoing discussion of the reforms needed to achieve a better balance between the legislative and judicial process.

Legislative revisions of case law can be so minor that they easily escape our attention. For example, while the CJEU had initially ruled that inspections of imported plants could not exceed 15 per cent of the consignments presented at the border,[245] the legislature subsequently passed legislation declaring that occasional inspections were allowed if 'made on no more than one-third of the consignments introduced from a given Member State'.[246] In *Rewe Zentral*, the CJEU held this intervention to be a legitimate exercise of legislative discretion.[247]

At other times, however, the choice of the legislature to revise established jurisprudence may be more significant, or at least more controversial. A good example is the 2004 Citizenship Directive, which overruled case law on jobseekers' right to social assistance. Until then, they could claim social assistance if 'a genuine link exists between the person seeking work and the employment market of that State'. Such a link was established by jobseekers that had 'for a reasonable period, in fact genuinely sought work'.[248] The Citizenship Directive does not mention these conditions and provides, instead, that Member States need not grant social assistance to Union citizens who reside in their territory to seek employment.[249] After initial hesitation, the CJEU accepted that it had been overruled, and disputes on claims by economically inactive citizens have since been settled in accordance with the

[245] Case 42/82 *Commission v France* ECLI:EU:C:1983:88.

[246] Article 11 (3) of Council Directive 77/93/EEC of 21 December 1976 on protective measures against the introduction into the Member States of harmful organisms of plants or plant products (OJ L26/20).

[247] Case 37/83 *Rewe Zentral* ECLI:EU:C:1984:89, para 20. For discussion, Ní Chaoimh (n 3) 93–94.

[248] Case C-138/02 *Collins* ECLI:EU:C:2004:172, paras 67–70. See also, Case C-258/04 *Ioannidis* ECLI:EU:C:2005:559, para 30.

[249] Articles 24(2) *juncto* 14(4)(b) of Directive 2004/38/EC (n 89).

Directive.[250] Another instructive example is the legislative response to the ill-judged *Sturgeon* ruling (discussed in section III.3). If the proposal to amend the Air Passenger Rights Regulation is passed without drastic changes, a distinction between passengers of delayed and cancelled flights in terms of their right to receive financial compensation will be reintroduced, contrary to the judgment.[251]

These examples would not be so interesting were it not for the fact that they illustrate something that can easily go unacknowledged: that the legislature is not inevitably bound by case law interpreting primary law. This, for those who are uncomfortable with it, is exactly as it should be, because not only is it fairer to settle disagreements about the course of EU law via the legislative rather than the judicial process, but also legislative decision-making normally enhances the quality of, and compliance with, EU law. As we saw in Chapter II, the legislative codification of case law carries the risk of inconsistent and unduly vague legislation. For this reason alone, legislative actors should not act as if they are strictly bound by judicial rulings interpreting primary law. This does not mean, of course, that they must pursue a different course from the one taken by the CJEU. It merely means they should enjoy the liberty to freely deliberate on the content of EU law and reject case law that they consider undesirable or that, if codified, would produce irrational legislative output.

My analysis also calls into question the notion that European integration suffers from an imbalance between legislative and judicial politics.[252] Or at least, this imbalance is less pronounced than is sometimes suggested. This, then, necessarily raises questions about the solutions proposed by critics of the presumed institutional asymmetry to strengthen the position of the legislature or, conversely, weaken that of the judiciary.[253] One solution not to be pursued, as it misunderstands the interplay between the legislature and judiciary, is to remove the Treaties from the Court's purview by 'de-constitutionalising' EU law. Dieter Grimm has famously argued that the Treaties 'should be limited to provisions regarding goals, institutions, powers, procedures, and fundamental rights. Provisions regarding policy should be relegated to the level of secondary European law'.[254] His proposal aims to free such policy areas from the constitutional constraints supposedly imposed by case law, placing these areas more firmly under the legislature's authority. Scharpf has elaborated on this proposal with the aim of also freeing national governments

[250] See section III.2.

[251] Proposal for a Regulation of the European Parliament and of the Council amending Regulation (EC) No 261/2004 establishing common rules on compensation and assistance to passengers in the event of denied boarding and of cancellation or long delay of flights and Regulation (EC) No 2027/97 on air carrier liability in respect of the carriage of passengers and their baggage by air (COM/2013/0130 final).

[252] van den Brink, Dawson, and Zglinski (n 180).

[253] For an extensive overview, Höpner and Schmidt (n 183).

[254] Grimm (n 175) 36. See also, Fritz W Scharpf, 'After the Crash: A Perspective on Multilevel European Democracy' (2015) 21 European Law Journal 384, 400–401.

from such constraints. He proposes to restrict the use of the preliminary reference and infringement proceedings to legislation enacted under arts 289, 290, and 291 of the TFEU. This should ensure that the power of the Commission and Court over national actors is limited to the confines laid down in secondary law.[255]

The first problem with these proposals is that they are supported by dubious assumptions. Both Grimm and Scharpf believe that the power to interpret the Treaties lies exclusively with the judiciary, but this is not the case. As we saw earlier, legislative revisions of case law are plausible in theory and possible in practice. Second, the proposals rest on an inadequate understanding of how EU law operates in practice, and therefore their consequences are not fully understood. According to Scharpf, 'there is no reason to fear that [de-constitutionalisation] could destroy the single market. The huge body of European legislation on economic integration . . . would of course remain in place.'[256] While it is true that the single market would not be destroyed, the regulatory scope of EU legislation is less comprehensive than his argument suggests, and leaving issues that are not regulated by legislation entirely unregulated is more problematic than it implies. Take the Citizenship Directive, the scope of which is limited to 'Union citizens who move to or reside in a Member State other than that of which they are a national.'[257] Since the legal position of mobile EU citizens who return to their state of nationality was unregulated, they would have been at the mercy of national governments if the CJEU had not plugged this regulatory gap by applying primary law.[258] In other words, de-constitutionalising EU law is not a desirable solution.

To strengthen the legislature's authority vis-à-vis the CJEU, the legislative process could be reformed to ease legislative action. Such reforms must not, however, undermine the virtues of the legislative process. For example, while it could be made more effective by abolishing qualified majority voting in the Council, this would weaken the normative legitimacy of the decisions taken. As we saw in Chapter II, qualified majority voting allows the national *demoi* to exercise shared and equal control over EU policy-making: it protects smaller *demoi* from domination. The abolition of qualified majority rule would thus promote effectiveness at the expense of legitimacy.[259]

An institutional change that is worth contemplating is to facilitate legislative override of case law, for example by a simple majority in the Council and Parliament.[260] This would be a modest change that would make it slightly easier to correct case law that is deemed inappropriate by a majority of states, which

[255] Fritz W Scharpf, 'De-Constitutionalisation and Majority Rule: A Democratic Vision for Europe' (2017) 23 European Law Journal 315, 322.
[256] ibid.
[257] Article 3(1) of Directive 2004/38/EC (n 89).
[258] Case C-35/20 *Syyttäjä* ECLI:EU:C:2021:813, paras 67–70; Case C-673/17 *Coman* ECLI:EU:C:2018:385, para 31; Case C-165/16 *Lounes* EU:C:2017:862, para 51.
[259] Scharpf, 'De-Constitutionalisation and Majority Rule' (n 255) 325–27.
[260] For a similar idea, Scharpf, 'After the Crash' (n 254) 403.

does not create the same legitimacy deficits. Of course, this would only marginally strengthen the legislature vis-à-vis the judiciary, but a more serious revision of their allocation of authority might not be necessary. As we have seen, the legislature can already exert significant influence over primary law, and the division of powers between the legislature and judiciary is better than critics have suggested. This suggests that no extensive reforms are needed to protect the legislative prerogative of Treaty interpretation. The legislature should just use the powers at its disposal.

This chapter examined the Treaties' negative and positive dimensions as regards the allocation of authority between the EU legislature and judiciary. On the one hand, it assessed the legitimacy of judicial review of legislation and, on the other, presented the legislature as an actor that should be allowed to shape the content of the Treaties and that actively does so. Regarding the legitimacy of judicial review, it found that the CJEU conducts *ultra vires* review according to appropriately deferential standards but also that it should afford more deference in fundamental rights cases. In the second half of the chapter, I argued for a better appreciation of the legislature, including a better awareness of its ability to autonomously steer the content of EU law.

PART 2

V

Out of Many, One

Legislative Intent in European Union Law

1. Introduction

How must those to whom European Union (EU) legislation is addressed—judicial officials, national governments, and private actors—interpret its provisions? This question has gained pertinence now that we know what authority legislative provisions should have: that, barring exceptional circumstances, they should be afforded deference by judicial officials and their other addressees. Chapters V–VII answer the question of how legislation ought to be interpreted.

Existing studies on the interpretation of EU law provide inadequate guidance. Most of these studies are descriptive in nature and only seek to identify and clarify how legal officials ascribe meaning to EU law. The few prescriptive studies that exist tend to conflate constitutional interpretation with legislative interpretation,[1] overlooking the fact that the two may raise distinct questions that set them apart. Moreover, these studies are often weighed down by misunderstandings about the interpretation of EU law in reality and about underlying conceptual issues in relation to legislative interpretation—such as the nature of legislative intent, the value of legislative rules, and the relative determinacy of the legislative plan—all of which have contributed to confusion about the proper object of legislative interpretation. How these misconceptions will be addressed as a theory of legislative interpretation is developed in Chapters V–VII, which I will do by establishing the conceptual plausibility of legislative intent in EU law, studying the nature of legislative rules, and, finally, identifying how legal officials can draw reasonable inferences of legislative intent from publicly available legislative material.

The logical starting point for the search for a cogent and compelling theory of legislative interpretation is the notion of legislative intent. Legislative intent is the legislature's intention in passing a legislative act or provision, that is not the intention to pass a certain act or provision but the intention to produce certain effects by

[1] See, eg Koen Lenaerts and José Gutiérrez-Fons, 'To Say What the Law of the EU Is: Methods of Interpretation and the European Court of Justice' (2013) 20 Columbia Journal of European Law 3; Miguel Poiares Maduro, 'Interpreting European Law—Judicial Adjudication in a Context of Constitutional Pluralism' (2008) 1 European Journal of Legal Studies 1; Gunnar Beck, *The Legal Reasoning of the Court of Justice of the EU* (Hart Publishing 2012); Suvi Sankari, *European Court of Justice Legal Reasoning in Context* (Europa Law Publishing 2013); Anthony Arnull, *The European Union and Its Court of Justice* (2nd edn, OUP 2006) ch 16.

Legislative Authority and Interpretation in the European Union. Martijn van den Brink, Oxford University Press.
 DOI: 10.1093/9780198900115.003.0005

passing that act or provision. In legal parlance, it is still said that interpreters must ascertain and respect legislative intent,[2] but many EU lawyers have come to regard the notion of legislative intent as unsound, not because they think that legislation is a product of unintentional action[3] but because they believe that a joint legislative intent cannot be formed or defined out of the individual intentions of legislative representatives. Piet Eeckhout, for example, argues that 'a single legislative intent may be lacking with such a complex of inputs',[4] expressing a view that many scholars working on the interpretation of EU law now seem to share.[5]

Some have gone further and expressed concern that this complex of inputs means that no coherent legislative action can be taken. Giandomenico Majone once suggested that the European Parliament 'is not yet institutionally suited to develop a coherent legislative strategy to achieve the objectives laid down in the Treaties'[6] and that, therefore, extensive power should be delegated to the EU judiciary. Similarly, Anand Menon and Stephen Weatherill have argued that such delegation could help avoid 'potentially damaging "cycling" between competing policy alternatives'.[7] What do they mean when they say this? Although they did not elaborate on their argument, an intuitively plausible version goes like this. Individual legislators have their own personal attitudes towards specific policies, which they aggregate into a joint legislative attitude by means of majority voting. Legislative majorities can shift, however, from one decision to another and over time, and as a result, the collective body of legislative acts passed may become internally incoherent. In other words, they seem to argue that since legislative representatives hold different attitudes, and since these attitudes will coalesce into fluctuating majorities, the idea of legislative intent is unintelligible, and, more worryingly, the integrity of legislative action may be compromised.[8]

[2] Not just among academics: Joined cases C-297/17, C-318/17, C-319/17 and C-438/17 *Ibrahim* ECLI:EU:C:2019:219, paras 64–65; Case C-480/08 *Texeira* ECLI:EU:C:2010:83, paras 56–57.

[3] Joseph Raz, *Between Authority and Interpretation: On the Theory of Law and Practical Reason* (OUP 2009) 275; Neil Duxbury, *Elements of Legislation* (CUP 2013) 107.

[4] Piet Eeckhout, 'The European Court of Justice and the Legislature' (1998) 18 Yearbook of European Law 1, 17.

[5] Elina Paunio, *Legal Certainty in Multilingual EU Law: Language, Discourse, and Reasoning at the European Court of Justice* (Ashgate 2013) 19–20; Sankari, (n 1) 170; Joxerramon Bengoetxea, 'Multilingual and Multicultural Legal Reasoning: The European Court of Justice' in Anne Lise Kjær and Silvia Adamo (eds), *Linguistic Diversity and European Democracy* (Ashgate 2011) 9; Phil Syrpis, 'The Relationship between Primary and Secondary Law in the EU' (2015) 52 Common Market Law Review 461, 485.

[6] Giandomenico Majone, 'Europe's "Democratic Deficit": The Question of Standards' (1998) 4 European Law Journal 5, 23. He refers to Paul Craig, 'Democracy and Rule-Making within the EC: An Empirical and Normative Assessment' (1997) 3 European Law Journal 105, 118.

[7] Anand Menon and Stephen Weatherill, 'Democratic Politics in a Globalising World: Supranationalism and Legitimacy in the European Union' (LSE Law, Society and Economy Working Paper No 2007/13, 2007) 18.

[8] See, eg Kenneth A Shepsle, 'Congress Is a "They," Not an "It": Legislative Intent as Oxymoron' (1992) 12 International Review of Law and Economics 239; Ronald M Dworkin, *Law's Empire* (Harvard UP 1995) ch 9; Jeremy Waldron, *Law and Disagreement* (OUP 1999) 119.

So, clearly, the question of legislative intent matters, and not just for our appreciation of the legislative process but also for our conception of what counts as reasonable legislative interpretation. EU lawyers writing on the issue have argued that if the object of interpretation cannot be legislative intent, then it must be the purpose behind the legislative act.[9] As Alexander Somek claims, 'textual interpretation can be claimed to be superior to purposive statutory construction if the legislature is thought to be a corporate body. Arguably, a body of this kind can form an intention and speak *uno voce* only by expressing itself in a text.'[10] He implies that purposive interpretation is superior to textualist interpretation if the legislature cannot form and express a joint legislative intention. As I will show, he is mistaken, both about the superiority of textualist interpretation in the event legislative intentions can be formed and in suggesting that textualism and purposivism are the only forms of legislative interpretation. To anticipate the argument that is developed in the coming chapters, I will argue that reasonable legislative interpretation is impossible without legislative intent. The object of legislative interpretation should be neither the literal meaning of legislative provisions nor the purpose behind them. It should be the intended meaning of legislation.

To that end, the aim of this chapter is to demonstrate that legislative intent can be the object of legislative interpretation by overcoming two objections to this idea, both of which follow from the fact that legislatures are pluralistic, multi-member assemblies. The first, raised by Eeckhout and Somek above, is that the legislature cannot form intentions, or at least not coherent ones, since legislation is a product of a process that involves many individuals with different intentions. The second, related objection is that even if it would be possible for the legislature to aggregate these individual intentions into a single legislative intent, there is no way to ascertain what it intended. This would, one might think, require us to know the intentions of every individual legislator who helped shape the legislature's intention, and since that is impossible, legislative intent cannot be known. This chapter rebuts both objections. I will show, first, that even an institution as complex as the EU legislature can aggregate the individual intentions of its members into coherent institutional intentions, rendering the notion of legislative intent in EU law plausible. Second, I will explain why the intentions of individual legislators are relevant for the formation of legislative intent but irrelevant for the identification of legislative intent. To be able to ascertain legislative intent, we do not need to ascertain these individual intentions. I show this by using social choice theory and its

[9] Contrary to the leading voices in legal theory, who take it that if the object of legislative interpretation cannot be legislative intent, it must be the literal meaning of legislative text: Waldron, *Law and Disagreement* (n 8) 142; Raz (n 3) 288; Dworkin (n 8) 322.

[10] Alexander Somek, 'The Emancipation of Legal Dissonance' in Henning Koch and others (eds), *Europe: The New Legal Realism: Essays in Honor of Hjalte Rasmussen* (Djøf Publishing 2010) 8. Others, who take it that the object of interpretation should not be legislative intent but legislative purpose, include Paunio (n 5) and Sankari (n 1).

application to legislative studies. Social choice theorists have shown that groups can have agency over and above the members composing them and that they can form coherent group attitudes out of the attitudes of their members;[11] legal theorists have shown that legislatures can be among such groups.[12] Drawing on their insights, I will show that the EU legislature meets the conditions for coherent intentional action.

The next three sections discuss the main findings of this literature, which can be technical and jargon laden. Section V.2 discusses the dilemma that groups that use an 'ideal' procedure to aggregate the individual attitudes of their members into a joint group attitude risk generating outcomes that are irrational. Section V.3 explains how groups can escape this dilemma by adjusting their decision-making. Section V.4 shows that legislatures, due to their internal organisation and the influence of political parties, can achieve collective rationality and legislate with integrity. Section V.5 applies these theoretical insights to the EU legislature and explains that the legislative process is structured to facilitate joint action and create intentional attitudes. For all that is unique about the EU legislature, its internal structure is comparable to that of contemporary legislatures elsewhere. It is organised hierarchically and according to a clear division of labour. This, I will explain, allows the formation of coherent legislative attitudes. Section V.6 clarifies the irrelevance of the intentions of the legislature's members for the identification of legislative intent in EU law.

2. The Discursive Dilemma

Each society needs an institution with the capacity to change the law. Without such an institution, its legal norms would be static, and it would be unable to respond to developments that demand legal change. While the legislature is the primary norm-creating institution in contemporary societies, other institutions play their part in the creation of legal norms. Courts, for example, produce new law when they adjudicate legal claims, yet we would not normally say that their primary purpose is to realise legal change. Indeed, the legitimacy of courts depends, in part, on the perception that they apply rather than make law.[13] In contrast, the primary purpose of legislatures is to amend existing legal norms and create new laws. They are uniquely situated to discharge this task because, contrary to courts, who are reactive institutions and depend on the disputes coming before them, legislatures

[11] This chapter draws on the following account in particular: Christian List and Philip Pettit, *Group Agency: The Possibility, Design, and Status of Corporate Agents* (OUP 2011).

[12] In particular, Richard Ekins, *The Nature of Legislative Intent* (OUP 2012). In addition, Duxbury (n 3).

[13] Jeremy Waldron, 'Legislating with Integrity' (2003) 72 Fordham Law Review 373, 379.

can respond directly, with an openness to all relevant facts, and initiate comprehensive reform when the situation so demands.[14]

This requires that legislatures can identify when there is a need for legal change and respond to such needs by amending the law in a manner consistent with their motivations and previous actions. Another way of putting this is that legislatures must meet standards of rationality. A rational decision-maker can form reasonably accurate representations of her environment and, in response, act in a way that is consistent with her intentions and previous behaviour.[15] We want legislatures to behave accordingly since we have little reason to trust a legislature that is unable to form a reasonably accurate representation of the state of affairs in society or is unable to respond thereto in a reasoned and consistent manner, and we would have little reason to respect its authority.[16] Realising consistency in legislative action is of particular importance. As Jeremy Waldron said, we want legislatures to 'legislate with integrity' and guarantee 'the coherence of the terms of the bills that are proposed and voted on in the legislature'.[17]

If the legislature were a single person, we would expect it to enjoy these facilities. Although individuals can act irrationally by forming inaccurate representations of the state of affairs around them or by failing to respond to this state of affairs in accordance with their intentions, we know that they are capable of rational action and, in the event they fall short, can recognise and correct their mistakes.[18] However, the modern legislature is a multi-member deliberative assembly, a body made up of hundreds of people that act jointly for the purpose of making the law. There are obvious advantages to an assembly over a single-person legislature: it reduces the potential for tyranny, creates room for citizen participation and representation, and allows groups to specialise and develop more expertise than individuals can alone[19]—but the complexity of assemblies also brings difficulties. For precisely with complex groups, doubts may arise about their capacity to act rationally.

The problem is one of attitude aggregation. Take, as example, the need for a judgement on three interrelated propositions: (a) whether a budget deficit will occur, (b) whether a balanced budget is desirable, and (c) whether action should be taken to achieve a balanced budget. A rational decision would be (c) action is required if (a) a budget deficit will occur and (b) a balanced budget is desirable (c

[14] This paragraph follows Ekins (n 12) 121–23, but see also the discussion in Chapter III. Others have emphasised the unique capabilities of legislatures too: Jeremy Waldron, 'The Dignity of Legislation' (1995) 54 Maryland Law Review 633; Richard Bellamy, *Political Constitutionalism: A Republican Defence of the Constitutionality of Democracy* (CUP 2007).

[15] These are 'attitude-to-fact', 'attitude-to-action', and 'attitude-to-attitude' standards of rationality. See, List and Pettit, *Group Agency* (n 11) 24. To be clear, rationality, as used here, does not refer to the desirability of a decision as determined by an external standard of, say, morality or economic efficiency.

[16] Ekins (n 12) 116.

[17] Waldron, 'Legislating with Integrity' (n 13) 373.

[18] List and Pettit, *Group Agency* (n 11) ch 1.

[19] Ekins (n 12) 144.

if a & b). Individuals can hold complete attitudes towards, and make consistent judgements about, such interrelated propositions. For example, our single-person legislature may find a budget deficit likely, prefer a balanced budget, and therefore decide to raise taxes or cut public spending. Groups, however, must aggregate the individual judgements of their members into a collective group judgement, which can be difficult when their members disagree. Within legislative assemblies, disagreement is the order of the day: legislative representatives may disagree, for example, about the likelihood of a budget deficit or the desirability of a balanced budget. Deliberation may resolve some of these disagreements but rarely leads to collective attitudes shared by all legislative representatives.[20] Hence, the need for an aggregation procedure by which legislatures can form a collective judgement on the propositions on the agenda based on the individual positions of their members. Most use majority voting, but different aggregation procedures are conceivable, including qualified majority and unanimity rule. The EU legislature is a case in point: it uses different aggregation rules as part of the same process—majority voting in the Parliament and qualified majority voting (and sometimes unanimity rule) in the Council.

I first want to abstract from the EU legislative process and focus on the aggregation procedure commonly used: majority rule. The problem with majority rule is that it can generate inconsistent collective judgements even when individuals hold consistent views on the propositions on the agenda. This is called the 'discursive dilemma'.[21] Christian List and Philip Pettit have shown that this dilemma can arise in any group of three or more members who make collective judgements on interrelated propositions by majority rule, including legislative assemblies.[22] Their impossibility theorem proves that groups that use an 'ideal' procedure to aggregate the attitudes of their members into a joint group attitude cannot act rationally. An ideal aggregation procedure is one that satisfies four conditions: 'universal domain', 'anonymity', 'systematicity', and 'collective rationality'. An aggregation procedure satisfies *collective rationality* if it produces consistent and complete group attitudes: if a group has a positive or negative attitude towards each proposition on the agenda (completeness) and if the collective attitudes towards the different propositions are co-realisable (consistency). It satisfies *universal domain* if it admits the complete and consistent judgements of all group members about the propositions on the agenda. It satisfies *anonymity* if it gives equal weight to the attitudes of all group members. And it satisfies *systematicity* if the group attitude towards

[20] According to List, 'most theorists recognise [that] we cannot rely on deliberation to generate consensus': Christian List, 'Democratic Deliberation and Social Choice: A Review' in André Bächtiger and others (eds), *The Oxford Handbook of Deliberative Democracy* (1st edn, OUP 2018) 470.

[21] List and Pettit, *Group Agency* (n 11) 45. For a less technical exploration of the discursive dilemma, read Philip Pettit, 'Collective Persons and Powers' (2002) 8 Legal Theory 443.

[22] List and Pettit, *Group Agency* (n 11) 47.

each proposition is determined only by the attitudes of their members towards that proposition, not by their attitudes towards other propositions on the agenda. List and Pettit's impossibility theorem shows that a decision-making procedure cannot meet the four criteria simultaneously. More specifically, an aggregation procedure that satisfies universal domain, anonymity, and systematicity cannot meet the fourth condition of collective rationality.

To illustrate this, take once again the example of a legislature having to decide whether to act to prevent a budget deficit. Assume, as in Table 5.1, that the legislature consists of three legislators who must make a judgement on the three interrelated propositions mentioned earlier: (a) whether a budget deficit will occur, (b) whether a balanced budget is desirable, and (c) whether action should be taken.

As Table 5.1 shows, this legislature uses a decision-making procedure that satisfies universal domain: it admits the attitudes of all three legislators on the propositions on the agenda; no attitudes are excluded. The procedure also satisfies anonymity, assigning equal weight to these attitudes, and it satisfies systematicity: the attitude of the entire legislature towards each proposition is determined only by the attitudes of the three members towards that proposition, not by their attitudes towards other propositions on the agenda. Thus, more concretely, the collective attitude on proposition (a) depends only on the individual attitudes on proposition (a), the collective attitude on proposition (b) depends only on the individual attitudes on proposition (b), and so forth.

Table 5.1 also shows that three legislators hold consistent attitudes at the individual level on the proposition that (c) action is required if (a) there will be a budget deficit and (b) a balanced budget is desirable. Indeed, their individual judgements are consistent (c if a & b). But, as the bottom row shows, if they were to decide on each proposition by majority vote, a majority of two legislators will judge that a budget deficit is likely and that a balanced budget is desirable, but only a minority of one legislator will favour action. So, as the example shows, individuals may hold consistent attitudes on interrelated propositions, but majority

Table 5.1 Legislature of three legislators, simple majority vote.

	(a) Budget deficit	(b) Balanced budget	(c) Action required
Legislator I	Yes	No	No
Legislator II	Yes	Yes	Yes
Legislator III	No	Yes	No
Collective decision	Yes	Yes	No

voting on these propositions may still produce inconsistent group judgements that undermine collective rationality (a & b, but not c). This dilemma is not merely a hypothetical one: it can arise in legislative assemblies that have to decide on many more interrelated propositions than the three in Table 5.1. The dilemma such assemblies face, therefore, is that they can either allow their members to act on their individual attitudes, in which case their collective decisions may be collectively irrational, or deprive their members of the ability to act on their attitudes to ensure collective rationality.

List and Pettit were not the first to show this. There are important parallels between their impossibility theorem and that of Kenneth Arrow,[23] which should be briefly discussed. Arrow universalised the majority voting paradox observed by the Marquis de Condorcet in the eighteenth century. The latter noted that collective preferences could be unstable in groups of three or more individuals that decide between three (or more) options (X, Y, and Z): one majority could prefer X over Y, a second Y over Z, and a third Z over Y—collective preferences could be cyclical. Arrow established that preference cycling could occur not just under majority rule: any aggregation procedure satisfying certain criteria would fail to produce coherent results. Although I am in no position to discuss the parallels between the theorems of Arrow and List and Pettit,[24] I mention Arrow because some have thought his theorem to prove the unintelligibility of the concept of legislative intent. Since the attitudes of individual legislators towards political propositions are aggregated into a joint legislative attitude by majority vote, and since the majorities that determine the legislative attitude on these propositions is likely to shift across time and policy area, it has been argued that the legislative attitude must logically be inconsistent. This would not only jeopardise the integrity of legislative action but also render unintelligible the notion of legislative intent. It shows, according to Kenneth Shepsle, that 'there is not a single legislative intent, but rather many legislators' intents'.[25]

Concrete examples of preference cycling in legislative assemblies are hard to find, suggesting that it is far less common than Arrow's theorem might seem to suggest.[26] However (and this is crucial), this does not refute the impossibility theorems. As we will see, legislative decision-making is stable in large part due to institutional constraints, such as agenda-setters and legislative procedures. Therefore, sceptics of legislative decision-making may point out that if it is institutions and

[23] Kenneth Joseph Arrow, *Social Choice and Individual Values* (Yale UP 1986). For a non-technical explanation of Arrow's theorem, Gerry Mackie, *Democracy Defended* (CUP 2003) 78–82.
[24] For a discussion, Christian List and Philip Pettit, 'Aggregating Sets of Judgments: Two Impossibility Results Compared' (2004) 140 Synthese 207.
[25] Shepsle (n 8) 244.
[26] Mackie (n 23).

not jointly held majoritarian attitudes that determine what policies prevail, legislative decision-making is primarily 'dependent on idiosyncratic, structural, procedural, and strategic factors, which are at best tenuously related to normative principles embraced by democratic theorists'.[27] In that case, the appeal of settling political questions through the EU legislative process would diminish rapidly. The challenge is thus twofold: to show that the EU legislature can form and act upon a consistent set of intentions and that it can form these intentions in non-arbitrary ways. Fortunately, as we shall see, it can do both.

3. Escaping the Discursive Dilemma

Before we continue, it should be made clear what the impossibility theorems tell us exactly. They do not say that collective decision-making is bound to be collectively irrational. Nor do they advise groups to use an aggregation procedure that satisfies the conditions 'collective rationality', 'universal domain', 'anonymity', and 'systematicity'. Rather, they provide a theoretical framework to make us understand how groups can aggregate individual preferences into collective judgements and the costs associated with alternative ways of doing so. As List and Pettit emphasise, their theorem proves that no aggregation procedure can satisfy all four conditions, not that groups cannot form rational attitudes. Instead, by relaxing one or more of the other three conditions, a group can aggregate the individual attitudes of its members into a rational group attitude.[28]

So, should legislatures that want to produce consistent legislative attitudes simply relax one of the other conditions? Unfortunately, it is not that easy: relaxing these conditions comes with a price that may be unacceptable. Which condition to relax depends, at least in part, on the nature of the group, but legislatures should not relax universal domain and anonymity alone, since these are conditions of democratic fairness. First, we expect democratic legislatures to be representative of the pluralism in our societies, in which case legislative representatives should be allowed to act upon their own attitudes towards political propositions (universal domain). By relaxing universal domain, a group excludes from the decision-making process individual attitudes that are too incohesive to produce consistent group attitudes. This would allow them to produce group attitudes that meet the condition of collective rationality, as well as anonymity and systematicity,[29] but

[27] Shepsle (n 8) 244.
[28] List and Pettit, *Group Agency* (n 11) 50; List and Pettit, 'Aggregating Sets of Judgments' (n 24) 223.
[29] List and Pettit, *Group Agency* (n 11) 51–52.

Table 5.2 Legislature of five legislators, simple majority vote.

	(a) Budget deficit	(b) Balanced budget	(c) Action required
Legislator I	Yes	No	No
Legislator II	Yes	Yes	Yes
Legislator III	No	Yes	No
Legislator IV	Yes	Yes	Yes
Legislator V	No	Yes	No
Collective decision	Yes	Yes	No

this solution is undemocratic: we cannot imagine democratic legislatures not admitting the views of individual legislators with outlying opinions. Second, it is also undemocratic to use an aggregation function that relaxes anonymity alone, that is that would treat its members unequally. While this would enable the formation of rational group attitudes, the only function that satisfies universal domain, collective rationality, and systematicity but relaxes anonymity is a dictatorship.[30] It may be evident why this is unattractive, democratically speaking.

As a rule of thumb, List and Pettit caution against relaxing collective rationality and advocate that groups relax systematicity, either alone or in combination with anonymity.[31] However, groups can form consistent attitudes by relaxing collective rationality. Recall that collective rationality consists of two components: consistency and completeness. A group's attitudes are consistent if its attitudes towards the propositions on the agenda are co-realisable; they are complete if it has a positive or negative attitude towards all propositions on the agenda.[32] Consistency is indispensable: legislatures should avoid enacting inconsistent provisions. Completeness, however, may be an overly demanding requirement. To see this, consider again the example of the legislature deciding whether to take action to prevent a budget deficit, but now suppose that it has five members who must form joint attitudes on the same three propositions as in Table 5.1. As Table 5.2 shows, this legislature uses a decision-making procedure that satisfies universal domain, anonymity, and systematicity.

Table 5.2 also shows that all five legislators hold a consistent attitude towards the proposition that (c) action is required if (a) there will be a budget deficit and (b) a balanced budget is preferable (c if a & b). However, if the five legislators were

30 ibid 53.
31 ibid.
32 ibid 49.

Table 5.3 Legislature of five legislators, four-fifth majority vote.

	(a) Budget deficit	(b) Balanced budget	(c) Action required
Legislator I	Yes	No	No
Legislator II	Yes	Yes	Yes
Legislator III	No	Yes	No
Legislator IV	Yes	Yes	Yes
Legislator V	No	Yes	No
Collective decision	–	Yes	–

to decide on each proposition by majority vote, a majority of three would accept proposition (a), a majority of four would accept proposition (b), but a majority of three would reject proposition (c). As in Table 5.1, the individual legislators hold consistent attitudes on interrelated propositions, but majority voting among them produces inconsistent group attitudes (a & b, but not c).

Now suppose that the legislature uses a procedure that requires a *four-fifths majority* to form a positive or negative attitude towards propositions (a), (b), and (c). Table 5.3 shows that if the attitudes of our legislators towards these propositions remain unchanged, this aggregation procedure generates a positive attitude towards proposition (b) but no attitude, either positive or negative, towards propositions (a) and (c), since no four legislators are for or against these propositions.

Indeed, the joint attitudes of the group using this aggregation procedure are *not inconsistent, but they are incomplete*, which is a direct result of the supermajority rule used. As List and Pettit point out, 'if the required supermajority rule is sufficiently high . . . this aggregation function produces consistent group attitudes, while satisfying universal domain, anonymity, and systematicity'.[33] But this comes at a cost too. While incompleteness may generally be preferable to inconsistency, groups that too often fail to form complete attitudes cannot react adequately when they have reason to act. EU scholars are well aware of the risk of indecisiveness associated with supermajority rule,[34] a risk famously encapsulated by Fritz Scharpf's account of the 'joint-decision trap'.[35] There is, ultimately, no single best aggregation procedure; the procedure a group should use depends on the interests it wants to

[33] ibid 53.

[34] Erik Jones, R Daniel Kelemen, and Sophie Meunier, 'Failing Forward? The Euro Crisis and the Incomplete Nature of European Integration' (2016) 49 Comparative Political Studies 1010.

[35] Fritz W Scharpf, 'The Joint-Decision Trap Revisited' (2006) 44 Journal of Common Market Studies 845. Note that the joint decision trap consists not just of a requirement of (near-)unanimity but also on the dependency of the central government on the agreement of constituent governments.

protect,[36] but while supermajority rule allows for consistent intentional attitudes, it makes the formation of group attitudes more difficult.

For most groups, the most attractive way of forming consistent collective attitudes is to relax systematicity. This condition is satisfied when the group's attitude towards a proposition depends only on its members' attitude towards that proposition and not towards other propositions. Thus, by relaxing systematicity, the group's attitude towards a proposition can depend on its members' attitudes towards other propositions. They can prioritise certain propositions over others and let the priority proposition condition the group's attitude towards secondary propositions.[37] Inconsistency can be addressed through forms of feedback between attitudes taking shape at the group level and the group member's individual attitudes. Members can prevent collective irrationality by adjusting their individual attitudes. Such attitude adjustments can be genuine, following deliberation and debate, but also strategic, if, for example, individuals prefer consistency and completeness at the group level to realising their own attitudes.[38]

Groups can also relax systematicity together with anonymity. This enables groups not only to prioritise certain propositions over others but also to form subgroups that can specialise in specific propositions and define the group's attitudes towards these propositions.[39] Specialisation offers several advantages, particularly for groups that must decide on a series of complex problems at the same time. Such groups may not have the time to collectively think through all relevant problems; specialisation allows them to assign responsibility for such problems to different subgroups. It also allows subgroup members to develop expertise on the issues within their purview, which, in turn, can improve the overall quality of the group's decisions.[40]

That said, relaxing systematicity can have drawbacks. Most of all, it may allow individual group members to manipulate decision-making in their favour. Members may disagree on the importance of different propositions and thus on which of them must be given priority. One way to settle such disagreements is to let agenda-setters determine the priority, but agenda-setters can set priorities in such a way that they realise their own preferred outcomes.[41] Moreover, specialisation distributes power unevenly: it privileges those who belong to the subgroup that shapes the group's collective attitude. The risk, at least in theory, is that the collective attitude that prevails is not supported by a majority of the group's members and is, instead, the result of strategic behaviour by agenda-setters or subgroup

[36] Robert E Goodin and Christian List, 'Special Majorities Rationalized' (2006) 36 British Journal of Political Science 213.
[37] List and Pettit, *Group Agency* (n 11) 55–56.
[38] ibid 61–63.
[39] ibid 57.
[40] ibid 95–97.
[41] ibid 57.

members. Nevertheless, relaxing systematicity, possibly together with anonymity, is usually the best way for groups to form rational attitudes—including, as we see now, for legislatures.

4. Rational Legislative Action

Legislatures are large and heterogeneous assemblies that are expected to act with reason when they identify the need for legal change. But how do they guarantee rational legislative action despite their complexity? This section shows that legislatures are capable of collective rationality not despite but thanks to their complex internal organisation. I will study institutions that contemporary legislatures share and explain how these institutions contribute to the aggregation of the individual attitudes of legislative representatives into coherent, collective legislative attitudes. As we will see, contemporary legislatures, for all their differences, are hierarchical and inegalitarian organisations. These hierarchies and inequalities relax the systematicity and anonymity of the legislative process, thereby enabling the aggregation of individual attitudes into joint legislative attitudes.

To that end, let us first imagine a simple legislature with no internal organisational divisions: the kind of legislature Gary Cox calls the 'legislative state of nature'.[42] The legislative state of nature consists of 'an assembly in which all business is conducted in the plenary session (no committees) and members' ability to talk and make motions is largely unrestricted and unregulated'.[43] This may sound appealing, but unregulated assemblies face a key problem: a scarcity of plenary time. Legislators could endlessly delay legislation if their right to speak and propose motions and amendments were unlimited; there would not be enough time left to debate societal problems worthy of their attention: the ability of the simple legislature to legislate would be weakened by the 'plenary bottleneck'.[44] This explains why all contemporary legislatures regulate plenary time and streamline the legislative process through agenda-setting offices. This, in turn, facilitates the formation of factions and parties, as access to such offices depends on the distribution of power among legislators.[45] This suggests that legislatures are inherently complex organisations, as they want to act effectively while plenary time is scarce.

Some believe that essential requirements of democratic fairness are met only in the legislative state of nature and that, therefore, internal legislative divisions of power are problematic; that is, some social choice theorists and deliberative democrats assume that a fair procedure is an unconstrained procedure: both 'demand

[42] Gary W Cox, 'The Organization of Democratic Legislatures' in Barry R Weingast and Donald A Wittman (eds), *The Oxford Handbook of Political Economy* (OUP 2008) 141.
[43] ibid.
[44] ibid.
[45] ibid.

equal access to debate, the absence of a powerful agenda setter, unrestrained access to raise and object to amendments and so on'.[46] But while deliberative democrats believe that unconstrained democracy is democracy in its ideal form, social choice theorists argue that it illustrates the impossibility of democratic fairness. As we saw earlier, they believe that policy-making will cycle if decisions are taken through unconstrained but fair democratic procedures. Cycling can be prevented, they say, but only through arbitrary institutional design.[47] However, as we saw in section V.2, cycling does not happen when decisions are taken by unanimity rule: political attitudes may be incomplete, but they are consistent. Thus, as law-making in the legislative state of nature can be infinitely frustrated without unanimous agreement among members of the legislature, cycling will not happen.[48] It does not happen either when legislative decision-making is constrained by agenda-setting offices, political parties, and legislative committees, since such institutions relax systematicity together with anonymity.

Inconsistent attitude formation is most likely in legislatures that seek to establish a direct link between citizens and representatives, unmediated by political parties. Legislative representatives are then directly delegated by citizens and are supposed to act as guardians of their constituents' interests. Political parties are anathema to theories of democracy which believe that elected representatives should act as delegates of citizens since parties increase the distance between voters and representatives and thwart the former's ability to control the latter. However, examples of successful democratic legislative assemblies unmediated by political parties are hard to find precisely because parties play such a vital role.[49] Simon Hix, Abdul Noury, and Gérard Roland have identified six benefits of strong parties for democracy, two relating to external electoral politics and four to internal legislative politics. Their contribution to external electoral politics lies in their ability to mobilise voters and strengthen citizens' identification with politics. They strengthen internal legislative politics by allowing representatives (a) to focus on issues falling within their areas of expertise and (b) to propose legislation that benefits a larger constituency and by reducing (3) the volatility and (4) dimensionality of politics.[50] The last two benefits enable stable legislative decision-making, as I will now discuss in more detail.

[46] The common assumptions behind social choice theory and some forms of deliberative democracy were explored by, David van Mill, 'The Possibility of Rational Outcomes from Democratic Discourse and Procedures' (1996) 58 Journal of Politics 734.

[47] Shepsle (n 8); Kenneth A Shepsle and Barry R Weingast, 'Why So Much Stability? Majority Voting, Legislative Institutions, and Gordon Tullock' (2012) 152 Public Choice 83.

[48] That cycling is not a problem in the legislative state of nature was emphasised also by Cox (n 42) 144.

[49] 'Their ubiquity suggests that they are virtually, if not actually, a necessity for a democracy to be viable': John A Aldrich, 'Political Parties In and Out of Legislatures' in Robert E Goodin (ed), *The Oxford Handbook of Political Science* (OUP 2011) 196.

[50] Simon Hix, Abdul G Noury, and Gérard Roland, *Democratic Politics in the European Parliament* (CUP 2007) ch 2.

First dimensionality: political conflicts are normally characterised by more than one dimension of conflict. Suppose there are two such dimensions: welfare distribution and standards of ecological protection. In that case, a proposal that seeks to provide high levels of redistribution and ecological protection may be defeated by another proposal for high levels of redistribution and low levels of ecological protection, which, in turn, may be defeated by a third proposal that favours low levels of both redistribution and ecological protection. In other words, political outcomes may cycle when more than one dimension of political conflict exists.[51] Political parties reduce the dimensionality of politics by presenting manifestos that integrate different dimensions into coherent policy proposals that are comprehensible to voters.[52] Parties thus reduce the myriad number of policy options that theoretically exists to a more limited number of distinct programmes whereby they manage to aggregate individual attitudes into coherent group attitudes. After all, parties expect their members to stick to the party line and will try to enforce party discipline by rewarding loyal members and punishing disobedient ones.[53]

The resulting cohesiveness, in turn, reduces volatility. Volatility can only occur when multiple members can propose legislation, which would allow a variety of inconsistent policies to be proposed and enacted.[54] However, because of the central role that political parties and agenda-setters play in the legislative process, the right to propose legislation is limited to only a few members. All legislatures have agenda-setting offices, as we saw earlier, because the time of individual representatives and the legislative plenary is scarce and because representatives will want to use the available time efficiently. Access to these offices is unevenly distributed among representatives, depending on party membership and strength. Parties with more seats or that are in government tend to have better access.[55] So, since the legislative agenda is set by a few parties, legislative politics will not be volatile.

Not only political parties but also legislative committees contribute to consistent legislative decisions. Modern legislatures assign responsibility for specific policy areas (social affairs, economic policy, etc) to such committees, by which they task a subgroup of legislators to draft or scrutinise legislation that falls within their area of expertise. This division of labour has several advantages. It allows the legislature to focus on multiple political issues at once and enables individual legislators to acquire expertise in specific policy areas, allowing them to exercise more effective control over the executive branch.[56] In addition, it allows subgroups of legislative representatives to determine the collective legislative attitude towards

[51] ibid 45.
[52] ibid 46; John M Carey, 'Legislative Organization' in Roderick AW Rhodes, Sarah A Binder, and Bert A Rockman (eds), *The Oxford Handbook of Political Institutions* (OUP 2008) 445.
[53] Hix, Noury, and Roland (n 50) ch 5.
[54] ibid 40–42.
[55] Cox (n 42) 148.
[56] List and Pettit, *Group Agency* (n 11) 95–97.

specific political propositions whereby they help aggregate the individual intentions of representatives into consistent legislative intentions.

The hierarchical organisation of legislatures creates real inequalities among its members. As Cox said, 'while legislators are everywhere equal in voting power, they are everywhere unequal in agenda-setting power'.[57] In the first place, these hierarchies may be a response to the scarcity of plenary time, but they also help aggregate the attitudes of legislative representatives into consistent legislative attitudes: they relax the systematicity and anonymity of the legislative process. Political parties help reduce the countless policy choices to a coherent set of policies, in part because they expect members to follow the party line and not their individual attitudes. Of course, legislators will often be prepared to sacrifice their individual attitudes in favour of coherent legislative policies of their own accord: they know that the effectiveness of their actions and respect for their office depends on the collective rationality of their decisions. The potential for inconsistency is further reduced by the influential role of agenda-setters and the internal division of labour between legislative committees. Such committees relax systematicity and anonymity by allowing a select group of representatives to define the collective attitude of the entire legislature. These inequalities (ie the restrictions placed on individual legislators' ability to act upon their individual attitudes) mean that legislatures are, in principle, capable of reasoned action when the situation demands.

5. The Formation of EU Legislative Intent

As we saw in the introduction, people question the EU legislature's capacity to integrate the complex inputs of its members into consistent legislative attitudes. My ambition in this section is to dispel such doubts by highlighting how the internal organisation of the institutions involved in the legislative process—the Commission, the Parliament, and the Council—facilitates the aggregation of the individual intentions of their members into joint institutional intentions and how the structure of the legislative process enables the aggregation of the intentions of these institutions into a joint legislative intention. This section focuses on ordinary legislative procedure, but its conclusions should apply to special legislative procedures as well.

The Commission, the EU's formal agenda-setter,[58] launches the legislative process when it submits a legislative proposal to the Parliament and the Council. The function of Commissioners and their Directorates General (DGs) is comparable

[57] Cox (n 42) 142.

[58] Although the European Council, which shall provide 'the Union with the necessary impetus for its development and shall define the general political directions and policies thereof' (art 15 of the Treaty on the Functioning of the European Union, TFEU) may well be the more powerful agenda-setter.

to that of ministers and their ministries in national parliamentary systems.[59] Commissioners and their cabinets form the political arm of the Commission, which is supported by a sizeable administration that is responsible for the Commission's day-to-day affairs, including drafting legislative proposals. Cutting across this horizontal division between political and bureaucratic functionaries is a vertical division of about thirty-five DGs that is responsible for specific policy areas, such as climate, competition, and economic and financial affairs.[60] Legislative proposals are drafted by a single DG, one or more of whose officials prepare a first draft, after gathering the required information and discussing the relevant issues with interested parties. This DG 'shall ensure from the beginning of the preparatory work that there is effective coordination between all the departments with a legitimate interest in the initiative by virtue of their powers or responsibilities or the nature of the subject'.[61] Other departments may respond to the draft proposal by expressing their disapproval, their agreement, or their agreement subject to substantial comments. The responsible DG then revises the draft proposal using the opinions expressed by other departments, after which outstanding issues are discussed and negotiated between the affected DGs at the political level.[62]

Coordination between DGs is essential to bridge differences of insight and interest and ensure consistency. The Commission did not always succeed in this due to its 'fragile internal coordination capacities',[63] but coordination between departments has improved.[64] The Commission's Rules of Procedure require its members to work 'in close cooperation and in coordinated fashion from the outset in the preparation and implementation of Commission decisions'.[65] The consistency of legislation is safeguarded by the Legal Service, which assesses draft proposals for their compatibility with the existing legal framework.[66] The fact that this framework acts as an influential constraint on what can be proposed shows that Commission officials in charge of preparing legislation understand that their proposals must be consistent with the law already in place.[67]

Once the proposal has been submitted to the Parliament and Council, the legislative process enters the first reading stage. Parliament is the first to form a position on the proposal. The Conference of Presidents, consisting of the President of the

[59] Hix, Noury, and Roland (n 50) 111.
[60] Miriam Hartlapp, Julia Metz, and Christian Rauh, *Which Policy for Europe? Power and Conflict Inside the European Commission* (OUP 2014) 15–16.
[61] Article 23(2) of the Commission Rules of Procedure.
[62] Hartlapp, Metz, and Rauh (n 60) 16–17.
[63] Andrew Jordan and Adriaan Schout, *The Coordination of the European Union: Exploring the Capacities of Networked Governance* (OUP 2006) 220.
[64] ibid; John Peterson, 'Playing the Transparency Game: Consultation and Policy-Making in the European Commission' (1995) 73 Public Administration 473.
[65] Article 23(1) of the Commission Rules of Procedure.
[66] ibid art 23(4).
[67] Hartlapp, Metz, and Rauh (n 60) 262–63.

European Parliament and the chairs of the political groups, decides which legislative committee will debate the proposed legislative act.[68] This committee selects one of its members to act as rapporteur,[69] which is done using a complex auction system that gives political groups a number of points in proportion to their size. As a result, the rapporteur is usually a Member of the European Parliament (MEP) from a larger political party.[70] The rapporteur is responsible for writing a report that defines the Parliament's position. This report includes a legislative resolution defining the position, the proposed legislative amendments, and an explanation of the amendments.[71] The legislative committee can debate and amend the report. Once approved, the report appears on the plenary session's agenda, at which point MEPs have the right to propose amendments, followed by a vote on the proposed amendments and then on the entire legislative proposal as amended. If the proposal obtains a majority of the votes cast, it is forwarded to the Council and the Commission.[72]

As long as the Council has not acted, the Commission can amend its proposal in response to the parliamentary position.[73] If the Commission exercises this right, the Parliament's President may request that it be resubmitted to Parliament.[74] If it does not, or if Parliament does not request a resubmission, the ball is in the Council's court. The Council can approve the Parliament's position, in which case the proposed act is adopted in the wording that corresponds to this position. It may also decide to propose amendments of its own.[75] Formal decisions are taken by the responsible national ministers, but preparatory work is carried out by the Committee of Permanent Representatives of the Member States (Coreper), which is 'responsible for preparing the work of the Council and for carrying out the tasks assigned to it by the latter'.[76] According to the Council's Rules of Procedure, Coreper shall 'ensure consistency of the European Union's policies and actions'[77] and 'endeavour to reach agreement at its level to be submitted to the Council for adoption'.[78] It does so by examining in advance all items on the agenda unless the Council decides otherwise.[79] Coreper consists of fifty-six members, a permanent

[68] Rules 26 and 27 of the Rules of Procedure of the European Parliament.
[69] ibid Rule 49.
[70] For an explanation, Richard Corbett, Francis Geoffrey Jacobs, and Michael Shackleton, *The European Parliament* (Harper 2011) 158–59; Nikoleta Yordanova, 'Inter-Institutional Rules and Division of Power in the European Parliament: Allocation of Consultation and Co-Decision Reports' (2011) 34 West European Politics 97, 101. For a perspective from within the European Parliament, Neil MacCormick, 'Legislative Deliberation: Notes from the European Parliament' in Luc Wintgens (ed), *The Theory and Practice of Legislation: Essays in Legisprudence* (Ashgate 2005) 291.
[71] Rule 49 of the Rules of Procedure of the European Parliament.
[72] ibid Rule 59.
[73] Article 293(2) of the TFEU.
[74] Rule 63 of the Rules of Procedure of the European Parliament.
[75] Article 294(4–5) of the TFEU.
[76] ibid art 240(1).
[77] Article 19(1) of the Council's Rules of Procedure.
[78] ibid art 19(2).
[79] ibid art 19(2).

representative, and deputy permanent representative from each Member State.[80] As these members cannot do the preparatory work alone, they are supported by their national delegations in Brussels and a dense network of committees and working parties that carry 'out certain preparatory work or studies defined in advance'.[81]

National officials sitting on working parties study every aspect of proposed legislative acts and Parliament's position on them, and they negotiate until they either reach a consensus on the proposal or decide that some issues are too divisive to be agreed upon at the working party level. The proposal then moves up the Council's decision-making chain, through Coreper, where it may or may not be discussed further, depending on the decision reached at the working party level, until it reaches the Council agenda. Items that appear on the agenda are divided into A and B items.[82] A items are those that can be approved by the national ministers without further discussion. B items, usually about one-third of the items on the agenda, will be subject to further debate and negotiation. If the ministers fail to agree on the proposal, it will return to Coreper and the supporting committees for further debate until it reappears on the Council agenda.[83] Most decisions are subject to qualified majority rule; in reality, they are almost always taken by consensus.

If the Council does not adopt Parliament's position, the proposal enters the second reading stage. Unlike the first stage, the second is subject to strict deadlines. Parliament has three months to decide on the Council's position,[84] though its President can extend this period by a month following a request by the Chair of the responsible legislative committee.[85] More importantly, unless the Council position differs from the proposal discussed at first reading, or unless a new fact or legal situation has arisen, amendments may only be adopted if they 'restore wholly or partly the position adopted . . . at its first reading' or if they 'reach compromise between the Council and Parliament'.[86] The goal is to find a compromise, unless Parliament insists on its original position. Responsibility for the proposal at the second reading lies with the committee and rapporteur responsible at the first stage.[87] The committee submits a recommendation to Parliament to approve, amend, or reject the Council's position.[88] If the position is approved, the proposal is adopted. If it is rejected, the legislative process is closed. If it is amended, the

[80] Jeffrey Lewis, 'Coreper: National Interests and the Logic of Appropriateness' in Dermor Hodson and John Peterson (eds), *The Institutions of the European Union* (4th edn, OUP 2017) 340.

[81] Article 19(3) of the Council's Rules of Procedure.

[82] ibid art 3.

[83] Fiona Hayes-Renshaw, 'The Council of Ministers: Conflict, Consensus, and Continuity' in Hodson and Peterson (n 80) 86.

[84] Article 294(7) of the TFEU.

[85] ibid art 294(14) and Rule 64 of the Parliament's Rules of Procedure.

[86] Rule 68 of the Parliament's Rules of Procedure.

[87] ibid Rules 63 and 65.

[88] ibid Rule 65.

proposed amendments are forwarded to the Council and Commission, who shall both put forward their respective opinions.[89]

The Council must respond to the amendments within three months. It must act unanimously on amendments on which the Commission has delivered a negative opinion.[90] Other amendments may be approved by qualified majority vote. If it does not approve the proposed amendments, the conciliation stage begins.[91] The conciliation committee consists of an equal number of Council representatives and MEPs. Taking the positions of the Parliament and Council at second reading as its point of departure, the committee has six weeks from its convening to reach agreement on a joint text, which must be approved by a qualified majority of members representing the Council and a majority of members representing the Parliament.[92] The Commission shall also participate and 'take all necessary initiatives with a view to reconciling the positions of the European Parliament and the Council'.[93] The six-week deadline may be extended by two weeks, but if no agreement is reached within that period, the proposal is not adopted.[94] If the committee agrees on a joint text, Parliament, acting by majority vote, and the Council, acting by qualified majority vote, have six weeks to approve the joint text.[95]

The entire legislative process is structured so that each institution can carefully study and debate proposed legislation but also so that they work together towards a final version that they can jointly agree upon. The internal organisation of the three institutions enables them to coordinate their collective actions and to take a coherent position towards the proposals before them, in line with the legislative framework already in place. The Commission's efforts to submit proposals that are in line with the law in place show that it is prepared to make its attitude dependent on the legislature's attitude on previous issues. As I will now show, the Parliament and Council can also aggregate their members' attitudes into consistent institutional attitudes.

The European Parliament is 'a normal parliament in a polity of a different kind'.[96] Like national parliaments, it allocates power unevenly among its members. Its internal proceedings are dominated by political groups, which determine the

89 Article 294(7) of the TFEU. See also Rule 67 of the Parliament's Rules of Procedure.
90 Article 294(9) of the TFEU.
91 ibid art 294(8).
92 ibid art 294(10).
93 ibid art 294(11).
94 ibid art 294(12).
95 ibid art 294(13).
96 Ariadna Ripoll Servent and Christilla Roederer-Rynning, 'The European Parliament: A Normal Parliament in a Polity of a Different Kind', Oxford Research Encyclopedias (2018) <https://oxfordre.com/politics/view/10.1093/acrefore/9780190228637.001.0001/acrefore-9780190228637-e-152> accessed 2 March 2024. See also Hix, Noury, and Roland (n 50); Mark Williams, 'The European Parliament: Political Groups, Minority Rights and the "Rationalisations" of Parliamentary Organisation' in Herbert Döring (ed), *Parliaments and Majority Rule in Western Europe* (St Martin's Press 1995).

division of power between and within legislative committees and agenda-setting offices.[97] Political groups and legislative committees are 'the two main aggregating institutions in the European Parliament'.[98] While the initial expectation was that MEPs would organise themselves along national lines, they immediately divided into Christian Democrats, Social Democrats, and Liberals, not unlike the main political divisions at the national level.[99] These groups were soon officially recognised, becoming the main actors aggregating the preferences of individual MEPs. Their ascent was so spectacular that '[b]y the time the first European elections were held, in 1979, the political groups dominated all aspects of the parliament's work, from deciding who is elected to be the parliament's president, to assigning committee positions, to organising the agenda of the plenary'.[100] The groups are remarkably cohesive. Despite their relatively weak agenda-setting powers, they manage to discipline their members, compelling them to give up individual attitudes that clash with their political position.[101] This makes parties 'an essential instrument in the EP [European Parliament] to help aggregate individual interests into a coherent whole'.[102]

If political groups are Parliament's 'lifeblood', then the legislative committees are its 'legislative backbone'.[103] By delegating legislative tasks to these committees and the MEPs acting as rapporteurs, Parliament can manage its plenary agenda and gain informational benefits through specialisation.[104] The committees exert an enormous influence on the drafting of legislative proposals, and so the joint attitude of Parliament is, to a large extent, determined by the attitudes of these committees and the MEPs sitting on them.[105] Parliament's internal decision-making thus relaxes both systematicity and anonymity: it gives unequal weight to the attitudes of MEPs (relaxing anonymity), and MEPs who are not involved in the

97 Ripoll Servent and Roederer-Rynning (n 96).

98 Simon Hix and Bjørn Høyland, 'Empowerment of the European Parliament' (2013) 16 Annual Review of Political Science 171, 178.

99 Hix, Noury, and Roland (n 50) 22.

100 ibid 23.

101 For a detailed empirical discussion of what explains party cohesiveness in the European Parliament, ibid chs 5–7. See also Shaun Bowler and Gail McElroy, 'Political Group Cohesion and "Hurrah" Voting in the European Parliament' (2015) 22 Journal of European Public Policy 1355. Cohesion varies, however, across political groups and tends to be lower among Eurosceptical groups. See Tapio Raunio and Wolfgang Wagner, 'Contestation over Development Policy in the European Parliament' (2021) 59 Journal of Common Market Studies 20, 28.

102 Ripoll Servent and Roederer-Rynning (n 96).

103 Christine Neuhold, 'The "Legislative Backbone" Keeping the Institution Upright? The Role of European Parliament Committees in the EU Policy-Making Process' (2001) 5 European Integration Online Papers <https://eiop.or.at/eiop/pdf/2001-010.pdf>.

104 It has been suggested that specialisation has reinforced its negotiating position vis-à-vis the Council: Gail McElroy, 'Committee Representation in the European Parliament' (2006) 7 European Union Politics 5, 10; Rory Costello and Robert Thomson, 'The Policy Impact of Leadership in Committees: Rapporteurs' Influence on the European Parliament's Opinions' (2010) 11 European Union Politics 219, 221.

105 Nikoleta Yordanova, *Organising the European Parliament: The Role of Committees and Their Legislative Influence* (ECPR Press 2013); Hix and Høyland (n 98) 182–84.

drafting process may be expected to adjust their attitudes so that they are consistent with the collective attitudes formed in the committees (relaxing systematicity). Allowing committees and rapporteurs to define Parliament's joint position reduces the chances of inconsistent preference aggregation and allows it to act with integrity.

The Council also succeeds in integrating the interests of its members into a joint position, but not in the same way as Parliament. At each of its decision-making levels, 'a culture of consensus-based decision-making' exists.[106] National delegations seek to iron out their main disagreements during the negotiations, and there is an apparent willingness among the delegations to accommodate each other's concerns and find solutions that are acceptable to everyone. Therefore, even when decisions can be taken according to qualified majority rule, the ambition is to bring everyone on board and integrate all national interests.[107] In this way, the Council can realise consistent group attitudes by relaxing what List and Pettit call the condition of completeness. The downside of deciding in such a consensual fashion is that it may be more difficult to reach political agreement,[108] but the Council has, on the whole, proven remarkably effective in integrating the various national interests in a joint position, which it then defends vis-à-vis the other institutions.

The same is true of the EU legislature collectively, which has been a prolific institution that still churns out a steady volume of legislative acts.[109] This is partly because the legislative process is structured to facilitate joint action but also because the institutions involved can usually overcome their differences and legislate in the EU's common interest. The requirement that they justify their positions and listen and respond to the other side enables them to work towards a common plan of action. The Interinstitutional Agreement on Better Law-Making states that 'the ordinary legislative procedure has developed on the basis of regular contacts at all stages of the procedure', with the Commission acting as 'facilitator by treating the two branches of the legislative authority equally'.[110] The Joint Declaration on Practical Arrangements for the Codecision Procedure (now the ordinary legislative procedure) fosters continuous cooperation between the three institutions at

[106] Lewis (n 80) 335. See also Hayes-Renshaw (n 83) 89. It still exists today: Stéphanie Novak, Olivier Rozenberg, and Selma Bendjaballah, 'Enduring Consensus: Why the EU Legislative Process Stays the Same' (2021) 43 Journal of European Integration 475; Renaud Dehousse, Stéphanie Novak, and Selma Bendjaballah, 'Consensus under Pressure: The Evolution of Conflict in the EU Legislative Process' (2018) 58 Politique européenne 44.

[107] Lewis (n 80); Hayes-Renshaw (n 83).

[108] List and Pettit, *Group Agency* (n 11) 53.

[109] Recent years have seen a decrease in legislative output, but this is more the result of the Commission's intention 'to do less and do it better' than anything else: Hayes-Renshaw (n 83) 90. If it is difficult to amend legislation, this is 'less a result of institutional constraints and more a product of the policy preferences of the EU governments and the European Parliaments': Christophe Crombez and Simon Hix, 'Treaty Reform and the Commission's Appointment and Policy-Making Role in the European Union' (2011) 12 European Union Politics 291, 293.

[110] Interinstitutional Agreement between the European Parliament, the Council of the European Union and the European Commission on Better Law-Making (OJ L123/1) para 23.

all stages of the legislative process 'with a view to reconciling their positions as far as possible and thereby clearing the way, where appropriate, for the adoption of the act concerned'.[111] An example of this is the practice of so-called 'trilogue' meetings between representatives of the Commission, Parliament, and Council, where Commission proposals are discussed and negotiated. These meetings have proven highly successful in integrating the joint intentions of these institutions into a coherent and unified intention held by the EU legislature as a whole.[112]

But while the EU legislative process can produce consistent legislative attitudes, the concern may be that such attitudes can only be produced through arbitrary institutional design: through internal legislative institutions and procedures such as time limits, restrictions on the amendments that can be proposed, and the decisions of agenda-setters and legislative committees. If indeed so, the legislature's intentions would merely represent the political preferences of agenda-setters or committee members and not those of the legislative majority. They would depend on 'idiosyncratic, structural, procedural, and strategic factors'[113] and therefore undermine the legitimacy of EU legislative decision-making.[114] However, while legislative committees and rapporteurs exert considerable influence on the drafting of legislative proposals, it has been shown that their choices are representative of the position of the Parliament as a whole.[115] Political groups who were not allocated the rapporteurship normally appoint shadow rapporteurs who act as 'the main interlocutors of the rapporteur'.[116] Moreover, rapporteurs and shadow rapporteurs are responsive to their political groups' partisan position, in part because 'the open amendment procedures in the committee and the plenary' significantly limit their agenda-setting powers.[117] Even during more informal trilogue meetings, when they can act more independently of their legislative committees and other MEPs, they do not push their individual agenda at the expense of that of the Parliament.[118] There is, indeed, a clearly visible 'shadow that majorities and coalitions cast over

[111] Joint Declaration on Practical Arrangements for the Codecision Procedure (OJ C145/5) para 4.

[112] So much so that trilogue meetings have been criticised for undermining the openness of the legislative process, eg in the Decision of the Ombudsman setting out proposals following her strategic inquiry OI/8/2015/JAS concerning the transparency of Trilogues of 25 May 2015.

[113] Shepsle (n 8) 244.

[114] Since the Council takes decisions consensually, this worry is potentially justified only regarding the Parliament.

[115] Costello and Thomson (n 104); McElroy (n 104); Thomas Jensen and Thom as Winzen, 'Legislative Negotiations in the European Parliament' (2012) 13 European Union Politics 118; Léa Roger and Thomas Winzen, 'Party Groups and Committee Negotiations in the European Parliament: Outside Attention and the Anticipation of Plenary Conflict' (2015) 22 Journal of European Public Policy 391. Somewhat more sceptical, Nikoleta Yordanova, 'The Rationale behind Committee Assignment in the European Parliament: Distributive, Informational and Partisan Perspectives' (2009) 10 European Union Politics 253.

[116] Jensen and Winzen (n 115) 121. Rule 205a of the Rules of Procedure of the European Parliament.

[117] Costello and Thomson (n 104) 235. See also Jensen and Winzen (n 115) 146; Neuhold (n 103) 8.

[118] Christine Reh, 'Is Informal Politics Undemocratic? Trilogues, Early Agreements and the Selection Model of Representation' (2014) 21 Journal of European Public Policy 822, 835.

committee decisions',[119] which indicates that individual attitudes are typically aggregated into a coherent legislative attitude in non-arbitrary ways.

6. The (Ir)Relevance of Individual Intentions for Legislative Intent

It is now clear that the legislature can aggregate the divergent attitudes of its members into consistent legislative intentions. But the question that remains, and which will interest interpreters of legislative provisions, is how we can ascertain these intentions. It may still be a mystifying thought that we should be able to understand legislation by reference to the intentions of the legislature. While it is the case that legislation expresses an intention on the part of the legislature to change the law and that this intention is the sum of the individual intentions of its members, common sense suggests that it cannot be the sum of the intentions of all members. They may have had different attitudes towards a legislative proposal or no specific intention at all and voted for or against it only because their political party told them to do so.[120] So how can legislative intent be ascertained if it is impossible to ascertain the intentions of the relevant legislators. This section clarifies how we should understand legislative intent, in particular the relationship between the joint intention of the legislature and the individual intentions of its members. These intentions, I will explain, are relevant to the formation of legislative intent but irrelevant to the identification of legislative intent.

It is logical to think that people who act together can have shared intentions. Two pianists may play a duet together, a group of football players may play a game together, and some friends may go on vacation together. Such activity typically implies an intention on the part of the people involved to act together. Intentions can thus be understood as plans of action that settle present and future conduct.[121] However, to speak of joint intentions, it is not sufficient that two or more persons are engaged in the same activity. As Michael Bratman has explained, these persons must know to be engaged in the same activity, and their intentions must be interlocking so that each has the intention to support the effectiveness of the intentions of the other.[122] Another characteristic of intentions is that they are hierarchical: they 'embed means and preliminary steps, and general intentions embed more specific intentions'.[123] Therefore, a group intention consists of not only

[119] Ripoll Servent and Roederer-Rynning (n 96).
[120] Duxbury (n 3) 95.
[121] Michael E Bratman, *Faces of Intention* (CUP 1999) 2. See also Michael Bratman, *Shared Agency: A Planning Theory of Acting Together* (OUP 2014) ch 1.
[122] Bratman, *Faces of Intention* (n 121) 116–19. See also Philip Pettit and David Schweikard, 'Joint Actions and Group Agents' (2006) 36 Philosophy of the Social Sciences 18.
[123] Bratman, *Faces of Intention* (n 121) 3.

interlocking individual intentions but also the means and more specific intentions that will allow the group to realise its more general intentions.[124]

Individuals can be involved in joint action and jointly intend to produce some effect without constituting a group agent. A joint intentional act can be the product of several individuals separately acting together. Consider a group of beachgoers who act together to save a swimmer in distress. To this end, they may perform one or several actions together but do not thereby establish common goals that define them as a group and that guide their future actions.[125] Indeed, their joint action does not turn them into a group agent that defines their future behaviour.

But individuals can also act together as a group agent. Contrary to what this may suggest, the intentions individuals must share to form a jointly intentional group are not very demanding. It only requires that they jointly intend that the group exists to achieve certain goals and that they perform the role assigned to them, believing that others will do the same.[126] They need not be equal participants in the formation of the group's intentions or be equally committed to the group. They certainly need not all intend that the group acts in the way it does.[127] Especially the intentions of more complex groups will almost inevitably differ to a degree from the intentions of their members. In fact, as the discussion of the discursive dilemma in earlier sections taught us, groups that want to form consistent intentional attitudes may need to act in ways that not all members agree with. Yet, the mere fact that group members may not share their group's intentions does not mean that they no longer jointly intend that the group exists to achieve certain goals or that the joint intention that has been formed is not the intention of the entire group.

To clarify this point, consider the example of a multinational company that makes a decision that is not shared by everyone with a say in the decision, for example, the cancellation of the sales of a particular product.[128] The fact that some people involved in the official procedures the company uses to make decisions disagree with this decision does not mean that it was no longer a company decision. It most certainly was. The decision expresses the intention on the part of the company to cancel the sales of one of its products, regardless of any disagreement among those authorised to take such decisions. Not only that, but the example also shows that we do not need to know the individual intentions of all employees of the company, or even of the employees involved in the decision-making process, to know the intentions of the company. The example precisely shows that we can know the intentions of a group without knowing the intentions of its members.

We can also bring the example closer to home and closer to legislative reality: a faculty board adopting its doctoral regulations that set conditions for admission

[124] ibid 99–122.
[125] List and Pettit, *Group Agency* (n 11) 34. See also Pettit and Schweikard (n 122) 30.
[126] List and Pettit, *Group Agency* (n 11) 33–34,
[127] ibid 35.
[128] This example is a modified version of that used by Ekins (n 12) 58–59.

to the doctoral programme, the transition from one year of the programme to the next, and the completion of the doctoral degree. Such regulations are likely drawn up by a subgroup of the faculty board (the PhD board) but must be approved by a majority of members of the faculty board to be the faculty's doctoral regulations. Anyone who has attended such meetings knows that, most likely, there has been disagreement about the content of the regulations, among members of both the PhD board and the faculty board. Some members might even have voted against the PhD regulations as adopted; yet, the decision to adopt them is a decision of the faculty board: it is the intention of the board to regulate its PhD programme in a specific way. However, to identify how it intends to regulate its PhD programme, students need not first figure out the intentions of those involved in drawing up the regulations. If that were needed, the regulations could not achieve what they exist for. To guide the behaviour of PhD students, they must be able to understand the regulations' intended consequences without knowing the intentions of their drafters.

Now, there surely are important differences between a faculty board and a legislative assembly. For instance, the distance between a faculty board and the doctoral students subject to its regulations is much smaller than that between a legislature and the citizens subject to its laws. A faculty board can respond to questions from doctoral students about the correct reading of its regulations in a way that a legislature cannot to interpretative uncertainty on the part of citizens. Nevertheless, the example also underlines essential similarities between faculty boards and legislatures. Both try to guide the behaviour of those subject to their norms, and both try to do this in a way that allows these persons to know the intention of these norms without having to know the intention of the drafters of these norms. Indeed, the intentions of the drafters of legislative norms are relevant for the formation of legislative intent but irrelevant for its identification. Rather, as I will explain now, legislative intent must be identified from the publicly available legislative material.

The legislature is a group agent of the kind envisaged by List and Pettit. Its members intend that they jointly act to achieve the end for which the legislature exists: to enact legislation and amend the existing legal framework when there are good reasons to do so. This intention stems from the interlocking intentions of its members and is shared by all of them, even those who disagree with the legislative course of action.[129] As Neil Duxbury said of recalcitrant members, '[t]heir participation in the legislative process demonstrates that they accept its legitimacy—that they intend, as a matter of general principle, that through the process of legislative enactment the law on particular matters should change'.[130] However, when we speak of legislative intent, we speak not of this intention but of the more particular intention formed and acted upon in the exercise of legislative authority. It is the

129 Here, I follow ibid 219–24.
130 Duxbury (n 3) 107.

plan of action established for the entire Union, consisting of both the ends the legislature wants to realise and the means of achieving these ends.[131]

While this plan arises out of the joint actions of individual legislators, not all legislators must intend that the legislature acts in the way it does. Indeed, as we already know, legislative intent is not the sum of the intentions of all legislators or even of the majority that voted in favour of the adopted legislative act. They may have no detailed knowledge of the proposed act and vote one way or another simply because their party instructed them to do so. Furthermore, the fact that important decisions in the European Parliament are made by legislative committees means that not all members contribute to the formation of the joint legislative intention in equal ways. In such circumstances, legislative intent is, by necessity, partly autonomous from the individual intentions of these members. However (and this is crucial), it does not follow that the enacted legislation is not the joint act of the EU legislature. Legal philosopher and former MEP Neil MacCormick understood this well. Speaking from his experience, he explained that all representatives work 'towards trying to reach a conclusion that is imputed to [the legislature] as its conclusion'.[132]

But how, then, is the conclusion imputed to the legislature to be understood? This conclusion depends on the individual intentions of some of its members, but we might not know which members and what their intentions were. So, while the legislature can form a joint legislative intention out of the individual intentions of its members, it might appear that we cannot know this legislative intention simply because we cannot know the individual intentions that contributed to the formation of the legislative intention. However, the crux is that we can know what intentions we can reasonably impute to the legislature without knowing the intentions of individual legislators, just as we can reasonably know the intentions of a faculty board without knowing the intentions of the persons who compose it. If that were not the case, legislative provisions could not achieve what they exist for. For a start, successful legislative action requires that members of the legislature can understand legislative proposals without them knowing the intentions of their proposers.[133] More importantly, citizens must be able to know the intended consequences of legislation without first having to know the individual intentions of legislators. Otherwise, legislation could not coordinate their conduct.

This shows, on the one hand, that the intentions of individual legislators *are relevant to the formation of the content* of legislation.[134] Indeed, as we have seen, the content of legislation does not exist independently of their intentions. Legislative intent is determined by individual intentions, particularly by the intentions of

[131] Ekins (n 12).
[132] MacCormick (n 70) 295.
[133] Ekins (n 12) 231.
[134] Jeffrey Goldsworthy, 'Legislative Intention Vindicated?' (2013) 33 Oxford Journal of Legal Studies 821, 827.

those members involved in drafting the act. It is just so, on the other hand, that these individual intentions *are irrelevant to knowing the content* of legislation. For interpretative purposes, it does not matter whose intentions influenced the content of legislation. EU citizens should be able to understand the legislature's intentions without studying the intentions of individual legislators. They should, as MacCormick rightly understood, be able to infer legislative intent 'from the limited range of textual and contextual evidence that is publicly available'.[135] Chapters VI and VII examine what this entails.

This chapter has laid the groundwork for the theory of legislative interpretation that is developed in Chapters VI and VII by showing that it is conceptually plausible to think that legislative intent should be the object of legislative interpretation. It did so by overcoming two objections to this idea. First, because EU legislation is the product of an aggregation of many individual intentions, the legislature cannot form consistent intentions. Second, because we cannot identify these individual intentions, we cannot identify legislative intent. In response to the first objection, I showed—focusing on the role of internal legislative procedures, legislative committees, and political parties, and the way in which the legislative process allows compromises between the institutions involved—that the individual intentions can be aggregated into coherent legislative intentions. I showed, in response to the second objection, that while the legislators' individual intentions of legislative representatives influence legislative intent, we do not need to know these individual intentions to identify the intended consequences of legislative acts. Instead, these consequences should be inferred from the publicly available legislative material.

[135] ibid 832.

VI

Legislative Rules

The Means to an End

1. Introduction

Legislative intent is the plan of action established by the legislature for the entire European Union. It consists of the ends the legislature pursues and the means it chooses to pursue these ends. In this chapter, I want to clarify this definition by zooming in on the legislative plan and clarifying by what means the legislature seeks to realise its chosen ends. These clarifications must be made before a theory of legislative interpretation is developed; they allow me to address the confusion that still exists in some circles of European Union (EU) law about the correct object of legislative interpretation. Those writing on the subject like to emphasise the open-ended nature of EU law, which, for some, means that legislative ends themselves—or what they call legislative purpose—must be the object of interpretation. In this chapter, I will, instead, explain that legislation establishes a rule-based system whose constraints may require decision-makers to make decisions that conflict with the purposes underlying the rules.

The organisation of this chapter is as follows. Section VI.2 discusses the rule-based nature of legislative acts and explains that the legislative text contains a complex set of legislative rules that, together, constitute the means whereby the legislature seeks to achieve its intended state of affairs. Section VI.3 discusses the difficulties and advantages inherent in any rule-based system of governance, emphasising, on the one hand, that rule-based decision-making can generate arbitrary outcomes, while showing, on the other hand, how rules help to attain predictability, certainty, and consistency. Section VI.4 argues that such values also derive from EU legislative rules and that the EU can only effectively coordinate the behaviour of its citizens if the addressees of legislation comply with the rules. While the rules generally seem to be followed in the interpretation of EU law, the last two sections highlight the unease that can arise when rule-based decision-making generates arbitrary results. Section VI.5 discusses the *Keck* and *Collins* judgments to show that such unease is not limited to legislation, while section VI.6 examines some cases of legislative interpretation affected by rule aversion.

Legislative Authority and Interpretation in the European Union. Martijn van den Brink, Oxford University Press.
 DOI: 10.1093/9780198900115.003.0006

2. EU Legislation as a System of Rules

In its *CILFIT* judgment, the Court of Justice of the European Union (CJEU) set out fundamental standards for the interpretation of EU law and underscored 'the particular difficulties to which its interpretation gives rise'.[1] Lawyers writing on the subject usually do the same and often as an important step towards concluding that EU law is unusually vague and, in any case, considerably less determinate than national law. The issue of legal vagueness and some of the factors that may exacerbate vagueness in EU law will be discussed in section VII.4. Here, I want to focus on an extreme conception of vagueness in EU law as put forward by constitutional pluralist theories of interpretation.[2] I discuss these theories as they show how an excessive focus on legal indeterminacy can present us with a misleading view of the legislative plan and its proper interpretation.

According to Miguel Maduro, whose pluralist theory of interpretation has been the most influential, the constitutional pluralist nature of the EU legal order affects 'the role of courts and the character of judicial adjudication'.[3] Because 'constitutional pluralism . . . entails an extreme form of political pluralism',[4] the political decisions reached will often resemble 'incompletely theorised agreements' that 'lead . . . to a delegation to courts of the final decisions on those issues'.[5] Whether it is the Treaties he has in mind or legislative provisions as well is not clear. Neither his theory nor pluralist theories of interpretation that have followed his distinguish clearly between constitutional and legislative interpretation. Some acknowledge that legislation can offer clarity when the Treaties do not,[6] but legal vagueness is clearly the focal point of these theories. For example, according to Elina Paunio, it is 'a *truism* of EU law that not only the EU Treaties but also other legal instruments, in particular directives, contain broad principles, goals and values'.[7]

Before we go on, note the debatable assumptions on which these theories rest. First, it is not evident that constitutional pluralism correlates with, or causes, political pluralism. Or rather, it is unclear how the nature of legal orders, whether

[1] Case C-283/81 *CILFIT* ECLI:EU:C:1982:335, para 17.

[2] Why constitutional pluralists have wanted to say anything about legal interpretation is unclear to me. Their theories are meant to describe the coexistence of different legal orders; it is not evident why the question of the relationship between the legal orders of the EU and the Member States has any bearing on the interpretation of EU law. See also Daniel Sarmiento, 'The Silent Lamb and the Deaf Wolves' in Matej Avbelj and Jan Komárek (eds), *Constitutional Pluralism in the European Union and Beyond* (Hart Publishing 2012).

[3] Miguel Poiares Maduro, 'Interpreting European Law—Judicial Adjudication in a Context of Constitutional Pluralism' (2008) 1 European Journal of Legal Studies 1.

[4] ibid 9.

[5] ibid.

[6] Elina Paunio, *Legal Certainty in Multilingual EU Law: Language, Discourse, and Reasoning at the European Court of Justice* (Ashgate 2013) 48.

[7] ibid (italics added). Similarly, Suvi Sankari, 'Constitutional Pluralism and Judicial Adjudication: On Legal Reasoning, Minimalism and Silence by the Court of Justice' in Gareth T Davies and Matej Avbelj (eds), *Research Handbook on Legal Pluralism and EU Law* (Edward Elgar 2018) 313–14.

pluralist or unitary, affects the degree of political pluralism we find within them. It is conceptually possible for two legal orders to stand to each other in a relationship of constitutional pluralism without either being very pluralistic in political terms. And vice versa, as the level of political polarisation in our national societies shows, unitary legal orders can politically be very pluralistic. Of course, uniting countries with their own histories, cultures, and identities, the EU is subject to plenty of political pluralism, but that is then a result of such socio-cultural diversity and not because of its constitutional pluralist order. Second, and more crucially, the result of political pluralism need not be incomplete political agreements. It can, on the contrary, motivate decision-makers to enact precise rules in an attempt to deprive lower decision-makers of their political discretion. As we saw in section III.2, the European Parliament persistently tries to make secondary legislation more precise in order to better guide and coordinate the conduct of Member States in the face of political pluralism.[8]

This gives us an idea of where constitutional pluralist theories of interpretation have gone wrong. There is no doubt that vagueness is inherent in EU legislation and that this, at times, causes serious disagreement about its interpretation, but these theories place too much emphasis on legal indeterminacy and the difficulties it would create. Legislation contains broad principles, goals, and values, but the belief that they are marred by ambiguity is contradicted by much of their content. As explained in section III.2, the legislative acquis is packed with norms that specify in great detail, and with appreciable precision, how the legislature intends to achieve its political ends,[9] imposing determinate regulatory standards that place weighty constraints on national decision-makers.[10]

Another way to put this is that the legislature seeks to realise its desired state of affairs by a system of rules. These rules may be more or less precise, but the rule-based nature of legislation may not be sufficiently appreciated if EU law is described in terms of principles, goals, and values. Our view of what constitutes proper legislative interpretation will suffer as a result. Constitutional pluralist theories advocate a purposive reading of legislation believing it will otherwise be 'difficult to ascertain the legislator's will with certainty'.[11] This view, as I shall explain in Chapter VII, underestimates the constraints rules place on how legislation can reasonably be understood, and quite significantly so. It neglects the unique features that rules possess and the specific challenges that arise for legal officials who deal with them. To understand what amounts to reasonable legislative interpretation, it is therefore important to be clear about the role of rules in legislation and identify how they seek to constrain the conduct of their addressees.

[8] Fabio Franchino, *The Powers of the Union: Delegation in the EU* (CUP 2007) 256.

[9] Excellently described in R Daniel Kelemen, *Eurolegalism: The Transformation of Law and Regulation in the European Union* (Harvard UP 2011) 43.

[10] Sacha Prechal, *Directives in EC Law* (2nd edn, OUP 2005) 14.

[11] Paunio (n 6) 46–47. See also Maduro (n 3) 7–8.

3. The Value of Rules

Rules are reasons for action.[12] People who are subject to their authority are expected to act in accordance with them. They may also have other reasons for action, however, and rules must be distinguished from two such reasons: from commands and from the purpose behind a rule. What distinguishes a rule from a command is that a rule prescribes to all members of a particular class how they must behave at all times. For example, a sign saying, 'Stay off the lawn' is a rule; someone telling you, 'Stay off the lawn' issues a command. So, the first condition of a rule is that it *generalises*: it dictates for all members of a particular class or category what must be done. What distinguishes a rule from a purpose behind a rule is that a rule remains applicable also when it no longer serves its purpose. Rules are enacted with the purpose of preventing certain calamities or achieving certain goals. For example, the rule 'Stay off the lawn' prohibits all people from walking on the lawn to protect the grass: it makes no distinction between persons who may destroy the lawn by walking on it and persons who take care of its maintenance. If, on the other hand, the rule 'Stay off the lawn' is applied only to persons who would destroy the lawn by walking on it, it is not the rule that is applied but the purpose behind the rule. Thus, the second condition of a rule is that it is an *entrenched* generalisation. This is why Joseph Raz conceived of rules as 'exclusionary reasons'.[13] Their addressees are expected to conform to the prescribed rule and exclude considerations not mentioned in it, even if such considerations may be relevant to attaining the purpose behind the rule—I am not allowed to walk on the lawn even when me doing so would not violate the rule's purpose.

Two important conclusions follow. First, rule-based decision-making is at odds with all-things-considered or particularistic decision-making. In the presence of rules, decision-makers may no longer be able to decide in accordance with all considerations that would otherwise be relevant to reaching a decision in a particular case. Second, decision-makers who decide in accordance with rules may arrive at decisions that are under- or over-inclusive in view of the purposes underlying them. Rules that extend to cases not falling within the direct application of their purpose are over-inclusive, while rules that do not extend to cases that would fall under a direct application of their purpose are under-inclusive.[14]

Despite the fact that rules generalise, a good rule has a level of specificity that is congruent with the purpose it serves.[15] A legislature can choose to adopt a flat tax rate (say, individuals pay 20 per cent tax on their personal income), but if it wants to distribute wealth from the rich to the poor, it should rather adopt a more specific

[12] The first paragraphs of this section follow closely Frederick Schauer, *Playing by the Rules: A Philosophical Examination of Rule-Based Decision-Making in Law and in Life* (Clarendon Press 2002).

[13] Joseph Raz, *Practical Reason and Norms* (OUP 2002) ch 2.

[14] Schauer, *Playing by the Rules* (n 12) 50.

[15] Tom Campbell, *The Legal Theory of Ethical Positivism* (Dartmouth 1996) 118.

tax regime with multiple tax brackets (say, individuals with an annual income of 'X or more' pay 40 per cent tax on their income and individuals with an annual income of 'less than X' pay 20 per cent tax on their income). But even such (more) specific rules are over- and/or under-inclusive to a degree. This is because rules depend on a probability assessment—in the example above, taxing individuals with an annual income of 'X or more' more heavily is likely to produce a fairer distribution of wealth.[16] Because the probability assessment may not always be accurate, over- and/or under-inclusion arises. Thus, the tax rule is over-inclusive because persons with an income of 'X or more' fall into the higher tax bracket under the assumption that they are wealthy, even if their financial situation is dire. It is under-inclusive because persons with an income of 'less than X' fall into the lower tax bracket on the assumption that they are relatively poor, even if they are financially well-to-do.

It is important to understand that over- and under-inclusiveness is an inevitable side effect of rule-based decision-making and that these effects cannot be entirely avoided by more carefully tailoring rules.[17] A more refined tax code that, besides measuring personal income and wealth, would include various tax exemptions and deductions, may lead to a fairer redistribution of wealth. But irrespective of how specific the rules are, it is likely that some of the affected people will be treated in ways inconsistent with the code's underlying justifications.[18] This is not to suggest that further specifications are unwelcome, just that following rules will lead to arbitrary outcomes, outcomes that are inconsistent with a rule's purpose and, in that sense, unfair to the persons affected.

The reason why one may think that the disadvantages of rule-based decision-making can be overcome by crafting rules more specifically is that the specificity/generality of rules is easily confused with their precision/vagueness.[19] A general rule applies to a large set of cases, as opposed to a more specific rule that applies to a smaller set of cases. A precise rule unambiguously defines to which cases it applies, while a vague rule has borderline cases where its application is unclear. Rules can be more or less precise/vague and thus leave behaviour more or less unregulated,[20] but generality does not imply vagueness. For example, a rule that says 'All citizens aged eighteen may exercise the right to vote' is more general than a rule that says 'All *male* citizens aged eighteen and over may exercise the right to vote',

[16] Schauer, *Playing by the Rules* (n 12) 27–30.

[17] ibid 50.

[18] Timothy Endicott, 'The Value of Vagueness' in Andrei Marmor and Scott Soames (eds), *Philosophical Foundations of Language in the Law* (OUP 2011) 23.

[19] Ralf Poscher, 'Ambiguity and Vagueness in Legal Interpretation' in Peter Meijes Tiersma and Lawrence Solan (eds), *The Oxford Handbook of Language and Law* (OUP 2012); Jeremy Waldron, 'Vagueness in Law and Language: Some Philosophical Issues' (1994) 82 California Law Review 509, 522.

[20] Also, vague standards can guide conduct: Jeremy Waldron, 'Vagueness and the Guidance of Action' in Marmor and Soames (n 18).

but both rules are very precise. By comparison, a rule that reads 'All *politically mature* citizens may exercise the right to vote' is both more specific and less precise than a rule that says 'All citizens may exercise the right to vote.' It is more specific because politically immature citizens (eg young children) do not fall within its application. It is less precise because there are borderline cases of political maturity when it is unclear whether citizens are sufficiently mature or not. So, legal acts that are written at a high level of generality are not automatically imprecise.

Only legal provisions that leave their addressees unfettered avoid the disadvantages of rule-based decision-making. A legal provision constrains its addressees if two cumulative conditions are met: it must be reasonably determinate *and* it must apply also when the result of its application is contrary to the rule's background purpose.[21] A provision does not constrain if one or both of the conditions is relaxed. First, provisions may be vaguely worded, using words such as 'reasonable' or 'genuine', in which case it underdetermines which considerations are relevant and to be applied by their addressees. Timothy Endicott gives the following example of a tax law that can be applied in a way that serves its underlying purposes: 'the taxpayer must pay a proportion of income that is reasonable in the light of the revenue needs of the government and the taxpayer's circumstances'.[22] This rule allows tax officials to determine for themselves how to apply the rule in a manner that is consistent with its underlying purposes. Second, rules do not constrain their addressees if they are allowed to deviate from them when their application produces results that are incompatible with their underlying purpose. Imagine a precise tax rule such as 'Persons with an annual personal income of X or more pay 40 per cent income tax.' When tax officials are allowed to deviate from the rule in case its application is inconsistent with its background purpose (say, achieving a more equitable distribution of wealth), it is not the rule that is being applied but its underlying purpose.

All this poses the crucial question: why require decision-makers to decide according to rules if that means them having to accept arbitrary results that are inconsistent with the purposes the rules are supposed to serve? In other words, what values are served by rule-based decision-making? It is difficult to determine this in an acontextual way because there are many situations in which precision is either unattainable or less desirable than using vague standards. Thus, to grasp the value of rules, it may help to first grasp the value of vagueness.[23] Vagueness can be an inevitable consequence of imprecision in language, but vagueness can also be a deliberate choice on the part of lawmakers. Evaluative legal standards such as 'genuine' or 'reasonable' are a major cause of vagueness. They give legal officials discretion to decide in a way that is consistent with the purposes underlying the

[21] Schauer, *Playing by the Rules* (n 12) 172–73.
[22] Endicott (n 18) 23–24.
[23] This paragraph follows Endicott (n 18).

standards in question, allowing them to avoid the arbitrariness that comes with the application of reasonably determinate rules. Granting such discretion may be desirable when legal officials can be trusted to take better decisions because of their expertise or closer proximity to the situation at hand.[24] Two examples from EU law illustrate this point. First, art 5(3) of the Air Passengers Regulation provides that no financial compensation is due in case of cancellation of a flight if 'the cancellation is caused by extraordinary circumstances which could not have been avoided even if all reasonable measures had been taken'.[25] It leaves a margin of discretion to authorities responsible for its application, as it may not be possible to determine in advance what counts as an extraordinary circumstance or when cancellation is beyond the control of air carriers. Second, art 5(1) of the Consumer Rights Directive provides that a consumer is only bound by a contract if he or she has been provided with the relevant information 'in a clear and comprehensible manner'.[26] This provision leaves discretion too, as the question of whether the information provided was clear and comprehensible can only be answered when all the relevant facts are known.

Precise legal standards do the opposite: they deprive decision-makers of the right to take into consideration factors that, seeing the rule's purpose, should otherwise have been considered.[27] The example of the voting age illustrates this well. The purpose of the voting age is to differentiate between citizens based on what we might call their political maturity. However, instead of allowing election officials to subject citizens to some sort of examination of their political maturity, the rule deprives them of this power. Voting eligibility depends solely on age. In this respect, the rule is arbitrary in the sense that its underlying purpose will not always be achieved: it is under-inclusive in that it denies the right to vote to citizens who are politically mature but not of age; it is over-inclusive in that it grants the right to vote to citizens who are of age but still politically immature. The value of a precise voting age should, however, be clear. First, it avoids the administrative burdens that would arise if election officials were required to measure political maturity by other means, such as a test of political knowledge. More importantly, possible alternatives to using a voting age may lead to more objectionable forms of arbitrariness. Requiring election officials to subject citizens to an examination of some kind would likely jeopardise the ideal of democratic equality by reinforcing status-based differences: it could lead them to consider factors that should not condition the political franchise, such as race, gender, or education.

[24] ibid 26.

[25] Regulation (EC) No 261/2004 of the European Parliament and of the Council of 11 February 2004 establishing common rules on compensation and assistance to passengers in the event of denied boarding and of cancellation or long delay of flights (OJ L46/1).

[26] Directive 2011/83/EU of the European Parliament and of the Council of 25 October 2011 on consumer rights (OJ L304/64)

[27] Schauer, *Playing by the Rules* (n 12) 158–62.

This example shows that rules can have 'process value' and 'guidance value'.[28] Rules have guidance value when they inform people of their legal rights and obligations; they have process value when they inform legal officials of the law's intended effects. Tax rules are an illustration of rules with both process and guidance value. Compared to the example of Endicott's vague tax law discussed above, more precise tax rules facilitate the work of tax officials by making it relatively easy to calculate the tax owed by citizens. They also allow citizens to familiarise themselves with their rights and obligations. Such precise rules are beneficial not only for administrative reasons but also because they reduce the chance that citizens are subjected to the arbitrary whims of public officials.

EU legislative rules have process and guidance value too. A good example is legislation that conditions rights and obligations on the criteria of *residence* and *time*. For example, EU citizens acquire the right of permanent residence when they legally reside 'for a continuous period of five years in the host Member State'; they lose this right 'only through absence from the host Member State for a period exceeding two consecutive years'.[29] Likewise, third-country nationals have a right of long-term residence after they 'have resided legally and continuously within [a Member State's] territory for five years';[30] they lose this status 'after six years of absence from the territory of the Member State that granted long-term resident status'.[31] Let us say that the purpose of these rules is to protect persons with sufficiently strong social ties to their state of residence. In respect of this purpose, their application may generate arbitrary (ie under- and over-inclusive) results. For example, they exclude citizens and third-country nationals who have established strong social ties already after three years of residence, and they include those who do not have sufficiently strong social ties even after five years of residence.

As we will see in sections VI.5 and VI.6, such arbitrariness can appear so problematic to legal officials that they decide to apply the rule's purpose rather than the rule itself. However, such rules are most beneficial to legal officials and to citizens because of their process and guidance value. In his work on the ethics of immigration, Joseph Carens makes this point in respect of rules that condition rights on the criteria of residence and time:

> If we want to institutionalize a principle that gives weight to the degree to which a person has become a member of society and if we expect to have to deal with a large number of cases, we will want to use indicators of social membership that

[28] Endicott (n 18) 19.

[29] Article 16 of Directive 2004/38/EC of the European Parliament and of the Council of 29 April 2004 on the right of citizens of the Union and their family members to move and reside freely within the territory of the Member States (OJ L158/77).

[30] Article 4(1) of Council Directive 2003/109/EC of 25 November 2003 concerning the status of third-country nationals who are long-term residents (OJ L16/44).

[31] ibid art 9(4).

> are relevant, objective, and easy to measure. Residence and time clearly meet these requirements. Other ways of assessing social membership do not.[32]

Residence and time are criteria that are easily and objectively measurable. Legal officials need not examine the individual circumstances of applicants to determine whether they have established genuine social ties—for example, whether they speak the language, what their family situation is, whether they have work, etc. In fact, they may not examine such individual circumstances but only consider the duration of someone's residence. Such rules not only provide citizens with a great deal of clarity about their rights and obligations but also ensure that they are not at the mercy of officials weighing various personal circumstances. Their legal position depends exclusively on the duration of their residence, the two criteria that determine the application of the rule. So, as this example shows, the disadvantages of rule-based decision-making can be more than offset by the process and guidance values that result from having and deciding according to a system of rules.

Another way of putting this is that rules serve purposes other than background purposes. To understand this, Frederick Schauer's distinction between the 'substantive justification' and the 'rule-generating justification' of a rule is helpful.[33] The substantive justification is the background purpose of a rule: the reason why the lawmaker decided to act in the first place. However, as we saw, rules can demand outcomes that are incompatible with their substantive justification, at which point their application becomes arbitrary. That their enforcement may nevertheless be desirable in such situations is due to their rule-generating justifications. These justifications include efficiency, clarity for citizens about permissible behaviour, the reduction of arbitrariness that can accompany discretionary decision-making, and a clearer allocation of authority between different decision-makers. Rules can serve several such rule-generating justifications at once, which explains their value. Since the regulation of factually diverse and normatively complex issues calls for different solutions at different times, one cannot determine in an acontextual way what form legal regulation should take—how precise or specific rules should be. It seems clear, however, that the degree of coordination and guidance of behaviour that is needed in our societies will be hard to achieve without a complex set of rules.

[32] Joseph H Carens, *The Ethics of Immigration* (OUP 2013) 165.
[33] Schauer, *Playing by the Rules* (n 12) 94–95. Likewise, Raz claimed that rules 'are, first, reasons for the acts they prescribe, but they are also, second, reasons not to act for some competing reasons': Joseph Raz, *Between Authority and Interpretation: On the Theory of Law and Practical Reason* (OUP 2009) 216.

4. Collaborating with the Legislative Plan

The legislature pursues substantive ends when it enacts legislation, but it also provides the means towards these ends. These are set out in the enacted legislative text and typically consist of a complex set of more or less specific and precise rules. The discussion in section VI.3 allows us to understand that legislative rules are not only the means to realise certain substantive justifications (or substantive purposes) but also meant to effect various rule-generating justifications. This picture gives us a more accurate view of the legislature's intentions and offers first insights into the proper interpretation of legislation. In rule-based systems, rules should be seen as entrenched, which is to say that they must be treated as the ends to be realised. Thus, while rules are the means to realise certain substantive ends, their addressees must treat those rules as if they were the ends for which the legislature acted. Only then can legislation achieve the intended combination of substantive justifications and rule-generating justifications.

Legislative rules can be valuable for all the reasons given in section VI.3, but their main value in the EU's composite political system is that they allow a clearer allocation of authority between decision-makers. The EU distributes decisional authority between its own institutions but also between itself and the Member States and between different domestic decision-makers. If legislative norms would consist mainly of open-ended principles and values, attempts to harmonise national standards and steer the behaviour of national authorities towards a common European standard would inevitably be ineffective. Political pluralism may hinder the enactment of clear and precise legal rules, but it is precisely in a context of political diversity and disagreement that rule-based decision-making can provide a welcome measure of clarity and agreement.[34] In this light, we can see why EU institutions often propose legislative amendments that tailor proposed legislative revisions more precisely. There are significant disparities between Member States, both in terms of their political orientation and their institutional capacity, so the national implementation of EU legislation would be uneven if they were required to implement only the substantive justifications that legislation pursues. Legislative rules prescribe by what means these substantive justifications must be achieved, so that legislation is more likely to achieve the desired level of harmonisation of national laws. They provide national officials with greater clarity on the intended effects of EU law and allow citizens to more easily invoke their rights when EU law is misapplied.

However, if the legislature wants to guide behaviour successfully, it is not enough that its legal norms are suitable for the ends it wishes to realise and can be enforced by other institutions. These institutions must also collaborate with the

[34] Schauer, *Playing by the Rules* (n 12) 139.

legislative plan, that is play their part in enforcing the legislative norms that were passed. This means that the national legislature must implement EU legislative acts with a view to respecting their rule-based nature, and the national judiciary and executive should apply legislative rules also when their substantive justification will not be realised by their application. Adherence to legislative rules should also be the norm for EU institutions. Commission guidelines on the correct implementation of legislative acts must respect the complex system of rules promulgated by the legislature, and the CJEU, when faced with situations in which the application of legislative rules may appear arbitrary, must normally apply these rules and fend off the desire to realise the most equitable outcome in every case. As we saw in Chapter III, the likelihood of EU law having its intended social effects domestically increases as EU institutions collaborate with the legislative plan. In exceptional cases, as we saw in Chapter IV, the application of a rule should be rejected if the result would be grossly unfair or otherwise nonsensical, but in general, the right decision is one that respects the legislative rule—both to obtain the benefits of rule-based decision-making and to respect the legislature's authority.

To what extent current practice corresponds to the view defended here is a hard question to answer. Although EU integration is seen as a compliance success story,[35] this success remains precarious. Errors and delays in the proper implementation of EU law show that compliance is not automatic: it depends on the political will and administrative capacity of both EU and national institutions.[36] While EU institutions seem generally willing to adhere to the system of rules set out in legislation, their willingness to enforce these norms can be influenced by their political interests and preferences.[37] As we will see in Chapter VII, the CJEU more consistently follows legislative rules than some theories of interpretation suggest. But at times, it is also reluctant to observe them, precisely because their application would lead to results that are at odds with their substantive purpose. The remainder of this chapter discusses some examples that show how concerns about the arbitrariness of rule-based decision-making can lead to a desire to be unconstrained by rules.

[35] Michael Zürn, 'Introduction: Law and Compliance at Different Levels' in Michael Zürn and Christian Joerges (eds), *Law and Governance in Postnational Europe Compliance beyond the Nation-State* (CUP 2005) 38. See also Lisa Conant, 'Compliance and What EU Member States Make of It' in Marise Cremona (ed), *Compliance and the Enforcement of EU Law* (OUP 2012).

[36] An extensive body of political science literature has emerged that studies Member State compliance with legislation, but there is still significant uncertainty and disagreement about the factors that affect compliance. For overviews, Oliver Treib, 'Implementing and Complying with EU Governance Outputs' (2014) 9 Living Reviews in European Governance; Mariyana Angelova, Tanja Dannwolf, and Thomas König, 'How Robust Are Compliance Findings? A Research Synthesis' (2012) 19 Journal of European Public Policy 1269.

[37] The Commission is less likely to start infringement proceedings against Member States if it disagrees with the content of legislation: Robert Thomson, René Torenvlied, and Javier Arregui, 'The Paradox of Compliance. Infringements and Delays in Transposing European Union Directives' (2007) 37 British Journal of Political Science 685.

5. *Keck* and *Collins*

Rule-based decision-making is firmly rooted in CJEU case law. As Elke Cloots has pointed out,

> Even a cursory glance at the case law readily reveals a number of examples of rule-like decision-making, such as the exemption of 'purely internal situations' from the scope of EU law, the exclusion of collective agreements between organizations representing employers and workers from the scope of EU competition law, the exclusion of regional tax reductions in a (quasi-)federal Member State from the European definition of 'State aid', ... etc.[38]

Yet, the challenges and contradictions involved in rule-based decision-making have occasionally led the CJEU to collapse rules into their underlying purpose. This section discusses two judgments that illustrate this tension: *Keck* and *Collins*. Neither involves legislative rules, but both show that unease with rule-based decision-making can easily translate into resistance to following rules.

The prohibition in art 34 of the Treaty on the Functioning of the European Union (TFEU) on measures having equivalent effect to quantitative import restrictions has always been interpreted widely.[39] Since the *Dassonville* case, the prohibition covers 'all trading rules enacted by Member States which are capable of hindering directly or indirectly, actually or potentially, intra-community trade'.[40] This formula is widely celebrated but has also given cause for concern,[41] especially as regards so-called *selling arrangements* that determine 'by whom, where, when, or how goods may be sold or used or at what price they may be sold'.[42] Such arrangements can adversely affect the volume of cross-border trade, but it was believed that they should not be deemed incompatible with the objective of creating an internal market as long as they apply indiscriminately to national and foreign products.

The CJEU addressed these concerns by limiting the scope of the *Dassonville* formula in the *Keck* judgment. It ruled that 'selling arrangements [do not] hinder trade between Member States ... so long as those provisions apply to all relevant traders operating within the national territory and so long as they affect in the same manner, in law and in fact, the marketing of domestic products and of those

[38] Elke Cloots, *National Identity in EU Law* (OUP 2015) 199.

[39] Article 34 of the TFEU.

[40] Case 8/75 *Dassonville* ECLI:EU:C:1974:82, para 5.

[41] For an excellent overview of the different concerns *Dassonville* gave rise to and how they contributed to *Keck*, Laurence W Gormley, 'Silver Threads among the Gold ... 50 Years of the Free Movement of Goods' 31 Fordham International Law Journal 1637.

[42] Eric L White, 'In Search of the Limits to Article 30 of the EEC Treaty' (1989) 26 Common Market Law Review 235, 259. See, in addition, Case C-292/92 *Hunermund* ECLI:EU:C:1993:863, Opinion of AG Tesauro.

from other Member States'.[43] What this amounted to, more specifically, was a generalisation from the particular fact that the selling arrangement at issue did not hinder cross-border trade to the universal rule that the application of selling arrangements to foreign products '*is not by nature* such as to prevent their access to the market or to impede access any more than it impedes the access of domestic products'.[44] In other words, the CJEU instantiated the rule that the prohibition of measures having an equivalent effect to import restrictions applies to measures regulating product characteristics but not to selling arrangements.[45]

But precisely because the findings in *Keck* were converted into a general rule, the decision met opposition. According to critics, the rule left too little room for a sufficiently particularistic assessment of the impact of national measures on trade: in other words, it allowed outcomes that were seemingly incompatible with the spirit of the internal market. The most articulate criticism came from Advocate General Jacobs, who considered it 'inappropriate to make rigid distinctions between different categories of rules, and to apply different tests depending on the category to which particular rules belong'.[46] He worried that '[m]easures affecting selling arrangements may create extremely serious obstacles to imports'.[47] Therefore, to correctly assess the lawfulness of those measures, an alternative standard was needed that could assesses such 'restrictions against a single test formulated in the light *of the purpose* of Article [34 of the TFEU]'.[48] He argued that the underlying purpose of this provision is to allow undertakings 'unfettered access' to the European market, so the correct test would be to assess 'whether there is a substantial restriction on that access'.[49] Put differently, he resisted using a clear rule to determine which measures fall under the prohibition on measures having equivalent effect. He proposed, instead, to assess whether national measures thwart its underlying purpose: realising the unfettered cross-border movement of goods.

Which of the two solutions is preferable—the generalisation established in *Keck* or the particularistic assessment advocated by Advocate General Jacobs—is not important here. Rather, the example is interesting because the principal actors of this story failed to ask the right questions, namely 'What degree of generalisation is desirable in this context?' and 'When is a particularistic assessment preferable?'.[50] The observation by Advocate General Jacobs that *Keck* introduced a rule

[43] Joined cases C-267/91 and C-268/91 *Keck and Mithouard* ECLI:EU:C:1993:905, para 16.
[44] ibid para 17.
[45] Peter Oliver, 'Some Further Reflections on the Scope of Articles 28–30 (Ex 30–36) EC' (1999) 36 Common Market Law Review 783, 793.
[46] Case C-412/93 *Leclerc-Siplec* ECLI:EU:C:1994:393, Opinion of AG Jacobs, para 38. See also Case C-110/05 *Commission v Italy* ECLI:EU:C:2006:646, Opinion of AG Bot, paras 79–81.
[47] Opinion of AG Jacobs (n 46) para 38.
[48] ibid (italics mine).
[49] ibid para 42.
[50] For this point, Sophia Moreau, 'Equality Rights and Stereotypes' in David Dyzenhaus and Malcolm Thorburn (eds), *Philosophical Foundations of Constitutional Law* (OUP 2016) 291.

that allowed outcomes that are inconsistent with the purpose underlying the free movement of goods is beside the point. He is not wrong, but it is in the nature of rules that they may demand outcomes that deviate from their substantive purpose, so his criticism does not allow him to conclude that the rule had to be abolished. Instead, he should have shown that it was undesirable or unnecessary to generalise in this particular context. On the other hand, the CJEU should not have inferred from the fact that not all selling arrangements restrict market access that no selling arrangement does. It could have said that there is a 'probabilistic relationship'[51] between a measure being a selling arrangement and there not being a barrier to market access and that, given the strength of this relationship, selling arrangements are not, as a rule, prohibited, provided they are applied without distinction between national and foreign products. This would have allowed the CJEU, on the one hand, to admit the costs of its decision—that selling arrangements are allowed even if they impede market access—and, on the other hand, to justify its decision by explaining that these costs are outweighed by the clarity the rule provides. Whether this justification would have been credible would have depended on the accuracy of the probabilistic assessment. The fact that the scope of *Keck* scope was limited in later judgments may indicate that the generalisation drawn in the case was too broad and that particularistic decision-making is, indeed, preferable in this context.[52] But it may also be that the CJEU gave in too easily to criticism and that the cost of excluding all selling arrangements from the scope of EU free movement law was, all things considered, acceptable.

Another judgment that illustrates how easily concerns about the arbitrariness of rule-based decision-making can create a desire to avoid rule-based constraints is *Collins*. This judgment also shows the problems that may arise out of such a desire. The facts of the case are as follows: with the exception of two short periods of residence in the United Kingdom—a semester in 1978 for study purposes and ten months between 1980 and 1981 for work purposes—Mr Collins, an Irish-American national, had never lived or worked in the EU. In 1998, he returned to the United Kingdom to find work. To support himself during his unemployment, he applied for a jobseeker allowance. The UK authorities denied him the allowance as he did not meet the habitual residence requirement.[53]

The CJEU was asked whether the UK authorities had violated Mr Collins's rights as an EU citizen. It replied that national authorities were, in principle, permitted to ensure that there is 'a genuine link between an applicant for an allowance

[51] Schauer, *Playing by the Rules* (n 12) 27–30.

[52] Case C-405/08 *Gourmet International Products* ECLI:EU:C:2001:135; Case C-322/01 *DocMorris* ECLI:EU:C:2003:664; Case C-239/02 *Douwe Egberts* ECLI:EU:C:2004:445. For an argument in favour of particularistic decision-making, Tarjei Bekkedal, 'The Reach of Free Movement. A Defence of Court Discretion' in Mads Tønnesson Andenæs, Tarjei Bekkedal, and Luca Pantaleo (eds), *The Reach of Free Movement* (TMC Asser Press 2017). For the opposite view, Oliver (n 45) 793.

[53] Case C-138/02 *Collins* ECLI:EU:C:2004:172, paras 18 and 19.

. . . and the geographic employment market in question'.[54] Such a link exists, it ruled, if the claimant has 'for a reasonable period, in fact genuinely sought work in the Member State',[55] in which case they must be allowed to claim benefits. Under UK law, entitlement to such benefits was made conditional on a habitual residence requirement, without verifying whether the jobseeker had genuinely sought work during that period. The CJEU held that such a residence requirement is 'in principle appropriate for the purpose of ensuring such a connection',[56] but it added that

> if it is to be proportionate . . . its application by the national authorities must rest on clear criteria known in advance and provision must be made for the possibility of a means of redress of a judicial nature. In any event, . . . the period must not exceed what is necessary in order for the national authorities to be able to satisfy themselves that the person concerned is genuinely seeking work in the employment market of the host Member State.[57]

This paragraph imposes contradictory expectations that are impossible to meet. On the one hand, national authorities must establish clear criteria that can be known in advance, which speaks in favour of a residence requirement: from the perspective of clarity and certainty, such a requirement is clearly superior to the criterion of 'genuinely seeking work'. On the other hand, they must ensure that this period is no longer than necessary to guarantee that the claimant is genuinely seeking work. The problem is that a habitual residence requirement provides no indication of efforts to find work, let alone of whether such efforts are genuine. This can only be established based on a case-by-case examination of each applicant's efforts.

If applicants with a genuine link with the employment market should be allowed to claim benefits, a habitual residence requirement cannot be used, not even as a proxy for the existence of a genuine link between an applicant and the employment market in question. Nor would a more specifically tailored rule suffice, for even such a rule might lead to under-inclusive outcomes: it may deny benefits to claimants who have, for a reasonable period, genuinely sought work but who do not meet the rule. *Collins*'s muddled reasoning makes it impossible to determine with certainty what result the CJEU intended to achieve, but it demonstrates that there is a fine line between being concerned about under-inclusive results and being opposed to rule-based decision-making altogether. Recall that a rule constrains if two conditions are met: it must be somewhat determinate, and it must hold also when it produces results that are contrary to its substantive justification. *Collins*

54 ibid para 67.
55 ibid para 70.
56 ibid para 72.
57 ibid.

can be read as weakening both conditions. First, the decision could be understood to require UK authorities to adopt a vague rule along the following lines: 'anyone who has genuinely sought work in the national employment market is entitled to a jobseeker allowance'. Second, it could also be taken to mean that the national rule should be disapplied when it fails to ensure that applicants who have genuinely sought work can claim benefits. The habitual residence requirement can be enforced unless it denies jobseekers with a genuine link to the employment market benefits. *Collins* may be open to different interpretations, but its seeming aversion to rule-based decision-making is the reason it imposes such unrealistic expectations on national authorities.

6. Rule Aversion in Legislative Interpretation

Rule aversion can also affect the interpretation of legislation. Legislative rules run the risk of being suppressed if their application is believed to generate results that are arbitrary given the purposes they serve. The magnitude of this risk should not be exaggerated, but there have been a few cases where the CJEU has sought to escape the rule-based constraints of legislation, either by collapsing legislative rules into their background purpose or by applying them proportionately in light of their purposes. The rules are thereby stripped of their process and guidance value, and the legislature is hence deprived of the authority to stipulate the EU's course of action.

EU citizenship case law illustrates how the CJEU may struggle with the challenges of rule-based decision-making. Previously, it was settled case law that whether Union citizens were entitled to social assistance in the host state had to be determined by making an individual assessment of their situation: social assistance had to be awarded to citizens 'who have demonstrated a certain degree of integration into the society of that State'.[58] National authorities, in determining whether a sufficient degree of integration had been established, had to take into account whether citizens had lived in their territory 'for a certain length of time'[59] or could prove 'representative elements' with their state.[60] Such elements included family, employment, and language skills;[61] the place where schooling was completed;[62] and the prospects of future links with the host society.[63] The CJEU

[58] Case C-209/03 *Bidar* ECLI:EU:C:2005:169, para 57.

[59] ibid para 59.

[60] Case C-75/11 *Commission v Austria* ECLI:EU:C:2012:605, para 62; Case C-503/09 *Stewart* ECLI:EU:C:2011:500, para 95.

[61] Case C-523/11 *Prinz and Seeberger* ECLI:EU:C:2013:524, para 38; Case C-367/11 *Prete* ECLI:EU:C:2012:668, para 48; *Stewart* (n 60) para 100.

[62] Joined cases C-11/06 and C-12/06 *Morgan and Bucher* ECLI:EU:C:2007:626, para 45; Case C-224/98 *D'Hoop* ECLI:EU:C:2002:432, para 39; *Prete* (n 61).

[63] Case C-20/12 *Giersch* ECLI:EU:C:2013:411, para 67; Case C-542/09 *Commission v The Netherlands* ECLI:EU:C:2012:346, para 77.

required, at the time, that legislative rules that denied social assistance to citizens with a certain degree of integration into the host state had to be ignored.[64] This approach had one advantage, at least in theory: the law could be applied fairly in each individual case since every citizen who could demonstrate a sufficient degree of integration could claim social assistance. Yet, this individualised approach had important drawbacks. First, it placed considerable administrative burdens on authorities responsible for applying the law.[65] Second, while enabling fairness in theory, it may weaken EU citizens' rights in practice. It leaves national authorities with broad discretion, which they may abuse when deciding which Union citizens qualify for social protection.

The legislature has taken a very different approach. The Citizenship Directive stipulates, for example, that the host state is under no obligation to grant social assistance to Union citizens during the first three months of residence or during the period in which they reside on the territory to seek employment.[66] Likewise, citizens who have been employed for less than a year and become involuntarily unemployed during this period are, according to the Directive, entitled to social assistance for a period of up to six months.[67] In section VI.3, I discussed similar provisions that use the criteria of 'residence' and 'time' to determine the legal status of citizen—criteria that come with considerable process and guidance value. The same is true of these provisions: they do not measure social integration as such—they are merely a proxy thereof—but they promote predictability, certainty, and consistency in ways that individual assessments do not. And thereby, they remove discretion from national authorities that could otherwise be abused in decisions on the award of social assistance.

In recent years, the CJEU began to observe these rules and, in turn, abolished the requirement to carry out individual assessments. The *Alimanovic* and *García-Nieto* judgments illustrate this most clearly. It ruled that social assistance can be lawfully denied to citizens who do not meet the criteria set forth in the Citizenship Directive, respectively the condition of more than one year of employment and more than three months of residence.[68] As I discussed in section III.2, these judgments contrast sharply with earlier case law that required individual assessments to be carried out. These judgments are interesting, however, not only because they display a different approach but also because they show how difficult the CJEU found it to justify its choice to decide in accordance with the Directive's rules.

[64] See, eg Case C-456/02 *Trojani* ECLI:EU:C:2004:488; Joined cases C-22/08 and C-23/08, *Vatsouras and Koupatantze* ECLI:EU:C:2009:344

[65] Floris de Witte, *Justice in the EU: The Emergence of Transnational Solidarity* (OUP 2015) 137–138.

[66] Article 24(2) of the Directive 2004/38/EC (n 29).

[67] ibid art 7(3)(b).

[68] Case C-67/14 *Alimanovic* ECLI:EU:C:2015:597; Case C-299/14 *García-Nieto* ECLI:EU:C:2016:114.

The applicable rule in *Alimanovic* was that EU citizens retain the right to social assistance if they have 'been employed for more than one year'.[69] The CJEU held that this rule removed the need for an individual assessment, as it established 'a gradual system ... which ... *itself takes into consideration various factors characterising the individual situation* of each applicant for social assistance and, in particular, the duration of the exercise of any economic activity'.[70] But this is incorrect: the rule does not consider factors that characterise the applicant's individual situation other than the duration of his or her employment. In fact, it does not allow any other factor to be considered. The CJEU, nevertheless, went on to say that this rule

> by enabling those concerned to know, without any ambiguity, what their rights and obligations are ... is ... such as to guarantee a significant level of legal certainty and transparency in the context of the award of social assistance ... while complying with *the principle of proportionality*.[71]

The first part of this statement is correct: the rule does, indeed, provide certainty and transparency. But the final part is misleading: the rule need not produce a result that is proportionate, or at least not proportionate in light of its underlying purpose of providing social protection to EU citizens who can demonstrate an adequate degree of social integration. In fact, the rule is under-inclusive in that it allows social assistance to be denied to EU citizens who are socially integrated but have not been employed for more than one year. In other words, while the CJEU was keen to emphasise the process and guidance values of legislative rules, it sought to deny the associated disadvantages of following them; that is, it refused to acknowledge that following rules might, in some situations, be disproportionate, contributing to the misperception that rules must be applied proportionately.

This misperception has often been behind advocacy for the use of individual assessments in EU citizenship law. Assuming that under-inclusiveness should be avoided, Advocate General Mazák once criticised the five-year residence requirement that students must meet before they can claim student maintenance aid.[72] In his view,

> it can reasonably be assumed that a number of students may have established a substantial degree of integration into society well before the expiry of that period. ... [A] residence requirement of five years may prevent students ... from benefiting from their right to equal treatment as citizens of the Union in respect

[69] Article 7(3)(b) of Directive 2004/38/EC (n 29).
[70] *Alimanovic* (n 68) para 60 (italics mine).
[71] ibid para 61 (italics mine).
[72] This requirement is included in art 24(2) of Directive 2004/38/EC (n 29).

> of study allowances, regardless of the actual link they may have established with the society of the host Member State. That cannot in my view be considered proportionate.[73]

He clearly finds individual assessments preferable to rule-like generalisations, and he is not alone to think so. For example, the *Förster* judgment, which upheld the five-year residence rule contrary to Advocate General Mazák's objections, faced considerable criticism along the lines of the position taken by the Advocate General.[74]

A similar aversion to rule-based decision-making underlies much academic criticism of the recent social assistance case law, including *Alimanovic* and *García-Nieto*. According to Charlotte O'Brien,

> The finding that individual assessments are not necessary to establish unreasonable burdens relies heavily upon generalizations, asserting that individual claims do not ever place unreasonable burdens on a system, so a reasonable burden test must be based on accumulated claims, not individual circumstances.[75]

She goes on to argue that this reliance on generalisations—that is, legislative rules—'is blithely at odds with *Brey*, with Recital 16 of the Directive, and with Commission guidance'.[76] She does not explain why previous case law or Commission guidance should have more authority than the decisions of the legislature (and indeed, there is no reason to think they should), but her position is illustrative of how EU citizenship scholars have approached legislative interpretation: faced with legislative rules they dislike, they advocate the application of the recitals to the legislative act. By collapsing the rules into their background purpose, as expressed in these recitals, they seek to eliminate the rule-like nature of EU citizenship law (see also section VII.2).

Why is this the wrong position to take? First, it does not correspond to the legislature's intentions in the Citizenship Directive. The Directive seeks to

[73] Case C-158/07 *Förster* ECLI:EU:C:2008:399, Opinion of AG Mazák, para 130.

[74] Case C-158/07 *Förster* ECLI:EU:C:2008:630. For criticism, de Witte (n 65) 160–61; Síofra O'Leary, 'Equal Treatment and EU Citizens: A New Chapter on Cross-Border Educational Mobility and Access to Student Financial Assistance' (2009) 34 European Law Review 612; Henri de Waele, 'EU Citizenship: Revisiting Its Meaning, Place and Potential' (2010) 12 European Journal of Migration and Law 319, 326–27; Ferdinand Wollenschläger, 'The Judiciary, the Legislature and the Evolution of Union Citizenship' in Phil Syrpis (ed), *The Judiciary, the Legislature and the EU Internal Market* (CUP 2012) 323.

[75] Charlotte O'Brien, 'Civis Capitalist Sum: Class as the New Guiding Principle of EU Free Movement Rights' (2016) 53 Common Market Law Review 937, 950. For similar criticism, Niamh Nic Shuibhne, 'Limits Rising, Duties Ascending: The Changing Legal Shape of Union Citizenship' (2015) 52 Common Market Law Review 889, 913; Herwig Verschueren, 'Preventing "Benefit Tourism" in the EU: A Narrow or Broad Interpretation of the Possibilities Offered by the ECJ in Dano?' (2015) 52 Common Market Law Review 363, 373.

[76] O'Brien (n 75) 950.

operationalise the principle that the award of social assistance can be made conditional on citizens having genuine social ties with the host state, but it does so by means of very precise rules that make the right to social assistance conditional on two criteria: time and residence/employment. The legislature intends these rules to be applied to achieve not only certain substantive justifications but also specific rule-generating justifications. As we saw in section VI.2, rules based on residence and time come with considerable process and guidance value, including, as the CJEU noted in *Alimanovic*, enhancing legal certainty and transparency. Moreover, as we saw in Chapter III, domestic compliance with legislation is most likely better than with case law, especially when the former sets rules that are precise and clear. There are thus ample reasons to think that decision-making in accordance with rules is preferable to individual, case-by-case assessments in the cases discussed here. The only reason that speaks against it is that it can lead to results that may be arbitrary in individual cases: it seems unfair that certain citizens cannot claim social assistance even if they have genuine social ties with the host state. This is a cost worth accepting, however, especially as citizens will be better protected by precise rules that remove discretion from national decision-makers.

The last point can perhaps be better illustrated by studying another area of EU citizenship law: the rules concerning expulsion from the host state. According to art 28 of the Citizenship Directive, protection against expulsion gradually increases the longer the citizen resides in the host state. A distinction is made between three classes of EU citizens: citizens who are not permanent residents, citizens who have acquired the right of permanent residence following five years of legal and continuous residence, and citizens who have resided in the host state for the previous ten years. An expulsion decision may be taken against the first group on grounds of public policy and security (art 28(1)),[77] against the second group only 'on serious grounds of public policy or public security' (art 28(2)),[78] and no expulsion decision may be taken against the third group 'except if the decision is based on imperative grounds of public security' (art 28(3)).[79] Finally, the right of

[77] Article 28(1) of Directive 2004/38/EC (n 29):

> [b]efore taking an expulsion decision on grounds of public policy or public security, the host Member State shall take account of considerations such as how long the individual concerned has resided on its territory, his/her age, state of health, family and economic situation, social and cultural integration into the host Member State and the extent of his/her links with the country of origin.

[78] ibid art 28(2): 'The host Member State may not take an expulsion decision against Union citizens or their family members, irrespective of nationality, who have the right of permanent residence on its territory, except on serious grounds of public policy or public security.' According to art 16(4) of the Directive, 'Union citizens who have resided legally for a continuous period of five years in the host Member State shall have the right of permanent residence there.'

[79] ibid art 28(3): 'An expulsion decision may not be taken against Union citizens, except if the decision is based on imperative grounds of public security, as defined by Member States, if they have resided in the host Member State for the previous 10 years.'

permanent residence, and thus the protection afforded by this status, expires after an absence of two consecutive years from the host state (art 16(4)).[80]

The objective of this graduated system is to increase citizens' protection against expulsion in accordance with their degree of integration in the host state. As Recital 24 of the Citizenship Directive states, 'the greater the degree of integration of Union citizens and their family members in the host Member State, the greater the degree of protection against expulsion should be'. But the Directive does not provide that national authorities must measure the degree of integration of EU citizens. Instead, it pursues this objective through precise rules that only take into account the duration of their period of residence: such periods serve as a proxy for integration and periods of absence as an indicator of the lack thereof.

The CJEU failed to see this and interpreted the rules in a way as to realise their underlying purpose; it thereby removed much of the protection that citizens facing expulsion measures would otherwise have enjoyed. In *Onuekwere*, it ruled that the legislature 'made the acquisition of the right of permanent residence . . . subject to the integration of the citizen of the Union'.[81] On that basis, and in flagrant contradiction to the written text (which provides that the acquisition of this right only depends on five years of legal and continuous residence), the CJEU ruled that

> Such integration, which is a precondition of the acquisition of the right of permanent residence . . . is based not only on *territorial* and *temporal* factors but also on *qualitative* elements . . . to such an extent that the undermining of the link of integration between the person concerned and the host Member State justifies the loss of the right of permanent residence *even outside* the circumstances mentioned in Article 16(4) of Directive 2004/38.[82]

Recall that, according to art 16(4) of the Citizenship Directive, the right of permanent residence is lost *only* after an absence of two consecutive years from the host state. However, unwilling to allow results contrary to the rule's purposes, the CJEU held that not only a continuous period of absence of two years but also any other qualitative element showing a lack of integration could lead to a loss of that right.[83]

This error has had dire consequences for citizens facing expulsion measures. It was the prelude to a thorough revision of the conditions justifying expulsion. The *MG* case was pivotal in this. The case concerned the interpretation of art 28(3), the provision that provides citizens who have resided in the host state for the previous ten years with the highest protection against expulsion. The CJEU, however, ruled

[80] ibid art 16(4): 'the right of permanent residence shall be lost only through absence from the host Member State for a period exceeding two consecutive years'.

[81] Case C-378/12 *Onuekwere* ECLI:EU:C:2014:13, para 24.

[82] ibid para 25 (italics added).

[83] For a similar analysis, Nic Shuibhne (n 75) 920.

that the condition 'previous ten years . . . must, in principle, be continuous'[84] and must 'be calculated by counting back from the date of the decision ordering the person's expulsion'.[85] Then, citing *Onuekwere*, it held that a custodial sentence may indicate a lack of integration and, therefore, interrupt the continuity of residence.[86] The legal consequence is that the protection afforded by art 28(3) can be enjoyed only by citizens who are issued with an expulsion order ten years after serving their sentence. The practical consequence is that this provision was rendered meaningless; no country will wait ten years before issuing an expulsion order.[87]

Ironically, the judgment's full implications were best visible in the part that sought to undo some of its perverse effects. In an attempt to retain some of the value of art 28(3), the CJEU ruled that non-continuous periods of residence in the ten years preceding the expulsion decision may still be relied on by citizens to claim enhanced protection but that this depends on an overall assessment 'of that person's situation on each occasion at the precise time when the question of expulsion arises'.[88] It once more preferred all-things-considered to rule-based decision-making: national authorities were expected to disregard the constraints of art 28 and instead take into account all individual factors that could be relevant to deciding whether taking an expulsion measure is appropriate.[89] Indeed, once a citizen is proven to be a threat to public policy or security, it all comes down to weighing up various individual circumstances, leaving already vulnerable persons entirely at the mercy of national authorities.

So far, I have only discussed EU citizenship case law, and for a reason. To my knowledge, the Court's attitude within this area is quite unusual, especially in terms of the intensity with which it has sought to unravel legislative rules. Having said that, we also find such behaviour in consumer protection cases on the labelling and presentation of products.[90] Consider, for example, the *Linhart and Biffl* case. According to art 6 of Directive 76/768/EEC, 'Member States shall take all measures necessary to ensure that, in the labelling, putting up for sale and advertising of cosmetic products, text, names, trade marks, pictures and figurative or other signs are not used to imply that these products have characteristics which they do

[84] Case C-400/12 *MG* ECLI:EU:C:2014:9, para 27.
[85] ibid para 24.
[86] ibid paras 31–33.
[87] For critical discussion, Dimitry Kochenov and Uladzislau Belavusau, 'Kirchberg Dispensing the Punishment: Inflicting "Civil Death" on Prisoners in Onuekwere (C-378/12) and M.G. (C-400/12)' (2016) 41 European Law Review 557; Nic Shuibhne (n 75) 922; Leandro Mancano, 'Criminal Conduct and Lack of Integration into the Society under EU Citizenship: This Marriage Is Not to Be Performed' (2015) 6 New Journal of European Criminal Law 53, 72–74.
[88] *MG* (n 84) para 35.
[89] ibid paras 36–38.
[90] The relevant cases are Case C-99/01 *Linhart and Biffl* ECLI:EU:C:2002:618; Case C-220/98 *Estée Lauder* ECLI:EU:C:2000:8; Case C-77/97 *Österreichische Unilever* ECLI:EU:C:1999:30; Case C-315/92 *Verband Sozialer Wettbewerb* ECLI:EU:C:1994:34; Case C-257/06 *Roby Profumi* ECLI:EU:C:2008:35; Case C-221/00 *Commission v Austria* ECLI:EU:C:2003:44.

not have.'[91] Thus, only national provisions that are *necessary* to prevent products being labelled and advertised in a misleading manner are allowed under this provision. However, the CJEU found that national measures—and, by implication, EU legislation—must 'observe the principle of proportionality'.[92] Therefore, national authorities were asked to weigh 'the risk of misleading consumers against the requirements of the free movement of goods'.[93] And because the national law precluded forms of labelling and advertising that 'could not mislead an average consumer who is reasonably well informed',[94] the law was found to be disproportionate and contrary to EU law.

This case is interesting, first, because it shows how the principle of proportionality can be used to dilute the authority of legislative rules. The same happened in *Baumbast*, where the principle was used to circumvent legislative conditions regulating the right to reside of mobile EU citizens.[95] The case is also interesting because it demonstrates that the extent to which the application of the principle of proportionality weakens the application of legislative rules depends on the precision of these rules. In *Linhart and Biffl*, the proportionality principle effectively demanded what the rule already required: that national measures are necessary to ensure that products are labelled and advertised in non-misleading ways.[96] More specifically, the reason why the proportionality principle did not prejudice the legislative rule in question was that the rule already granted a very large margin of discretion to local decision-makers, which could hardly be increased by applying the principle of proportionality on top. However, if the principle is applied to a more precise rule, as in the *Baumbast* case, the rule may lose its capacity to constrain decision-makers and legislation will be deprived of its rule-generating justifications.

Therefore, unless legislative provisions expressly call for a proportionality assessment, the CJEU should not require its application. Because the principle of proportionality allows—no, requires—open-ended moral reasoning, as opposed to rules that are designed precisely to constrain decision-makers,[97] legislation risks being deprived of its rule-like capacity when subjected to this principle. Indeed, the idea of proportionate rule-based decision-making is an oxymoron, one that

[91] Article 6(3) of Directive 76/768 on the approximation of the laws of the Member States relating to cosmetic products (OJ L262/169).

[92] *Linhart and Biffl* (n 90) para 26.

[93] The Court said so explicitly in *Estée Lauder* (n 90) para 27 but suggested the same in ibid para 25.

[94] *Linhart and Biffl* (n 90) para 35. See also= *Estée Lauder* (n 90) paras 28–30.

[95] Famously, Case C-413/99 *Baumbast* ECLI:EU:C:2002:493.

[96] Karsten Engsig Sørensen, 'Reconciling Secondary Legislation with the Treaty Rights of Free Movement' (2011) 36 European Law Review 339, 344.

[97] On the difference between proportionality and rule-based decision-making, Frederick Schauer, 'Balancing, Subsumption, and the Constraining Role of Legal Text' in Matthias Klatt (ed), *Institutionalized Reason: The Jurisprudence of Robert Alexy* (OUP 2012).

essentially conflates constitutional and legislative interpretation.[98] Treaty interpretation is primarily about whether a restriction on a Treaty right is proportionate and therefore justified. Legislative interpretation, on the other hand, involves determining the meaning of legislative provisions and deciding on their application. Of course, it is easy to see how the two can be confused. Sometimes, the validity of a national law depends on whether it is a legitimate restriction on a Treaty provision, other times on whether it is compatible with the legislative provisions adopted. And a judgment concerning the proportionality of a national measure under the Treaties may serve as a precedent in a later dispute on the correct interpretation over a particular legislative provision.[99] However, it is one thing to examine whether a national measure constitutes a proportionate restriction on a Treaty right and quite another to insist on the proportionate application of legislative rules. The latter deprives legislation of its rule-like nature and draws wrong inferences about legislative intent.

When it passes legislation, the legislature adds to or amends the complex set of rules that together make up the legislative framework. This chapter explored the rule-based nature of this framework and the values the legislature aspires to in trying to attain its political ends by means of legislative rules. We saw that rules give legislation greater process and guidance value and that the legislature, through these rules, seeks to achieve certain substantive ends but also rule-specific ends, including a more precise and effective allocation of authority between EU and national institutions. This has important ramifications for how legislation ought to be interpreted. It shows that legislative intent must be inferred from both the substantive and rule-generating justifications.

[98] Paul Yowell, *Constitutional Rights and Constitutional Design: Moral and Empirical Reasoning in Judicial Review* (Hart Publishing 2018) 14.

[99] As, in fact, happened in the consumer law cases, where the proportionality test was introduced by reference to a case that examined the proportionality of a national measure that constituted an obstacle to movement. See *Verband Sozialer Wettbewerb* (n 90) para 16 and the reference to Case C-382/87 *Buet* ECLI:EU:C:1989:198 therein.

VII
Identifying Intent
A Theory of Legislative Interpretation

1. Introduction

If, as I have argued in Chapters V and VI, the goal of legislative interpretation is to infer legislative intent from publicly available legislative material, how should legal officials interpret legislation if they want to respect legislation's intended meaning and consequences? Chapter V explained that the intention in a legislative act consists of both the ends the legislature wants to achieve and the means by which it seeks to achieve these ends. Chapter VI explained that the means used by the legislature to achieve its desired state of affairs consists, in large part, of the enacted legislative rules. Building on these insights, this chapter develops a theory of legislative interpretation in European Union (EU) law, thereby addressing the lack of interest EU law scholarship has shown for what counts as reasonable legislative interpretation.[1] Through a discussion of Court of Justice of the European Union (CJEU) case law and some of the inconsistencies we find in it, this chapter improves our view of what counts as reasonable legislative interpretation.

First, I explain why an instrumentalist interpretation of legislation, the aim of which is to achieve desirable results, is unattractive and undesirable. Second, building on my analysis in Chapter VI, I rebut purposive legislative interpretation, which attaches too little weight to written rules in the legislative plan of action. I then conceptualise legal indeterminacy in EU law and argue that there must be more agreement on its meaning than is commonly assumed. It does not follow, however, that legislative provisions must necessarily be read literally, since literal interpretation might misidentify the intention in legal provisions. The object of interpretation must be legislative intent, not the legislative purpose behind or the literal meaning of this provision. I finally explain that to discern legislative intent, the legislature must be treated as an ordinary language user. This means that the literal meaning of legislative text must be placed in the context in which the legislature expressed itself.

[1] For the same observation, Elke Cloots, *National Identity in EU Law* (OUP 2015) ch 10.

Legislative Authority and Interpretation in the European Union. Martijn van den Brink, Oxford University Press.
 DOI: 10.1093/9780198900115.003.0007

2. Against Instrumentalist Interpretation

How nice it would be if the point of interpretation could be to achieve desirable results, as defined by (say) some theory of justice or economic welfare.[2] Gone would be the difficulties of trying to decipher the legislature's intentions, figuring out the precise constraints of legislative rules, and the like. Judges' only task would be to ensure that the law is applied in a morally or economically sound way. Some constitutional pluralists, whose ideas we discovered in section VI.2, may have found this idea appealing at some level: their theories, they say, are meant to foster 'debate among alternative normative preferences in interpreting EU law'.[3] Yet, even they are not fervent instrumentalists. That EU lawyers do not favour instrumentalism seems evident: it would mean that judges should be bound by some extra-legal normative standard, such as justice or economic welfare, and that no method of interpretation has any independent force. The interpretation of legislation would have to proceed according to incompatible methods of interpretation, depending on what outcome is the best outcome, however defined. Still, while most EU lawyers will reject instrumentalism if asked about its desirability, it is more popular than might appear at first sight. As Alexander Somek has observed, EU lawyers are unwittingly 'inclined to tolerate reasoning flaws so long as policy results are to their liking'.[4] This section discusses an example of instrumentalism to illustrate its shortcomings.

Let us begin with a hypothetical scenario. An EU citizen with Dutch nationality moves to Germany to pursue her studies at a German university. She makes a concerted effort to integrate into Germany and has a fluent command of the German language after two years (not an easy feat, not even for Dutch people!). But since her prosperous social life is draining her finances, she fears that she will not have the means to finish her studies and therefore applies for social assistance. The German authorities reject her application on the basis of arts 16(1) and 24(2) of the Citizenship Directive:[5]

1. Article 16(1): 'Union citizens who have resided legally for a continuous period of *five years* in the host Member State shall have the right of permanent residence there.'

[2] Part of this section draws on Martijn van den Brink, 'Justice, Legitimacy and the Authority of Legislation within the European Union' (2019) 82 Modern Law Review 293.
[3] Elina Paunio, *Legal Certainty in Multilingual EU Law: Language, Discourse, and Reasoning at the European Court of Justice* (Ashgate 2013) 47; Miguel Poiares Maduro, 'Interpreting European Law—Judicial Adjudication in a Context of Constitutional Pluralism' (2008) 1 European Journal of Legal Studies 11.
[4] Alexander Somek, 'The Emancipation of Legal Dissonance' in Henning Koch and others (eds), *Europe: The New Legal Realism: Essays in Honor of Hjalte Rasmussen* (Djøf Publishing 2010) 28.
[5] Directive 2004/38 of the European Parliament and of the Council of 29 April 2004 on the right of citizens of the Union and their family members to move and reside freely within the territory of the Member States (OJ L158/77).

2. Article 24(2): 'the host Member State shall not be obliged to confer . . . prior to acquisition of the right of permanent residence, to grant maintenance aid for studies.'

They tell her that she does not qualify for the right of permanent residence under art 16(1) as she has resided in Germany for only two years; therefore, she is not entitled to claim maintenance aid for her studies in accordance with art 24(2).

The Dutch national contests this interpretation, believing that it is incompatible with the purpose of these provisions. She has read the Directive carefully and discovered that, according to the tenth Recital, their purpose is to ensure that EU citizens do not become 'an unreasonable burden on the social assistance system of the host Member State'.[6] She claims that whether someone is an unreasonable burden cannot depend on periods of residence in the host state alone, without taking into account the individual circumstances of the person claiming social assistance, including the extent of that person's integration in the host state. In her view, her demonstrated commitment to integrate into the German society means that she will not be an unreasonable burden and that the German authorities thus violate the purpose behind the Directive by blindly applying the five-year residence requirement.

She eventually manages to complete her studies without recourse to maintenance aid and subsequently finds work in Germany. However, after six years of legal and continuous residence, it is discovered that she occasionally sells drugs to friends and relatives, in small quantities but enough for the German authorities to issue her an expulsion order on grounds of public policy. She once again disagrees with their interpretation of the Citizenship Directive, this time that of arts 16(1) (provision (1) above), 16(4), and 28(2):

3. Article 16(4): 'the right of permanent residence shall be lost *only* through absence from the host Member State for a period exceeding *two consecutive years*.'
4. Article 28(2): 'The host Member State may not take an expulsion decision against Union citizens or their family members, irrespective of nationality, who have *the right of permanent residence* on its territory, except on *serious grounds* of public policy or public security.'

Unlike before, she now advocates a literal reading of the relevant legal provisions. She claims she has a right of permanent residence within the meaning of art 16(1), having resided in Germany for six years. She can lose this right, but according to art 16(4), only through an absence of a period exceeding two consecutive years.

[6] Recital 10 of ibid.

And since she has not resided outside Germany in the previous six years, she has a right of a permanent resident and therefore enjoys protection under art 28(2). She acknowledges that her conduct constituted a violation of German public policy but contends that the expulsion order was unlawful because it did not violate a *serious ground* of public policy.

This puts the German authorities in a difficult position. Her conduct did not constitute a serious violation of public policy that would justify expulsion under art 28(2), but they are adamant that they want to expel her. They therefore advocate a purposive interpretation of the relevant provisions, arguing that a literal reading would, in this instance, produce a result incompatible with their purpose. They refer to the eighteenth Recital of the Citizenship Directive, according to which the status of permanent residence is meant to be a 'genuine vehicle for integration', and they argue that this requires that permanent residence can be enjoyed only by citizens who are fully integrated. Therefore, to decide who enjoys a right of permanent residence and the privileges attached thereto, regard must be had not only to their period of residence but also to other personal circumstances that offer an indication of their integration in the host state. The authorities argue that criminal behaviour is a strong indication that a citizen is not well integrated so that the Dutch citizen should not enjoy the right of permanent residence under art 16(1) and the protection against expulsion that art 28(2) confers in that case.

Note the great similarities between the two situations. Both involve disagreement on the correct interpretation of the Citizenship Directive. Does the legal position of an EU citizen depend exclusively on her period of residence in the territory of the host state or (also) on other criteria that are indicative of her integration there? The answer to this question depends on the chosen method of interpretation. Are decision-makers constrained by the written rules (a more textualist approach), or should they interpret these rules in the light of their purpose, as expressed in the recitals to the legislative act (a more purposive approach)? Which method we prefer depends either on what we regard to be the most reliable method for identifying legislative intent or on what is the most desirable result, which some may find more important than respecting the choices of the legislature. In any case, both situations clearly raise important questions concerning the allocation of responsibility between the EU legislature and judiciary.

However, there is one aspect that distinguishes both situations: purposive interpretation will benefit citizens in need of social assistance but harm those who face expulsion measures, while textualist interpretation will disadvantage citizens who seek social assistance but work in favour of those at risk of being expelled. A consistent theory of interpretation cannot simultaneously provide the highest protection to citizens who need social assistance and those facing expulsion, unless, of course, legislation must be interpreted with a view to achieving the best substantive result (for the citizens in question). As implausible as it is to think that our view of legal interpretation should depend on the outcome we prefer, it turns out that

EU lawyers do take such instrumentalist views on such institutional questions and that the CJEU does so too.

Let me first discuss some relevant case law. Chapter VI has already shown that there has been a shift in the social assistance case law, from the use of individual assessments to rule-based decision-making. The latter approach is reflected in the *Alimanovic* verdict, which held that Member States may deny social assistance to EU citizens who do not meet the conditions set out in the following provisions:[7]

5. Article 7(3) of the Citizenship Directive: 'a Union citizen who is no longer a worker or self-employed person shall retain the status of worker or self-employed person in the following circumstances:
   (a) ...
   (b) 'he/she is in duly recorded involuntary unemployment after having been employed for *more than one year*'
   (c) 'he/she is in duly recorded involuntary unemployment after completing a fixed-term employment contract of *less than a year* ... In this case, the status of worker shall be retained for *no less than six months*'.

Note that an EU citizen with the status of worker can claim social assistance benefits. In *Alimanovic*, two Swedish nationals living in Germany challenged the decision of the local authorities to refuse them social assistance after they became unemployed, having worked for eleven months. Seeing the plain meaning of these provisions, the lawfulness of this decision was beyond reasonable doubt. The applicants had worked for less than one year, which meant that, under art 7(3)(c), they had a right to retain their status of worker for no less than six months. The German authorities had complied with this provision. Since the applicants had not been employed for more than one year, the authorities were not obliged to offer social assistance for the longer period referred to in art 7(3)(b). The CJEU read these provisions according to their ordinary meaning and ruled in favour of the authorities.

Chapter VI also discussed the expulsion case law, which stands in stark contrast to the approach in recent social assistance case law. This contrast becomes clear again when we compare *Alimanovic* with *Onuekwere*, one of the expulsion cases. The CJEU was asked about the correct interpretation of art 16(4) of the Citizenship Directive, according to which the right of permanent residence shall be lost *only* through absence from the host Member State for a period exceeding *two consecutive years* (provision (3) above). It ruled, contrary to the literal meaning of Article 16(4), that the protection EU citizens enjoy depends 'not only on territorial and temporal factors but also on qualitative elements, relating to the level of integration

[7] Case C-67/14 *Alimanovic* ECLI:EU:C:2015:597. See also Case C-299/14 *García-Nieto* ECLI:EU:C:2016:114.

in the host Member State'.[8] It therefore concluded that 'the undermining of the link of integration between the person concerned and the host Member State justifies the loss of the right of permanent residence *even outside the circumstances* mentioned in Article 16(4) of Directive 2004/38'.[9]

Indeed, the interpretation of the provisions on the right to claim social assistance and the provisions on protection against expulsion is blatantly inconsistent: social assistance can be claimed only if the written legislative conditions are met, while meeting very similar textual conditions does not provide protection against expulsion. The inconsistency is so glaring that one wonders why it is rarely seen. The reason is, without a doubt, that scholars hold equally inconsistent views yet, interestingly, views that are diametrically opposed to the CJEU's: they criticise the social assistance case law for failing to take into account citizens' individual circumstances[10] while condemning the expulsion case law for applying individual assessments contrary to legislation's express meaning.[11] Curiously, moreover, it is not just different scholars advocating different methods of interpretation in different situations; it is the same scholars taking inconsistent positions. For example, Eleanor Spaventa denounces the social assistance case law for the fact that 'Union citizens who do not satisfy *the black letter conditions* contained in the Directive are excluded from the right to equal treatment'.[12] Yet, she also argues that the individual assessments in the expulsion case law violate the text of the Directive.[13] Likewise, while Niamh Nic Shuibhne castigates the social assistance case law for downgrading 'the formerly central place of individual assessments',[14] she also criticises the individual assessments in the expulsion case law for restricting rights 'in disruption of the will of the legislature'.[15] Indeed, their views suggest that legislative provisions should be interpreted in a way that is advantageous to the citizens concerned.

[8] Case C-378/12 *Onuekwere* ECLI:EU:C:2014:13, para 25. See also Case C-400/12 *MG* ECLI:EU:C:2014:9, para 31.

[9] *Onuekwere* (n 8) para 25 (italics added).

[10] Floris de Witte, *Justice in the EU: The Emergence of Transnational Solidarity* (OUP 2015) 160–61; Síofra O'Leary, 'Equal Treatment and EU Citizens: A New Chapter on Cross-Border Educational Mobility and Access to Student Financial Assistance' (2009) 34 European Law Review 612; Henri de Waele, 'EU Citizenship: Revisiting Its Meaning, Place and Potential' (2010) 12 European Journal of Migration and Law 319, 326–27.

[11] Stephen Coutts, 'Union Citizenship as Probationary Citizenship: *Onuekwere*' (2015) 52 Common Market Law Review 531; Dimitry Kochenov and Uladzislau Belavusau, 'Kirchberg Dispensing the Punishment: Inflicting "Civil Death" on Prisoners in Onuekwere (C-378/12) and M.G. (C-400/12)' (2016) 41 European Law Review 557; Dora Kostakopoulou, 'When EU Citizens Become Foreigners' (2014) 20 European Law Journal 447.

[12] Eleanor Spaventa, 'Once a Foreigner Always a Foreigner: Who Does Not Belong Here Anymore? Expulsion Measures' in Herwig Verschueren (ed), *Residence, Employment and Social Rights of Mobile Persons: On How EU Law Defines Where They Belong* (Intersentia 2016) 96 (italics added).

[13] ibid 105–106.

[14] Niamh Nic Shuibhne, 'Limits Rising, Duties Ascending: The Changing Legal Shape of Union Citizenship' (2015) 52 Common Market Law Review 889, 913.

[15] ibid 921 (italics omitted).

This is not to point fingers, but only to show how easy it is to succumb to the temptations of instrumentalist interpretation: the very best EU citizenship lawyers do so. Their output-oriented thinking gets in the way of serious consideration of legislative interpretation. It thereby runs into the same problems as the output-oriented conceptions of legitimacy discussed in Chapter II: it relies on substantive standards that are too contentious to determine proper institutional behaviour. It also precludes genuine debate about the quality and consistency of judicial reasoning and even encourages inconsistency in furtherance of desirable outcomes. EU legal scholars are, indeed rightly, not outspoken advocates of instrumentalism.

3. The Problem with Purposive Interpretation

We have seen that the CJEU adhered to the purposive method in *Onuekwere* and that scholars believe that this method should have been applied in *Alimanovic*. What explains the popularity of purposive interpretation? Why do people assume, that is, that to respect the intended meaning of legislation, interpreters must act in accordance with the substantive purposes the legislature sought to achieve? Part of the answer, as we saw, is that it might give them the result they desire. Another part of the answer, as we saw in Chapter VI, is that decision-makers can avoid seemingly arbitrary and formalistic results by collapsing rules into their background purpose. There are, however, other reasons that explain the popularity of purposive theory, which is more refined than my discussion of it in Chapter VI may have suggested. This section discusses the theory's underlying assumptions and explains why they do not vindicate purposive reasoning.

Our preference for a certain method of interpretation depends partly on our understanding of legislatures. Modern legislatures are complex institutions that consist of many individuals who, representing different interests and political views, collectively decide on the political direction of their society.[16] What this complexity means for legislative interpretation is, however, an issue on which different theorists disagree. Purposive theorists are inclined to emphasise that legislatures have neither the time nor the ability to concern themselves with individual legislative provisions and their semantics details. Their task is to decide on the overall direction their society takes, which they do by passing legislation for specific purposes. This is why, purposive theory argues, courts must accord priority to these purposes if they want to respect the legislature's intentions.[17]

[16] On the complex nature of legislatures, Jeremy Waldron, *The Dignity of Legislation* (CUP 1999).
[17] For a brief summary of this position, John F Manning, 'What Divides Textualists from Purposivists?' (2006) 106 Columbia Law Review 70, 96–99.

The most influential account of purpose interpretation in EU law, developed by Miguel Maduro, rests on such assumptions. His position has radical edges that not all EU lawyers tempted by purposivism's promises will share, but for lack of other equally influential theories of purposive interpretation, this section will examine his. According to Maduro,

> Teleological interpretation can also be seen as more faithful to the democratic outcome, since it prevents textual manipulation of the legal rules. In fact, an interpretation that pays attention to the goals of the rule, and not simply its wording, prevents opportunistic behaviours and minimises the risk of an interpretative manipulation of the legislation. Such a manipulation would derive, in practice, effects from those rules which were neither wished for nor debated in the political process.[18]

Not all aspects of this position are clear. What a textual manipulation of legal rules consists of is mysterious, given that rules are usually textual. Maybe Maduro meant the textual manipulation of legislative intent. Moreover, why teleological, or purposive interpretation prevents opportunistic behaviour remains underspecified. Nevertheless, his theory is quintessentially purposive: judges should pay careful attention to the goals behind legislative rules if they want to be faithful to the legislature's choices.

The cited paragraph contains two arguments in support of purposive interpretation. I call the first the 'substantive purpose argument'. It holds that since the legislature acts to achieve certain substantive ends, judges should focus on those ends when they seek to identify legislative intent (as Maduro says, 'an interpretation that pays attention to the goals of the rule . . . minimises the risk of an interpretative manipulation of the legislation'). The second argument is the 'legislative capacity argument'. It holds that legislative proposals are too lengthy and complex to be considered in detail by legislative representatives, so judges risk interpreting legislation in ways never envisaged by the legislature if they prioritise legislative rules over legislative purpose (as Maduro says, 'such a manipulation would derive, in practice, effects from those rules which were neither wished for nor debated in the political process'). Both arguments are plausible: not all legislators will have studied the legislative proposals they vote on (the legislative capacity argument), and the legislature obviously pursues certain substantive goals (the substantive purpose argument) when it passes an act. However, we can accept both arguments without having to accept purposive theory as such.

The legislative division of labour means that legislative representatives will not know the ins and outs of every legislative act they vote on. As we saw in Chapter V,

[18] Maduro (n 4) 10.

legislators sit on a select number of legislative committees and do not have the time or expertise to familiarise themselves with and understand the details of proposals being discussed by colleagues in other committees. Not even all members of the committee responsible for a particular proposal are equally closely involved in the drafting of legislative acts; they may therefore not understand the full implications of the acts being debated. This may be why purposive theorists worry that deference to legislative text will lead judicial officials to follow rules 'which were neither wished for nor debated in the political process'.[19]

However, while possible, the legislative capacity argument does not justify legislative rules being read in the light of their underlying purposes. After all, purposive theory stipulates a general method of interpretation that expects judges to read the content of legislative rules in a way that most closely realises the substantive ends to which the legislature acted, including, indeed, rules that were wished for and debated in the legislative process. This point may not trouble purposive theorists at face value; they may assume that carefully drafted legislation will achieve the purposes the legislature intended to realise. This assumption is incorrect, however, certainly on the narrow conception of purpose that underlies their theories.

To see why, let's reconsider some of the provisions discussed in section VII.2. Provisions (1) and (3) establish the conditions for the acquisition and loss of the right of permanent residence; provision (5) sets the conditions for the enjoyment of social assistance. The substantive purpose of provisions (1) and (3) is to protect Union citizens who are well integrated in the host state and support their further integration,[20] while provision (5) seeks to prevent EU citizens from becoming an unreasonable burden on the social assistance system of the host state.[21] However, the legislature did not make the right of permanent residence conditional on EU citizens being able to prove that they are sufficiently integrated; and it did not make access to social assistance conditional on them not imposing an unreasonable burden on the host state. Instead, the enjoyment of these rights was conditioned on two criteria alone: *residence/employment* and *time*. Five years of legal and continuous residence is sufficient to claim permanent residence, and one year of employment is enough to claim social assistance.

As we saw in section VII.2, purposive interpretation risks collapsing legislative rules into their background purpose: the criteria of residence/employment and time would be enforced only when the outcome is compatible with these purposes. Thus, the CJEU suggested, in *Onuekwere*, that the right of permanent residence could be lost outside the circumstances mentioned in the Citizenship Directive: it should be reserved for those who are sufficiently integrated into the host society—a result that is more consistent with the purpose behind the rule than the rule itself.

[19] ibid.
[20] Recitals 23 and 24 of Directive 2004/38 (n 5).
[21] ibid Recital 10.

As a result, purposive reasoning risks misreading legislative intent. As Chapters V and VI have made clear, the intention in a legislative act is the joint plan of action legislators intend to realise. This plan consists of certain ends but also embeds the means chosen by the legislature to attain these ends, which consists, in large part, of the body of legislative rules laid down in the enacted legislative text. In Chapter VI, we saw that legislative rules must, in principle, entrench decision-making, even when their application generates results incompatible with the ends pursued by the legislature. The reason was that rules are the means not only to 'substantive justifications' but also to various 'rule-generating justifications'.[22] Purposive theory is too fixated on the former and neglects the latter. To identify the intent in an act, it may be necessary to take into consideration substantive legislative purposes, but the entire legislative plan, not just these purposes, must be respected in legislative interpretation.[23] Otherwise, the plan may collapse under the weight of substantive justifications, wrongly causing the object of interpretation to be legislative purpose rather than legislative intent.

The legislative capacity argument cannot salvage purposive theory. It is one thing to think that legislators occasionally fail to understand the practical consequences of the provisions they vote on; it is another thing entirely to assume that they cannot make the law they intend to make. It is the latter assumption that must be credible for purposive theory to be plausible. After all, the mere possibility that the adopted plan of action contains rules that are not congruent with the ends pursued by the legislature cannot support a general theory of interpretation that attaches so little weight to legislative text and legislative rules. Such a theory can be justified only if it is plausible to think that members of the legislature are rather unconcerned with the textual details of legislation. But this is not credible. Most legislative provisions will have been examined by its members, at least by those sitting on the legislative committee scrutinising the proposed legislative act.

One important reason why the adopted legislative text is the text the legislature intended to adopt is that legislative text is central to successful legislative decision-making. Decision-making by a large group of persons representing different interests and beliefs can only proceed in an orderly fashion if the procedure by which decisions are taken is relatively clear. This explains why the Treaties clearly define the stages of the ordinary legislative procedure and the responsibilities of the institutions involved. And it explains why they explicitly define what these institutions vote on: the 'wording' and 'text' proposed by other institutions.[24] Indeed, the legislative text is the main source for legislative representatives to know what legal changes the Commission proposes and what amendments the Council and

[22] Frederick Schauer, *Playing by the Rules: A Philosophical Examination of Rule-Based Decision-Making in Law and in Life* (Clarendon Press 2002) 94–95.
[23] Richard Ekins, *The Nature of Legislative Intent* (OUP 2012) 251.
[24] Article 294 of the Treaty on the Functioning of the European Union.

Parliament want to introduce. This, then, explains why it is impossible to ascertain legislative intent without paying close attention to the legislative text and also why the successful transposition of Directives into national law depends, to a large extent, on the proper transposition of the enacted text.[25] Without the publicly promulgated set of textual provisions, the legislature could not guide the behaviour of Member States and inform them and their citizens about the intended effects of its decisions. It is clearly implausible, therefore, to think that the legislature is not as concerned with the wording of legislative provisions as it is with the realisation of certain substantive purposes.

The main shortcoming of purposive theory is the disconnect between its premises and its conclusions. It is true that the legislature acts to realise certain substantive goals and that it may, at times, enact provisions that are inconsistent with these goals. This does not support purposive legal reasoning, however, which tends to overlook the rule-generating justifications legislation serves. Moreover, while legislation may include provisions that were not wished for or debated in the legislative process, most legislative rules will have been adopted intentionally. In other words, the problem with purposive theory is that it focuses on only a part of the legislative plan and ignores the central role of written legislative rules. Interpreters who believe that legislative purpose should be the object of interpretation are therefore likely to misunderstand the legislature's intentions.

4. Indeterminacy in EU Law

In section VI.2, I noted that purposive theory relies on an inflated notion of indeterminacy in EU law. Legislation is replete with detailed and precise provisions that unmistakably constrain its addressees. This may be uncontroversial, and many legal scholars who stress the indeterminacy of EU law may have something less extreme in mind than the purposive views discussed in Chapter VI. They may merely contend that EU law is less determinate than domestic law so that the text enacted by the EU legislature is less indicative of legislative intent than the text enacted by domestic legislatures.[26] It seems to me that the truth of such arguments depends on the vigour by which they are asserted. On the one hand, it is, indeed, plausible to think that there are additional causes of indeterminacy in EU law,[27] such as the multilingual nature of the European legal order and the possibility that

[25] As the CJEU has said itself, 'the preamble to a Community act has no binding legal force and cannot be relied on as a ground for derogating from the actual provisions of the act in question': Case C-162/97 *Nilsson* ECLI:EU:C:1998:554, para 54.

[26] Gunnar Beck, *The Legal Reasoning of the Court of Justice of the EU* (Hart Publishing 2012); Jan Komárek, 'Legal Reasoning in EU Law' in Anthony Arnull and Damian Chalmers (eds), *The Oxford Handbook of European Union Law* (1st edn, OUP 2015) 41.

[27] Trevor C Hartley, *Constitutional Problems of the European Union* (Hart Publishing 1999) ch 4.

issues are left open if the legislature is unable to reach agreement. On the other hand, misconceptions about both the degree of indeterminacy in EU law and its causes still exist, which I wish to address in this section.

First some preliminary observations about indeterminacy—an essential feature of law. An indeterminate provision is one that has borderline cases in which its application is unclear.[28] Indeterminacy has different sources, the most important of which is imprecision. An imprecise word has no clear boundary to its application,[29] such as the concept of 'worker' for the purposes of EU law: it is unclear, for example, whether it applies to persons working four hours a week or not. There is some debate as to whether there are other sources of indeterminacy and whether they are distinguishable from imprecision,[30] but incompleteness is arguably a distinct source. The following provision is fairly precise, yet incomplete: 'Union citizens who have resided legally for a continuous period of five years in the host Member State shall have the right of permanent residence there.' It is incomplete because it is unclear whether the provision applies to periods of residence accumulated before its entry into force.[31] Thus, the provision is incomplete insofar as it does not fully answer which citizens enjoy the right of permanent residence.[32] Other possible sources of indeterminacy are ambiguity, a feature of words with more than one meaning (such as chair or right),[33] and the use of dummy standards, which call on others to define the applicable standard (such as genuine or sufficient).[34]

There can be misconceptions about when a provision is indeterminate. First, disagreement about a provision's application does not entail indeterminacy. Disagreement can be disingenuous or arise due to a genuine misunderstanding about the law's application. To illustrate: earlier, we saw that, according to art 16(4) of the Citizenship Directive, 'the right of permanent residence shall be lost *only* through absence from the host Member State for a period exceeding *two consecutive years*.' In contrast, the CJEU held that 'the undermining of the link of integration between the person concerned and the host Member State justifies the loss of the right of permanent residence *even outside the circumstances* mentioned in Article 16(4)'.[35] That this provision was interpreted contrary to its plain meaning does not mean that it was more indefinite than would appear at first sight. It only means that it was interpreted contrary to determinate language. Second, indeterminacy is not

[28] Timothy Endicott, *Vagueness in Law* (OUP 2000); Timothy Endicott, 'The Value of Vagueness' in Andrei Marmor and Scott Soames (eds), *Philosophical Foundations of Language in the Law* (OUP 2011).

[29] Endicott, *Vagueness in Law* (n 28) 33–36.

[30] ibid.

[31] Case C-162/09 *Lassal* ECLI:EU:C:2010:592; Case C-325/09 *Dias* ECLI:EU:C:2011:498.

[32] The distinction between imprecision and incompleteness is not sharp: Endicott, *Vagueness in Law* (n 28) 38–41.

[33] ibid 54.

[34] ibid 48–49.

[35] *Onuekwere* (n 8) para 25 (italics added).

due to ignorance of the meaning of language.[36] A CJEU judge once replied to my question of whether the disregard for legislative text in *Onuekwere* was appropriate by saying that only judges can determine whether a provision is determinate. His suggestion about my ignorance of the English language probably reflected his unease about my question, not his belief that only people donned in burgundy robes have sufficient knowledge of language to know the meaning of linguistic expressions. Finally, indeterminacy does not depend on political constraints, at least not in the ordinary sense of linguistic indeterminacy. Judges may enjoy considerable political discretion because of the environment they operate in, but this should not be confused with the discretion that may result from vague legal norms. How they use their political discretion depends on what behaviour is deemed appropriate, not on the determinacy of the enacted legal provisions.[37] Of course, certain non-linguistic indeterminacies may affect legal interpretation. Think, for example, of unresolved conflicts between different rules or doubts about the application of precise rules when they lead to absurd results.[38] But there is no reason to think that there is a smaller number of clear cases in which legal provisions clearly do or do not apply when judges are subject to weaker political constraints.

Indeterminacy is an essential feature of EU law, but there are also good reasons to think that there is considerable agreement about EU law. First, a provision that has borderline cases need not be radically indeterminate: there may not be one right answer, but that does not justify the conclusion that there are no wrong answers.[39] In addition, while the presence of EU law is felt in ever-increasing policy areas, the Court receives only 550 preliminary references annually.[40] EU judges face an immense workload because of these references, but their number is minuscule if we consider the reach of EU law. There are several reasons for this. Citizens may not have an adequate understanding of their legal position or ability to enforce their rights, and national courts may think they can resolve disputes themselves even when they should have submitted a preliminary ruling to ask for clarification.[41] However, the low number is difficult to fathom without accepting that there is significant agreement about the meaning of EU law.[42] If this were not

[36] Endicott, *Vagueness in Law* (n 28) 32.

[37] It is not institutional features alone that explain the position of courts. Also important is the judicial behaviour of judges and their attitude towards judicial decision-making: Ran Hirschl, 'The Judicialization of Politics' in Keith E Whittington, R Daniel Kelemen, and Gregory A Caldeira (eds), *The Oxford Handbook of Law and Politics* (OUP 2008).

[38] Endicott, *Vagueness in Law* (n 28) 7 and 55.

[39] ibid ch 2; Herbert Lionel Adolphus Hart, *The Concept of Law* (Clarendon Press 1998) 126.

[40] An accessible overview of the statistics of judicial activity from 2022 is available from CJEU, 'Annual Report 2022: Statistics Concerning the Judicial Activity of the Court of Justice' (2022) <https://curia.europa.eu/jcms/upload/docs/application/pdf/2023-03/stats_cour_2022_en.pdf> accessed 17 April 2023.

[41] Anna Wallerman, 'Who Is the National Judge? A Typology of Judicial Attitudes and Behaviours Regarding Preliminary References' in Clara Rauchegger and Anna Wallerman (eds), *The Eurosceptic Challenge: National Implementation and Interpretation of EU Law* (Hart Publishing 2019).

[42] Just as there is a great deal of legal agreement in general: Bill Watson, 'Explaining Legal Agreement' (2023) 14 Jurisprudence 221.

the case, the number of preliminary references should be much higher than it is. In fact, we should expect the European legal order to be on the verge of collapse if there is immense uncertainty about EU law's intended effects. That would mean that it would be virtually impossible for Member States to comply with the law without inundating the CJEU with questions about its meaning. That this has not happened suggests that citizens will often understand that a particular standard of EU law has been correctly applied and that it is pointless to challenge that decision. It also suggests that national courts that hear disputes about the correct application of EU law are often able to resolve such cases without having to ask the Court for clarification.[43] There are, of course, plenty of 'hard' cases,[44] but most cases are so easy that they never appear in court.[45]

Of course, agreement about EU law's meaning is not just due to the linguistic expressions of legislation. Legislative context (discussed in the following sections) and case law also contribute to the agreement that exists. The *Keck* judgment, discussed in section VI.5, illustrates how case law can achieve this. The prohibition on measures having an equivalent effect to quantitative restrictions was interpreted as not prohibiting selling arrangements that apply indiscriminately to foreign and domestic goods. This may not settle all legal disputes; there may be borderline cases when it is unclear whether a national practice is a selling arrangement and, therefore, whether the rule applies or not. Nevertheless, the judgment did reduce uncertainty about the types of measures permitted under EU free movement law. In the same vein, most other judgments foster agreement on the effects of EU law (if not agreement on what these effects should be).

Legislative interpretation has the same effects. We know, for example, that the concept of worker extends to '[a]ny person who pursues activities which are real and genuine, to the exclusion of activities on such a small scale as to be regarded as purely marginal and ancillary';[46] that the concept of spouse includes married same-sex couples;[47] that the concept of social assistance refers 'to all assistance schemes established by the public authorities . . . to which recourse may be had by an individual who does not have resources sufficient to meet his own basic needs

[43] Case C-283/81 *CILFIT* ECLI:EU:C:1982:335.
[44] As suggested by Komárek (n 26) 41.
[45] According to Solum,

> the reason that easiest cases are not 'cases' at all is that the law's relative determinacy does not permit us to make a 'case' out of them. The very determinacy of the law prevents us from even recognizing them as cases in any grand empirical study to determine the percentages of hard and easy cases.

Lawrence B Solum, 'On the Indeterminacy Crisis: Critiquing Critical Dogma' (1987) 54 University of Chicago Law Review 462, 495. For a similar point, Brian Leiter, 'Explaining Theoretical Disagreement' (2009) 76 University of Chicago Law Review 1215; Andrei Marmor, *The Language of Law* (1st edn, OUP 2014) 109.
[46] Case 53/81 *Levin* ECLI:EU:C:1982:105, para 17; Case C-456/02 *Trojani* ECLI:EU:C:2004:488, para 15.
[47] Case C-673/16 *Coman* ECLI:EU:C:2018:385.

and those of his family'.[48] I could go on, but the point should be clear. Case law allows for agreement on the law, either by stipulating further criteria to determine whether inherently vague concepts (such as worker and social assistance) apply or by filling gaps left open by the legislature (such as whether married same-sex couples are spouses within the meaning of EU free movement law).

Legal provisions may be open not to one but several interpretations. In that case, different meanings can be reasonably inferred from the same provision. For instance, the CJEU could have interpreted the concept of worker as applying to every person carrying out an economic activity for at least 50 per cent of the statutory working week without it being open to the accusation of misinterpretation. However, since the law is usually only underdeterminate and not indeterminate with respect to a given dispute, the range of results compatible with some legal provision is smaller than the range of all conceivable results.[49] For instance, while the application of the concept of 'spouse' to same-sex couples was contested, no one doubted its application to opposite-sex couples. And while there are borderline cases for social assistance and social security, many social benefits are clearly instances of either social assistance or social security, in which case it is clear whether EU law applies.[50] All this is to say that a range of textual and contextual factors allow decision-makers to determine which outcomes can reasonably be inferred from the legislative material.

The final two sections of this chapter highlight the importance of context in interpretation, namely that good interpretation requires the enacted text to be read in the context in which the legislature expressed itself. Nevertheless, the starting point of reasonable legislative interpretation cannot be anything but the written words enacted by the legislature. This conclusion finds support in legal practice as well. Contrary to the belief that purposive legal reasoning must be the hallmark method of interpretation,[51] many disputes get resolved by reference to the law's

[48] Case C-140/12 *Brey* ECLI: EU:C:2013:565, para 61; Case C-333/13 *Dano* ECLI:EU:C:2014:2358, para 63; *Alimanovic* (n 7) para 44.

[49] I borrow this distinction between indeterminacy and underdeterminacy from Solum (n 45) 473.

[50] For some, this statement may be begging the question of why so many disputes on social assistance and social security came before the Court in the past. In part, this happened because there are benefits that have features of both social assistance and social security (see, eg *Coman*, cited in n 46), but also because of the Court's willingness to offer a very broad (narrow) definition of social security (assistance) to aid mobile Union citizens. For example, it defined a national benefit as social security that was social assistance in Case C-139/82 *Pisticello* ECLI:EU:C:1983:126. And it excluded from the concept social assistance national benefits 'intended to facilitate access to the labour market' (Joined cases C-22/08 and C-23/08 *Vatsouras and Koupatantze* ECLI:EU:C:2009:344, para 42), even though these benefits were social assistance according to our common understanding of the term. For discussion, Anne Pieter van der Mei, 'Regulation 1408/71 and Coordination of Special Non-Contributory Benefit Schemes' (2002) 5 European Law Review 551.

[51] See, in addition to constitutional pluralist theories of interpretation, Komárek (n 26) 41; Nial Fennelly, 'Legal Interpretation at the European Court of Justice' (1996) 20 Fordham International law Journal 656; Anthony Arnull, *The European Union and Its Court of Justice* (2nd edn, OUP 2006) ch 16; Oreste Pollicino, 'Legal Reasoning of the Court of Justice in the Context of the Principle of Equality between Judicial Activism and Self-Restraint' (2004) 5 German Law Journal 283, 289.

plain meaning.[52] Indeed, it appears that even disputed legal provisions in hard cases—cases that national courts cannot resolve without the help of the CJEU—are rarely so indeterminate that they provide no guidance about the legislature's intended consequences. This suggests that legislative interpretation involves greater textuality than is sometimes acknowledged.

5. The Limits of Literal Interpretation

To say that there is considerable textuality to legislative interpretation is not the same as saying that the linguistic or literal meaning of legislation must be the object of legislative interpretation. Some EU lawyers have advocated literal interpretation. For Gerard Conway, for example, EU law should be read in accordance with the 'ordinary, literal meaning of the words used'.[53] And Phil Syrpis argues that the CJEU 'should, as far as possible, try to read secondary legislation literally'.[54] Both scholars rightly appreciate that the written text forms the basis for legislative interpretation, but I will show that whether its meaning corresponds with legislative intent cannot be determined out of legislative context.

There are vast differences between purposive and literal theories of interpretation. These differences stem, in large part, from their conception of legislative language use. As we have seen, purposive theorists like Maduro assume that the legislature is an ineffectual language user who cares little for the written rules it adopts. Hence, his belief that an interpretation that prioritises a rule's linguistic meaning over its purposes might be mistaken about the intended consequences of legislation. Conway, in contrast, claims that legislative language use is incredibly straightforward: 'The context of legal communication from the officials of the legal system to the legal audience, i.e. the citizens in general, is clearly of a direct and uncomplicated public communication.'[55] He assumes that legislative language use is not as complex as communication among ordinary people: 'there is no hidden meaning or no indirect language, such as irony, allegory, or metaphor in legal expression. Unlike in every day conversation, non-verbal communication is

[52] Beck (n 26) 285–87; Albertina Albors-Llorens, 'The European Court of Justice, More Than a Teleological Court' (1999) 2 Cambridge Yearbook of European Legal Studies 373; Cornelis JW Baaij, 'Fifty Years of Multilingual Interpretation in the European Union' in Peter Meijes Tiersma and Lawrence Solan (eds), *The Oxford Handbook of Language and Law* (OUP 2012).

[53] Gerard Conway, *The Limits of Legal Reasoning and the European Court of Justice* (CUP 2013) 130. Similar views have been expressed by Trevor C Hartley, *The Foundations of European Union Law: An Introduction to the Constitutional and Administrative Law of the European Union* (8th edn, OUP 2014) 72–78.

[54] Phil Syrpis, 'The Relationship between Primary and Secondary Law in the EU' (2015) 52 Common Market Law Review 461, 484.

[55] Conway (n 53) 130.

not central to the communication.'[56] He therefore believes that reading legislation literally is the best way to pursue the wishes of the legislature.[57]

There would be good reasons to favour literal interpretation if it were the only alternative to purposive interpretation. Most importantly, legislative text is central to successful legislative decision-making. What speaks for literal interpretation, as Jeremy Waldron observed, is that '[t]he rule that has been posited by the legislature is the rule expressed by the very words that are used in the bill that the legislature has passed'.[58] In addition, literal interpretation would probably be the best method if the legislature could not form legislative intentions. In that case, as Joseph Raz said, knowing legislation's envisaged meaning would involve nothing but knowing '[w]hat the legislator said [and] what his words mean, given the circumstances of the promulgation of the legislation, and the conventions of interpretation prevailing at the time'.[59]

However, as Richard Ekins has shown, theories that advocate a literal reading of legislation 'are unable to explain how judges and legislators understand real statutes'.[60] This is due to the fact that meaning is not just a function of linguistic conventions, such as semantics and syntax, which form the literal or semantic meaning of a sentence. While the literal meaning of words is relevant to determine the meaning a speaker intends to convey, literal meaning often underdetermines speaker meaning.[61] Even grammatically correct sentences with an unambiguous literal meaning can underdetermine speaker meaning, including in legislative language use.[62] As I will show next, EU legislative interpretation risks becoming an irrational exercise if its object is the literal meaning and not the intended meaning of legislation. Indeed, it is difficult to conceive of a plausible theory of legislative interpretation without the notion of legislative intent.

It should be obvious, I think, that legislative intent cannot be deduced from the semantic meaning of a legislative provision in case of discrepancies between different language versions. It has been said that the CJEU is inclined to resolve linguistic discrepancies between two or more legislative provisions by reading legislation literally rather than purposively,[63] but this just cannot be the case. It is logically impossible. What such studies show is that the correct language version

[56] ibid.

[57] For a similar view, Syrpis (n 54) 484.

[58] Jeremy Waldron, 'The Dignity of Legislation' (1995) 54 Maryland Law Review 633, 652. See also Jeremy Waldron, *Law and Disagreement* (OUP 1999) 143.

[59] Joseph Raz, *Between Authority and Interpretation: On the Theory of Law and Practical Reason* (OUP 2009) 288. See also Waldron, *Law and Disagreement* (n 58) 142.

[60] Ekins (n 23) 191.

[61] Kent Bach, 'Context Ex Machina' in Zoltán Gendler Szabó (ed), *Semantics vs. Pragmatics* (Clarendon Press 2005); Scott Soames, *Philosophical Essays, Volume 1—Natural Language: What It Means and How We Use It* (Princeton UP 2009) 278–83; Ekins (n 23) 196–97.

[62] Ekins (n 23) ch 7.

[63] Baaij (n 52); Mattias Derlén, *Multilingual Interpretation of European Union Law* (Wolters Kluwer 2009) 37; Case C-265/03 *Igor Simutenkov* ECLI:EU:C:2005:6, Opinion of AG Stix-Hackl, para 18.

can be identified without reading legislation purposively, but this does not mean that it can be done by reading the text literally. After all, a literal reading of discrepant language versions would not resolve the discrepancy but merely lead to the discrepant application of EU law in the national legal orders.

The *Lubella* verdict illustrates this. The case concerned a discrepancy between different language versions of Regulation No 1932/93, which established protective measures as regards the import of sour cherries.[64] All language versions referred to sour cherries, except for the German-language version, which referred to sweet cherries. A literal interpretation of the different language versions would have established protective measures as regards the import of sweet cherries in Germany and of sour cherries in all other Member States. The decision that the Regulation sought to establish protective measures regarding sour cherries in Germany followed not from a literal reading of the legislative provisions but from an understanding of the wider legislative context. The CJEU mentioned the corrigendum that had been issued to the German translation, noted that all other language versions clearly applied to sour cherries, and referred to the Combined Nomenclature codes for the classification of goods mentioned by the Regulation.[65]

As this case shows, interpreters must, when faced with linguistic discrepancies, refer to non-linguistic features of the law to decide which language version prevails. As the CJEU itself has noted, linguistic discrepancies do not allow 'the text of a provision to be considered in isolation'.[66] Indeed, when asked which language version reflects legislative intent, it reads the text not literally but in context, which it does 'by reference to the purpose and general scheme of the rules of which it forms part'.[67] It studies the 'structure and history' of a legislative act,[68] 'the versions existing in the other official languages',[69] as well as legislative preambles.[70] Even when the decision of which language version is correct is made by reference to 'the clear wording of the great majority of the language versions',[71] legislation is read not literally but contextually.

[64] Commission Regulation (EEC) No 1932/93 of 16 July 1993 establishing protective measures as regards the import of sour cherries (OJ L174/35).

[65] Case C-64/95 *Lubella* ECLI:EU:C:1996:388, paras 16–18.

[66] Case C-353/04 *Nowaco* ECLI:EU:C:2006:522, para 41; Case C-174/05 *Stichting Zuid-Hollandse Milieufederatie* ECLI:EU:C:2006:170, para 20; Case C-63/06 *UAB Profisa* ECLI:EU:C:2007:233 para 13.

[67] Case C-30/77 *Bouchereau* ECLI:EU:C:1977:172, para 14. Similarly, Case C-6/74 *Moulijn* ECLI:EU:C:1974:129, paras 10–11; Case C-11/76 *Netherlands v Commission* ECLI:EU:C:1979:28, para 6; *Lubella* (n 65) para 26; Case C-449/93 *Rockfon* ECLI:EU:C:1995:420 para 28; *UAB Profisa* (n 66) para 14.

[68] *Nowaco* (n 66) para 42.

[69] ibid para 41; *Stichting Zuid-Hollandse Milieufederatie* (n 66) para 20; *UAB Profisa* (n 66) paras 13 and 15. See also Case C-298/94 *Annette Henke* ECLI:EU:C:1996:382 para 15.

[70] *Rockfon* (n 67) para 30; *Lubella* (n 65) para 27; *Stichting Zuid-Hollandse Milieufederatie* (n 66) para 21; *Annette Henke* (n 69) para 13.

[71] C-236/97 *Codan* ECLI:EU:C:1998:617, para 29.

Literal interpretation is also inadequate when legislation's meaning is underdetermined by its literal meaning. Some examples suffice to illustrate this.

6. Article 47(2) of the Act Concerning the Conditions of Accession of Spain and Portugal: 'This [patent] right may be invoked for the products referred to in paragraph 1 until the end of the third year after Spain has made these products patentable.'

In *Merck and Beecham*, the CJEU was asked to decide when the patent right expires: exactly three years after pharmaceutical products had become patentable or by the end of the third calendar year after the date on which the products had become patentable. The provision's wording could support either reading. Based on the scheme and purpose of the Act, the CJEU decided that the right expired exactly three years after the product had become patentable.[72]

7. Article 3(7) of Directive 96/71/EC on the posting of workers in the framework of the provision of services: 'Paragraphs 1 to 6 shall not prevent application of terms and conditions of employment which are more favourable to workers.'

It was not clear from the literal meaning whether it allows the *home* state, where posted workers come from, or the *host* state, where posted workers are sent to, to apply employment conditions that are more favourable than those set out in paragraphs 1–6 of the Directive. In *Laval*, the CJEU ruled, consistent with the Directive's drafting history, that this should not be the standards of the host state.[73]

8. Article 5(2) of Council Directive 90/314/EEC on package travel, package holidays and package tours: 'With regard to *the damage* resulting for the consumer from the failure to perform or the improper performance of the contract, Member States shall take the necessary steps to ensure that the organizer and/or retailer is/are liable unless such failure to perform or improper performance is attributable neither to any fault of theirs nor to that of another supplier of services.'

In *Leiter*, the question was whether 'non-material damage' constituted damage within the meaning of art 5(2). No answer could be inferred from the literal meaning of this provision. Looking at the general scheme of which it was part,

[72] Joined cases C-267/95 and C-268/95 *Merck and Beecham* ECLI:EU:C:1996:468. This case serves as an illustration of the limits of literal interpretation, however, not as an example of good interpretation. The Court's arguments are rather thin.

[73] Case C-341/05 *Laval un Partneri* ECLI:EU:C:2007:809. For detailed discussion, section IV.8.

the CJEU held that 'the Directive implicitly recognises the existence of a right to compensation for damage other than personal injury, including non-material damage'.[74]

9. Article 24 of the Citizenship Directive
   1) 'Subject to such specific provisions as are expressly provided for in . . . secondary law, all Union citizens residing on the basis of this Directive in the territory of the host Member State shall enjoy equal treatment with the nationals of that Member State.'
   2) 'By way of derogation from paragraph 1, the host Member State shall not be obliged to confer entitlement to social assistance during the first three months of residence or, where appropriate, the longer period provided for in Article 14(4)(b).'
10. Article 14(4)(b) of the Citizenship Directive: 'the Union citizens and their family members may not be expelled for as long as the Union citizens can provide evidence that they are continuing to seek employment and that they have a genuine chance of being engaged'.

EU citizens enjoy equal treatment with the host state's nationals 'subject to such specific provisions as are expressly provided' (9(1)). By way of derogation from this provision, they cannot claim social assistance during their first three months of residence (9(2)) and, beyond this period, if they have a right of residence as work seekers ((9(2)) and (10)). The legislature overlooked, however, that EU citizens may reside in the host state for more than three months without seeking employment there. It did not exempt this group of EU citizens from the right to equal treatment, which is why a literal reading of provisions (9) and (10) would lead to the paradoxical result that citizens who do not seek work in the host state can claim social assistance, while those who try to find work cannot.[75] The CJEU must have understood that this could not have been the outcome envisaged by the legislature. It ruled, in *Dano*, that assistance may also be denied to EU citizens who reside in the host state for more than three months without seeking work.[76]

These examples show that the linguistic meaning of the written text can underdetermine legislative intent, even when literal interpretation is, in principle, possible. The discrepant language versions of the Regulation in *Lubella* and provisions (9) and (10) could have been read literally, but the CJEU decided not to, knowing this would be an unreasonable inference of legislative intent. Advocates of literal interpretation must assume, by contrast, that the legislature intended these

[74] Case C-168/00 *Leiter* ECLI:EU:C:2002:163, para 23.
[75] Case C-333/13 *Dano* ECLI:EU:C:2014:341, Opinion of AG Wathelet, para 16.
[76] *Dano* (n 48).

provisions to produce the irrational consequences suggested by their linguistic meaning and that it did not intend the meaning of provisions (6), (7), and (8) to be more specific than its linguistic meaning. A more plausible conclusion is that the examples just discussed show the limits of literal interpretation.

6. The Intended Meaning of EU Legislation

Theories of legislative interpretation rest on a particular view of legislative language use. Advocates of purposive reasoning believe that the legislature is an ineffectual language user and that the way to respect legislative intent is, therefore, to attain the substantive purpose underlying a legislative act rather than to follow its linguistic meaning. Proponents of literal interpretation assume that the legislature is a simple language user and that legislative intent can reasonably be inferred from the literal meaning of the legislative text. As we have seen, neither view of legislative language use—nor, therefore, either theory—is adequate. In this section, I argue that the legislature should, instead, be treated as an ordinary language user and explain what that means for the reasonable interpretation of legislative acts.

While his preference for literal interpretation is unfounded, Conway is right that legislation will not use 'indirect language, such as irony, allegory or metaphor'.[77] Nor will it normally rely on unnecessarily vague expressions: numerical standards such as sixty-five years old or 120 kilometre per hour will, for example, be preferred over terms like old/young or fast/slow.[78] However, as Ekins has made clear, 'legislators and interpreters are persons and they understand language as a natural language, in which speakers act to convey their intended meaning to others'.[79] Indeed, there is no reason to think that ordinary people will use language in unordinary ways when acting as legislative representatives. They should try not to use stylistic devices and other language that is detrimental to the legislative task, but we can safely assume that they convey meaning as they normally would—as ordinary language users.

So how do ordinary language users convey meaning? It was once thought that the meaning conveyed corresponds to the semantic content of the sentence a speaker utters,[80] but philosophers of language today recognise that semantic meaning often (and some say always) underdetermines the meaning a speaker intends to convey.[81] Instead, speaker meaning is a pragmatically enriched version

[77] Conway (n 53) 130.
[78] Scott Soames, 'What Vagueness and Inconsistency Tell Us about Interpretation' in Marmor and Soames (n 27) 33–34; Ekins (n 23) 212. This does not deny that vague expressions can serve useful purposes for legislatures: Endicott, 'The Value of Vagueness' (n 28).
[79] Ekins (n 23) 213.
[80] Scott Soames, *Philosophy of Language* (Princeton UP 2010) ch 7.
[81] Whether the semantic meaning frequently or always underdetermines speaker meaning is not very relevant, I believe, for our discussion. What matters is that it underdetermines speaker meaning

of the uttered sentence's semantic meaning. Pragmatic enrichment refers to the process of inferring the meaning the speaker intends to convey based on what he or she literally said and the context that speaker and hearer share.[82] Following this understanding, both semantic meaning and shared context constrain rather than determine what the speaker might reasonably have meant: both factors contribute to the hearer's ability to infer the meaning the speaker intended to convey.[83]

This understanding of language use explains, on the one hand, the problems of purposive reasoning as encountered in sections VII.2 and VII.3, which pays insufficient attention to the semantic constraints imposed by legislative text. On the other hand, as we just saw, theories of legislative interpretation that instruct interpreters to resolve disputes based on the linguistic meaning of the enacted words ignore that semantic meaning often underdetermines the intended meaning. The chosen text may be unintentionally imprecise or incorrect, but more importantly, legislation would become too lengthy and complex if the legislature tried writing out its intentions in full.[84] For this reason, interpreters must not limit themselves to identifying the literal meaning of legislation but try to ascertain the meaning the legislature intended to convey. The literal meaning is relevant: it constrains what interpreters can reasonably judge the legislature to have intended, and a provision's literal meaning maybe consistent with its intended meaning, but whether this is so will depend on legislative context.

What to understand by legislative context? Philosophers of language define context as the 'conversational setting broadly construed',[85] meaning that what the hearer can reasonably identify the speaker to mean is 'influenced by many factors, including the purpose and direction of the conversation, remarks previously made, contextually salient information [and] shared background assumptions'.[86] The concept of legislative context has been understood as such by the CJEU in *CILFIT*, where it offered the following definition of legislative context:

> every provision of EU law must be placed in its context and interpreted in the light of the provisions of EU law as a whole, regard being had to the objectives thereof and to its state of evolution at the date on which the provision in question is to be applied.[87]

often enough to dismiss the notion that interpreters should focus solely on the semantic meaning of legislative provisions. For further discussion, Bach (n 61) 26–27.

[82] On pragmatics, Bach (n 61); Soames, *Philosophy of Language* (n 80) ch 7; Marmor (n 45) 22–27; Ekins (n 23) 205–11.
[83] Bach (n 61); Soames, *Philosophy of Language* (n 80) ch 7.
[84] Ekins (n 23) 214–15. I will return to this issue at the end of this section.
[85] Bach (n 61) 21.
[86] Soames, *Philosophy of Language* (n 80) 157.
[87] *CILFIT* (n 43) para 20.

This definition is almost accurate, though not entirely complete. As I explain later in this section, the phrase 'EU law as a whole' must not be understood to entail an obligation to interpret all legislative acts conform the Treaties (see also section IV.7). But let me first examine in some detail the relevant aspects of legislative context, including those identified in *CILFIT*.

One element *not* mentioned in *CILFIT* is the drafting history of legislative acts. This may be because the Court's position on using legislative history in interpretation seems to have shifted. In the past, it rejected invocations of legislative history, ruling, for instance, that reservations and objections made at the time of legislative negotiations cannot be used in legislative interpretation[88] and that unpublished minutes of Council meetings cannot be relied upon by the applicants.[89] This conclusion could be justified on the basis that this material was either not publicly available or consisted of statements of individual Member States that did not provide a reliable indication of the intended meaning of the provisions in question. But what about publicly available material that seems reliable? According to Advocate General Warner, it would never be appropriate to look at legislative history since legislative representatives 'may agree on a text without necessarily having the same views as to its meaning'.[90] However, since the views of individual legislators are irrelevant in the identification of legislative intent (section V.6), this argument does not justify his idea that legislative history must be ignored. Instead, insofar as it is publicly available and appears indicative of the legislature's state of mind on the legislation under discussion, no obvious justification exists for excluding it in the process of attributing meaning to legislation. For example, it was clear from the drafting history of the Posted Workers Directive that the reason for introducing provision (7) was to allow the home state to apply its more favourable employment standards.[91] It would make little sense to ignore such reliable evidence of legislative intent. In this sense, it is right that the CJEU has come to attach greater importance to legislative history than before.[92]

[88] Case 39/72 *Commission v Italy* ECLI:EU:C:1973:13, para 22. Similarly, Case C-402/03 *Skov and Bilka* ECLI:EU:C:2006:6, para 43.

[89] Case 9/56 *Meroni v High Authority* ECLI:EU:C:1958:7; Case 38/69 *Commission v Italy* ECLI:EU:C:1970:11. See also Joined cases C-197/94 and C-252/94 *Bautiaa and Société française maritime* ECLI:EU:C:1996:47, para 51; Case C-292/89 *Antonissen* ECLI:EU:C:1991:80, para 18; Case C-375/98 *Epson Europe* ECLI:EU:C:2000:302, para 26; Case C-242/08 *Swiss Re Germany Holding* ECLI:EU:C:2009:647, para 62.

[90] Case C-28/76 *Milac v Hauptzollamt Freiburg* ECLI:EU:C:1976:144, Opinion of AG Warner at 1664. See also Case 155/79 *AM and S Europe v Commission* ECLI:EU:C:1981:9, Opinion of AG Warner at 1620–21.

[91] Discussed in section VII.5 and in section IV.7.

[92] Karin Frick and Soren Schonberg, "Finishing, Refining, Polishing: On the Use of Travaux Preparatoires as an Aid to the Interpretation of Community Legislation' (2003) 28 European Law Review 149; Koen Lenaerts and José A Gutiérrez-Fons, 'To Say What the Law of the EU Is: Methods of Interpretation and the European Court of Justice' (2013) 20 Columbia Journal of European law 3, 21–23.

An element of legislative context mentioned in *CILFIT* is 'provisions of EU law as a whole'. Legislative provisions should not be read in isolation but in the light of the whole legislative act. This presupposes that different parts of a legislative act are meant to form a coherent whole: they should not impose contradictory obligations or illogical results.[93] This justifies what is called a systemic interpretation of EU law, whereby rules are interpreted by reference to the general scheme of which they are part.[94] It justifies, for instance, the ruling in the *Dano* case that provisions (9) and (10) should be read to mean that unemployed EU citizens residing in the host country for more than three months are not entitled to social assistance if they are not looking for work, the same as unemployed citizens who try finding employment. Indeed, the Court ruled that the provisions should not be read literally but systematically, in a way that avoids illogical outcomes.

In contrast, as the EU citizens' expulsion case law demonstrates, failures to read legislative acts in their entirety may lead to unreasonable inferences of legislative intent. These provisions protect against expulsion:

11. Article 28 of the Citizenship Directive
    1) Before taking an expulsion decision on grounds of *public policy or public security*, the host Member State shall take account of considerations such as how long the individual concerned has resided on its territory, his/her age, state of health, family and economic situation, social and cultural integration into the host Member State and the extent of his/her links with the country of origin.
    2) The host Member State may not take an expulsion decision against Union citizens or their family members, irrespective of nationality, who have *the right of permanent residence* on its territory, except on *serious grounds* of *public policy or public security.*
    3) An expulsion decision may not be taken against Union citizens, except if the decision is based on *imperative grounds* of *public security*, as defined by Member States, if they have resided in the host Member State for *the previous 10 years.*

Taken together, these provisions establish a three-stage assessment that Member States must carry out before they can issue an expulsion order. First, they must measure the duration of residence of the citizen in question, which determines which of the three paragraphs applies and what level of protection citizens enjoy. Paragraph 1 applies to citizens without the right of permanent residence (less than

[93] Ekins (n 23) 257.

[94] Case C-275/98 *Unitron Scandinacia* ECLI:EU:C:1999:567, para 30; Case C-66/99 *Wandel* ECLI:EU:C:2001:69, para 47.

five years of lawful and continuous residence); paragraph 2 applies to citizens with the right of permanent residence (five years of lawful and continuous residence);[95] and paragraph 3 applies to citizens who have enjoyed the right to reside for the previous ten years. Second, the national authorities must assess whether the conduct of the citizen facing an expulsion decision is so serious that it meets the grounds for expulsion. Citizens to whom the first paragraph applies may be expelled on the grounds of public policy and security; citizens to whom the second paragraph applies cannot be expelled except on *serious grounds* of public policy or public security; and citizens to whom the third paragraph applies may not be expelled, except if the decision is based on *imperative grounds* of public security. Third, in case citizens meet the conditions justifying expulsion, Member States are required to assess their individual circumstances to decide whether an expulsion decision would be proportionate, that is whether the seriousness of the threat they pose outweighs their personal interests (see paragraph 1).[96]

As we already saw in section VI.6, the CJEU has failed to read the three provisions jointly. First, it ruled in respect of the sentence 'for the previous ten years' in art 28(3) that 'the decisive criterion is whether the Union citizen has lived in that Member State for the 10 years *preceding the expulsion decision*'.[97] This meant that 'the 10-year period of residence . . . must be calculated by *counting back* from the date of the decision ordering that person's expulsion'.[98] To this, it added that 'a period of imprisonment is, in principle, capable . . . of interrupting the continuity of the period of residence'.[99] The effect of deciding, on the one hand, that periods of continuous residence must be counted backward and, on the other hand, that periods of imprisonment may interrupt this period is that only citizens who obtain an expulsion order more than ten years after serving their sentence can invoke art 28(3). As a result, the judgment effectively rendered this provision meaningless, simply because no Member State will wait for ten years before issuing an expulsion order against serious offenders of public security. Since we can safely assume that the legislature did not intend a provision offering enhanced protection against expulsion to be without effect, the CJEU failed to respect the legislative intentions in this provision. This conclusion finds additional support in the recitals of the legislative act, which expressly state that the expulsion of permanent residents may only take place in highly exceptional circumstances.[100] Thus, by failing to read

[95] Provision (1) in section 1.
[96] This reading is affirmed by art 27(2) of Directive 2004/38/EC (n 5).
[97] Case C-145/09 *Tsakouridis* ECLI:EU:C:2010:708, para 31 (italics mine); *MG* (n 8) para 23.
[98] *MG* (n 8) para 24.
[99] ibid para 38.
[100] Recital 24 reads as follows: 'Only in exceptional circumstances, where there are imperative grounds of public security, should an expulsion measure be taken against Union citizens who have resided for many years in the territory of the host Member State, in particular when they were born and have resided there throughout their life.'

individual provisions in the context of the entire legislative act, the CJEU weakened the intended safeguards against expulsion.

To identify the intended meaning of legislation, interpreters must not just read legislative provisions in the context of the legislative act of which they are part. In addition, as was recognised in *CILFIT*, they must also have regard to the state of evolution of the law at the date on which it is to be applied. It follows, inter alia, that if the legislature wanted to change the law by amending existing legislation, we should expect this to be reflected in the amendments it adopts. Hence, if newly introduced legislative provisions are worded in the same way as the provisions they amend or replace, it can be assumed, absent evidence to the contrary, that the legislature did not intend to change the envisaged consequences of the law. The CJEU seems, in principle, to be working on the same assumption. In *Ibrahim*, it said that

> in contrast to what was done in the case of Articles 10 and 11 of Regulation No 1612/68, Directive 2004/38 did not repeal Article 12 of that regulation. Such a choice necessarily reveals the intention of the European Union legislature not to introduce restrictions of the scope of that article, as interpreted by the Court.[101]

Indeed, from the fact that the legislature repealed only part of Regulation No 1612/68, it could be inferred that the provisions that had not been repealed were left unaffected. In the same vein, it held, in *Alemo-Herron*, that

> It is important to note at the outset that several aspects of the judgment in *Werhof*, in relation to Article 3 of Directive 77/187, are relevant to the case in the main proceedings. Although the case in the main proceedings concerns Directive 2001/23, those aspects are fully transposable to it, in so far as that directive codifies Directive 77/187 and the wording of the relevant provisions of Article 3 of each of those directives is identical.[102]

The fact that the new provisions were worded in an identical way as the amended provisions indeed indicates that the legislature did not intend to amend the law's envisioned meaning.

However, the state of evolution of legislation is not always adequately taken account of, as the Court's understanding of the following two provisions shows:

[101] Case C-310/08 *Ibrahim* ECLI:EU:C:2010:80, para 46. See also Case C-480/08 *Teixeira* ECLI:EU:C:2010:83, para 57.

[102] Case C-426/11 *Alemo-Herron* ECLI:EU:C:2013:521, para 21.

12. Article 10 of Regulation No 1612/68
    a. The following shall, irrespective of their nationality, have the right to install themselves with a worker who is a national of one Member State and who is employed in the territory of another Member State
        i. his spouse and their descendants who are under the age of 21 years or are dependents.
13. Article 7 of Directive 2004/38
    a. ...
    b. All Union citizens shall have the right of residence on the territory of another Member State for a period of longer than three months if they:
        i. are workers or self-employed persons in the host Member State; or
    c. The right of residence provided for in paragraph 1 shall extend to family members who are not nationals of a Member State, accompanying or joining the Union citizen in the host Member State.

In *Akrich*, the Court held that provision (12) applies on the condition that 'the national of a non-Member State [is] *lawfully resident* in a Member State when he moves to another Member State to which the citizen of the Union is migrating or has migrated'.[103] After provision (12) had been replaced by provision (13), the CJEU decided, in *Metock*, to reverse *Akrich*, saying that 'the benefit of such rights *cannot depend on the prior lawful residence* of such a spouse in another Member State'.[104]

Metock has always been immensely popular for its legal result but highly unconvincing in terms of legal reasoning.[105] First, it cannot be inferred from the wording of both provisions that the legislature intended to change the law's meaning by replacing provision (12) with provision (13): both provide that family members can accompany Member State nationals that take up residence in the host Member State.[106] In other words, the state of evolution of the legislative text strongly suggests that there was *no* intention on the part of the legislature to amend provision (12).

Nevertheless, the CJEU decided to reverse *Akrich*, saying that the *purpose* of the amending legislative act was to 'strengthen the right of free movement and residence of all Union citizens'.[107] More specifically, it ruled that

[103] Case C-109/01 *Akrich* ECLI:EU:C:2003:491, para 50 (italics added).

[104] Case C-127/08 *Metock* ECLI:EU:C:2008:449, para 58.

[105] I discuss the shortcomings more extensively in, Martijn van den Brink, 'A Typology of Reverse Discrimination in EU Citizenship Law' (2023) 2 European Law Open 57.

[106] In his Opinion in the *Metock* case, Advocate General Maduro also pointed out that a reversal of *Akrich* could not be justified based on the text of provision (13): Case C-127/08 *Metock* ECLI:EU:C:2008:335, Opinion of AG Maduro, para 5.

[107] *Metock* (n 104) para 59.

> the refusal of the host Member State to grant rights of entry and residence to the family members of a Union citizen is such as to *discourage that citizen from moving to or residing in that Member State*, even if his family members are not already lawfully resident in the territory of another Member State.[108]

However, this purposive argument does not justify the decision either, simply because *Metock* did not strengthen, or even protect, the right of free movement and residence. Note that the decision in *Akrich* to introduce a prior lawful residence requirement was taken precisely because provision (12) was understood as covering 'only freedom of movement within the Community'.[109] That is to say, the Court invoked the same legislative purpose first to introduce the requirement in *Akrich* and then, curiously, to abolish it in *Metock*.

A closer look reveals, furthermore, that the right to free movement and residence provides much stronger arguments for than against the prior lawful residence requirement. After all, if the EU citizen's partner did not reside within the EU before settling with the citizen in the host state, the host state's refusal to grant the partner a right to reside does not—indeed, logically cannot—be a barrier to the citizen's right of free movement. It is possible that the partner was already living in the host state when he or she met the EU citizen, namely after the latter had moved to the host state. In that case, the decision not to award the partner a right to reside cannot be regarded as an obstacle to the EU citizen's free movement rights—he or she could successfully exercise their rights after all.[110] Therefore, since a decision not to grant family members a residence permit when they meet after the citizen has exercised his or her right of free movement does not constitute a restriction of that right, the CJEU wrongly ruled that reversing *Akrich* was necessary to strengthen the right of free movement and residence. Indeed, as the legislative text's state of evolution suggests, there was no intention on the part of the legislature to amend provision (12) and reverse *Akrich*.

We have seen that interpreters must focus on the linguistic meaning of legislation having regard to legislative context. Legislative context may include drafting history, legislative purpose, the general scheme of which a provision forms part, and the law's state of evolution. In addition, the CJEU ruled, in *CILFIT*, that a reasonable interpretation of legislation requires that legislative provisions be interpreted in accordance with 'EU law as a whole'. This is not wrong. Legislative

[108] ibid para 64 (italics mine).

[109] *Akrich* (n 103) para 49.

[110] For this conclusion, Alina Tryfonidou, 'Family Reunification Rights of (Migrant) Union Citizens: Towards a More Liberal Approach' (2009) 15 European Law Journal 634; Pedro Caro Sousa, 'Quest for the Holy Grail—Is a Unified Approach to the Market Freedoms and European Citizenship Justified?' (2014) 20 European Law Journal 499, 511; van den Brink, 'A Typology of Reverse Discrimination in EU Citizenship Law' (n 105).

provisions must be read in relation to other provisions of secondary legislation, and, as shown in section IV.7, it is not, by definition, unreasonable to read legislative provisions in accordance with primary law. For example, the CJEU is right that 'if the wording of secondary . . . law is open to more than one interpretation, preference should be given to the interpretation which renders the provision consistent with the . . . Treaty rather than to the interpretation which leads it to being incompatible with the Treaty'.[111] Indeed, where legislation lends itself to two or more different interpretations, it is reasonable to assume that it seeks to realise a result that is compatible with prevailing interpretations of primary law.[112]

However, not all EU law is part of legislative context. As we saw in Chapter III, this idea can easily be abused to deprive the legislature of its power to determine the EU's political course of action. There, we saw that the practice of Treaty-conform interpretation has led the CJEU to interpret legislation contrary to legislative intent. We also saw that this is, in principle, illegitimate. For some EU lawyers, however, this amounts to reasonable and rational legislative interpretation. Koen Lenaerts and José Gutiérrez-Fons have argued, on the 'premise that the EU legislator is a rational actor', that it 'favours an interpretation which seeks to preserve the validity of his acts over one which would lead to their annulment'.[113] This misunderstands what amounts to rational legislative decision-making. Instead, the *CILFIT* requirement that legislation must be interpreted 'in light of the provisions of EU law as a whole' must be construed narrowly so that EU law is not part of legislative context when this would prejudice legislative intent. Let me explain.

From the rational legislature's point of view, Lenaerts's and José Gutiérrez-Fons's argument is misleading for two reasons. First, the legislature is not necessarily acting rationally by observing and implementing CJEU case law. As we saw in Chapter II, the legislative codification of case law can lead to inconsistent legal rules and provisions that are so vague as to be almost impossible to implement. On the contrary, a rational legislature will reflect on which of the principles established by the CJEU are desirable and which should be rejected. Second, the legislature is not necessarily treated as a rational actor if its choices are interpreted in conformity with the CJEU's preferred understanding of primary law. The *Sturgeon* judgment illustrates this well.

[111] Case C-305/05 *Ordre des barreaux francophones et germanophone* ECLI:EU:C:2007:383, para 28; Case C-135/93 *Spain v Commission* ECLI:EU:C:1995:201, para 37; Case C-90/92 *Dr Tretter GmbH* ECLI:EU:C:1993:264, para 11.

[112] Such as prevailing interpretations of the Charter of Fundamental Rights or the European Convention of Human Rights. See, for instance, Case C-465/07 *Elgafaji* ECLI:EU:C:2009:94, para 28: 'the case-law of the European Court of Human Rights is taken into consideration in interpreting the scope of that right in the Community legal order'.

[113] Lenaerts and Gutiérrez-Fons (n 92) 13–14.

Regulation (EC) No 261/2004 establishes rules on compensation and assistance to air passengers in case of denied boarding and cancellation or long delay of flights.[114]

14. Article 5 of Regulation (EC) No 261/2004
    1. In case of cancellation of a flight, the passengers concerned shall:
        (a) be offered assistance by the operating air carrier in accordance with Article 8; and
        (b) be offered assistance by the operating air carrier in accordance with Article 9(1)(a) and 9(2) . . . and;
        (c) have the right to compensation by the operating air carrier in accordance with Article 7.
15. Article 6 of Regulation (EC) No 261/2004
    1. When an operating air carrier reasonably expects a flight to be delayed beyond its scheduled time of departure . . . passengers shall be offered by the operating air carrier:
        (i) the assistance specified in Article 9(1)(a) and 9(2); and
        (ii) when the reasonably expected time of departure is at least the day after the time of departure previously announced, the assistance specified in Article 9(1)(b) and 9(1)(c); and
        (iii) when the delay is at least five hours, the assistance specified in Article 8(1)(a).

The important distinction these provisions draw between flight cancellations and delays is that passengers have a right to receive assistance and compensation in case of cancellation (provision (14)) and only a right to receive assistance in case of delay (provision (15)). The distinction was set aside in *Sturgeon*. Finding that 'the damage sustained by air passengers in cases of cancellation or long delay is comparable',[115] the distinction between delayed and cancelled flights was ruled to be contrary to the principle of equal treatment in primary law.[116] The two categories of passengers were not to be treated differently: delayed passengers had to have a right to financial compensation as well.

Lenaerts and Gutiérrez-Fons have defended this judgment, not on the grounds that it was legitimate for the CJEU to override legislation but by arguing that the interpretation of provision (15) was a reasonable inference of legislative intent based on legislative silence. More specifically, they argue that we cannot infer from the fact that provision (15) makes no mention of the right to compensation that the

[114] Regulation (EC) No 261/2004 of the European Parliament and of the Council of 11 February 2004 establishing common rules on compensation and assistance to passengers in the event of denied boarding and of cancellation or long delay of flights (OJ L46/1).

[115] ibid para 60.

[116] Case C-432/07 *Sturgeon* ECLI:EU:C:2009:716, para 48.

legislature intended that passengers should not have this right in the event of delays.[117] Indeed, they essentially argue that a legislative act can reasonably be attributed any meaning that is not literally excluded by its text, which implies that the legislature must expressly enumerate any result it does not intend to achieve. This is clearly not how rational legislatures act: legislation would become excessively lengthy and complex if legislatures attempted to expressly exclude any result they do not wish to achieve. It is precisely because this would be irrational that legislation's linguistic meaning underdetermines its intended meaning. On the contrary, the only logical inference about the legislature's intent based on provisions (14) and (15) is that the silence on compensation regarding delayed passengers meant that these passengers were not meant to have a right to compensation. Indeed, if judges want to treat the legislature as a rational actor, they must treat it as a rational language user and accept that it does not always intend to legislate in accordance with their preferred understanding of primary law. They must, in other words, treat the legislature as an ordinary language user and determine the intention that it conveyed based on the enacted legislative material.

This chapter examined how legal officials must interpret the publicly available legislative material to ascertain and respect the intended consequences of legislation. It rejected three approaches to legislative interpretation that do not allow them to do so properly: instrumentalist, purposive interpretation, and textualist interpretation. Instead, I clarified why, in order to identify legislative intent, the legislature must be treated as an ordinary language user and why, therefore, the literal meaning of the words chosen by the legislature must be placed in the context in which it expressed itself. Relevant context encompasses the objectives pursued by legislation, its state of evolution, the publicly available drafting history, and other provisions of EU law. Taking this context into account may not provide a uniquely correct answer, but it will allow legal officials to draw reasonable inferences of legislative intent from the publicly available material.

[117] Lenaerts and Gutiérrez-Fons (n 92) 15–16.

VIII
Conclusion
The Dignity of International Legislation?

Three decades ago, Jeremy Waldron called out legal philosophers for having failed to take note of the 'dignity of legislation'.[1] In his view, 'analytical jurisprudence . . . with its emphasis on courts and its depiction of the legislature as a disreputable, embarrassing and inconvenient sideshow, contrives to present the political provenance of our laws as a matter unworthy of philosophical notice'.[2] More importantly, in this particular essay and in much of his later work, he attempted to bring to light

> a glimpse of the opportunities that may open up for jurisprudence when we pose questions about the composition of legislative institutions and take seriously the possibility that law made by an assembly of persons may differ significantly, in concept as well as in quality, from law made by one person [and, of course, by courts].[3]

Numerous scholars from the disciplines of political, legal, and constitutional theory have since heeded his invitation, studying the opportunities that arise when laws are made by diverse, representative, and democratically elected assemblies—for academic scholarship, but also, more importantly, for societies that are in need of tackling vast social and political challenges in the face of serious disagreement about the correct way of tackling them.[4]

This book can be placed in this tradition. Drawing on what has become a thriving academic debate about the province of legislation in constitutional democratic societies, it has sought to draw attention to the dignity of legislation within the European Union. It has hopefully furnished more than just 'a glimpse of the opportunities' that arise for the study of European Union (EU) law when we reflect seriously on the structure of the legislative process and the unique value of legislative acts. And it has hopefully brought to light the opportunities that legislative decision-making offers for European integration. Until very recently, EU legal

[1] Jeremy Waldron, 'The Dignity of Legislation' (1995) 54 Maryland Law Review 633; Jeremy Waldron, *The Dignity of Legislation* (Cambridge University Press 1999).
[2] Waldron, 'The Dignity of Legislation' (n 1) 665.
[3] ibid.
[4] See especially Chapters II, III, and IV for references to this literature.

Legislative Authority and Interpretation in the European Union. Martijn van den Brink, Oxford University Press.
 DOI: 10.1093/9780198900115.003.0008

discourse suffered from the same deficiencies that plagued analytical jurisprudence until the 1990s, namely that 'there is nothing about legislatures or legislation in [EU legal scholarship] remotely comparable to the discussion of decision-making by judges'.[5] When legislation was discussed, it was portrayed in an unappealing manner and associated with poor decision-making. Attention was drawn to the undemocratic character of the legislative process; the risk that the legislature would thread on the limits of EU competence or on individual rights; its inability to take rational and coherent decisions, or any decision at all in the face of political pluralism; and so forth. The implication of these discussions was often that we should rather put our faith in the judiciary.

This book has sought to rectify this picture. The legislative process should be associated with important values that the judicial process cannot be associated with at all or to the same extent. It lends demo(i)cratic legitimacy to EU law, and legislative acts are conducive to the rule of law thanks to the relative clarity and precision of the norms embedded in them. The legislature is also better at processing the information that is relevant to undertaking the complex political and socio-economic issues underlying the question of how EU law ought to evolve. Finally, even if more research is needed to validate this conclusion, legislation seems, all things being equal, better at guiding the conduct of citizens than case law. I have also shown that the legislature should be disassociated from connotations of ineffective decision-making and a disregard for the limits of EU competence or individual rights. The legislative process is plagued by deadlock from time to time, but it has been remarkably effective at harmonising large areas of domestic law and has, in doing so, navigated the discretion the Treaties have given it with great care. In the areas of law studied in this book, the legislature has observed the limits of EU competence and shown respect for individual rights affected by its decisions.

This does not mean that the proper limits of EU legislative authority should not be discussed, but this discussion should take place after, and be informed by, our discussion of the nature of the legislative process and the value of legislative decision-making. It then turns out that the justification for judicial deference is far stronger than the justification for judicial review. Judicial officials must grant the legislature wide discretionary powers and, in almost all circumstances, defer to the legislature's choices, a decision they can justify by one or more of three reasons: institutional legitimacy, institutional capacity, and institutional collaboration. Accordingly, deference is justified by virtue of the legitimacy with which the legislative process endows EU law, the legislature's superior law-making capacities, and the fact that judicial collaboration with the legislative plan furthers the promotion of a shared vision of EU governance. Conversely, the judicial power to review the legality of legislative acts should be used sparingly.

[5] Waldron, *The Dignity of Legislation* (n 1) 664.

In the book's second part, I explained how addressees of legislative instructions must interpret them. Legislative interpretation is a systematically neglected subject in EU law scholarship, and the theoretical work on the interpretation of EU law that exists is mired in the false dichotomy between purposivism and textualism. It is, moreover, so detached from how EU law is interpreted in fact that this alone casts doubt on the credibility of the claims of this scholarship. For instance, the EU judiciary is not nearly as purposive in adjudicating the claims before it as this literature suggests, and purposive theories of interpretation fail to account for the vast agreement that exists on EU law. However, while there is significant textuality to legislative interpretation, this should not lead us to stray into textualism or literalism, which also cannot explain how judges must act. I have argued, instead, that the legislature is able to aggregate the individual intentions of its members into a single legislative intent and that the object of legislative interpretation should be to identify and act in line with legislative intent. The theory of legislative interpretation developed appreciates legislation's textuality, yet also understands that the text's intended meaning can be misunderstood if it is not placed in the broader context in which the legislature expressed itself. This requires that judges have regard also to other provisions of EU law, their development over time, and the objectives for which they were adopted. This theory is consistent not only with the structure of the legislative process and the nature of legislative acts but also, it seems, with how legislation is usually interpreted by the Court of Justice of the European Union (CJEU).

These conclusions, like the book's overall thinking and argumentation, have benefited greatly from a wealth of scholarship from the disciplines of law, philosophy, and the political sciences on the domestic legislative process. As Chapter I explained, an important part of my intellectual exercise was to translate the theoretical concepts and empirical findings of these bodies of literature to the EU setting. I believe that this methodological choice has paid off. Writing this book would have been an impossible task had I not been able to rely on neighbouring academic disciplines—or at least the book would have been worse for it. This prompts both a conclusion and a question. The conclusion is that EU lawyers will deprive their community of new insights by not crossing their disciplinary boundaries and venturing into domestic legal debates and extra-legal scholarship. Our understanding of legislative authority and interpretation in the EU context would already have been more accurate had EU lawyers drawn on the insights from these bodies of literature long ago. I am convinced, moreover, that the allocation of EU legislative and judicial authority is far from the only EU legal debate that can benefit from an incorporation of the insights of related disciplines.[6]

[6] The concept of EU citizenship is another evident example. See, eg Martijn van den Brink, 'EU Citizenship and (Fundamental) Rights: Empirical, Normative, and Conceptual Problems' (2019) 25 European Law Journal 21.

The question, which I will not attempt to answer, but which is interesting to raise nevertheless, is how far non-state judicial actors other than the EU judiciary can be evaluated through the lens of state-centred constitutional law. As has become clear, the legitimacy of international courts is not just a European dilemma. A significant development in international politics in the past three decades has been the rapid proliferation of international courts. Until the end of the Cold War, the EU was the only international organisation with a court with compulsory jurisdiction that was accessible to private litigants. But now, after a period of successful regional and global integration, there are over twenty international courts with compulsory jurisdiction and sixteen that allow private actors to initiate legal proceedings.[7] Important issues from human rights to international trade and environmental protection, which were once the exclusive jurisdiction of states, are nowadays settled by international tribunals, which wield significant influence over domestic politics and constrain democratically elected actors while often escaping democratic accountability themselves. This raised no serious concerns for as long as it could be assumed that courts merely enforced the rules states had voluntarily consented to, but international agreements tend to evolve dynamically over time and outside of the provisions required for their amendment.

The key question, thus, is this: if state consent is an insufficient condition for the legitimacy of international courts,[8] how to theorise and conceptualise the legitimacy of international courts instead? Answering this question has always been difficult because the basic principles against which to evaluate the exercise of judicial authority beyond the state remain unsettled. The normative principles of the democratic state might seem compelling but also demanding as appropriate yardsticks for the allocation of authority beyond the state. This, as we saw in Chapter I, fuelled the search for alternative, non-democratic standards of legitimacy that would be more appropriate, but these could not command more support than the democratic standards we apply to domestic judiciaries. The answer to this dilemma, I hope to have shown, lies not in substituting the normative principles of the democratic constitutional state for non-democratic alternatives but in translating these principles to new contexts without them losing their normative qualities—or at least in the EU context.

If there is value in translating the concepts of domestic constitutionalism to the EU context, what about other international courts and tribunals? Since international courts come in different shapes and sizes, conclusions drawn in respect of one court can only be generalised with prudence to others. This note of caution should certainly be flagged in relation to the CJEU, which is a unique international court in terms of the scale of its tasks, the breadth of its authority, and the

[7] Karen J Alter, *The New Terrain of International Law: Courts, Politics, Rights* (Princeton UP 2014).
[8] Andreas Follesdal, 'Survey Article: The Legitimacy of International Courts' (2020) 28 Journal of Political Philosophy 476.

organisation in which it is embedded.[9] I believe, however, that this book contains some lessons about how we should theorise the legitimacy of international courts more generally, especially as the EU is not the only transnational separation-of-powers system that divides authority between a legislature, a judiciary, and an executive: the Andean Community (AC) and the Economic Community of West African States (ECOWAS) do so too. Their courts are embedded in a complex institutional architecture and enjoy authority relative to other institutions of these communities. We know that these communities pass secondary legislation to harmonise regulatory standards and that their courts interpret, apply, and occasionally invalidate the enacted legislative provisions. We also know that such provisions influence and constrain the conduct of international courts,[10] while also creating new avenues for litigation that can strengthen their position.[11] However, we know very little about how international courts should act in relation to international legislatures: is there a dignity to international legislation that should compel courts to defer thereto, just as there is a dignity to domestic and, as this book has shown, European legislation?

This book does not answer this question, but it might contain some clues as to how it can be answered. As I indicated in Chapter I, I believe that my analysis shows that in evaluating international courts, we must be sensitive to the context in which they operate. Institutional context, as we saw, matters a lot. International courts that operate as standalone courts may have to be evaluated according to different standards than international courts that are embedded in a complex institutional architecture. If so, it matters that the courts of the AC and ECOWAS exercise power in relation to a legislative branch. Other contextual factors might also impact the evaluation of international court authority. One might think it matters in what domain (eg human rights or international trade) they exert authority.[12] Chapter I suggested as much, indeed: because the EU regulates areas that cannot be regulated (equally well) by states individually means that judicial review by the CJEU must proceed from a position of deference to EU legislation. Finally, one might also assume that the societal context in which international courts operate is a relevant factor in our evaluation of how they ought to behave. It has been credibly argued, for instance, that they should 'calibrate' their decisions to the rise of populism.[13] These concluding remarks are not the place to discuss more extensively in

[9] Mark A Pollack, 'The Legitimacy of the European Court of Justice' in Nienke Grossman and others (eds), *Legitimacy and International Courts* (CUP 2018) 143–44.

[10] Clifford J Carrubba and Matthew Gabel, 'International Courts: A Theoretical Assessment' (2017) 20 Annual Review of Political Science 55.

[11] Alter (n 7) 108; Karen J Alter and Laurence R Helfer, *Transplanting International Courts: The Law and Politics of the Andean Tribunal of Justice* (1st edn, OUP 2017).

[12] John Tasioulas, 'The Legitimacy of International Law' in Samantha Besson and John Tasioulas (eds), *The Philosophy of International Law* (OUP 2010).

[13] Alain Zysset, 'Calibrating the Response to Populism at the European Court of Human Rights' (2022) 20 International Journal of Constitutional Law 976.

what ways the legitimacy of international courts is, indeed, context-dependent. I merely wanted to draw attention to this question, hoping that this book has something meaningful to contribute to the broader debate on the legitimacy of international law.

The central ambition of this book was to deepen our appreciation of the EU legislative process. It is a curious fact, I think, that EU case law shows a greater appreciation for it than our academic scholarship and teaching. The EU judiciary is, for the most part, highly deferential towards legislation when it can be, its activist reputation notwithstanding. The vast reach of harmonising legislation also means that more complex political judgements can be left to the legislature and that fewer disputes over EU law arise, or need to be resolved, through the preliminary reference procedure.[14] This reality has not yet sufficiently permeated our understanding of EU law and our teaching of it. Case law remains the focal point of our academic debates and the main source of EU law that we teach to students, even though the course and content of EU law are determined to a more considerable extent by Brussels than by Luxembourg. It is perfectly logical, and probably somewhat inevitable, that legal debates concentrate on the latest and most controversial rulings of our highest courts, but just as hard cases can make bad law, a focus on hard cases can make for a bad understanding of the law. Most EU law is not made by the EU judiciary, and most of it is not subject to the kind of disagreements that often come before the CJEU. Instead, there is ubiquitous agreement among legal officials on EU law, which exists largely thanks to the legislature's tremendous harmonisation efforts. This is but one of the virtues of the legislative process, in addition to the legitimacy that it bestows on and the quality of decision-making it brings to EU law. These virtues should be valued as such, in legal practice, in academic scholarship, and in our teaching of future students of EU law.

[14] Jan Zglinski, 'The End of Negative Market Integration: 60 Years of Free Movement of Goods Litigation in the EU (1961–2020)' [2023] Journal of European Public Policy 1.

Bibliography

Abbott KW and others, 'The Concept of Legalization' (2000) 54 International Organization 401

Albors-Llorens A, 'The European Court of Justice, More Than a Teleological Court' (1999) 2 Cambridge Yearbook of European Legal Studies 373

Albors-Llorens A, 'Edging towards Closer Scrutiny? The Court of Justice and Its Review of the Compatibility of General Measures with the Protection of Economic Rights and Freedoms' in A Arnull and others (eds), *A Constitutional Order of States? Essays in EU Law in Honour of Alan Dashwood* (Hart Publishing 2011)

Aldrich JA, 'Political Parties In and Out of Legislatures' in RE Goodin (ed), *The Oxford Handbook of Political Science* (OUP 2011)

Alter KJ, *Establishing the Supremacy of European Law: The Making of an International Rule of Law in Europe* (OUP 2006)

Alter KJ, *The New Terrain of International Law: Courts, Politics, Rights* (Princeton UP 2014)

Alter KJ and Helfer LR, *Transplanting International Courts: The Law and Politics of the Andean Tribunal of Justice* (1st edn, OUP 2017)

Amhlaigh CM, *New Constitutional Horizons: Towards a Pluralist Constitutional Theory* (OUP 2022)

Angelova M, Dannwolf T, and König T, 'How Robust Are Compliance Findings? A Research Synthesis' (2012) 19 Journal of European Public Policy 1269

Arnull A, 'Owning Up to Fallibility: Precedent and the Court of Justice' (1993) 247 Common Market Law Review 247

Arnull A, *The European Union and Its Court of Justice* (2nd edn, OUP 2006)

Arnull A, 'Judicial Review in the European Union' in D Chalmers and A Arnull (eds), *The Oxford Handbook of European Union Law* (OUP 2015)

Arrow KJ, *Social Choice and Individual Values* (Yale UP 1986)

Auel K and Christiansen T, 'After Lisbon: National Parliaments in the European Union' (2015) 38 West European Politics 261

Auer S, Bergsen P, and Kundnani H, 'The Law as a Tool for Integration Could Be Ending' (2021) <www.chathamhouse.org/2021/10/law-tool-eu-integration-could-be-ending> accessed 3 July 2023

Augenstein D and Dawson M, 'Introduction: What Law for What Polity? "Integration through Law" in the European Union Revisited' in D Augenstein (ed), *'Integration through Law' Revisited: The Making of the European Polity* (Routledge 2016)

Azoulai L, 'The European Court of Justice and the Duty to Respect Sensitive National Interests' in M Dawson, B de Witte and E Muir (eds), *Judicial Activism at the European Court of Justice* (Edward Elgar 2013)

Baaij CJ, 'Fifty Years of Multilingual Interpretation in the European Union' in P Meijes Tiersma and L Solan (eds), *The Oxford Handbook of Language and Law* (OUP 2012)

Bach K, 'Context Ex Machina' in Z Gendler Szabó (ed), *Semantics vs. Pragmatics* (Clarendon Press 2005)

Barber NW, *The Principles of Constitutionalism* (OUP 2018)

Barnard C, 'The UK and Posted Workers: The Effect of Commission v Luxembourg on the Territorial Application of British Labour Law: Case C-319/06 Commission v Luxembourg, Judgment 19 June 2008' (2009) 38 Industrial Law Journal 122

Barnard C, 'The Calm after the Storm: Time to Reflect on EU (Labour) Law Scholarship following the Decisions in *Viking* and *Laval*' in A Bogg, C Costello, and ACL Davies (eds), *Research Handbook on EU Labour Law* (Edward Elgar 2016)

Baroncelli S and Mooij AAM, 'What Kind of Judicial Review for the European Central Bank?: All Institutions Are Equal But Some Are More Technical Than Others' (2022) 29 Maastricht Journal of European and Comparative Law 413

Bartolini S, *Restructuring Europe: Centre Formation, System Building and Political Structuring between the Nation-State and the European Union* (OUP 2005)

Bast J, 'Is There a Hierarchy of Legislative, Delegated, and Implementing Acts?' in C Fredrik Bergström and D Ritleng (eds), *Rulemaking by the European Commission: The New System for Delegation of Powers* (OUP 2016)

Beck G, *The Legal Reasoning of the Court of Justice of the EU* (Hart Publishing 2012)

Bekkedal T, 'The Reach of Free Movement. A Defence of Court Discretion' in M Tønnesson Andenæs, T Bekkedal, and L Pantaleo (eds), *The Reach of Free Movement* (TMC Asser Press 2017)

Bellamy R, *Political Constitutionalism: A Republican Defence of the Constitutionality of Democracy* (CUP 2007)

Bellamy R, *A Republican Europe of States: Cosmopolitanism, Intergovernmentalism and Demoicracy in the EU* (CUP 2019)

Bengoetxea J, 'Multilingual and Multicultural Legal Reasoning: The European Court of Justice' in A Lise Kjær and S Adamo (eds), *Linguistic Diversity and European Democracy* (Ashgate 2011)

Bernitz U, 'Epilogue' in MR Freedland and J Prassl (eds), *Viking, Laval and Beyond* (Hart Publishing 2014)

Biagi M, 'Guest Editorial—Fortune Smiles on the Italian EU Presidency: Talking Half-Seriously about the Posted Workers and Parental Leave Directives' (1996) 12 International Journal of Comparative Labour Law and Industrial Relations 97

Bickel AM, *The Least Dangerous Branch: The Supreme Court at the Bar of Politics* (2nd edn, Yale UP 1986)

Blauberger M, 'With Luxembourg in Mind . . . the Remaking of National Policies in the Face of ECJ Jurisprudence' (2012) 19 Journal of European Public Policy 109

Blauberger M, 'National Responses to European Court Jurisprudence' (2014) 37 West European Politics 457

Blauberger M and Schmidt SK, 'Welfare Migration? Free Movement of EU Citizens and Access to Social Benefits' (2014) 1 Research & Politics 1

Blauberger M and Schmidt SK, 'The European Court of Justice and Its Political Impact' (2017) 40 West European Politics 907

Bobek M, 'Joined Cases C-92 & 93/09, *Volker und Markus Schecke GbR and Hartmut Eifert*, Judgment of the Court of Justice (Grand Chamber) of 9 November 2010' (2011) 48 Common Market Law Review 2005

Bobek M, 'Of Feasibility and Silent Elephants: The Legitimacy of the Court of Justice through the Eyes of National Courts' in M Adams and others (eds), *Judging Europe's Judges: The Legitimacy of the Case Law of the European Court of Justice* (Hart Publishing 2013)

Bobek M, 'EU Law in National Courts: *Viking, Laval* and Beyond' in MR Freedland and J Prassl (eds), *Viking, Laval and Beyond* (Hart Publishing 2016)

Bobek M, 'Uniform Rights? The Nature of Regulations Revisited' in M Bobek and J Prassl (eds), *Air Passenger Rights: Ten Years On* (Hart Publishing 2016)

Bodansky D, 'Legitimacy in International Law and International Relations' in JL Dunoff and MA Pollack (eds), *'Interdisciplinary Perspectives on International Law and International Relations': 'The State of the Art'* (CUP 2013)

Boeger N, 'Minimum Harmonisation, Free Movement and Proportionality' in P Syrpis (ed), *The Judiciary, the Legislature and the EU Internal Market* (CUP 2012)

Bourdieu P, 'The Force of Law: Toward a Sociology of the Juridical Field' (1987) 38 Hastings Law Journal 805

Bowler S and McElroy G, 'Political Group Cohesion and "Hurrah" Voting in the European Parliament' (2015) 22 Journal of European Public Policy 1355

Bradford A, *The Brussels Effect: How the European Union Rules the World* (OUP 2020)

Bratman M, *Shared Agency: A Planning Theory of Acting Together* (OUP 2014)

Bratman ME, *Faces of Intention* (CUP 1999)
Brunkhorst H, 'A Curtain of Gloom Is Descending on the Continent: Capitalism, Democracy and Europe' (2017) 23 European Law Journal 335
Buchanan A, 'Political Legitimacy and Democracy' (2002) 112 Ethics 689
Buchanan A, 'The Legitimacy of International Law' in S Besson and J Tasioulas (eds), *The Philosophy of International Law* (OUP 2010)
Buchanan A and Keohane RO, 'The Legitimacy of Global Governance Institutions' (2006) 20 Ethics & International Affairs 405
Campbell T, *The Legal Theory of Ethical Positivism* (Dartmouth 1996)
Camporesi F, 'The European Parliament and the EU Charter of Fundamental Rights' in G Di Federico (ed), *The EU Charter of Fundamental Rights: From Declaration to Binding Instrument* (Springer 2011)
Cappelletti M, Seccombe M, and Weiler JH (eds), *Integration through Law: Methods, Tools and Institutions*, vol 1 (De Gruyter 1986)
Carens JH, *The Ethics of Immigration* (OUP 2013)
Carey JM, 'Legislative Organization' in RAW Rhodes, SA Binder, and BA Rockman (eds), *The Oxford Handbook of Political Institutions* (OUP 2008)
Carrubba CJ and Gabel M, 'International Courts: A Theoretical Assessment' (2017) 20 Annual Review of Political Science 55
Carrubba CJ and Gabel MJ, *International Courts and the Performance of International Agreements: A General Theory with Evidence from the European Union* (CUP 2015)
Chalmers D, Davies G, and Monti G, *European Union Law: Cases and Materials* (2nd edn, CUP 2010)
Cheneval F and Nicolaidis K, 'The Social Construction of Demoicracy in the European Union' (2017) 16 European Journal of Political Theory 235
Cheneval F and Schimmelfennig F, 'The Case for Demoicracy in the European Union' (2013) 51 Journal of Common Market Studies 334
Cheneval F, Lavenex S, and Schimmelfennig F, '*Demoi*-Cracy in the European Union: Principles, Institutions, Policies' (2015) 22 Journal of European Public Policy 1
Christiano T, *The Rule of the Many: Fundamental Issues in Democratic Theory* (Westview Press 1996)
Christiano T, *The Constitution of Equality: Democratic Authority and Its Limits* (OUP 2008)
Christiano T, 'Democratic Legitimacy and International Institutions' in S Besson and J Tasioulas (eds), *The Philosophy of International Law* (OUP 2010)
Christiano T, 'An Instrumental Argument for a Human Right to Democracy' (2011) 39 Philosophy & Public Affairs 142
Cichowski RA, 'Introduction: Courts, Democracy, and Governance' (2006) 39 Comparative Political Studies 3
Cichowski RA, *The European Court and Civil Society Litigation, Mobilization and Governance* (CUP 2007)
Claassen J, 'Attitude or Aptitude? Explaining the Lack of Preliminary References in Dutch Competition Law Cases' in C Rauchegger and A Wallerman (eds), *The Eurosceptic Challenge: National Implementation and Interpretation of EU Law* (Hart Publishing 2019)
Cloots E, *National Identity in EU Law* (OUP 2015)
Cloots E, 'Safe Harbour or Open Sea for Corporate Headscarf Bans? *Achbita* and *Bougnaoui*' (2018) 55 Common Market Law Review 589
Conant L, 'Compliance and What EU Member States Make of It' in M Cremona (ed), *Compliance and the Enforcement of EU Law* (OUP 2012)
Conant LJ, *Justice Contained: Law and Politics in the European Union* (CUP 2002)
Conway G, *The Limits of Legal Reasoning and the European Court of Justice* (CUP 2013)
Cooper I, 'A Yellow Card for the Striker: National Parliaments and the Defeat of EU Legislation on the Right to Strike' (2015) 22 Journal of European Public Policy 1406
Corbett R, Jacobs FG, and Shackleton M, *The European Parliament* (Harper 2011)

Costello R and Thomson R, 'The Policy Impact of Leadership in Committees: Rapporteurs' Influence on the European Parliament's Opinions' (2010) 11 European Union Politics 219
Costello R, Thomassen J, and Rosema M, 'European Parliament Elections and Political Representation: Policy Congruence between Voters and Parties' (2012) 35 West European Politics 1226
Court of Justice of the European Union (CJEU), 'Annual Report 2022: Statistics Concerning the Judicial Activity of the Court of Justice' (2022) <https://curia.europa.eu/jcms/upload/docs/application/pdf/2023-03/stats_cour_2022_en.pdf> accessed 1 March 2024
Coutts S, 'Union Citizenship as Probationary Citizenship: *Onuekwere*' (2015) 52 Common Market Law Review 531
Cox GW, 'The Organization of Democratic Legislatures' in BR Weingast and DA Wittman (eds), *The Oxford Handbook of Political Economy* (OUP 2008)
Craig P, 'Democracy and Rule-Making within the EC: An Empirical and Normative Assessment' (1997) 3 European Law Journal 105
Craig P, 'Institutions, Power, and Institutional Balance' in P Craig and G de Búrca (eds), *The Evolution of EU Law* (2nd edn, OUP 2011)
Craig P, 'The ECJ and *Ultra Vires* Action: A Conceptual Analysis' (2011) 48 Common Market Law Review 395
Craig P, 'Subsidiarity: A Political and Legal Analysis' (2012) 2012 Journal of Common Market Studies 72
Craig P, *The Lisbon Treaty: Law, Politics, and Treaty Reform* (OUP 2013)
Craig P, 'Judicial Review and Judicial Deference' in M Scholten and AFM Brenninkmeijer (eds), *Controlling EU Agencies: The Rule of Law in a Multi-Jurisdictional Legal Order* (Edward Elgar 2020)
Crombez C and Hix S, 'Treaty Reform and the Commission's Appointment and Policy-Making Role in the European Union' (2011) 12 European Union Politics 291
Currie S, 'Pregnancy-Related Employment Breaks, the Gender Dynamics of Free Movement Law and Curtailed Citizenship: *Jessy Saint Prix*' (2016) 53 Common Market Law Review 543
Curtin D, 'Challenging Executive Dominance in European Democracy' (2014) 77 Modern Law Review 1
Dahl RA, *Democracy and Its Critics* (Yale UP 1991)
Davies G, 'Legislative Control of the European Court of Justice' (2014) 51 Common Market Law Review 1579
Davies G, 'Democracy and Legitimacy in the Shadow of Purposive Competence' (2015) 22 European Law Journal 2
Davies G, 'The European Union Legislature as an Agent of the European Court of Justice' (2016) 54 Journal of Common Market Studies 846
Davies G, 'Has the Court Changed, or Have the Cases? The Deservingness of Litigants as an Element in Court of Justice Citizenship Adjudication' (2018) 25 Journal of European Public Policy 1442
Davies G and Kramer D, 'The Posting of Workers' in R Schutze and T Tridimas (eds), *Oxford Principles of European Union Law Vol 2: The Internal Market* (OUP forthcoming)
Davies P, 'Posted Workers: Single Market or Protection of National Labour Law Systems?' (1997) 34 Common Market Law Review 571
Dawson M, *The Governance of EU Fundamental Rights* (CUP 2017)
Dawson M, 'Re-Visiting Europe's "Law–Politics Imbalance"' in M Dawson, E Muir, and B de Witte (eds), *Revisiting Judicial Politics in the European Union* (Edward Elgar 2023)
Dawson M and De Witte F, 'Constitutional Balance in the EU after the Euro-Crisis' (2013) 76 Modern Law Review 817
Dawson M, Maricut-Akbik A, and Bobić A, 'Reconciling Independence and Accountability at the European Central Bank: The False Promise of Proceduralism' (2017) 23 European Law Journal 118
van den Brink M, Dawson M, and Zglinski J, 'Revisiting the Asymmetry Thesis: Negative and Positive Integration in the EU' (2023) Journal of European Public Policy 1

De Búrca G, 'Giving Effect to European Community Directives' (1992) 55 Modern Law Review 215
De Búrca G, 'The Quest for Legitimacy in the European Union' (1996) 59 Modern Law Review 349
De la Rosa S, 'The Directive on Cross-Border Healthcare or the Art of Codifying Complex Case Law' (2012) 49 Common Market Law Review 15
De Waele H, 'EU Citizenship: Revisiting Its Meaning, Place and Potential' (2010) 12 European Journal of Migration and Law 319
De Witte B, 'Setting the Scene: How Did Services Get to Bolkestein and Why?' (European University Institute Working Paper Law No 2007/20, 2007)
De Witte B, 'Exclusive Member State Competences—Is There Such a Thing?' in S Garben and I Govaere (eds), *The Division of Competences between the EU and the Member States: Reflections on the Past, the Present and the Future* (Hart Publishing 2017)
De Witte B, 'Legal Methods for the Study of EU Institutional Practice' (2022) 18 European Constitutional Law Review 637
de Witte F, 'Sex, Drugs & EU Law: The Recognition of Moral and Ethical Diversity in EU Law' (2013) 50 Common Market Law Review 1545
de Witte F, *Justice in the EU: The Emergence of Transnational Solidarity* (OUP 2015)
Dehousse R, Novak S, and Bendjaballah S, 'Consensus under Pressure: The Evolution of Conflict in the EU Legislative Process' (2018) 58 Politique européenne 44
Derlén M, *Multilingual Interpretation of European Union Law* (Wolters Kluwer 2009)
Dougan M, 'The Court Helps Those Who Help Themselves . . . The Legal Status of Migrant Work-Seekers under Community Law in the Light of the Collins Judgment' (2005) 7 European Journal of Social Security 7
Dougan M, 'The Constitutional Dimension to the Case Law on Union Citizenship' (2006) 31 European Law Review 613
Dougan M, 'The Treaty of Lisbon 2007: Winning Minds, Not Hearts' (2008) 45 Common Market Law Review 617
Dougan M, 'The Bubble That Burst: Exploring the Legitimacy of the Case Law on the Free Movement of Union Citizens' in M Adams and others (eds), *Judging Europe's Judges: The Legitimacy of the Case Law of the European Court of Justice* (Hart Publishing 2013)
Duxbury N, *Elements of Legislation* (CUP 2013)
Dworkin R, *Taking Rights Seriously* (Bloomsbury 2013)
Dworkin RM, *Law's Empire* (Harvard UP 1995)
Dyevre A, Glavina M, and Ovadek M, 'Raising the Bar: The Development of Docket Control on the Court of Justice' (2021) Zeitschrift für öffentliches Recht 523
Edward D, 'Guest Editorial: Will There Be Honey Still for Tea?' (2006) 43 Common Market Law Review 623
Eeckhout P, 'The European Court of Justice and the Legislature' (1998) 18 Yearbook of European Law 1
Ekins R, *The Nature of Legislative Intent* (OUP 2012)
Ellis E and Watson P, *EU Anti-Discrimination Law* (2nd edn, OUP 2012)
Ely JH, *Democracy and Distrust* (Harvard UP 1981)
Endicott T, *Vagueness in Law* (OUP 2000)
Endicott T, 'The Value of Vagueness' in A Marmor and S Soames (eds), *Philosophical Foundations of Language in the Law* (OUP 2011)
Ensig Sørensen K, 'Reconciling Secondary Legislation with the Treaty Rights of Free Movement' (2011) 36 European Law Review 339
Epstein RA, 'The ECJ's Fatal Imbalance: Its Cavalier Treatment of National Security Issues Poses Serious Risk to Public Safety and Sound Commercial Practices' (2016) 12 European Constitutional Law Review 330
Estlund DM, *Democratic Authority: A Philosophical Framework* (Princeton UP 2009)
European Equality Law Network, 'Sweden—Country Report on Non-Discrimination 2019' (2019) 51 www.equalitylaw.eu/downloads/4973-sweden-country-report-non-discriminat ion-2019-pdf-1-44-mb> accessed 1 March 2024

European Equality Law Network, ‘Austria—Country Report on Non-Discrimination 2020’ (2020) 43–44 < www.equalitylaw.eu/downloads/5264-austria-country-report-non-discrimination-2020-1-37-mb> accessed 1 March 2024

European Equality Law Network, ‘Germany—Country Report on Non-Discrimination 2020’ (2020) 56–62 <www.equalitylaw.eu/downloads/5226-germany-country-report-non-discrimination-2020-1-96-mb> accessed 1 March 2024

Evju S, ‘Revisiting the Posted Workers Directive: Conflict of Laws and Laws in Contrast’ (2010) 12 Cambridge Yearbook of European Legal Studies 151

Fabre C, ‘The Dignity of Rights’ (2000) 20 Oxford Journal of Legal Studies 271

Falke J and Joerges C, ‘The New Approach to Technical Harmonization and Standards, Its Preparation through ECJ Case Law on Articles 30, 36 EEC and the Low-Voltage Directive, and the Clarification of Its Operating Environment by the Single European Act’ (2010) 6 Hanse Law Review 289

Fennelly N, ‘Legal Interpretation at the European Court of Justice’ (1996) 20 Fordham International Law Journal 656

Ferrera M, *The Boundaries of Welfare: European Integration and the New Spatial Politics of Social Protection* (OUP 2005)

Follesdal A, ‘Survey Article: The Legitimacy of International Courts’ (2020) 28 Journal of Political Philosophy 476

Follesdal A and Hix S, ‘Why There Is a Democratic Deficit in the EU: A Response to Majone and Moravcsik’ (2006) 44 Journal of Common Market Studies 533

Franchino F, *The Powers of the Union: Delegation in the EU* (CUP 2007)

Frick K and Schonberg S, ‘Finishing, Refining, Polishing: On the Use of Travaux Preparatoires as an Aid to the Interpretation of Community Legislation’ (2003) 28 European Law Review 149

Garben S, ‘Sky-High Controversy and High-Flying Claims? The Sturgeon Case Law in Light of Judicial Activism, Euroscepticism and Eurolegalism’ (2013) 50 Common Market Law Review 15

Garben S, ‘The Turbulent Life of Regulation 261: Continuing Controversies Surrounding EU Air Passenger Rights’ in M Bobek and J Prassl (eds), *Air Passenger Rights: Ten Years On* (Hart Publishing 2016)

Garben S, ‘The Constitutional (Im)Balance between “the Market” and “the Social” in the European Union’ (2017) 13 European Constitutional Law Review 23

Gardner J, ‘Legal Positivism: 5½ Myths’ (2001) 46 American Journal of Jurisprudence 199

Gerards J, ‘Pluralism, Deference and the Margin of Appreciation Doctrine’ (2011) 17 European Law Journal 80

Gill-Pedro E, ‘’ (2017) 9 European Journal of Legal Studies 103

Goldsworthy J, ‘Structural Judicial Review and the Objection from Democracy’ (2010) 60 University of Toronto Law Journal 137

Goldsworthy J, ‘Legislative Intention Vindicated?’ (2013) 33 Oxford Journal of Legal Studies 821

Goodin RE, ‘Enfranchising All Affected Interests, and Its Alternatives’ (2007) 35 Philosophy & Public Affairs 40

Goodin RE and List C, ‘Special Majorities Rationalized’ (2006) 36 British Journal of Political Science 213

Gordon M, ‘A Positivist and Political Approach to Public Law’ in D Kyritsis and S Lakin (eds), *The Methodology of Constitutional Theory* (Hart Publishing 2022)

Gormley LW, ‘Free Movement of Goods and EU Legislation in the Court of Justice’ in P Syrpis (ed), *The Judiciary, the Legislature and the EU Internal Market* (CUP 2012)

Gormley LW, ‘Silver Threads among the Gold . . . 50 Years of the Free Movement of Goods’ (2007) 31 Fordham International law Journal 1637

Gornitzka Å and Sverdrup U, ‘Access of Experts: Information and EU Decision-Making’ (2011) 34 West European Politics 48

Grimm D, *The Constitution of European Democracy* (OUP 2017)

Guinan J and Hanna TM, ‘Forbidden Fruit: The Neglected Political Economy of Lexit’ (2017) 24 Institute for Public Policy Research Progressive Review 14

Habermas J, 'Citizen and State Equality in a Supranational Political Community: Degressive Proportionality and the *Pouvoir Constituant Mixte*: Citizen and State Equality' (2017) 55 Journal of Common Market Studies 171
Hart HLA, *The Concept of Law* (Clarendon Press 1998)
Hartlapp M, 'Power Shifts via the Judicial Arena: How Annulments Cases between EU Institutions Shape Competence Allocation' (2018) 56 Journal of Common Market Studies 1429
Hartlapp M, Metz J, and Rauh C, *Which Policy for Europe? Power and Conflict Inside the European Commission* (OUP 2014)
Hartley TC, *Constitutional Problems of the European Union* (Hart Publishing1999)
Hartley TC, *The Foundations of European Union Law: An Introduction to the Constitutional and Administrative Law of the European Union* (8th edn, OUP 2014)
Hayes-Renshaw F, 'The Council of Ministers: Conflict, Consensus, and Continuity' in D Hodson and J Peterson (eds), *The Institutions of the European Union* (4th edn, OUP 2017)
Heisenberg D, 'The Institution of "Consensus" in the European Union: Formal versus Informal Decision-Making in the Council' (2005) 44 European Journal of Political Research 65
Hennette-Vauchez S, 'Equality and the Market: The Unhappy Fate of Religious Discrimination in Europe' (2017) 13 European Constitutional Law Review 744
Héritier A, *Policy-Making and Diversity in Europe: Escape from Deadlock* (CUP 1999)
Héritier A, 'Mutual Recognition: Comparing Policy Areas' (2007) 14 Journal of European Public Policy 800
Himsworth CM, 'Things Fall Apart: The Harmonisation of Community Judicial Procedural Protection Revisited' (1997) 22 European Law Review 292
Hirschl R, 'The Judicialization of Politics' in KE Whittington, RD Kelemen, and GA Caldeira (eds), *The Oxford Handbook of Law and Politics* (OUP 2008)
Hix S and Høyland B, 'Empowerment of the European Parliament' (2013) 16 Annual Review of Political Science 171
Hix S and Marsh M, 'Second-Order Effects plus Pan-European Political Swings: An Analysis of European Parliament Elections across Time' (2011) 30 Electoral Studies 4
Hix S, Noury AG, and Roland G, *Democratic Politics in the European Parliament* (CUP 2007)
Hofmann A, 'Resistance against the Court of Justice of the European Union' (2018) 14 International Journal of Law in Context 258
Höpner M and Schmidt SK, 'Can We Make the European Fundamental Freedoms Less Constraining? A Literature Review' (2020) 22 Cambridge Yearbook of European Legal Studies 182
Horsley T, 'Subsidiarity and the European Court of Justice: Missing Pieces in the Subsidiarity Jigsaw?' (2012) 50 Journal of Common Market Studies 267
Horsley T, *The Court of Justice of the European Union as an Institutional Actor: Judicial Lawmaking and Its Limits* (CUP 2018)
Howard E, 'Islamic Headscarves and the CJEU: *Achbita* and *Bougnaoui*' (2017) 24 Maastricht Journal of European and Comparative Law 348
Hurrelmann A, '*Demoi*-Cratic Citizenship in Europe: An Impossible Ideal?' (2014) 22 Journal of European Public Policy 19
Isiksel T, *Europe's Functional Constitution: A Theory of Constitutionalism beyond the State* (OUP 2016)
Jacob MA, *Precedents and Case-Based Reasoning in the European Court of Justice: Unfinished Business* (CUP 2014)
Jans J, 'Minimum Harmonisation and the Role of the Principle of Proportionality' in M Führ and E Rehbinder (eds), *Umweltrecht und Umweltwissenschaft: Festschrift für Eckard Rehbinder* (Schmidt 2007)
Janssens C, *The Principle of Mutual Recognition in EU Law* (OUP 2013)
Jensen T and Winzen T, 'Legislative Negotiations in the European Parliament' (2012) 13 European Union Politics 118
Joerges C, 'European Law as Conflict of Laws' in C Joerges and J Neyer (eds), *'Deliberative Supranationalism' Revisited* (2006)

Jones B, 'United Kingdom and Ireland: Passenger Protection Turns a Corner' in M Bobek and J Prassl (eds), *Air Passenger Rights: Ten Years On* (Hart Publishing 2016)
Jones E, Kelemen RD, and Meunier S, 'Failing Forward? The Euro Crisis and the Incomplete Nature of European Integration' (2016) 49 Comparative Political Studies 1010
Jordan A and Schout A, *The Coordination of the European Union: Exploring the Capacities of Networked Governance* (OUP 2006)
Jubb R, 'Realism' in A Blau (ed), *Methods in Analytical Political Theory* (CUP 2017)
Kaczyński PM, 'Paper Tigers or Sleeping Beauties? National Parliaments in the Post-Lisbon European Political System' (Centre for European Policy Studies Special Report, February 2011)
Kavanagh A, 'Deference or Defiance?: The Limits of the Judicial Role in Constitutional Adjudication' in G Huscroft (ed), *Expounding the Constitution: Essays in Constitutional Theory* (CUP 2008)
Kelemen RD, *Eurolegalism: The Transformation of Law and Regulation in the European Union* (Harvard UP 2011)
Kelemen RD, 'Europe's Other Democratic Deficit: National Authoritarianism in Europe's Democratic Union' (2017) 52 Government and Opposition 211
Khaitan T and Calderwood NJ, 'The Right to Freedom of Religion and the Right against Religious Discrimination: Theoretical Distinctions' (2019) 17 International Journal of Constitutional Law 1125
Kilpatrick C, 'Internal Market Architecture and the Accommodation of Labour Rights: As Good as It Gets?' (European Union Institute Working Paper Law No 2011/04, 2011)
King J, *Judging Social Rights* (CUP 2012)
Klamert M, 'What We Talk about When We Talk about Harmonisation' (2015) 17 Cambridge Yearbook of European Legal Studies 360
Kochenov D, 'Citizenship without Respect: The EU's Troubled Equality Ideal' (Jean Monet Working Paper No 08/10, 2011)
Kochenov D and Belavusau U, 'Kirchberg Dispensing the Punishment: Inflicting "Civil Death" on Prisoners in Onuekwere (C-378/12) and M.G. (C-400/12)' (2016) 41 European Law Review 557
Kochenov D and Pech L, 'Respect for the Rule of Law in the Case Law of the European Court of Justice: A Casebook Overview of Key Judgments since the Portuguese Judges Case' (Swedish Institute for European Policy Studies Report, 2021)
Kochenov D and Plender SR, 'EU Citizenship: From an Incipient Form to an Incipient Substance? The Discovery of the Treaty Text' (2012) 37 European Law Review 369
Komárek J, 'Legal Reasoning in EU Law' in A Arnull and D Chalmers (eds), *The Oxford handbook of European Union law* (1st edn, OUP 2015)
Komesar NK, *Imperfect Alternatives: Choosing Institutions in Law, Economics and Public Policy* (University of Chicago Press 1997)
Köpcke Tinturé M, *Legal Validity: The Fabric of Justice* (Hart Publishing 2018)
Kostakopoulou D, 'European Union Citizenship: Writing the Future' (2007) 13 European Law Journal 623
Kostakopoulou D, 'When EU Citizens Become Foreigners' (2014) 20 European Law Journal 447
Koukiadaki A, 'The Far-Reaching Implications of the Laval Quartet: The Case of the UK Living Wage' (2014) 43 Industrial Law Journal 91
Krajewski M, 'Judicial and Extra-Judicial Review: The Quest for Epistemic Certainty' in Merijn Chamon and others (eds), *The Boards of Appeal of EU Agencies: A New Paradigm of Legal Protection?* (OUP 2022)
Kramer D, 'EU-Studenten en de Nederlandse Studiefinanciering: Assertiviteit in de Schaduw van Het Europees Hof van Justitie' [2020] Nederlands Tijdschrift voor Onderwijsrecht en Onderwijsbeleid 29
Kymlicka W, *Politics in the Vernacular: Nationalism, Multiculturalism, and Citizenship* (OUP 2001)
Laborde C, 'Republicanism and Global Justice: A Sketch' (2010) 9 European Journal of Political Theory 48

Laborde C and Ronzoni M, 'What Is a Free State? Republican Internationalism and Globalisation' (2016) 64 Political Studies 279
Landemore H, *Democratic Reason: Politics, Collective Intelligence, and the Rule of the Many* (Princeton UP 2017)
Larsen SR, *The Constitutional Theory of the Federation and the European Union* (OUP 2021)
Larsson O and Naurin D, 'Judicial Independence and Political Uncertainty: How the Risk of Override Affects the Court of Justice of the EU' (2016) 70 International Organization 377
Lassalle M, 'Op-Ed: "Who Cares about Financial Privacy?: The Court of Justice in *WM, Sovim SA v Luxembourg Business Registers* (C-37/20 and C-601/20)"' [2022] European Law Live
Le Bot F, 'France: Air Passengers Facing Long-Haul Judicial Journeys' in M Bobek and J Prassl (eds), *Air Passenger Rights: Ten Years On* (Hart Publishing 2016)
Lefkofridi Z and Katsanidou A, 'Multilevel Representation in the European Parliament' (2014) 15 European Union Politics 108
Leiter B, 'Explaining Theoretical Disagreement' (2009) 76 University of Chicago Law Review 1215
Lenaerts K, 'The Court's Outer and Inner Selves: Exploring the External and Internal Legitimacy of the European Court of Justice' in M Adams and others (eds), *Judging Europe's Judges: The Legitimacy of the Case Law of the European Court of Justice* (Hart Publishing 2013)
Lenaerts K, 'The Principle of Democracy in the Case Law of the European Court of Justice' (2013) 62 International and Comparative Law Quarterly 271
Lenaerts K and Gutiérrez-Fons JA, 'To Say What the Law of the EU Is: Methods of Interpretation and the European Court of Justice' (2013) 20 Columbia Journal of European law 3
Lewis J, 'Coreper: National Interests and the Logic of Appropriateness' in D Hodson and J Peterson (eds), *The Institutions of the European Union* (4th edn, OUP 2017)
List C, 'Democratic Deliberation and Social Choice: A Review' in A Bächtiger and others (eds), *The Oxford Handbook of Deliberative Democracy* (1st edn, OUP 2018)
List C and Pettit P, 'Aggregating Sets of Judgments: Two Impossibility Results Compared' (2004) 140 Synthese 207
List C and Pettit P, *Group Agency: The Possibility, Design, and Status of Corporate Agents* (OUP 2011)
Loughlin M, 'Constitutional Pluralism: An Oxymoron?' (2014) 3 Global Constitutionalism 9
Loughlin M, *Political Jurisprudence* (OUP 2017)
Lynskey O, 'The Data Retention Directive Is Incompatible with the Rights to Privacy and Data Protection and Is Invalid in Its Entirety: *Digital Rights Ireland*' (2014) 51 Common Market Law Review 1789
MacCormick N, 'Legislative Deliberation: Notes from the European Parliament' in L Wintgens (ed), *The Theory and Practice of Legislation: Essays in Legisprudence* (Ashgate 2005)
Mackie G, *Democracy Defended* (CUP 2003)
Maduro M, *We the Court: The European Court of Justice and the European Economic Constitution* (Hart Publishing 1998)
Maduro MP, 'Interpreting European Law—Judicial Adjudication in a Context of Constitutional Pluralism' (2008) 1 European Journal of Legal Studies 1
Maduro MP, 'Interpreting European Law—On Why and How Law and Policy Meet at the European Court of Justice' in H Koch and others (eds), *Europe: The New Legal Realism: Essays in Honor of Hjalte Rasmussen* (Djøf Publishing 2010)
Majone G, 'Europe's "Democratic Deficit": The Question of Standards' (1998) 4 European Law Journal 5
Majone G, 'From Regulatory State to a Democratic Default' (2014) 52 Journal of Common Market Studies 1216
Mancano L, 'Criminal Conduct and Lack of Integration into the Society under EU Citizenship: This Marriage Is Not to Be Performed' (2015) 6 New Journal of European Criminal Law 53
Mancini GF, 'The Making of a Constitution for Europe' in RO Keohane and S Hoffmann (eds), *The New European Community: Decisionmaking and Institutional Change* (Westview Press 1991)

Manning JF, 'What Divides Textualists from Purposivists?' (2006) 106 Columbia Law Review 70

Marmor A, *The Language of Law* (1st edn, OUP 2014)

Martinsen DS, *An Ever More Powerful Court? The Political Constraints of Legal Integration in the European Union* (OUP 2015)

Martinsen DS, 'The European Union and EU Legislative Politics' in F Vandenbroucke, C Barnard, and G de Baere (eds), *A European Social Union after the Crisis* (CUP 2017)

Martinsen DS and Blauberger M, 'The Court of Justice of the European Union and the Mega-Politics of Posted Workers' (2021) 84 Law and Contemporary Problems 29

Martinsen DS and Pons Rotger G, 'The Fiscal Impact of EU Immigration on the Tax-Financed Welfare State: Testing the "Welfare Burden" Thesis' (2017) 18 European Union Politics 620

Martinsen DS and Werner B, 'No Welfare Magnets—Free Movement and Cross-Border Welfare in Germany and Denmark Compared' (2019) 26 Journal of European Public Policy 637

McCown M, 'The European Parliament before the Bench: ECJ Precedent and EP Litigation Strategies' (2003) 10 Journal of European Public Policy 974

McElroy G, 'Committee Representation in the European Parliament' (2006) 7 European Union Politics 5

Mendes J, 'Bounded Discretion in EU Law: A Limited Judicial Paradigm in a Changing EU: Bounded Discretion in EU Law' (2017) 80 Modern Law Review 443

Menon A and Weatherill S, 'Democratic Politics in a Globalising World: Supranationalism and Legitimacy in the European Union' (LSE Law, Society and Economy Working Paper No 2007/13, 2007)

Meunier S and Alter KJ, 'Judicial Politics in the European Community: European Integration and the Pathbreaking Cassis de Dijon Decision' (1994) 26 Comparative Political Studies 535

Meuwese AC, *Impact Assessment in EU Lawmaking* (Wolters Kluwer Law 2008)

Miller D, 'Democracy's Domain' (2009) 37 Philosophy & Public Affairs 201

Moravcsik A, 'In Defence of the "Democratic Deficit": Reassessing Legitimacy in the European Union' (2002) 40 Journal of Common Market Studies 603

Moreau S, 'Equality Rights and Stereotypes' in D Dyzenhaus and M Thorburn (eds), *Philosophical Foundations of Constitutional Law* (OUP 2016)

Morvillo M and Weimer M, 'Who Shapes the CJEU Regulatory Jurisprudence? On the Epistemic Power of Economic Actors and Ways to Counter It' (2022) 1 European Law Open 510

Mühlböck M and Tosun J, 'Responsiveness to Different National Interests: Voting Behaviour on Genetically Modified Organisms in the Council of the European Union: Responsiveness to National Interests' (2018) 56 Journal of Common Market Studies 385

Muir E, 'The Fundamental Rights Implications of EU Legislation: Some Constitutional Challenges' (2014) 51 Common Market Law Review 219

Muir E, *EU Equality Law: The First Fundamental Rights Policy of the EU* (OUP 2018)

Nehl HP, 'Judicial Review of Complex Socio-Economic, Technical, and Scientific Assessments' in J Mendes (ed), *EU Executive Discretion and the Limits of Law* (OUP 2019)

Neuhold C, 'The "Legislative Backbone" Keeping the Institution Upright? The Role of European Parliament Committees in the EU Policy-Making Process' (2001) 5 European Integration Online Papers

Neuvonen PJ, *Equal Citizenship and Its Limits in EU Law: We the Burden* (Hart Publishing 2016)

Newdick C, 'Citizenship, Free Movement and Health Care: Cementing Individual Rights by Corroding Social Solidarity' (2006) 43 Common Market Law Review 1645

Neyer J, *The Justification of Europe: A Political Theory of Supranational Integration* (OUP 2012)

Ní Chaoimh E, *The Legislative Priority Rule and the EU Internal Market for Goods: A Constitutional Approach* (OUP 2022)

Nic Shuibhne N, '(Some of) The Kids Are All Right: Comment on McCarthy and Dereci' (2012) 39 Common Market Law Review 349

Nic Shuibhne N, 'Limits Rising, Duties Ascending: The Changing Legal Shape of Union Citizenship' (2015) 52 Common Market Law Review 889

Nicol D, 'Europe's Lochner Moment' (2011) Public Law 308

Nicolaïdis K, 'European Demoicracy and Its Crisis' (2013) 51 Journal of Common Market Studies 351

Nicolaïdis K and Schmidt SK, 'Mutual Recognition "on Trial": The Long Road to Services Liberalization' (2007) 14 Journal of European Public Policy 717

Nicolaïdis K and Watson M, 'Sharing the Eurocrats' Dream: A Demoicratic Approach to EMU Governance in the Post-Crisis Era' in D Chalmers, M Jachtenfuchs, and C Joerges (eds), *The End of the Eurocrats' Dream: Adjusting to European Diversity* (CUP 2016)

Novak S, Rozenberg O, and Bendjaballah S, 'Enduring Consensus: Why the EU Legislative Process Stays the Same' (2021) 43 Journal of European Integration 475

Nyikos SA, 'The Preliminary Reference Process: National Court Implementation, Changing Opportunity Structures and Litigant Desistment' (2003) 4 European Union Politics 397

Öberg J, 'The Rise of the Procedural Paradigm: Judicial Review of EU Legislation in Vertical Competence Disputes' (2017) 13 European Constitutional Law Review 248

O'Brien C, 'Real Links, Abstract Rights and False Alarms: The Relationship between the ECJ's "Real Link" Case Law and National Solidarity' (2008) 33 European Law Review 125

O'Brien C, 'I Trade, Therefore I Am: Legal Personhood in the European Union' (2013) 50 Common Market Law Review 1643

O'Brien C, 'Civis Capitalist Sum: Class as the New Guiding Principle of EU Free Movement Rights' (2016) 53 Common Market Law Review 937

O'Brien C, 'The ECJ Sacrifices EU Citizenship in Vain: *Commission v. United Kingdom*' (2017) 54 Common Market Law Review 209

O'Brien C, *Unity in Adversity: EU Citizenship, Social Justice and the Cautionary Tale of the UK* (Hart Publishing 2017)

O'Leary S, 'Putting Flesh on the Bones of European Union Citizenship' (1999) 24 European Law Review 68

O'Leary S, 'Equal Treatment and EU Citizens: A New Chapter on Cross-Border Educational Mobility and Access to Student Financial Assistance' (2009) 34 European Law Review 612

Oliver P, 'Some Further Reflections on the Scope of Articles 28–30 (Ex 30–36) EC' (1999) 36 Common Market Law Review 783

Panke D, 'The European Court of Justice as an Agent of Europeanization? Restoring Compliance with EU Law' (2007) 14 Journal of European Public Policy 847

Paunio E, *Legal Certainty in Multilingual EU Law: Language, Discourse, and Reasoning at the European Court of Justice* (Ashgate 2013)

Pavone T, *The Ghostwriters: Lawyers and the Politics behind the Judicial Construction of Europe* (CUP 2022)

Pennings F, 'The Draft Patient Mobility Directive and the Coordination Regulations of Social Security' in JW van de Gronden, E Szyszczak, and U Neergaard (eds), *Health Care and EU Law* (TMC Asser Press 2011)

Peterson J, 'Playing the Transparency Game: Consultation and Policy-Making in the European Commission' (1995) 73 Public Administration 473

Pettit P, *Republicanism: A Theory of Freedom and Government* (OUP 1999)

Pettit P, 'Collective Persons and Powers' (2002) 8 Legal Theory 443

Pettit P, 'Legitimate International Institutions: A Neo-Republican Perspective' in S Besson and J Tasioulas (eds), *The Philosophy of International Law* (OUP 2010)

Pettit P, *On the People's Terms: A Republican Theory and Model of Democracy* (CUP 2012)

Pettit P and Schweikard D, 'Joint Actions and Group Agents' (2006) 36 Philosophy of the Social Sciences 18

Pirker B, *Proportionality Analysis and Models of Judicial Review: A Theoretical and Comparative Study* (Europa Law Publishing 2013)

Pollack MA, 'The Legitimacy of the European Court of Justice' in N Grossman and others (eds), *Legitimacy and International Courts* (CUP 2018)

Pollicino O, 'Legal Reasoning of the Court of Justice in the Context of the Principle of Equality Between Judicial Activism and Self-Restraint' (2004) 5 German Law Journal 283

Poscher R, 'Ambiguity and Vagueness in Legal Interpretation' in P Meijes Tiersma and L Solan (eds), *The Oxford Handbook of Language and Law* (OUP 2012)

Prassl J, 'Tackling Diversity through Uniformity? Revisiting the Reform of Regulation 261/2004' in M Bobek and J Prassl (eds), *Air Passenger Rights: Ten Years On* (Hart Publishing 2016)

Prechal S, *Directives in EC Law* (2nd edn, OUP 2005)

Prek M and Lefèvre S, 'Administrative Discretion, Power of Appraisal and Margin of Appraisal in Judicial Review Proceedings before the General Court' (2019) 56 Common Market Law Review 339

Rauchegger C, 'National Constitutional Rights and the Primacy of EU Law: M.A.S.' (2018) 55 Common Market Law Review 1521

Raunio T, 'Destined for Irrelevance? Subsidiarity Control by National Parliaments (WP)' (Real Institute Elcano Working Paper No 36/2010, 2010)

Raunio T and Wagner W, 'Contestation over Development Policy in the European Parliament' (2021) 59 Journal of Common Market Studies 20

Rawls J, *Political Liberalism* (Columbia UP 1993)

Raz J, *Practical Reason and Norms* (OUP 2002)

Raz J, *Between Authority and Interpretation: On the Theory of Law and Practical Reason* (OUP 2009)

Reh C, 'Is Informal Politics Undemocratic? Trilogues, Early Agreements and the Selection Model of Representation' (2014) 21 Journal of European Public Policy 822

Reich N, 'How Proportionate Is the Proportionality Principle? Some Critical Remarks on the Use and Methodology of the Proportionality Principle in the Internal Market Case Law of the ECJ' in H-W Micklitz and B de Witte (eds), *The European Court of Justice and the Autonomy of the Member States* (Intersentia 2012)

Rennuy N, 'The Emergence of a Parallel System of Social Security Coordination' (2013) 50 Common Market Law Review 1221

Ripoll Servent A and Roederer-Rynning C, 'The European Parliament: A Normal Parliament in a Polity of a Different Kind', Oxford Research Encyclopedias (2018) <https://oxfordre.com/politics/view/10.1093/acrefore/9780190228637.001.0001/acrefore-9780190228637-e-1 52> accessed 29 February 2024

Risse-Kappen T (ed), *European Public Spheres: Politics Is Back* (CUP 2015)

Ritleng D, 'The Independence and Legitimacy of the European Court of Justice' in D Ritleng (ed), *Independence and Legitimacy in the Institutional System of the European Union* (OUP 2016)

Ritzer C, Ruttloff M, and Linhart K, 'How to Sharpen a Dull Sword—The Principle of Subsidiarity and Its Control' (2006) 7 German Law Journal 734

Roger L and Winzen T, 'Party Groups and Committee Negotiations in the European Parliament: Outside Attention and the Anticipation of Plenary Conflict' (2015) 22 Journal of European Public Policy 391

Ronzoni M, 'The European Union as a Demoicracy: Really a Third Way?' (2017) 16 European Journal of Political Theory 210

Rosenberg GN, *The Hollow Hope: Can Courts Bring about Social Change?* (University of Chicago Press 2008)

Sadurski W, 'Judicial Review and the Protection of Constitutional Rights' (2002) 22 Oxford Journal of Legal Studies 275

Sadurski W, 'Rights and Moral Reasoning: An Unstated Assumption' (2008) 7 International Journal of Constitutional Law 25

Sánchez Barrueco M-L, 'Litigation as a Means to Solve Conflicts between the European Parliament and the Council: One Size Does Not Fit All' in PJ Cardwell and M-P Granger (eds), *Research Handbook on the Politics of EU Law* (Edward Elgar 2020)

Sánchez-Tabernero SR, 'The Choice of Legal Basis and the Principle of Consistency in the Procedure for Conclusion of International Agreements in CFSP Contexts: *Parliament v. Council* (Pirate-Transfer Agreement with Tanzania)' (2017) 54 Common Market Law Review 899

Sandholtz W and Stone Sweet A, 'Integration, Supranational Governance, and the Institutionalization of the European Polity' in W Sandholtz and A Stone Sweet (eds), *European Integration and Supranational Governance* (OUP 1998)

Sandhu A, 'Das EU-Antidiskriminierungsrecht zwischen ökonomischer und sozialer Integration: Zu den Grenzen unternehmerischer Freiheit—Anmerkung zu EuGH, Rs. C-188/15 (Bougnaoui) und C-157/15 (Achbita)' (2017) 50 Kritische Justiz 517

Sangiovanni A, 'Global Justice, Reciprocity, and the State' (2007) 35 Philosophy & Public Affairs 3

Sangiovanni A, 'Justice and the Free Movement of Persons: Educational Mobility in the European Union and the United States' in DA Hicks and T Williamson (eds), *Leadership and Global Justice* (Palgrave Macmillan 2012)

Sankari S, *European Court of Justice Legal Reasoning in Context* (Europa Law Publishing 2013)

Sankari S, 'Constitutional Pluralism and Judicial Adjudication: On Legal Reasoning, Minimalism and Silence by the Court of Justice' in GT Davies and M Avbelj (eds), *Research Handbook on Legal Pluralism and EU Law* (Edward Elgar 2018)

Sarmiento D, 'The Silent Lamb and the Deaf Wolves' in M Avbelj and J Komárek (eds), *Constitutional Pluralism in the European Union and Beyond* (Hart Publishing 2012)

Sarmiento D and Sharpston E, 'European Citizenship and Its Union: Time to Move On?' in D Kochenov (ed), *EU Citizenship and Federalism: The Role of Rights* (CUP 2017)

Scharpf FW, *Governing in Europe: Effective and Democratic?* (OUP 1999)

Scharpf FW, 'The Joint-Decision Trap Revisited' (2006) 44 JCMS: Journal of Common Market Studies 845

Scharpf FW, 'Legitimacy in the Multi-Level European Polity' in P Dobner and M Loughlin (eds), *The Twilight of Constitutionalism?* (OUP 2010)

Scharpf FW, 'The Asymmetry of European Integration, or Why the EU Cannot Be a "Social Market Economy"' (2010) 8 Socio-Economic Review 211

Scharpf FW, 'Perpetual Momentum: Directed and Unconstrained?' (2012) 19 Journal of European Public Policy 127

Scharpf FW, 'After the Crash: A Perspective on Multilevel European Democracy' (2015) 21 European Law Journal 384

Scharpf FW, 'De-Constitutionalisation and Majority Rule: A Democratic Vision for Europe' (2017) 23 European Law Journal 315

Schauer F, *Playing by the Rules: A Philosophical Examination of Rule-Based Decision-Making in Law and in Life* (Clarendon Press 2002)

Schauer F, 'Balancing, Subsumption, and the Constraining Role of Legal Text' in M Klatt (ed), *Institutionalized Reason: The Jurisprudence of Robert Alexy* (OUP 2012)

Schenk A and Schmidt SK, 'Failing on the Social Dimension: Judicial Law-Making and Student Mobility in the EU' (2018) 25 Journal of European Public Policy 1522

Scherz A, 'Representation in Multilateral Democracy: How to Represent Individuals in the EU While Guaranteeing the Mutual Recognition of Peoples' (2017) 23 European Law Journal 495

Schmidt SK, 'Beyond Compliance: The Europeanization of Member States through Negative Integration and Legal Uncertainty' (2008) 10 Journal of Comparative Policy Analysis: Research and Practice 299

Schmidt SK, 'Who Cares about Nationality? The Path-Dependent Case Law of the ECJ from Goods to Citizens' (2012) 19 Journal of European Public Policy 8

Schmidt SK, *The European Court of Justice and the Policy Process: The Shadow of Case Law* (OUP 2018)

Schmidt SK, 'Governing by Judicial Fiat? Over-Constitutionalisation and Its Constraints on EU Legislation' (European Union Studies Association International Biennial Conference, Denver, 9–11 May 2019)

Schmidt VA, 'Democracy and Legitimacy in the European Union Revisited: Input, Output *and* "Throughput"' (2013) 61 Political Studies 2

Schmidtz D, 'Realistic Idealism' in A Blau (ed), *Methods in Analytical Political Theory* (CUP 2017)

Schütze R, 'Limits to the Union's "Internal Market" Competence(s)' in L Azoulai (ed), *The Question of Competence in the European Union* (1st edn, OUP 2014)

Scicluna N and Auer S, 'Europe's Constitutional Unsettlement: Testing the Political Limits of Legal Integration' (2023) 99 International Affairs 769

Shapiro M, 'Comparative Law and Comparative Politics' (1980) 53 Southern California Law Review 537

Shaw J and Wiener A, 'The Paradox of the "European Polity"' in M Green Cowles and M Smith (eds), *The State of the European Union: Risks, Reforms, Renewals, and Revival* (OUP 2000)

Shepsle KA, 'Congress Is a "They," Not an "It": Legislative Intent as Oxymoron' (1992) 12 International Review of Law and Economics 239

Shepsle KA and Weingast BR, 'Why So Much Stability? Majority Voting, Legislative Institutions, and Gordon Tullock' (2012) 152 Public Choice 83

Shore C, '"European Governance" or Governmentality? The European Commission and the Future of Democratic Government' (2011) 17 European Law Journal 287

Skinner Q, 'On the Slogans of Republican Political Theory' (2010) 9 European Journal of Political Theory 95

Snell J, 'The Internal Market and the Philosophies of Market Integration' in C Barnard and S Peers (eds), *European Union Law* (OUP 2014)

Snell J, 'Economic Justifications and the Role of the State' in P Koutrakos, N Nic Shuibhne, and P Syrpis (eds), *Exceptions from EU Free Movement Law: Derogation, Justification, and Proportionality* (Hart Publishing 2016)

Soames S, *Philosophical Essays, Volume 1—Natural Language: What It Means and How We Use It* (Princeton UP 2009)

Soames S, *Philosophy of Language* (Princeton UP 2010)

Soames S, 'What Vagueness and Inconsistency Tell Us About Interpretation' in A Marmor and S Soames (eds), *Philosophical Foundations of Language in the Law* (OUP 2011)

Solum LB, 'On the Indeterminacy Crisis: Critiquing Critical Dogma' (1987) 54 University of Chicago Law Review 462

Somek A, 'Solidarity Decomposed: Being and Time in European Citizenship' (2007) 32 European Law Review 787

Somek A, *Individualism: An Essay on the Authority of the European Union* (OUP 2008)

Somek A, 'The Argument from Transnational Effects I: Representing Outsiders through Freedom of Movement' (2010) 16 European Law Journal 315

Somek A, 'The Argument from Transnational Effects II: Establishing Transnational Democracy' (2010) 16 European Law Journal 375

Somek A, 'The Emancipation of Legal Dissonance' in H Koch and others (eds), *Europe: The New Legal Realism: Essays in Honor of Hjalte Rasmussen* (Djøf Publishing 2010)

Sousa PC, 'Quest for the Holy Grail—Is a Unified Approach to the Market Freedoms and European Citizenship Justified?' (2014) 20 European Law Journal 499

Spaventa E, 'Once a Foreigner Always a Foreigner: Who Does Not Belong Here Anymore? Expulsion Measures' in Herwig Verschueren (ed), *Residence, Employment and Social Rights of Mobile Persons: On How EU Law Defines Where They Belong* (Intersentia 2016)

St Clair Bradley K, 'Powers and Procedures in the EU Constitution: Legal Bases and the Court' in P Craig and G de Búrca (eds), *The Evolution of EU Law* (2nd edn, OUP 2011)

Stein E, 'Lawyers, Judges, and the Making of a Transnational Constitution' (1981) 75 American Journal of International Law 1

Stone A, 'Judicial Review without Rights: Some Problems for the Democratic Legitimacy of Structural Judicial Review' (2008) 28 Oxford Journal of Legal Studies 1

Stone A, 'Democratic Objections to Structural Judicial Review and the Judicial Role in Constitutional Law' (2010) 60 University of Toronto Law Journal 109

Stone Sweet A, *The Judicial Construction of Europe* (OUP 2004)

Strban G and others, 'FreSsco Analytical Report 2016: Access to Healthcare in Cross-Border Situations' (European Commission 2017)

Streeck W, 'Progressive Regression' (2019) 118 New Left Review 117

Syrpis P, 'Theorising the Relationship between the Judiciary and the Legislature in the EU Internal Market' in P Syrpis (ed), *The Judiciary, the Legislature and the EU Internal Market* (CUP 2012)
Syrpis P, 'The Relationship between Primary and Secondary Law in the EU' (2015) 52 Common Market Law Review 461
Tasioulas J, 'The Legitimacy of International Law' in S Besson and J Tasioulas (eds), *The Philosophy of International Law* (OUP 2010)
Tecqmenne M, 'Minimum Harmonisation and Fundamental Rights: A Test-Case for the Identification of the Scope of EU Law in Situations Involving National Discretion?' [2020] European Constitutional Law Review 20
Thomas CA, 'The Uses and Abuses of Legitimacy in International Law' (2014) 34 Oxford Journal of Legal Studies 729
Thomson R, Torenvlied R, and Arregui J, 'The Paradox of Compliance: Infringements and Delays in Transposing European Union Directives' (2007) 37 British Journal of Political Science 685
Thym D, 'The Elusive Limits of Solidarity: Residence Rights of and Social Benefits for Economically Inactive Union Citizens' (2015) 52 Common Market Law Review 17
Thym D, 'The Constitutional Dimension of Public Policy Justifications' in P Koutrakos, N Nic Shuibhne, and P Syrpis (eds), *Exceptions from EU Free Movement Law: Derogation, Justification and Proportionality* (Hart Publishing 2016)
Treib O, 'Implementing and Complying with EU Governance Outputs' (2014) 9 Living Reviews in European Governance
Tripkovic B, 'A New Philosophy for the Margin of Appreciation and European Consensus' [2021] Oxford Journal of Legal Studies 207
Tryfonidou A, 'Family Reunification Rights of (Migrant) Union Citizens: Towards a More Liberal Approach' (2009) 15 European Law Journal 634
Tushnet MV, *Taking the Constitution Away from the Courts* (Princeton UP 1999)
van den Brink M, 'EU Citizenship and (Fundamental) Rights: Empirical, Normative, and Conceptual Problems' (2019) 25 European Law Journal 21
van den Brink M, 'Justice, Legitimacy and the Authority of Legislation within the European Union' (2019) 82 Modern Law Review 293
van den Brink M, 'The European Union's Demoicratic Legislature' (2021) 19 International Journal of Constitutional Law 914
van den Brink M, 'Is It Time to Abolish the Substance of EU Citizenship Rights Test?' (2021) 23 European Journal of Migration and Law 13
van den Brink M, 'When Can Religious Employers Discriminate? The Scope of the Religious Ethos Exemption in EU Law' (2022) 1 European Law Open 89
van den Brink M, 'Off Track, Again? EU Citizenship and the Right to Social Assistance' (2023) 11 Hungarian Yearbook of International and European Law 18
van den Brink M, 'The Protected Grounds of Religion and Belief: Lessons for EU Non-Discrimination Law' (2023) 24 German Law Journal 855
van den Brink M, 'A Typology of Reverse Discrimination in EU Citizenship Law' (2023) 2 European Law Open 57
van den Brink M, 'Institutional Choice in the Internal Market: A Review Essay' Modern Law Review (forthcoming)
van den Brink M, 'Political, Not (Just) Legal Judgment: Studying EU Institutional Balance' European Law Open (forthcoming)
van der Mei AP, 'Regulation 1408/71 and Coordination of Special Non-Contributory Benefit Schemes' (2002) 5 European Law Review 551
van der Vossen B, 'The Asymmetry of Legitimacy' (2012) 31 Law and Philosophy 565
van Mill D, 'The Possibility of Rational Outcomes from Democratic Discourse and Procedures' (1996) 58 Journal of Politics 734
Varga Z, *The Effectiveness of the Köbler Liability in National Courts* (Hart Publishing 2020)
Vauchez A, *Brokering Europe Euro-Lawyers and the Making of a Transnational Polity* (CUP 2018)

Vauchez A, 'The Genie of Independence and the European Bottle. How Independence Became Europe's Most Contentious Political and Legal Category' (iCourts Working Paper No 2021/266, 2001)

Velyvyte V, *Judicial Authority in EU Internal Market Law: Implications for the Balance of Competences and Powers* (Hart Publishing 2022)

Venzke I and Mendes J, 'The Idea of Relative Authority in European and International Law' (2018) 16 International Journal of Constitutional Law 75

Veraldi J and Hassall M, 'Corporate Power and the Constitutionalisation of the EU Internal Market Project' in MV Tushnet and D Kochenov (eds), *Research Handbook on the Politics of Constitutional Law* (Edward Elgar 2023)

Vermeule A, *Judging under Uncertainty: An Institutional Theory of Legal Interpretation* (Harvard UP 2006)

Verschueren H, 'The EU Social Security Co-Ordination System: A Close Interplay between the EU Legislature and Judiciary' in P Syrpis (ed), *The Judiciary, the Legislature and the EU Internal Market* (CUP 2012)

Verschueren H, 'Preventing "Benefit Tourism" in the EU: A Narrow or Broad Interpretation of the Possibilities Offered by the ECJ in Dano?' (2015) 52 Common Market Law Review 363

Vickers L, '*Achbita* and *Bougnaoui*: One Step Forward and Two Steps Back for Religious Diversity in the Workplace' (2017) 8 European Labour Law Journal 232

von Achenbach J, 'The European Parliament as a Forum of National Interest? A Transnationalist Critique of Jürgen Habermas' Reconstruction of Degressive Proportionality' (2017) 55 Journal of Common Market Studies 193

von Bogdandy A, 'The Past and Promise of Doctrinal Constructivism: A Strategy for Responding to the Challenges Facing Constitutional Scholarship in Europe' (2009) 7 International Journal of Constitutional Law 364

von Bogdandy A, 'Founding Principles of EU Law: A Theoretical and Doctrinal Sketch' (2010) 16 European Law Journal 95

Waldron J, 'Vagueness in Law and Language: Some Philosophical Issues' (1994) 82 California Law Review 509

Waldron J, 'The Dignity of Legislation' (1995) 54 Maryland Law Review 633

Waldron J, *The Dignity of Legislation* (CUP 1999)

Waldron J, *Law and Disagreement* (OUP 1999)

Waldron J, 'Legislating with Integrity' (2003) 72 Fordham Law Review 373

Waldron J, 'The Core of the Case against Judicial Review' (2006) 115 Yale Law Journal 1246

Waldron J, 'Judges as Moral Reasoners' (2008) 7 International Journal of Constitutional Law 2

Waldron J, 'Vagueness and the Guidance of Action' in A Marmor and S Soames (eds), *Philosophical Foundations of Language in the Law* (OUP 2011)

Walker N, 'Postnational Constitutionalism and the Problem of Translation' in JHH Weiler and M Wind (eds), *European Constitutionalism beyond the State* (CUP 2001)

Walker N, 'The White Paper in Constitutional Context' (Jean Monnet Working Paper No 6/01, 2001)

Wallerman A, 'Who Is the National Judge? A Typology of Judicial Attitudes and Behaviours Regarding Preliminary References' in C Rauchegger and A Wallerman (eds), *The Eurosceptic Challenge: National Implementation and Interpretation of EU Law* (Hart Publishing 2019)

Wasserfallen F, 'The Judiciary as Legislator? How the European Court of Justice Shapes Policy-Making in the European Union' (2010) 17 Journal of European Public Policy 1128

Watson B, 'Explaining Legal Agreement' (2023) 14 Jurisprudence 221

Weale A, *Democracy* (2nd edn, Palgrave Macmillan 2007)

Weatherill S, 'The Limits of Legislative Harmonization Ten Years after *Tobacco Advertising*: How the Court's Case Law Has Become a "Drafting Guide"' (2011) 12 German Law Journal 827

Weatherill S, 'Use and Abuse of the EU's Charter of Fundamental Rights: On the Improper Veneration of "Freedom of Contract"' (2014) 10 European Review of Contract Law 167

Weatherill S, 'Justification, Proportionality and Consumer Protection' in P Koutrakos, N Nic Shuibhne, and P Syrpis (eds), *Exceptions from EU Free Movement Law: Derogation, Justification, and Proportionality* (Hart Publishing 2016)
Weatherill S, 'The Principle of Mutual Recognition: It Doesn't Work Because It Doesn't Exist' (2018) 43 European Law Review 224
Weatherill S, 'The Fundamental Question of Minimum or Maximum Harmonisation' in S Garben and I Govaere (eds), *The Internal Market 2.0* (Hart Publishing, an imprint of Bloomsbury Publishing 2020)
Weatherill S, 'Did *Cassis de Dijon* Make a Difference?' in A Albors-Llorens, C Barnard, and Brigitte Leucht (eds), *Cassis de Dijon: 40 Years On* (Hart Publishing, an imprint of Bloomsbury Publishing 2021)
Weatherill S, 'The Beauty and the Beast: Is EU Internal Market Law Over-Constitutionalised?' in T Ćapeta, Iris Goldner Lang, and T Perišin (eds), *The Changing European Union: A Critical View on the Role of Law and the Courts* (Hart Publishing 2022)
Weiler J, 'Epilogue: Judging the Judges—Apology and Critique' in M Adams and others (eds), *Judging Europe's Judges: The Legitimacy of the Case Law of the European Court of Justice* (Hart Publishing 2013)
Weiler JH, 'Fundamental Rights and Fundamental Boundaries: On Standards and Values in the Protection of Human Rights' in NA Neuwahl and A Rosas (eds), *The European Union and Human Rights* (Martinus Nijhoff 1995)
Weiler JHH, 'The Transformation of Europe' (1991) 100 Yale Law Journal 2403
Weiler JHH, 'The Political and Legal Culture of European Integration: An Exploratory Essay' (2011) 9 International Journal of Constitutional Law 678
Weiler JHH, 'Europe in Crisis—On "Political Messianism", "Legitimacy" and the "Rule of Law" ' [2012] Singapore Journal of Legal Studies 248
Weiler JHH, 'Je Suis Achbita!' (2017) 15 International Journal of Constitutional Law 879
Wessel R, 'Legality in EU Common Foreign and Security Policy: The Choice of the Appropriate Legal Basis' in C Kilpatrick and J Scott (eds), *Contemporary Challenges to EU Legality* (OUP 2021)
White EL, 'In Search of the Limits to Article 30 of the EEC Treaty' (1989) 26 Common Market Law Review 235
Wilkinson MA, *Authoritarian Liberalism and the Transformation of Modern Europe* (1st edn, OUP 2021)
Williams M, 'The European Parliament: Political Groups, Minority Rights and the "Rationalisations" of Parliamentary Organisation' in H Döring (ed), *Parliaments and Majority Rule in Western Europe* (St Martin's Press 1995)
Wind M, 'The Nordics, the EU and the Reluctance towards Supranational Judicial Review' (2010) 48 Journal of Common Market Studies 1039
Wollenschläger F, 'A New Fundamental Freedom beyond Market Integration: Union Citizenship and Its Dynamics for Shifting the Economic Paradigm of European Integration' (2011) 17 European Law Journal 1
Wollenschläger F, 'The Judiciary, the Legislature and the Evolution of Union Citizenship' in P Syrpis (ed), *The Judiciary, the Legislature and the EU Internal Market* (CUP 2012)
Wyatt D, 'Could a "Yellow Card" for National Parliaments Strengthen Judicial as Well as Political Policing of Subsidiarity?' (2006) 2 Croatian Yearbook of European Law and Policy 1
Yordanova N, 'The Rationale behind Committee Assignment in the European Parliament: Distributive, Informational and Partisan Perspectives' (2009) 10 European Union Politics 253
Yordanova N, 'Inter-Institutional Rules and Division of Power in the European Parliament: Allocation of Consultation and Co-Decision Reports' (2011) 34 West European Politics 97
Yordanova N, *Organising the European Parliament: The Role of Committees and Their Legislative Influence* (ECPR Press 2013)
Yowell P, *Constitutional Rights and Constitutional Design: Moral and Empirical Reasoning in Judicial Review* (Hart Publishing 2018)

Zglinski J, *Europe's Passive Virtues: Deference to National Authorities in EU Free Movement Law* (OUP 2020)

Zglinski J, 'The End of Negative Market Integration: 60 Years of Free Movement of Goods Litigation in the EU (1961–2020)' [2023] Journal of European Public Policy 1

Zglinski J, 'The Internal Market: From Judicial Politics to Ordinary Politics?' in M Dawson, E Muir, and B De Witte (eds), *Revisiting Judicial Politics in the European Union* (Edward Elgar 2023)

Zürn M, 'Introduction: Law and Compliance at Different Levels' in M Zürn and C Joerges (eds), *Law and Governance in Postnational Europe Compliance beyond the Nation-State* (CUP 2005)

Zysset A, 'Calibrating the Response to Populism at the European Court of Human Rights' (2022) 20 International Journal of Constitutional Law 976

Index

For the benefit of digital users, indexed terms that span two pages (e.g., 52–53) may, on occasion, appear on only one of those pages.

agenda setters 148–49, 152–54, 155, 156–57, 163–64
air passenger rights 11–12, 65–66, 71, 72–73, 174–75, 221–23
Alimanovic 36, 62, 64–65, 75, 185–86, 187–88, 197–98, 199
Andean Community 227–29
anti-discrimination 104, 119–22
  religious discrimination 104–5, 119–22
  see also equality
Article 114 TFEU 16, 82, 94–99
Article 352 TFEU 94–95, 97
attitude aggregation 142, 143–44, 145–47, 149–51, 156, 160–61, 164, 226

Cassis de Dijon 126–27, 135
Charter of Fundamental Rights 81–82, 83–84, 100, 103–4, 106–7, 110–11, 119–21
CILFIT 170, 214–15, 216, 218, 221
coherence/consistency 26, 142, 143–45, 150, 157, 158–59, 160, 161–62, 163–64, 165, 224–25
Collins 16–17, 75–76, 135–36, 169, 182–84
Commission 14–15, 28–29, 30–31, 41–42, 54, 90–93, 104, 117–18, 131–32, 156–57, 158–59, 160, 162–63, 178–79, 187, 202–3
comparative institutional analysis 27–28, 45–46, 51, 109
competences 16, 86, 93–95, 96, 97–98, 224–25
compliance 63–65, 66, 179
conferral 26, 94–95, 96–97
consensus 16, 77–78, 104, 159, 162
consent 26–27, 45
constitutional identity 9, 77–79
constitutional pluralism 170–71, 194
consumer protection 16–17, 81–82, 127–28, 174–75, 190–91
containment 29–30, 32–35
contextualist institutionalism 70–72
Coreper 158–59
Council of Ministers 10–11, 14–15, 16, 30–31, 38, 42–43, 44, 94–95, 137–38, 156, 157–60, 162–63, 202–3
cycling 142, 148–49, 153–55

Dano 62, 64–65, 75, 78, 90–93
de-constitutionalisation 74, 125, 136–37
degressive proportionality 38, 42
delegated acts 117–18
democratic deficit 23, 25–26, 28–29, 38
*demoi*cracy 15, 37–44, 46, 49, 137, 225
demos 22–23, 33–34, 38, 40–42
Digital Rights Ireland 100, 102–3, 108, 109, 110–11
disagreement 30, 31–32, 35, 36–37, 51, 83–84, 89–90, 97–98, 101–2, 105–6, 136, 145–46, 165–66, 171, 178, 204–5, 229
discretion 61, 71–72, 89–90, 96, 100–2, 110–12, 113–15, 116–17, 118, 135, 184–85, 191, 204–5
discursive dilemma 146–47, 165
diversity 29, 37, 41, 42, 55–56, 81, 83–84, 97, 105–6, 170–71, 178
doctrinal reasoning 9–11
domination 38–40, 42, 44, 45, 49, 50, 99–100, 103–4, 107–8, 137
drafting history 130–31, 211, 215, 223

Early Warning Mechanism 42, 43–44
Economic Community of West African States 227–29
effectiveness 2, 22–23, 30–32, 63–64, 69–70
Ekins, Richard 54, 144–45, 209, 213
EMU crisis 31–32, 41–42
environmental protection 8, 67, 81–82, 91, 94
equality 11–12, 33–34, 65–66, 104–5, 108, 119–21
EU citizenship 2–3, 5, 36, 47–48, 58–63, 72–73, 74–76, 106–7, 135–36, 137, 176, 182–92, 194–99, 201, 204, 206–7, 212, 216–17, 218–20
  expulsion 47–48, 62–63, 188–90, 195–98, 216–17
  family reunification 62–63, 218–20
  social assistance 2–3, 36, 47, 58–63, 64–65, 71–72, 74–76, 78–79, 106–7, 135–36, 182–88, 194–95, 196–98, 201, 206–7, 212
European Central Bank 41–42, 115–16
European Convention of Human Rights 7, 8, 111
European Court of Human Rights 7, 8, 111–12

European Parliament 10–11, 14–15, 16, 30–31, 38, 42–43, 44, 90–93, 133, 137–38, 156, 157–64, 167, 170–71, 202–3
Executive (EU) 115–18

free movement 32–33, 76–77, 78–79, 84, 126–30, 220
  goods 78–79, 126–27, 180–81
  services 127–28, 131–33
  workers 76–77, 204, 206–7
freedom to conduct a business 82, 83–84, 102–3, 119–21
fundamental rights 8–9, 16, 87, 99–114, 115–16, 121–22, 136–37

group agency 143–44, 165, 166–67

harmonisation 1, 51–52, 81–85, 126–28, 178, 229
  maximum 15, 81–82, 83, 84–85
  minimum 15, 51–52, 81–85, 130–31
headscarf 119–21
hierarchy primary law-secondary law 11–13, 74–75, 79–80, 118–19

impact assessment 54, 103–4
impossibility theorem 146–47, 148–49
incrementalism (judicial) 53–54, 56–57
indeterminacy 80, 109–10, 141, 170, 171, 173–75, 203–8
  see also vagueness
individual assessments 61, 177, 184–85, 186, 190, 195, 198
institutional balance 2–3, 27, 30–31, 88–89, 90–91, 93
institutional capacity 7–8, 15, 21–22, 50, 51–52, 69–70, 72–73, 84–85, 88, 89–90, 96–97, 101–2, 107–8, 109, 178, 225
  capacity to realise legal change 51, 52–63, 68, 84–85
  capacity to realise social change 51–52, 63–68, 84–85
institutional collaboration 3, 15, 21, 51–52, 69–70, 73, 84–85, 225
integration through law 5–6, 52
internal market 3, 8–9, 11, 16, 47, 78–79, 82, 84, 91, 94–96, 97–99, 100–1, 125–34, 180
international courts 1–2, 227–29
interpretation 17, 52, 74, 125, 141–42, 169–70, 171, 178, 184, 191–92, 193–97, 198–202, 208–23, 226
  constitutional 141, 170, 191–92
  instrumentalist 17, 193–99
  legislative 17, 118–38, 169, 170, 171, 178, 184, 191–92, 193–97, 198–202, 206–23, 226
  literal 195–96, 208–13
  primary law conform 11–12, 73, 221
  purposive 17, 143, 169, 171, 193, 196–97, 199–203, 207–10, 214, 226
  systemic 216
  textual 17, 143, 193, 196–97, 207–8, 226

judicial deference 2–3, 8, 15, 21–22, 49, 51–52, 53–54, 68–75, 77, 78, 80, 84–85, 93, 107–8, 141, 225, 229
judicial review 16, 86–114, 116–18, 225
  fundamental rights review 87, 88–89, 90, 92–93, 99–114
  legislative process review 87, 88–89, 90–93
  ultra vires review 87, 88–89, 90, 92–99, 100–1
justice 22–23, 35–37, 51

Keck 16–17, 169, 180–82, 206
King, Jeff 52–53, 68–70

Laval 16, 87, 125, 129–35, 211
legal basis 82, 90–93
legal certainty 56–57, 61, 73
legislated rights 86–87, 118–19, 123, 125
legislative committee 16, 153–54, 155–56, 159–62, 163–64, 167, 201
legislative context 206, 214–15, 218, 220–21, 226
legislative integrity 142–43, 145, 148, 153, 161–62
legislative intent 16, 84, 118–19, 122, 141–44, 148, 156, 164, 166–68, 169, 187–88, 193–94, 199, 201–2, 209–10, 215, 217–18, 222–23, 226
legislative language use 17, 208–9, 213–14
legislative text 193, 201–3, 204–5, 207–8, 209
legitimacy 7–8, 11, 15, 21–44, 49, 50, 51–52, 68, 69–70, 72, 84–85, 88, 89–90, 97, 99–100, 101–2, 107–8, 111–12, 163–64, 199, 225, 227
  democratic 13–14, 22–23, 28–29, 38, 89, 100, 116–17
  external 33
  input-oriented 15, 23, 28–29, 30, 37, 38–40, 44, 49
  internal 33–34
  legal 24–25, 26–27
  normative 24–25, 27–28
  output-oriented 15, 22–23, 28–30, 38, 199
  sociological 24–26
linguistic discrepancy 209–10
Lisbon Treaty 14–15, 42, 43–44, 91–92
List, Christian 146–47, 149, 151–52, 162, 166–67

Maastricht Treaty 125
majority rule 38, 145–48, 160

margin of appreciation 7–8, 111–12
methodology 9–14, 226
mutual recognition 16, 87, 125–28

national identity *see* constitutional identity
national parliaments 26–27, 42, 43–44, 114–15
negative integration 5–6, 33–34
non-domination *see* domination

ordinary legislative procedure 14–15, 16, 90–91, 156, 162–63, 202–3
over-constitutionalisation 46, 134–35
over-inclusion 172–74, 176

patient mobility 48
permanent residence 176, 188–89, 194–96, 197–98, 201, 204–5, 216–17
Pettit, Philip 146–47, 149, 151–52, 162, 166–67
political equality 38, 40–41, 99–100
political judgement 9, 12–13, 27
political parties 16, 41, 144, 153–56, 160–62
positive integration 5–6
  see also harmonization
posted workers 5, 129–35, 211, 215
pragmatic enrichment 17, 213–14
precedent 56–57, 62, 123–24
precision 57, 58, 67, 171, 173–74, 175, 178, 189
preliminary reference 53–54, 63–65, 66, 67, 205–6
proportionality 76–78, 82, 94–95, 114–15, 183, 186–87, 190–92
public sphere 38, 40–41, 44

qualified majority 38, 91, 98, 123–24, 137, 145–46, 159, 160, 162

rapporteur 157–58, 159–60, 163–64
religion 104–5, 119–21
remedies (EU law) 64, 73
restrictive institutionalism 51–52, 70–72, 73, 74–75, 80
right to private life 100, 102–3, 108, 110–11, 112
rule-based decision-making 169, 172–75, 177, 178–80, 183–84, 187, 190
rule of law 15, 26, 52, 56–57, 58, 225
rules 16–17, 51–52, 141, 169, 170–82, 187–88, 189, 190–92, 193, 194, 201–3

Scharpf, Fritz 46, 123–24, 136–37, 151–52
separation of powers 3–4, 66–67, 227–28
Single European Act 91
social choice theory 16, 143–44, 153–54
social security coordination 76–79
special legislative procedure 14–15, 156
standard of review 88, 89, 100–1, 108, 109, 111–12, 113–14, 115–17, 118
subsidiarity 94–95, 96–97, 133
Sturgeon 11–12, 65–67, 71, 72–73, 135–36, 221–22

Trilogues 162–64
tyranny of the majority 102, 103, 104–5

ultra vires 16, 26, 87, 88–89, 90, 93–99
unanimity 91, 94–95, 145–46, 153–54
under-inclusion 172–74, 176, 183–84, 186

vagueness *see* indeterminacy

Waldron, Jeremy 36, 144–45, 209, 224
workload 55, 67–68, 199, 205–6